INTERNATIONAL FINANCIAL POLICY AND ECONOMIC DEVELOPMENT

INTERNATIONAL FINANCIAL POLICY AND ECONOMIC DEVELOPMENT

A Disaggregated Approach

Graham Bird
Senior Lecturer in Economics
University of Surrey

St. Martin's Press   New York

Folio Bradley Fund

© Graham Bird 1987

Barnard

First published in the United States of America in 1987

Printed in Hong Kong

ISBN 0-312-42213-X

Library of Congress Cataloguing-in-Publication Data
Bird, Graham R.
International financial policy and economic
development.
Bibliography: p.
Includes index.
1. International finance. 2. Finance—Developing
countries. 3. International Monetary Fund—Developing
countries. I. Title.
HG3881.B536   1987   332'.042'091724   86-10195
ISBN 0-312-42213-X

To the memory of my father

To the memory of my father

Contents

List of Tables

Preface

This book focuses on the international financial problems of developing countries and the ways in which international financial policy might be used to help alleviate them. However, an attempt is made throughout to maintain a sharp distinction between considerations of equity and efficiency. Conclusions are drawn on the basis of underlying economic analysis rather than from a desire simply to 'throw more money' at Less Developed Countries (LDCs) in the belief that this will miraculously bring about their economic development. At the same time, it needs to be acknowledged that the advocacy of international policies to assist LDCs reflects a belief that leaving things exclusively to the private markets is an inadequate solution.

A strong theme that emerges, warranting the book's subtitle, is that developing countries cannot be treated as a homogeneous group from the point of view of their international financial problems. At the very least, a distinction needs to be drawn between the better-off LDCs of Latin America and Southeast Asia (the Newly Industrialised Countries or NICs) on the one hand and the Low Income Countries (LICs) of Africa and Asia on the other. This distinction, of course, immediately begs the question of definition. Rather than getting into this admittedly important, but also highly complex, area, the book tends to use the classifications adopted by the principal international agencies – in particular the International Monetary Fund and the World Bank.

It is beyond the scope of the book to discuss the question of measuring the level of development though clearly this issue is closely related to anything which stresses the importance of distinguishing between different developing countries. By consulting a recent copy of the IMF's *World Economic Outlook* or the World Bank's *World Development Report*, readers can easily find out which countries are included in which categories, and can then form their own view as to whether these classifications are adequate.

The chapters of the book reflect the heterogeneity of LDCs. Some focus on policies that would be of most benefit to LICs, such as interest rate subsidies and the Special Drawing Rights (SDR) link, while other focus on policies that would be of more direct benefit to the NICs, such as measures to support private bank lending. Much of the material covered has been published by the author elsewhere, mostly in journal articles. However, the book is not merely a collection of previously published papers. Although one or two chapters are heavily based on a particular article, others draw together the analysis contained in a number of papers and extend it, while others are completely new.

Early chapters (1, 2 and 3) set the scene by raising the principal issues involved, by examining the extent to which it is legitimate to treat LDCs as a special case in international financial reform, and by painting an historical and empirical picture of the position of developing countries within the international financial regime. Chapters 4, 5, 7 and 8 examine various aspects of the IMF in its relations with developing countries, covering questions of IMF conditionality, the IMF's lending facilities, interest rate subsidies, and the problem of financing the Fund's activities. Chapter 6 examines certain aspects of the problem of commodity price stabilisation as it relates to international financial policy, contrasting a buffer stocking approach to the compensatory financing one reviewed in Chapter 5.

The next part of the book, Chapters 9 and 10, examines the Special Drawing Rights facility and ways in which this might be modified to the advantage of LDCs. While such modifications would be of principal advantage to the poorest developing countries, Chapters 11, 12, 13 and 14 focus on questions that are of more relevance to the NICs, examining various aspects of private lending to developing countries, including the role of the banks and the problem of debt.

Since most of the book supports an incremental approach to reform, building on the institutional arrangements that are already in place, Chapter 15 briefly examines an alternative approach based on more exclusively 'Southern' solutions. Chapter 16 then attempts to bring together many of the conclusions reached throughout the book to answer the questions posed in the first chapter. While the chapters are interrelated, it should be possible to read most of them independently of one another.

Although the hope is that the book is reasonably rigorous in its analysis and empirical in its approach, it is not at all mathematical. However, an attempt has been made throughout to show an awareness of the political economy of reform and of what is and is not feasible in practice. These features taken together should make the book of some interest to both students and practitioners. Although constituting a textbook for courses which narrowly focus on the subject matter it covers, the book is perhaps more likely to be useful as supplementary reading on courses in both international and development economics. In many ways it is a cross between a textbook and a research monograph. Clearly the author's hope is that it incorporates the best qualities of these two types of book – involving both breadth and depth – but readers will have to judge for themselves. One aspect of this hybrid status relates to the notes and references. Notes have only been included where considered unavoidable. Similarly the list of references, while quite lengthy, should not be regarded as a bibliography of the literature in this area. In fact it is a literature that has expanded dramatically in the last ten years. The growing literature reflects a rapidly growing interest in the position of LDCs in the international financial system, an interest which is also reflected by the increased amount of media coverage and public debate.

Although many of the issues discussed in the book are topical, the temptation to refer, as a matter of course, to current negotiations and deliberations has been resisted. For one thing, these would no longer be current by the time the book is published, and for another, it is hoped that the durability of the book's relevance will be maximised by concentrating on underlying issues which probably change less rapidly than the details of any specific scheme that is in vogue at any one moment in time. In any case, it will not be difficult for readers to relate the analysis contained here to those discussions that are current at the time of the book's publication.

One of the nicest aspects of writing a book is to be able to thank all the people who have helped. I have been helped in writing this book in a number of ways and by a number of people. First, the editors of various journals have allowed me to use material previously published by them. The journals are the *Banca Nazionale del Lavoro Quarterly Review*, *De Economist*, *Lloyds Bank Review*, and *World Development*. Second, many people have commented on sections of the text at different stages and have discussed various issues with me, though I must admit that I have not always taken their advice. These people are Gerry Helleiner, Nicholas Hope, Peter Kenen, Tony Killick, Danny Leipziger, Geoffrey Maynard, Bahram Nowzad, John Spraos, Frances Stewart, Tony Thirlwall and John Williamson. In particular, I should like thank Heydar Pourian, who not only read and commented in depth on most of the book, but also helped me with the final preparation of the manuscript. Useful research assistance was also given to me by Jane Redfern in the preparation of Chapter 2, and by Jeremy Oppenheim, with whom Chapter 15 was jointly written. Jeremy and I also had lengthy discussions about many of the issues raised in the book which I found helpful and rewarding. Much of the typing was done by Alberta Langley and my thanks go to her for the kind and friendly way in which she persisted with the task of mastering my handwriting.

Most of this book was written while I was a Visiting Professor of International Economic Affairs at the Fletcher School of Law and Diplomacy at Tufts University in the United States. My thanks go to the entire Fletcher community, faculty, staff and students, for making my stay with them such an enjoyable one. Particular thanks go to Benjamin J. Cohen, who made the necessary arrangements, and to the University of Surrey for granting me a sabbatical from my duties in England. As always, my thanks ultimately go to my wife, Heather, and my children, Alan, Anne and Simon, who make such a major contribution to everything I do. Finally, as noted in the dedication, this book is in memory of my father, who died in June 1985, while I was in the US. He was one of the nicest and best men I have ever known, and I consider myself exceedingly lucky to have had him as a father.

Boston, Mass. GRAHAM BIRD

1 Introduction: the Issues Involved

This book sets out to identify and analyse some of the principal issues involved in discussing international financial policy from the viewpoint of the developing world. That such a perspective receives specific attention is a relatively recent phenomenon. Certainly at the time of the Bretton Woods conference in 1944 the generally held view was that developing countries did not warrant any form of special treatment within the context of the international financial system. However, since then the evolution of the system – or in recent years some would argue the 'non-system' – has shown a gradual acceptance of the hypothesis that developing countries experience balance of payments difficulties that are different in nature or in degree from those experienced by developed countries and that their ability to deal with them is more circumscribed.

In the main this has been reflected by the introduction of a series of special facilities within the International Monetary Fund (IMF) designed to help alleviate problems that are particularly acute in developing countries. During the 1960s the Compensatory Financing Facility was introduced to provide countries with compensation for shortfalls in export receipts and the Buffer Stock Financing Facility was set up to provide indirect financial support for international commodity schemes. During the 1970s the CFF was liberalised and the Extended Fund Facility and Trust Fund were established, the former to provide larger amounts of Fund finance in support of programmes designed to correct structural payments imbalances and the latter to provide concessionary assistance, financed by selling Fund gold, to the least developed countries of the world. The 1970s also witnessed other significant developments in relations between the International Monetary Fund and the Third World. In its Final Report the Committee of Twenty argued strongly that international monetary reform should promote the net flow of real resources to developing countries, and to encourage this the Development Committee (formally

1

the Joint Ministerial Committee of the Fund and World Bank on the Transfer of Real Resources to Developing Countries) was subsequently established. Furthermore, towards the end of the 1970s, the Fund reviewed its approach to the conditions it attaches to many of its loans and gave some indications that it was adopting a more flexible attitude. It also introduced two Subsidy Accounts to reduce the cost of Fund borrowing under the Oil Facility and the Supplementary Financing Facility for its least developed member countries. These changes took place against a backdrop of increasing interest in and pressure for a new international economic order which would discriminate in favour of, or at least not discriminate against, developing countries.

The early 1980s seemed to suggest that this trend of gradual modification to the needs of developing countries would continue, since, in 1981, there were further changes in the CFF to allow the Fund to compensate countries for excesses in the cost of cereal imports. As with the Oil Facility of the mid-1970s, it appeared to be recognised that balance of payments difficulties could arise just as much through sudden and exogenously caused increases in import payments as from shortfalls in export receipts.

However, this pattern of gradual adaptation was soon to be interrupted. First, political changes in a number of important developed countries led to a change in attitude towards the Fund and its dealings with developing countries, and in particular with the poorest amongst them, which by then formed its almost exclusive clientele. This was reflected by a significant increase in the strictness and form of Fund conditionality, and by the increasing emphasis that was being placed on the private international banks as the mechanism for providing balance of payments financing. Second, but related to this latter point, the 'debt crisis' emerged in 1982 with the problems encountered by Mexico and a series of other, mainly Latin American, countries. The debt problem and its resolution subsequently dominated discussion of international financial reform and most other issues were either pushed to one side or were redefined in terms of their contribution to dealing with debt.

Meanwhile international financial arrangements, more widely perceived, have undergone fundamental changes, especially with the move to flexible exchange rates. Established to oversee the operation of the Bretton Woods system, the Fund has been searching for a different role following the collapse of the old system. Significantly it has been the debt crisis that has provided it with a new lease of life as its task of vetting and validating the adjustment programmes of debtor countries has become a central component of debt rescheduling.

Although brief, this review of the evolution of international financial arrangements with reference to the developing world identifies a number of key issues with which any future policies will have to deal.

1. SETTING THE SCENE: THE POLICY ISSUES

1.1 The Fund and economic development

The Fund's traditional role involved overseeing what was an essentially fixed exchange rate system, providing short-term finance to assist countries facing temporary balance of payments difficulties, and encouraging the development of a liberal system of international trade and payments. Since 1973, however, the Fund has generally exerted little influence over the direction or size of exchange rate movements (even though it has made efforts to provide a degree of surveillance over these and to come up with an acceptable set of guidelines for government intervention in foreign exchange markets), there has been a massive increase in the size of balance of payments disequilibria with most of the associated 'recycling' taking place through the banks rather than the Fund, and there has been a period of growing protectionism as countries have tried to ameliorate the effects of recession on their external accounts and to offset the implications of increased competition from the newly industrialising countries (NICs) on their traditional industries and thereby on employment. What is more, changes in the quantity of international liquidity have had very little to do with the Fund and much more to do with the macroeconomic policies pursued in the United States, the operation of the Eurocurrency market and fluctuations in the price of gold.

Yet there remain a number of channels through which the Fund may still exert a significant influence over economic development. First, it is a direct source of finance at either near-market or concessionary rates of interest. Second, because a large proportion of its finance is conditional, it has an effect on the conduct of economic policy in those countries turning to it for help. Third, and primarily through its conditionality, it may help to sustain private bank lending to countries that would otherwise be deemed less creditworthy – the so-called catalytic effect.

Identifying these channels of influence in turn poses a series of questions about the Fund's relationship with the developing world. Should it be an adjustment or financing institution? Should it direct its resources primarily to those least developed countries with little access to private loans or to the better-off developing countries in support of private lending? What is the appropriate division of functions between the Fund and the banks?

Depending on the answers to these questions it is possible to imagine very different types of IMF. At one extreme it would possess very few resources of its own, and merely approve countries' economic programmes in advance of private loans. This would almost inevitably mean that it would have relatively few dealings with the poorer African and Asian countries. At the other extreme it would be a major source of balance of payments finance to such countries. Of course these roles need not be mutually exclusive, although the question of the correct balance between them remains.

Having defined a role for the Fund, we must next decide how to provide it with sufficient resources? At present Fund activities are mainly financed by subscriptions, which, in turn, are determined by countries' quotas. However, borrowing from member countries has been used as a way of supplementing resources. There has also been discussion of the possibility of the Fund borrowing from private capital markets. Yet the impression is sometimes created that the Fund's financing is organised on the basis of expediency rather than either efficiency or equity. It is therefore an issue worthy of further consideration. If it is felt that subscriptions should be the dominant, if not exclusive, source of finance for the Fund, then a related question is whether existing quotas form the ideal framework upon which these should be based. If not, what changes should be made?

While there is some debate about how much finance it should provide to countries encountering balance of payments difficulties, there is general consensus that the Fund does contribute an important input into payments adjustment through its conditionality. Beyond this, however, there is considerable disagreement over what form conditionality should take. This relates not only to the proportions of low as opposed to high conditionality finance, but also to the nature of the conditions themselves.

As far as the division between low and high conditionality is concerned, one view is that low conditionality finance should cover those payments imbalances that are exogenously caused. Another is that causation is largely irrelevant and that strict conditions are appropriate for all imbalances that are 'permanent' rather than 'temporary.' Certainly there are legitimate grounds for debate about the appropriate division between the two types of finance, not least because of the ambiguity in the terms used (for example, what is temporary?).

Turning to the nature of high conditionality, we find that the principal emphasis of IMF stabilisation programmes is on credit restraint, which is internally consistent with the Fund's view that over-expansionary demand policies are more often than not the prime cause of payments problems. In circumstances where fiscal deficits have been allowed to grow, and have been financed by domestic credit creation, there can be little doubt that the imposition of financial discipline is crucial to payments correction. But in other circumstances there may be more doubt about whether credit control should be allocated the prime role or whether it should adopt only a secondary role.

If there are circumstances in which existing Fund conditionality is inappropriate, the next question is how should it be modified? Should ceilings on credit creation be abandoned or should a richer mix of policies be used?

1.2 Structural changes to the international financial regime

1.2.1 Existing Fund facilities

As mentioned earlier, the Fund's range of activities has evolved in response to recognising a number of specific problems in developing countries. Legitimate questions are, first, whether the problems have been correctly defined, and, second, whether the measures introduced provide the best way of dealing with them.

Looking first of all at the Compensatory Financing Facility, a number of questions may be asked. Why does the CFF focus on export shortfalls when exogenously caused balance of payments instability may equally arise from variations in imports? Why has CFF finance, especially net drawings, covered only a relatively small proportion of those payments deficits caused by externally generated

terms of trade movements, and does not expansion of the CFF offer a
better way of increasing the amount of low conditionality finance
available from the Fund than expanding the lower credit tranches,
since its emphasis on external causation avoids the problem of 'moral
hazard?' Why have nominal instead of real values been used in
estimating export shortfalls? Why has more flexibility not been
shown in organising the repayment of CFF loans to enable net
drawings to reflect the current needs of deficit countries? Has the
facility encouraged the basic causes of export instability to be corrected? If criticisms are accepted, a related question is how best the
CFF might be reformed?

Turning to the Extended Fund Facility we may query the extent to
which it has actually helped the structural balance of payments
problems it was designed to alleviate. Its usage has been somewhat
patchy over the years since its introduction in 1974, and analysis of
the programmes associated with EFF loans suggests that these differ
little from conventional stand-by programmes which concentrate on
demand side financial variables rather than supply side real ones. Is
there then an argument for reassessing and reforming the EFF?

The Buffer Stock Financing Facility has been very little used by
Fund members. Although its title is rather misleading, since the
Facility does not provide direct finance for buffer stocking, its existence, as well as subsequent attempts to set up an integrated programme of commodity stabilisation agreements outside the Fund,
raises the question of the best way of dealing with commodity
instability. Is this best tackled by trying to eliminate it via buffer
stocks or production agreements, or does compensatory financing
offer a superior policy alternative?

While there may be scope for modifying existing facilities, there is
also the question of whether there are other specific problems which
would benefit from having a special Fund facility addressed to them.
For example, could the difficulties caused for debtor countries by
unanticipated increases in interest rates be ameliorated by introducing a facility which enables countries affected to receive financial
compensation along similar lines to the CFF?

1.2.2 Interest rate subsidies

Whereas it could be argued that introducing an interest rate compensation scheme would have an undesirable element in terms of the

distribution of its benefits, which would, in the main, go to those countries with the largest amounts of private debt, i.e. the better-off developing countries, the Fund could offer more help to its poorer members by extending the use of interest rate subsidies, which, in the past, have been restricted to drawings under the Oil Facility and the Supplementary Financing Facility. Questions, of course, remain about the details of such subsidy arrangements, including their coverage, the size of subsidy payments and the rate of subsidy, and the method of financing. Furthermore, since the Fund would in effect be granting aid to recipients of subsidies, a more central question relates to the costs and benefits of subsidies by comparison with other conventional forms of aid.

1.2.3 The quota system

Quotas are fundamental to the Fund's operations, since they help to determine (a) access to General Account finance, (b) the distribution of SDRs, (c) subscriptions to the Fund, and (d) voting rights. However, there are reasons for arguing that current quota arrangements represent a structural deficiency of the IMF system. One such reason is that quotas are used for more than one purpose. This would not be a problem if these purposes were perfectly positively correlated. But in fact they may be in direct conflict. Countries in the strongest economic position to provide the resources necessary to run the Fund are, almost by definition, unlikely to be the ones in greatest need of the Fund's financial assistance.

Quotas, as currently used, may be insufficiently subtle and flexible to perform the various jobs that they have been given to do. More than this, it is perhaps doubtful whether any single set of individual country quotas could successfully fulfil such a multipurpose role. Rather than a country having one multipurpose Fund quota, is there a case for having what are, in effect, multiple quotas?

Second, while it is the size of the overall global quota that constrains the Fund's activities, the precise mechanism by which this is determined remains unclear to those not involved in the decision making. Although statements from the Fund refer to vague concepts such as 'the financing and adjustment role envisaged for the Fund', the details of how such concepts are translated into a specific global quota are not explained. If the economic underpinning of the global quota is ill-defined, the process by which its value is changed, by means of periodic reviews, may have become increasingly unsatisfactory in a world where global economic variables can and do change rapidly.

The system used for changing quotas limits the ability of the Fund to respond to a changing global economic environment. Instead the Fund is forced into using *ad hoc* measures to increase its resources and therefore to raise the amount of financial assistance it can offer deficit countries. Although such measures allow the Fund to be more flexible than it could otherwise be, they may have deficiencies of their own. Is there then a case for increasing flexibility by modifying the arrangements through which the global quota is changed?

While the global quota effects the amount of resources the Fund has at its disposal, individual country quotas determine the distribution of subscriptions to the Fund, voting rights and SDR allocations. They also set an upper limit on the quantity of General Account finance that members can borrow. That quotas do not determine countries' actual drawings from the Fund is because these are also affected by various eligibility criteria. Members without a 'balance of payments need' cannot borrow from the Fund irrespective of their quota. Similarly members' access to finance through the Fund's various special facilities depends both qualitatively and quantitatively on the nature of their payments deficits. For example, members not experiencing a temporary shortfall in export receipts are ineligible to draw from the Fund under the CFF. Furthermore, in the case of upper credit tranche drawings or drawings under the EFF, the Fund's financial assistance depends on the ability of a member's government satisfactorily to negotiate a detailed programme of economic measures with the Fund.

However, this is not to deny that individual country quotas are of considerable significance. The key issue is whether the way in which quotas are arrived at accurately summarises the various facets of a member's relationship with the Fund. One part of this question is the extent to which actual quotas differ from those calculated on the basis of various formulas used within the Fund. Another related part of the question is the extent to which the 'calculated quotas' provide a satisfactory objective means of determining individual quotas; are all relevant economic variables considered, and are they given appropriate weights?

1.2.4 An SDR link and reserve currency consolidation

One specific aspect of modifying the quota system would be to change the distribution formula for SDRs so that a larger proportion of any given SDR allocation goes to developing countries. But even if it is accepted that there should be some form of link, a number of other questions follow on from this. What precise form should the SDR distribution formula take from the range of alternatives that could be suggested? Would developing country recipients really stand to gain that much from a link, given that the interest rate on net use is now at a market-related level? Moreover, given that the link will only be beneficial if SDRs are actually created, does the international economy warrant an extra allocation of SDRs? Furthermore, how can the SDR be made more attractive and established as the principal reserve asset? Does this objective require the setting up of a Substitution Account to change the composition of reserves, and, if so, can this be organised in such a way as to induce a net flow of resources to developing countries? Again, if net resource flows would result from the link and from other reforms, what would be the size of these flows?

2. THE DIFFERENT INTERESTS OF DIFFERENT DEVELOPING COUNTRIES

To group all developing countries together and imply thereby that they have common interests in international financial reform is highly misleading. Moreover, any simple form of country disaggregation is likely to suggest a community of interests that in fact does not exist. But what are the special interests of particular groups and how can they be best served? Furthermore, are there areas of common ground? For example, might developing countries be expected to share a view on the desirability of a specific global exchange rate regime?

3. THE TYPE, METHOD, AND PACE OF REFORM

The lack of uniformly common interests amongst developing countries is likely to slow down the pace of reform. Even if agreement can be reached between them as to what reforms are desirable, an important question relates to the best way in which such reforms may be achieved. One approach would be to push for a whole range of reforms which, at an instant, restructures existing arrangements and establishes some type of new international order. A second approach would be to opt for more gradual, piecemeal, and evolutionary reform. Which of these approaches is more likely to succeed? A third possibility could be for the developing world to try and 'go it alone' through South–South co-operation. But is this a sensible policy for developing countries to adopt?

4. A CHECKLIST OF KEY POLICY QUESTIONS

Let us conclude this chapter by re-emphasising some of the key international financial policy issues for the developing world.

   (i) What should be the Fund's role in its dealing with developing countries?

  (ii) What should be the nature of the Fund's relationship with the banks in the context of dealings with the developing world?

 (iii) What mechanism should be used for providing the Fund with resources?

 (iv) Should Fund conditionality be modified to reflect better the needs of developing countries, and, if so, in what ways?

  (v) What is the correct balance between low and high conditionality finance within the Fund?

 (vi) Is the existing set of IMF facilities satisfactory? If not, what changes should be made to existing ones and what new ones should be introduced?

 (vii) What is the best way of dealing with the problem of commodity instability?

(viii) Is there a case for extending the use of interest rate subsidies within the Fund, and, if so, how might this be best arranged?

 (ix) In what ways, if any, should the quotas that underpin the Fund's operations be modified?

  (x) Should an SDR link be introduced and would this really benefit developing countries?

 (xi) How best can the SDR be established as the system's principal reserve asset and can the process be used to benefit developing countries?

(xii) What are the different interests of different developing countries in international financial reform?

(xiii) Do developing countries share common interests in issues such as the nature of the global exchange rate regime?

(xiv) What approach to achieving reforms is likely to be most successful?

(xv) How best can the debt problems of the developing world be handled?

(xvi) Is there an argument for South–South financial policies?

(xvii) What would be the quantitative significance of the policies discussed?

There are, no doubt, other questions which could be raised, but the foregoing provide enough to be going on with.

The remainder of this book assesses these questions in more detail and attempts to provide some kind of answer to them. However, space is an effective constraint and some questions are therefore more fully discussed than others.

Furthermore, many issues that are of related importance are neglected. There is, for example, very little discussion of aid policy or of trade policy as it applies to the developing world. Similarly neglected are questions of stabilisation policy within developing countries. Clearly all these have a bearing on the LDCs' balance of payments position and may influence the need for or the feasibility of international financial policy. However, the line has to be drawn somewhere and international financial policies seem to offer a sufficiently self-contained area for discussion to warrant the exclusion of aid, trade, and stabilisation policy from this book. Yet their considerable importance should not be overlooked.

2 The Developing World: a Special Case?

The argument that developing countries are a special case and warrant special treatment within the international financial system draws on a number of factors related both to equity and efficiency. On the equity side the argument is that people in developing countries have lower living standards than those in the rest of the world and that the international financial system could and should be used as a vehicle for directing a larger volume of aid to them. This immediately raises the whole question of the pros and cons of foreign aid. However, if it is decided that aid is to be encouraged, another question is whether the international financial system offers the best way of securing a desirable flow of aid. This is a matter of efficiency.

More generally, however, considerations of international financial efficiency as applied to developing countries focus on their balance of payments problems rather than their level of development. In the real world, of course, such distinctions are difficult to sustain, for developmental and balance of payments problems become inexorably interrelated. Furthermore, balance of payments policies have implications for the distribution of income, and this again raises the question of equity.

A further efficiency consideration involves the effect that international financial policies directed towards benefiting the developing world may have on the operation of the international financial system as a whole. Are equity gains being bought at the cost of global inefficiency? The principal problem here is to define what is an 'efficient' international financial system. In theory this may be one that generates the optimum combination of balance of payments adjustment and financing: with the optimum reflecting the maximisation of an underlying welfare function comprising both micro elements in terms of the allocation of resources and macro elements in terms of economic growth, full employment and price stability.

Yet making such theoretical concepts operational is fraught with difficulty. Although views may frequently be expressed, the rigour with which they are supported often leaves something to be desired. The IMF has, for example, maintained that the international financial system placed too little emphasis on adjustment during the 1970s and too much on financing, whereas during the early 1980s the balance was more appropriate. The argument is supported by claiming that the disequilibria of the 1970s were not temporary and required adjustment. However, on the basis of other criteria, such as world output and trade, the counter-claim could be made that, from a world efficiency point of view, adjustment was excessive in the early 1980s. The issues are complex. What is clear is that it is important not to lose sight of efficiency in an attempt to realise equity objectives. The developing world has an undoubted interest in securing an efficient and smoothly running international financial system.

Rather than examining various indicators of poverty, which would emphasise equity considerations, this chapter concentrates on criteria for assessing the size and nature of balance of payments problems. An attempt is made to see whether these efficiency criteria show that developing countries may legitimately be regarded as a special case within the international financial system, and therefore singled out for specific attention. The final part of the chapter goes on to examine other aspects of the international financial regime from the viewpoint of the developing world.

1. THE CRITERIA FOR SPECIAL TREATMENT

Without constructing a full model of the balance of payments, it may be observed that payments difficulties emanate from a number of sources. First, there may be secular changes in exports, imports and long term capital flows. For example, a country producing and exporting goods which have a low income elasticity of demand and importing goods which have a higher one will tend to encounter balance of payments problems. Such factors reflect payments deficits and surpluses as essentially structural phenomena whose resolution depends on a reorganisation of production and trade.

Differing income elasticities of demand for imports and exports may also lead to movements in a country's commodity terms of trade. The extent of these will depend not only on the size of changes in demand, induced by factors other than price, but also on the price elasticity of supply. A given shift in demand will have a greater impact on price the lower the supply elasticity. Of course where the demand for a good is unstable because of instability in its underlying determinants (other than price), the extent to which this is reflected in price instability will also depend on the elasticity of supply. A second aspect of countries' balance of payments problems, then, relates to instability in export earnings and in imports payments. In part such instability reflects vulnerability to exogenous shocks. However, vulnerability will also be affected by the exchange rate regime, the conventional view being that countries with fixed exchange rates are more exposed to outside shocks than those with flexible rates.

Both of the above factors influence the incidence of payments deficits and surpluses. Other important aspects of the balance of payments relate to the speed and efficiency with which deficits may be financed or corrected. The capacity of a country to finance a payments deficit depends on the level of its reserve holdings and the availability of finance from the private international banks and the International Monetary Fund (IMF). In turn the scope for payments correction varies with the capacity for adjustment within the economy. This depends on a number of factors, including the extent to which domestic consumption may be switched into exports and more generally the scope for short run export expansion and efficient import substitution, the degree of money illusion, the flexibility of domestic economic policy, the level of infrastructural investment, and, not unrelated to the above, the values of export supply and import and export demand price elasticities.

For example, with low elasticities and a high degree of real wage resistance the scope for balance of payments adjustment will be strictly constrained. Clearly to the extent that the adaptability of an economy is positively related to its level of economic development it is likely that developing countries will encounter more difficulty in coping with balance of payments problems than do developed economies. However, the presumption may not always be valid. It is not difficult to think of developing countries that have been characterised by their ability to respond to a changing world economic environment. Similarly one can think of developed countries that find change difficult to accommodate because of their stymied socio-economic and political systems. Against this background a number of indicators may be assembled to provide some reflection of the size and nature of a country's, or country group's, payments problem.

1.1 Balance of payments: export and import trends

Table 2.1 summarises the current account position of the main country groupings over 1977–85. Aside from short periods of time following the large increases in oil prices in 1973–4 and 1978–9, many industrial countries maintained a surplus on current account. Up until 1982 the OPEC countries as a group were in surplus, even though, as in the case of the industrial countries, there is considerable variation within the group. The non-oil developing countries by contrast were in deficit on their current account throughout the period. Again, however, there are significant differences within the group. Although the absolute value of the low income countries' (LICs') deficit has been less than that of the other non-oil LDCs when it is expressed as a percentage of exports of goods and services, as is done in Table 2.2, it emerges that, on a weighted average basis, the size of the LIC deficit has been much greater than that for NOLDCs as a whole. A similar comparison with respect to merchandise trade presented in Table 2.3 shows that while NICs experienced a fall in export volume only in 1982 and a fall in import volume in 1982 and 1983, LICs experienced a fall in export volume in three years between 1977 and 1983 and a fall in import volume in 1981 and 1983. In the years prior to 1973 LICs had a heavier incidence of import volume contraction than NICs.

Of course care has to be exercised in glibly concluding that the size of payments deficits stands as a pure guide to the size of balance of payments problems. While the argument that the deficits may be temporary and self-reversing does not seem to hold in the case of much of the developing world, other arguments that permanent capital inflows, for example in the form of aid, may permit a current account deficit to be sustained, and that *ex post* payments data conceal the extent to which other macroeconomic policy objectives have been subjugated, are valid. The former would result in data on current account deficits overstating the size of payments problems while the latter would lead to underestimation.

However, care is still needed in interpreting these factors. Experience in the 1970s and 1980s clearly demonstrated that the financing of current account deficits by private borrowing will not be sustainable unless accompanied by an increased capacity to service the related debt. Current account deficits which in the short term seem to create relatively few problems may in the longer run appear far

TABLE 2.1 *Summary of payments balances on current account, 1977–85[1] (in billions of US dollars)*

	1977	1978	1979	1980	1981	1982	1983	1984	1985
Industrial countries	-2.1	32.7	-5.1	-38.1	4.8	3.2	2.8	-31.2	-46.2
Canada	-4.1	-4.0	-4.2	-1.2	-5.4	1.9	1.3	-0.2	—
United States	-11.7	-12.3	2.6	6.6	10.7	-3.8	-35.5	-84.3	-109.0
Japan	11.1	17.0	-8.1	-9.9	6.3	8.8	22.2	36.4	41.5
France	1.0	8.5	6.9	-2.5	-2.8	-9.5	-1.8	-0.2	2.6
Germany, Fed. Rep. of	8.5	13.4	0.1	-8.3	0.8	10.2	9.8	9.6	12.0
Italy	3.1	7.9	6.4	-9.5	-7.5	-4.9	1.0	—	-1.8
United Kingdom	2.0	5.5	3.0	12.7	18.1	13.3	7.5	4.9	4.2
Other industrial countries	-12.0	-3.2	-11.8	-26.0	-15.6	-13.0	-1.6	2.5	4.4
Developing countries	-1.0	-37.3	-1.0	21.8	-55.0	-99.0	-70.1	-53.0	-54.0
Of which, major borrowers	-9.5	-18.4	-22.3	-26.6	-35.7	-39.8	-11.0	-11.5	-9.7
Oil exporting countries	29.4	5.7	62.3	110.4	53.5	-13.1	-17.5	-8.0	-9.0
Middle Eastern countries	36.7	20.6	61.8	99.7	57.8	3.7	-10.3	-5.5	-6.5
Other	-7.3	-14.9	0.5	10.7	-4.3	-16.8	-7.2	-2.5	-2.5
Non-oil developing countries	-30.4	-42.9	-63.3	-88.7	-108.5	-85.9	-52.6	-45.0	-45.0
By analytical group[2]									
Net oil exporters	-6.4	-7.9	-8.6	-11.0	-23.4	-17.3	-4.4	-6.5	-7.6
Net oil importers	-25.0	-34.3	-52.5	-74.4	-86.4	-74.3	-51.8	-40.6	-37.4
Major exporters of manufactures	-8.9	-10.8	-23.0	-32.8	-37.8	-34.6	-15.9	-8.6	-5.3
Low-income countries	-3.7	-8.2	-10.6	-14.2	-15.5	-15.0	-12.4	-12.8	-13.8
Other net oil importers	-12.5	-15.3	-18.9	-27.4	-33.1	-24.7	-23.5	-19.2	-18.2

By area									
Africa[3]	−6.6	−9.3	−9.6	−12.6	−14.1	−13.0	−10.2	−9.4	−9.6
Asia	−1.6	−8.3	−17.1	−25.3	−22.7	−14.3	−11.5	−6.2	−6.5
Europe	−9.1	−7.2	−10.1	−12.7	−10.4	−6.9	−5.4	−3.1	−3.0
Middle East	−5.1	−6.2	−8.4	−8.1	−10.6	−9.6	−10.2	−9.3	−10.6
Western Hemisphere	−8.5	−13.3	−21.3	−33.1	−45.9	−38.9	−15.5	−17.1	−15.5
Total[4]	−3.1	−4.6	−6.0	−16.3	−50.3	−95.9	−67.3	−84.2	−100.2

1. On goods, services, and private transfers.
2. China, which is classified as a low-income country but is also a net oil exporter, is included in the total but not in the subgroups.
3. Excluding South Africa.
4. Reflects errors, omissions, and asymmetries in reported balance of payments statistics on current account, plus balance of listed groups with other countries (mainly the USSR and other nonmember countries of Eastern Europe).

SOURCE: *World Economic Outlook*, IMF, Washington, 1984.

TABLE 2.2 Developing countries: current account balances as percentage of exports of goods and services, 1967–85

	Average 1967–76[1]	1977	1978	1979	1980	1981	1982	1983	1984	1985
Developing countries										
Weighted average	-6.7	-0.3	-8.7	-0.2	2.9	-7.1	-14.2	-10.6	-7.6	-6.9
Median	-19.9	-20.5	-29.6	-27.0	-30.4	-37.5	-35.4	-31.0	-25.9	-24.3
Oil exporting countries										
Weighted average	11.3	17.9	3.5	26.3	33.2	16.6	-5.1	-8.1	-4.2	-3.8
Median	8.4	19.3	3.5	24.2	31.8	5.4	1.5	-1.6	-2.5	-3.8
Non-oil developing countries										
Weighted average	-17.1	-13.7	-16.4	-18.7	-20.7	-23.7	-19.6	-11.9	-9.1	-8.2
Median	-22.0	-21.5	-30.7	-29.1	-34.1	-42.4	-36.9	-33.9	-29.4	-25.9
By analytical group										
Weighted averages										
Net oil exporters	-22.6	-9.3	-20.2	-15.3	-14.5	-28.7	-22.3	-5.6	-7.6	-8.0
Net oil importers	-16.2	-12.7	-15.7	-19.4	-22.0	-22.6	-19.0	-13.2	-9.4	-8.3
Major exporters of manufactures	-15.5	-8.7	-8.8	-14.7	-16.5	-17.4	-16.9	-7.5	-3.6	-2.0
Low-income countries	-22.7	-9.1	-26.7	-29.8	-32.8	-25.3	-16.6	-15.4	-17.2	-20.7
Excluding China and India	-46.5	-41.9	-59.0	-58.3	-59.6	-66.3	-65.6	-51.6	-50.4	-47.5
Other net oil importers	-13.5	-21.6	-23.0	-23.1	-27.3	-32.3	-24.7	-24.4	-18.2	-15.8
Medians										
Net oil exporters	-19.5	-21.9	-24.4	-16.2	-5.7	-25.6	-23.3	-18.7	-14.2	-13.8
Net oil importers	-22.4	-21.5	-32.7	-30.4	-36.7	-42.5	-42.0	-36.1	-32.5	-27.6

Major exporters of manufactures	-13.9	-2.9	-9.7	-7.1	-18.7	-19.9	-15.6	-5.5	-2.5	—
Low-income countries	-41.1	-41.8	-69.5	-69.0	-67.5	-66.4	-87.5	-74.8	-59.7	-58.7
Other net oil importers	-16.9	-17.8	-23.8	-24.5	-27.9	-36.3	-32.1	-30.8	-25.7	-24.1
By area										
Weighted averages										
Africa (excluding South Africa)	-20.6	-29.0	-38.1	-31.7	-35.1	-42.9	-42.3	-34.0	-28.7	-26.8
Asia	-12.9	-1.9	-8.0	-12.6	-14.9	-11.9	-7.5	-5.7	-2.7	-2.6
Europe	-8.5	-27.7	-18.9	-21.2	-22.2	-16.2	-11.4	-9.1	-4.7	-4.3
Middle East	-34.2	-32.6	-32.6	-34.8	-24.3	-30.7	-28.3	-31.8	-26.4	-27.5
Western Hemisphere	-24.1	-15.9	-21.9	-26.8	-32.2	-41.0	-38.3	-15.6	-15.5	-12.5
Medians										
Africa (excluding South Africa)	-26.8	-22.9	-46.8	-38.8	-51.6	-55.4	-62.1	-53.0	-41.4	-35.2
Asia	-21.8	-22.5	-32.5	-28.7	-36.4	-35.1	-30.5	-31.6	-27.2	-25.7
Europe	-7.7	-21.5	-18.0	-20.4	-19.3	-11.8	-9.4	-10.0	-7.5	-8.5
Middle East	-30.9	-28.0	-45.9	-53.6	-41.9	-52.1	-51.7	-52.0	-45.4	-47.3
Western Hemisphere	-21.1	-20.1	-12.7	-18.9	-24.3	-37.5	-30.9	-25.0	-24.8	-21.5
Memorandum item										
Major borrowers										
Weighted average	-20.0	-13.9	-23.6	-22.0	-19.7	-23.1	-28.5	-8.0	-7.4	-5.6
Median	-20.3	-20.2	-26.4	-21.5	-25.4	-25.6	-24.1	-25.0	-16.5	-10.2

1. Excludes China.

SOURCE: *World Economic Outlook*, IMF, Washington, 1984.

TABLE 2.3 *Non-oil developing countries – by analytical subgroup: merchandise trade, 1967–85, (percentage changes, except as indicated)*

	Average	Change from Preceding Year								
	1967–76[1]	1977	1978	1979	1980	1981	1982	1983	1984	1985
Major exporters of manufactures										
Value (in US dollar terms)										
Exports	17.7	21.9	19.5	26.9	27.8	7.6	-6.8	7.0	14.9	12.2
Imports	18.5	12.7	19.2	33.5	28.1	6.9	-10.0	-4.2	9.1	10.4
Volume										
Exports	9.9	7.2	12.3	9.9	12.6	9.0	-2.2	9.7	11.7	7.2
Imports	9.4	4.1	8.3	11.8	6.5	3.7	-7.8	-0.7	7.4	5.9
Unit value (in US dollar terms)										
Exports	7.1	13.7	6.4	15.5	13.5	-1.4	-4.7	-2.4	2.9	4.7
Imports	8.3	8.3	10.1	19.4	20.2	3.1	-2.4	-3.6	1.5	4.3
Terms of trade	-1.1	5.0	-3.3	-3.3	-5.6	-4.3	-2.4	1.2	1.4	0.4
Purchasing power of exports[2]	8.7	12.5	8.5	6.3	6.3	4.4	-4.5	11.0	13.2	7.6

Low-Income countries
(excluding China and India)

Value (in US dollar terms)										
Exports	9.1	21.0	7.3	19.3	15.0	−7.2	−7.3	7.5	8.8	9.5
Imports	9.3	15.6	30.8	17.5	22.8	−1.4	−4.0	−3.3	5.9	5.8
Volume										
Exports	1.3	−4.6	5.2	2.8	6.4	−3.0	−1.2	5.1	2.9	5.9
Imports	0.8	6.0	18.7	0.7	1.6	−4.4	0.3	−0.8	3.6	2.3
Unit value (in US dollar terms)										
Exports	7.7	26.9	2.0	16.1	8.1	−4.4	−6.1	2.2	5.7	3.4
Imports	8.4	9.0	10.1	16.7	20.9	3.1	−4.3	−2.4	2.2	3.4
Terms of trade	−0.6	16.4	−7.3	−0.5	−10.6	−7.3	−1.9	4.8	3.4	—
Purchasing power of exports[2]	0.6	11.1	−2.6	2.2	−4.9	−10.0	−3.1	10.2	6.4	5.9

1. Compound annual rates of change.
2. Export earnings deflated by import prices.

SOURCE: *World Economic Outlook.* IMF, Washington, 1984.

more problematical. One part of the longer term problem is the domestic sacrifices that need to be made. These are reflected by the drop in import volume amongst the major exporters of manufactures in 1982. Although the effect was to strengthen statistically the current account of these countries, to argue that there was an equivalent reduction in the size of the balance of payments problem is to take a very narrow view. On the basis of the data in Tables 2.1, 2.2, and 2.3 it seems reasonable to conclude that the developing world has experienced payments problems that are relatively severe compared with the rest of the world. However, amongst developing countries significant differences are to be found.

1.2 Commodity terms of trade, export concentration and export instability

Table 2.3 also shows that over 1978–82 there was a marked decline in the terms of trade of NOLDCs. In general this reflected a weakening in the prices of primary products relative to manufactures. Bearing this in mind, it is not surprising to find that LICs with a much heavier concentration of exports on primary products than other non-oil developing countries experienced a sharper deterioration. Data over a longer period suggest that the long run trend in LDCs' terms of trade is downwards. There is also some evidence to suggest that export concentration on primary products brings with it considerable instability in export earnings, and that this in turn creates problems for the management of the balance of payments, even though, in principle, it should be possible to use the reserve accumulations permitted by above trend performance to finance the deficits associated with shortfalls in export earnings.[1]

1.3 Reserve holdings

Table 2.4 expresses reserves in relation to imports of goods and services. On the basis of this criterion developing countries have generally held rather fewer reserves than industrial countries. Again, however, the average conceals considerable variety. While the LICs possessed more reserves than other non-oil developing countries, the LIC average is heavily weighted by India, which holds relatively large reserves. When India (and China) are excluded, LICs' reserve holdings emerge as being less than two-thirds of the average of all NOLDCs.

However, it is not simply a matter of whether developing countries hold relatively few reserves, there is also the question of whether reserve holdings are adequate. Some countries may need fewer reserves than others. Factors affecting the need for reserves include the instability of the balance of payments, the costs of adjustment, the opportunity cost of holding reserves, the availability of non-reserve finance from both the official and private sectors, and the nature of exchange rate policy.[2] If developing countries encounter frequent and large payments problems, high adjustment costs, little access to private capital and operate fixed exchange rates, the argument can be made that they require more reserves than countries with the opposite characteristics. The problem is that LDCs do not fit into such a neat pigeon-hole. Again there is a strong case for disaggregation.[3]

Yet there is little reason to believe that developing countries need *fewer* reserves relative to their imports than do developed countries, except perhaps in the sense that their opportunity cost of holding reserves may be higher. Having a relatively low reserve import ratio may then provide some *prima facie* evidence of reserve inadequacy.

1.4 Access to private capital

Faced with a payments deficit a country has essentially two financing options. One is to run down reserves. The second is to borrow. Quantitatively the most important source of payments finance is the private capital market. However, with the onset of the so-called debt crisis, even developing countries that had been regarded as creditworthy by the banks encountered difficulties in securing loans. Table 2.5 shows clearly how the flow of private loans to developing countries levelled and declined in the 1980s after the rapid growth of the late 1970s.

Lurking behind this observation is the question of the optimum value of private bank lending to the developing world. A possible response to a fall in bank lending is to argue that there had been 'overlending' in the past. Whatever one's conclusion about this complex issue, there is reason to believe that, at least for a while,

TABLE 2.4 *Non-oil developing countries: reserves and ratios of reserves to imports of goods and services, 1977–85*[1]

	1977	1978	1979	1980	1981	1982	1983	1984	1985
Official reserve holdings					*(In billions of US dollars)*				
All non-oil developing countries	68.6	84.7	94.8	96.1	96.9	92.4	100.2	116.6	131.3
By analytical group									
Net oil exporters	9.3	10.4	13.4	16.8	17.3	13.3	15.2	18.8	22.5
Net oil importers	59.3	74.3	81.4	79.3	79.6	79.1	85.1	97.7	108.8
Major exporters of manufactures	28.1	38.0	39.9	35.7	38.0	35.8	38.8	50.7	63.9
Low-income countries	12.5	13.2	15.4	14.9	14.8	20.3	25.7	28.1	27.7
Excluding China and India	4.5	4.3	4.8	4.5	4.2	3.8	5.1	4.8	3.8
Other net oil importers	18.6	23.1	26.2	28.7	26.7	22.9	20.6	18.9	17.2
By area									
Africa (excluding South Africa)	4.5	4.8	5.4	5.0	4.4	3.8	3.8	3.6	2.6
Asia	27.2	30.4	34.2	35.8	40.5	47.9	55.9	65.1	73.1
Europe	8.6	10.6	9.7	10.3	9.5	7.6	8.6	9.4	9.3
Middle East	7.1	9.0	9.8	10.6	10.5	11.2	9.6	8.6	8.4
Western Hemisphere	20.3	28.9	34.8	33.1	31.0	21.1	21.2	28.7	36.8
Memorandum item									
Major borrowers[2]	27.5	32.8	38.0	34.3	33.0	22.4	24.8	33.1	42.8

(In per cent)

Ratios of reserves to imports of goods and services[3]

All non-oil developing countries	26.0	26.6	22.7	17.9	16.5	17.0	19.4	20.8	21.4
By analytical group									
Net oil exporters	23.5	22.0	20.8	19.3	16.4	14.0	18.5	20.3	21.9
Net oil importers	26.4	27.4	23.1	17.6	16.5	17.6	19.6	20.9	21.2
Major exporters of manufactures	24.4	27.2	21.3	14.9	14.4	14.5	16.5	19.8	22.7
Low-income countries	36.2	28.7	25.7	19.3	19.2	28.2	35.1	35.2	31.6
Excluding China and India	23.0	17.3	16.5	12.6	12.0	11.2	15.3	13.6	10.0
Other net oil importers	25.0	27.1	24.8	21.5	18.8	17.5	16.3	14.4	12.2
By area									
Africa (excluding South Africa)	15.3	14.0	13.3	10.2	9.1	8.6	9.3	8.4	5.7
Asia	30.4	26.1	21.7	17.7	18.5	22.5	25.3	26.8	27.1
Europe	18.5	20.9	15.0	13.2	11.3	10.1	12.1	12.7	11.6
Middle East	29.7	33.0	27.8	23.9	21.5	23.9	21.1	17.9	16.0
Western Hemisphere	32.2	38.6	34.2	24.2	19.5	15.0	18.2	22.4	26.2
Memorandum item									
Major borrowers[2]	35.2	33.8	30.6	21.2	17.3	12.5	16.6	19.8	23.3

1. For this table, official holdings of gold are valued at SDR 35 an ounce. This convention results in a significant underestimate of the reserves of those groups of countries that have substantial holdings of gold.
2. Includes two oil exporting countries: Indonesia and Venezuela.
3. Ratio of year-end reserves to imports of goods and services during the year indicated.

SOURCE: *World Economic Outlook*, IMF, Washington, 1984.

TABLE 2.5 *International bond issues and Eurocurrency bank credits – by country of borrower (millions of dollars)*

International bond issues

	1981	1982	1983
Developing countries	4,886	5,003	2,535
Latin American countries	3,658	2,480	71
Argentina	195	—	—
Brazil	60	91	—
Chile	30	—	—
Colombia	20	35	—
Mexico	3,012	1,919	—
Panama	25	—	21
Venezuela	291	385	—
Other	25	50	50
Asian countries	1,068	2,075	2,252
Hongkong	70	40	50
India	271	250	60
Indonesia	97	412	328
Korea	323	172	556
Malaysia	—	807	883
Philippines	99	50	—
Singapore	30	125	70
Thailand	93	63	265
Other	85	156	40
Middle Eastern and African countries	160	448	212
Egypt	—	75	—
Israel	117	200	135
United Arab Emirates	—	20	—
Other	43	153	77

Eurocurrency bank credits

	1981	1982	1983
Developing countries	45,264	41,519	32,937
Latin American countries	30,152	26,719	15,406
Argentina	2,534	1,565	1,750
Brazil	5,751	5,716	4,475
Chile	2,204	1,194	1,319
Colombia	1,030	741	549
Ecuador	934	815	431
Mexico	7,530	7,953	5,138
Peru	1,407	1,069	500
Venezuela	7,559	6,799	237
Other	1,203	867	1,007

TABLE 2.5—*continued*

Eurocurrency bank credits

	1981	1982	1983
Asian countries	10,288	8,403	8,828
India	377	284	809
Indonesia	725	1,250	1,467
Korea	2,824	2,923	3,250
Malaysia	1,725	1,909	950
Pakistan	350	455	365
Philippines	1,257	635	819
Thailand	692	268	349
Other	2,338	679	819
Middle Eastern and African			
* countries*	4,824	6,397	8,703
Algeria	—	26	1,934
Egypt	63	353	335
Morocco	774	326	226
Nigeria	1,802	2,042	1,775
Turkey	100	277	1,106
United Arab Emirates	363	93	876
Other	1,722	3,280	2,451

SOURCE: *World Financial Markets, Morgan Guaranty.*

TABLE 2.6 *Access to bank loans (in millions US dollars normalised for country size)*[1]

	1973	1975	1977	1979	1981	1982
Major borrowers	17,361	34,144	65,002	113,405	141,063	161,480
Middle income oil						
importers	29,131	51,811	93,933	164,402	224,545	236,974
Low income						
countries	4,377	7,753	10,811	17,021	27,117	32,482

1. The figures are deflated by relative GDPs.

bankers may be generally reluctant to increase their exposure in developing countries. The psychological impact of the debt crisis may incline them towards 'underlending'.

From amongst the developing world some countries may seem less creditworthy than others. It is frequently argued that LICs have had relatively little access to bank loans. Tables 2.5 and 2.6 test this claim. It transpires that (even after normalisation for country size) the distribution of bank lending has been skewed towards a fairly

narrow elite of developing countries. The poorer countries within the
developing world have indeed been largely by-passed.

1.5 Debt

The relatively low level of private borrowing by LICs, however, has
not meant that they have escaped the debt difficulties more commonly associated with many of the better-off developing countries.
Indeed as Tables 2.7 and 2.8 reveal, both in terms of their debt ratios
and debt service ratios LICs have encountered problems more severe
than those of the major exporters of manufactures. Although the
nature of their debt, and the fact that a high proportion of it is
official, may mean that such comparisons overstate the relative size
and acuteness of the LIC debt problem, it can hardly imply other
than their balance of payments position is severely constrained. Debt
problems are certainly not the *exclusive* preserve of the Latin American LDCs, as much media coverage seems to suggest.

1.6 Structural flexibility, the level of development and the costs of adjustment

Although not lending itself to easy empirical confirmation, there is a
reasonable presumption that the poorest developing countries possess a relatively low degree of structural flexibility. With poorly
developed markets and price structures and a low degree of infrastructural investment, along with the nature of many of the products
produced, price elasticities are likely to be relatively low in the short
run. The scope for correcting payments deficits by switching resources rapidly into the production of traded goods may therefore be
constrained and, as the evidence on import volume presented in
Table 2.3 suggests, there may often seem to be few alternatives to
deflationary programmes of balance of payments stabilisation. The
costs of such programmes in terms of lost output and unemployment
will depend on the value of the marginal propensity to import. Where
the propensity is small, the costs will be high, and it may be particularly low for just those economies which are most likely to have to
correct their deficits through deflationary policies.[4]

Other developing countries, in particular the NICs, are notorious
for their adaptability. For these more open economies the cost of

adjustment might be expected to be significantly lower. At the same time, of course, their superior access to borrowing also means that they may have less need to adjust quickly.

1.7 The international financial system and inequity

A final reason why it may be warranted to treat the developing world as a special case is if the international financial system has in the past discriminated against it, both by the distribution of seigniorage and by imposing a disproportionate share of the adjustment burden on non-reserve currency deficit countries.

While there is some legitimate debate over precisely how much seigniorage specific developed countries have gained, the argument that developing countries have gained relatively little seems to have foundation.[5] As far as the burden of adjustment is concerned, however, the picture is less clear cut. The burden of adjustment tends to fall on those deficit countries that cannot finance their deficits either by running down reserves or by borrowing. For this burden to be unevenly placed on the developing world, LDCs need to encounter the most deficits, have relatively few reserves and little access to finance. As seen above, on these criteria there are significant differences across developing countries and over time.

1.8 Conclusion on the basis of the criteria

What emerges from this overview of the criteria for treating the developing world as a special case? The main conclusion is that there is no single entity the 'developing world' which shares similar and exclusive problems. It is therefore the variety amongst developing countries which needs to be reflected in international financial policy.

Many of the better-off, yet still so-called developing, nations do not have a strong case to be treated separately, except perhaps in the sense that measures to support bank lending may be of particular relevance to them. On the other hand, the poorest countries in the developing world have experienced a marked structural deterioration in their balance of payments, are exposed to the problems of payments instability associated with export concentration, lack reserves and access to finance, and therefore are under pressure to achieve short run payments correction, even though rapid adjustment may be

TABLE 2.7 Developing countries: long term and short term external debt relative to exports and to GDP, 1977–85[1] (in per cent)

	1977	1978	1979	1980	1981	1982	1983	1984	1985
Ratio of external debt to exports of goods and services[2]									
Developing countries[3]	124.4	131.0	118.0	108.6	120.1	145.8	154.5	146.8	139.2
Of which, major borrowers	185.8	199.7	188.2	173.6	184.8	241.9	254.5	238.6	222.0
Non-oil developing countries	129.5	131.0	119.5	113.1	125.0	148.3	154.4	147.4	139.8
By analytical group									
Net oil exporters	181.4	185.9	151.8	135.0	163.5	198.4	210.8	201.5	190.8
Net oil importers	120.4	121.3	113.1	108.4	116.7	137.5	142.4	136.0	129.1
Major exporters of manufactures	109.9	108.0	100.1	96.3	103.1	126.8	127.6	119.1	111.3
Low-income countries	166.0	164.7	146.3	134.8	136.2	148.1	154.8	155.8	156.3
Excluding China and India	220.1	228.0	222.0	220.6	265.2	307.1	311.6	311.3	300.7
Other net oil importers	115.7	124.1	120.6	118.5	134.8	153.4	167.9	163.1	154.9
By area									
Africa (excluding South Africa)	136.4	151.6	149.2	141.2	170.9	204.0	220.7	212.0	201.4
Asia	81.9	76.1	68.9	68.1	70.4	80.6	83.1	81.0	78.4
Europe	115.7	123.7	115.2	116.1	109.5	119.5	127.2	119.9	113.1
Middle East	138.9	162.2	149.4	124.4	133.3	149.8	173.2	165.5	163.4
Western Hemisphere	203.9	217.8	198.8	187.9	220.3	283.2	300.0	285.9	264.4

Ratio of external debt to GDP[2]

Developing countries[3]	24.6	25.5	25.4	25.5	28.5	32.8	35.3	35.6	34.2
Of which, major borrowers	29.7	30.6	32.5	32.7	35.3	42.5	47.5	47.8	46.5
Non-oil developing countries	24.4	24.7	24.4	25.0	28.4	32.8	34.9	35.4	34.3
By analytical group									
Net oil exporters	38.9	41.4	39.7	36.3	38.7	50.1	60.4	57.7	56.1
Net oil importers	22.2	22.3	22.2	23.1	26.3	29.6	30.9	31.6	30.6
Major exporters of manufactures	26.2	26.3	26.7	28.2	31.6	35.8	37.4	37.8	36.6
Low-income countries	14.1	13.2	12.9	12.7	13.9	15.1	15.3	15.7	15.3
Excluding China and India	35.4	34.0	35.1	35.3	42.2	45.8	47.6	48.4	45.0
Other net oil importers	26.5	28.5	27.0	29.1	33.8	38.0	42.0	45.0	44.3
By area									
Africa (excluding South Africa)	36.0	36.7	37.9	35.7	43.4	49.7	54.6	57.7	54.0
Asia	15.9	15.0	14.9	16.0	18.2	20.6	21.3	21.8	21.3
Europe	21.4	23.1	20.8	24.6	27.9	28.9	34.4	37.3	36.7
Middle East	45.0	55.3	63.4	59.1	59.4	58.6	56.4	55.3	52.2
Western Hemisphere	28.0	29.4	30.1	29.9	33.7	41.1	45.9	45.6	45.0

1. Does not include debt owed to the Fund.
2. Ratio of year-end debt to exports or GDP for year indicated.
3. Excludes, for purposes of this table, eight oil exporting countries: the Islamic Republic of Iran, Iraq, Kuwait, the Libyan Arab Jamahiriya, Oman, Qatar, Saudi Arabia, and the United Arab Emirates.

SOURCE: *World Economic Outlook,* IMF, Washington, 1984.

TABLE 2.8 Developing countries: debt service payments on short term and long term external debt, 1977–85 (values in billions of US dollars; ratios in per cent)

	1977	1978	1979	1980	1981	1982	1983	1984	1985
Developing countries									
Value of debt service payments	19.8	57.7	75.4	89.6	109.3	124.1	111.7	121.3	142.9
Interest payments	15.4	21.9	32.3	45.8	60.6	71.4	65.1	71.5	80.7
Amortisation	24.4	35.8	43.1	43.8	48.7	52.7	46.7	49.8	62.2
Debt service ratio[1]	15.1	19.1	19.0	17.4	20.2	24.4	22.1	21.5	23.0
Interest payments ratio	5.9	7.3	8.1	8.9	11.2	14.1	12.9	12.7	13.0
Amortisation ratio	9.2	11.8	10.8	8.5	9.0	10.4	9.2	8.8	10.0
Of which, major borrowers									
Value of debt service payments	17.0	26.3	35.7	40.0	52.0	61.6	53.3	55.1	65.7
Interest payments	6.7	10.2	15.6	22.9	30.6	38.7	34.9	38.2	42.0
Amortisation	10.3	16.0	20.1	17.1	21.4	22.9	18.5	16.9	23.7
Debt service ratio	24.8	33.7	35.2	19.7	33.6	44.1	38.8	35.5	37.9
Interest payments ratio	9.9	13.1	15.4	17.0	19.7	27.7	25.3	24.6	24.2
Amortisation ratio	15.0	20.6	19.8	12.7	13.8	16.4	13.4	10.9	13.7
All non-oil developing countries									
Value of debt service payments	35.8	51.8	66.6	77.4	98.1	109.7	98.9	107.2	124.2
Interest payments	13.7	19.2	27.5	39.4	55.2	63.9	59.0	64.7	71.7
Amortisation	22.1	32.6	39.0	38.1	42.9	45.8	39.9	42.5	52.5
Debt service ratio	16.1	19.8	19.7	18.1	21.4	25.0	22.3	21.7	22.7
Interest payments ratio	6.2	7.3	8.2	9.2	12.1	14.6	13.3	13.1	13.1
Amortisation ratio	9.9	12.5	11.6	8.9	9.4	10.5	9.0	8.6	9.6

By analytical group									
Net oil exporters									
Debt service ratio	26.4	32.3	32.9	23.4	28.5	34.9	34.5	34.2	36.3
Interest payments ratio	9.0	11.2	12.1	12.3	16.6	21.7	19.7	20.4	20.0
Amortisation ratio	17.4	21.2	20.8	11.1	11.9	13.2	14.8	13.8	16.3
Major exporters of manufactures									
Debt service ratio	15.9	19.2	19.1	18.7	21.9	25.6	20.5	18.8	18.7
Interest payments ratio	6.2	7.4	8.3	9.6	12.5	15.1	13.3	12.3	12.0
Amortisation ratio	9.7	11.8	10.8	9.1	9.4	10.6	7.1	6.5	6.7
Low-income countries									
Debt service ratio[4]	12.2	12.0	10.3	10.5	12.5	14.2	10.9	12.0	13.1
Interest payments ratio	4.5	4.7	4.3	4.5	5.0	5.5	4.8	5.4	6.2
Amortisation ratio	7.7	7.2	6.1	6.1	7.4	8.7	6.1	6.6	6.9
Low-income countries (excluding China and India)									
Debt service ratio	14.5	14.3	13.3	14.9	18.2	20.2	18.1	22.2	23.7
Interest payments ratio	5.7	6.2	5.9	6.4	7.9	9.7	8.5	10.2	11.4
Amortisation ratio	8.8	8.1	7.4	8.5	10.3	10.5	9.6	11.9	12.3
Other net oil importers									
Debt service ratio	12.5	17.4	16.8	16.9	19.7	22.3	23.2	23.6	26.4
Interest payments ratio	5.3	6.2	7.1	8.6	11.4	13.1	13.1	13.4	14.0
Amortisation ratio	7.3	11.1	9.6	8.3	8.3	9.1	10.1	10.3	12.4

1. Payments (interest, amortisation, or both) as percentages of exports of goods and services.

SOURCE: *World Economic Outlook*, IMF, Washington, 1984.

particularly costly and may be difficult to implement. It follows that it is these countries that warrant special category status because of the size and nature of their balance of payments problems. It is hardly coincidental then that most of the reforms discussed in this book focus on the special needs of the poorest countries. It is also true, of course, that reforms motivated solely out of equity considerations will tend to favour the same group of countries.[6]

2. MUTUAL INTERESTS AMONGST DEVELOPING COUNTRIES

However, while different LDCs have different problems, they may still have mutual interests in certain areas of international finance. Let us examine three specific issues: first, the extent to which there is an international financial *system* rather than a much looser set of arrangements; second, the nature of the generalised exchange rate regime; and third, the international economic environment under which attempts are made to resolve international financial problems, and the degree of macroeconomic policy harmonisation in the developed world.

2.1 A structured system based on the official sector

The relatively structured Bretton Woods system was replaced in 1973 by a much looser set of international financial arrangements which put greater emphasis on the role of the private international financial sector. Initially this may have been to the advantage of the more creditworthy LDCs, which were able to tap the Eurocurrency market for finance and maintain better standards of living than would have been possible otherwise. However, the very success of such countries in raising finance was to the disadvantage of the rest of the developing world inasmuch as the impression was created that no official action, or certainly only more muted official action, was required. Reforms to assist poorer LDCs are largely set within the context of the official sector and their significance therefore rests on the relative size of this sector.

With the onset of debt problems in the principal borrowers, the official sector regained its importance. Resolution of, or more accurately the capacity to cope with, their payments difficulties has hinged on the involvement of the IMF. As a result, the debtor nations have been drawn back into the official sector and they therefore have interests in a structured system as well.

But while the developing world as a whole may favour a more highly structured system, different groups of countries will wish to structure it in different ways. The principal debtors might be expected to favour reforms that support bank lending and provide refinancing, whereas the poorest countries that would, at best, only benefit indirectly from such modifications may instead prefer a form of restructuring which more directly assists them. Their concern will be that in the competition for resources a preoccupation with highly visible debt difficulties may preclude such reforms.

2.2 The nature of the exchange-rate regime

The initial scepticism that developing countries showed over a system of generalised floating has to some extent been borne out by the evidence since 1973, and developing countries as a group may therefore be expected to favour a move towards a greater degree of exchange rate management. Their scepticism hinged on a number of areas of concern. First it was felt that floating rates produce uncertainty, and that uncertainty in turn discourages international trade and investment. It may of course be countered that a flexible exchange-rate system may be more stable and may involve less uncertainty than an adjustable-peg system which operates imperfectly. The Bretton Woods system, which, especially in the 1960s, fitted into this latter category, incorporated features which acted against the interests of LDCs. In addition to putting an asymmetrical adjustment burden on LDCs, the system also had a globally deflationary bias. Furthermore, exchange risk was not absent.

A standard way of compensating for the uncertainty caused by prospective movements in exchange rates and the risk of receiving a devalued currency or having to buy an appreciated currency is by making use of forward exchange markets. With forward exchange cover the parameters of any trading transaction may be fixed in advance and uncertainty may be removed. Indeed, it is the purpose of the forward exchange market to buy and sell uncertainty. Traders may thus eliminate exchange risk. A reservation held by LDCs about flexible rates was that they had inadequate access to forward exchange markets. For dealings which employ foreign currencies forward exchange facilities in developed countries might be used, but for dealings involving domestic currency domestic facilities are required. However, even where forward cover is available, it is not free of charge. The additional cost of covering foreign exchange transactions may therefore still discriminate against trade and in favour of the non-traded sector, in which productivity growth may be relatively slow.

A second area of concern was that the real opportunity cost of imports would rise under a flexible-rate system. This may be the outcome either of a devaluation in the currency of export quotation or of a revaluation in the currency of import quotation. Where LDC exports and imports are sold and bought from different markets and using different currencies, it is possible that, in the absence of offsetting foreign-currency price changes, the LDCs' terms of trade will deteriorate as a result of exchange-rate flexibility. The impact of floating amongst foreign currencies on any particular LDC's terms of trade will clearly depend on the pattern of the LDC's trade. Where, for instance, trade is concentrated in one currency bloc, depreciation of that currency will exert no adverse effect: the real relative price of exports and imports will remain unchanged. However, where developing countries have a diversified pattern of trade and yet peg the value of their currency to one major currency which is floating against the rest of the world, it is quite possible that their real effective exchange rate will change in ways that are quite inappropriate in terms of their own underlying payments position.

A third area of concern focused on reserve management with problems relating both to the appropriate level and composition of reserves. A combination of currency pegging by LDCs and generalised floating elsewhere which leads to inappropriate effective exchange-rate movements may induce balance of payments deficits which then require financing. In these circumstances generalised floating can increase the need for reserves in developing countries.[7]

With regard to the optimal composition of the reserve portfolio, a flexible exchange-rate system introduces the extra risk of exchange loss resulting from depreciation, and the extra opportunity for exchange gain resulting from appreciation. LDCs holding a high proportion of their reserves in currencies which depreciate will suffer a reduction in the real value of their reserves. In principle, LDCs might neutralise the implications of a flexible exchange-rate system for the value of reserves by holding a diversified portfolio of reserve assets. The portfolio could be apportioned on the basis of the shares of various developed countries in the LDC's imports or on the basis of expected deficits with certain currency areas. But, in practice, the scope for such sophisticated reserve management is almost certainly strictly constrained in most developing countries.

A fourth reason why LDCs were opposed to a flexible exchange-rate system was the worry that their debt was denominated in currencies which might appreciate, thus causing its real value to rise. Since the real value of debt denominated in depreciating currencies will fall, the structure of an LDC's debt burden will be a major determinant of its attitude toward the adoption of exchange-rate flexibility by developed countries. LDCs might attempt to offset the effect of appreciation on their real debt burden by distributing their debt amongst developed countries in proportions similar to their export trade shares; this would tend to ensure that export earnings would rise to offset any rise in debt payments, but again the scope for such debt management is almost certainly small.

A fifth reason for concern amongst LDCs over generalised floating was the belief that a permanent move towards fairly freely floating exchange rates would represent a decisive move away from a centrally managed monetary and trading system, which could be designed to provide substantial benefits to them in the form of resource transfers. To the extent that greater exchange-rate flexibility reduces the international monetary system's need for reserve assets, there would be less reason for further SDR emissions; as a result LDCs might forgo actual and potential benefits. Paradoxically, at the same time as reducing the likelihood of future SDR emissions, exchange-rate flexibility amongst developed countries could also, as noted above, increase LDCs' need for reserves.

The costs of generalised exchange-rate flexibility as outlined are not independent of developing countries' own exchange-rate policies. While the thinness of foreign exchange markets and, some would argue, the low value of trade elasticities may advise against adopting flexible rates, the choice of the currency peg will effect the degree of instability in the effective exchange rate. Yet while recognising this, developing countries will be unable to eliminate all the problems created for them by generalised floating simply through the choice of their own exchange-rate policy.[8]

There is a growing amount of evidence that generalised floating has been unstable and that 'third currency instability' has, in turn, caused significant changes in the real effective exchange rates of developing countries.[9] Furthermore, evidence is emerging that flexible exchange rates have an anti-trade bias because of the risks associated with them.[10] Nor does the evidence seem to support the claim that flexible rates benefit developing countries because they enable the developed world to sustain policies of demand expansion and trade liberalisation. Indeed, it would appear to be just the opposite. Meanwhile flexible exchange rates have accommodated considerable currency misalignment which may have been caused by factors that are disadvantageous to LDCs – something taken up in the next section. At the same time the advent of flexible rates has undoubtedly affected the perceived need for reserve creation.

These observations would suggest that developing countries share a common interest in reforming the global exchange-rate regime and in removing 'excessive' flexibility. To the extent that they are less able to cope with the effects of exchange-rate flexibility they stand to gain more than others from such reform.

Yet, of course, exchange-rate flexibility has undoubtedly had an uneven impact within the developing world. Although much depends on the details relating to the pattern of trade, the denomination of debt and reserves, and LDCs' own exchange-rate policy, the cost of generalised floating will tend to be greater the more unstable are effective exchange rates as a result of the third currency phenomenon, the less is access to, or the higher the price of forward cover, and the lower are reserve holdings. What this means in effect is that it has again been the least developed countries that have suffered most from generalised flexible exchange rates.

Appropriate policies that emerge from this analysis fall into two categories. The first involves measures to reduce the degree of exchange-rate instability by working on its underlying causes. Such measures could relate to managing the exchange-rate system itself via government intervention in foreign exchange markets to keep rates within predetermined 'target zones.'[11] However, other measures could relate to modifying the monetary and fiscal policies pursued in the most significant developed countries. There is an argument that it is misguided domestic macroeconomic policy which lies at the heart of exchange-rate instability.[12]

The second involves LDCs in trying to provide themselves with more protection against the problems which generalised floating creates. Such policies include using their own exchange-rate policy to minimise instabilities in their effective exchange rates, providing more and cheaper access to forward cover, building up expertise in reserve and debt management, and encouraging the use of the SDR as a unit of account, since the SDR's value is more stable than that of individual currencies. Clearly international agencies and in particular the IMF could offer assistance in these directions.

2.3 The international economic environment: micro- and macroeconomic policy in developed countries

There are some environments that are more conducive to solving the balance of payments problems of developing countries than others. Given the central significance of exports, LDCs will be anxious to see sustained economic growth in the developed world as well as a dismantling of protectionist tariff and non-tariff barriers.

At the same time the policy means by which expansion is achieved will be a matter of some concern to them. They may reasonably be expected to prefer methods of expansion that do not result in increasing world interest rates and which do not crowd out their own borrowing from international capital markets. Thus they will have an interest in the size of fiscal deficits in the developed world and the ways in which such deficits are financed. High interest rates will, of course, in any case tend to neutralise the expansionary effects of fiscal deficits.

To the extent that high interest rates, recession, and exchange-rate misalignment amongst the principal currencies in the world result from a failure to co-ordinate macroeconomic policy, LDCs will favour the closer harmonisation of monetary and fiscal policy within the developed world. But, the attitude of individual LDCs will also depend on the differential economic performance of developed countries, according to the structure of their trading and financial links.[13]

Leading on from this, but also bearing in mind the demand deflationary implications of a system which permits some countries to run persistent surpluses and the fact that the unwillingness of surplus countries to allow their surpluses to fall constrains the ability of deficit countries to reduce their deficits, LDCs will favour policies which encourage a reduction in surpluses elsewhere in the system. Significantly the introduction of flexible exchange rates has failed to eliminate them, even though in principle they should offer one way of removing adjustment asymmetries. How then can pressure be brought to bear on surplus countries?

One option would be to use a version of the scare currency clause under which countries may take protective action against imports from persistent surplus countries. An appealing feature of this scheme is that it attempts to resolve financial problems by working on the trade problems which underscore them. A second option would be to penalise surplus countries by refusing to allocate additional SDRs to them or by reducing the rate of interest on any new acquisition of SDRs. However, unless the international monetary system is more fully based on the SDR as its principal reserve asset, such measures are unlikely to have much impact.[14] A third and rather different option would be to down play the idea of pressurising surplus countries and merely provide developing countries with the SDRs necessary to finance their deficits. This would amount to arguing that the unwillingness of surplus countries to adjust precludes deficit nations from adjusting, or means that they can only adjust at an excessively high welfare cost. If adjustment cannot be accommodated, greater emphasis should perhaps be placed on financing. Extra allocations of SDRs could then be used to break the foreign exchange constraint in developing countries and to overcome the zero sum nature of the international financial system under which some countries can strengthen their balance of payments only if others are prepared to see theirs weaken. Under the financing alternative, surplus countries would not be required to give up their surpluses. They would, however, have to be prepared to accept the related and perpetual net outflow of real resources.[15]

3. CONCLUDING REMARKS

The discussion in this chapter suggests that the developing world will favour a return to a more structured international financial system, the elimination of exchange-rate instability and of the misalignment of key currencies, and the pursuit of a more co-ordinated approach to macroeconomic policy amongst developed countries – in particular one which encourages surplus countries to adjust. Indeed, the argument can legitimately be made that developing countries stand to gain more from such changes than from the more specific reforms which are the main subject matter of this book. However, the point needs to be stressed that the two groups of changes are not mutually exclusive. To concede that developing countries would benefit from greater exchange-rate stability, for example, is not to argue that they will fail to benefit from more specifically LDC-oriented reforms. Yet the distinction between the two groups of changes becomes relevant in circumstances where LDC representatives in international fora have to decide how to allocate their time between arguing for general reforms to the system and more specific reforms. It is clearly in this context that some estimation of relative gains needs to be made.

Should LDCs decide to press for reforms that are specific to themselves, examination of the evidence suggests that a strong case can be made that such special treatment is warranted on the basis of their payments difficulties. However, the evidence also clearly shows that different groups of LDCs have different problems and some LDCs have a stronger case than others. This suggests that policy will need to be sufficiently subtle to reflect these differences. Of course it also suggests that the harmony of view required to mount an effective campaign for reform may be lacking with different LDCs favouring different reforms. The political economy of international financial policy as it relates to the developing world is something to which we shall return in the final chapter of the book. Yet it may be noted here that the policies advocated presuppose an incrementalist and marginalist type of reform rather than the grander but less realistic approach associated with the introduction of a new international economic order.

3 The IMF and the Developing World: History, Relationships and Resource Uses

The purpose of this chapter is to provide an institutional and historical background to the discussion contained in subsequent ones. However, the temptation to provide a comprehensive glossary of IMF facilities or a detailed statistical picture of the use of these facilities by developing countries has been resisted, the reason being that such information is conveniently available elsewhere.[1]

The chapter concentrates on relations between the Fund and LDCs through the operation of the General Account. The SDR Account is discussed later in the book.

1. THE INSTITUTIONAL FRAMEWORK AND HISTORICAL BACKGROUND

While LDCs exerted only a minimal influence at the 1944 Bretton Woods conference which led to the creation of the IMF, they were not completely excluded from it, and there was some debate on the problems of development. Also, of course, it needs to be remembered that the World Bank was simultaneously established in order to help deal more directly with developmental problems. While the Fund's Articles of Agreement were being drafted India pushed hard for a reference to LDCs against the opposition of the USA, and there was an element of compromise in the final version. Thus, while the Articles did not make any distinction between developed and less developed countries, there was a direct reference to development, although whether the precise wording of the Articles has made any difference in Fund attitudes towards LDCs is unclear. Certainly the uniform legal position of all member countries has not prevented it from adopting policies which have primarily favoured developing countries.

During its early years the Fund showed limited concern with the problems of developing countries, regarding development as a relatively unimportant issue which was, in any case, outside its terms of reference. In 1947–9 Western Europe accounted for three-quarters of total drawings from the IMF and LDCs for well under a quarter, even though post-war reconstruction in Europe was then being financed by Marshall Aid, the conditions of which limited recourse to the IMF to 'exceptional and unforeseen circumstances'.

Even so, certain changes in the early 1950s were beneficial to LDCs. Drawings on the gold tranche were made automatic and the first credit tranche became more easily available. In 1952 the stand-by concept was introduced. Upon the acceptance of a package of economic policies, stand-bys provided countries with an assured line of credit. In the same year it was announced that an agreed par value would no longer necessarily be a precondition of Fund assistance.

Its annual reports during the early and mid-1950s, however, confirm that the Fund had little specific interest in the particular problems of LDCs as such and indeed LDCs were not seen as constituting a separate class. Fund policy continued to rest on the notion that monetary stabilisation and free trade were in the interests of all members alike.

In the late 1950s and through the 1960s there was a significant shift in the Fund's attitude towards development. This resulted in innovations intended to alleviate the monetary aspects of economic problems faced by LDCs. First, quotas were increased, especially small quotas. Second, the geographical distribution of Fund lending shifted towards LDCs. Third, in 1961 the Managing Director stated that the IMF had a positive role to play in promoting development through the provision of short-term finance to countries experiencing temporary payments difficulties. Monetary stability was still viewed as the Fund's main objective but this was now presented as necessary for stable development. Fourth, and after some initial resistance, the Fund accepted that export instability constituted a special problem for developing countries that was not covered by existing facilities, and in 1963 the Compensatory Financing Facility (CFF) was introduced. Although open to all members, the CFF was of greatest benefit to primary product exporting countries, and represented perhaps the first institutional response to the demands of LDCs. Initially compensation was available only on relatively restrictive terms, but in 1966 lobbying by LDCs resulted in a liberalisation, although the Fund continued to resist making the facility automatically available. As a fifth innovation the Buffer Stock Financing Facility (BSFF) was set up in 1969 to assist members facing payments difficulties as a result of participation in international buffer stock schemes. Also during the mid-1960s the Fund began to show concern over LDCs' indebtedness and participated in negotiations concerning the debts of several LDC members (de Vries, 1976, 1977).

Perhaps, not coincidentally, as the Fund was beginning to show greater awareness of LDC problems, its influence over international monetary reform in general was diminishing. The General Arrangement to Borrow, the Basle Agreements and a system of bilateral swap agreements were all established in the 1960s and these modifications were organised by industrial countries with the latter two lying largely outside the auspices of the IMF. Even the early negotiations which eventually led to the introduction of the Special Drawing Rights scheme were largely conducted outside the IMF, though it was as a result of pressure from the Fund that developing countries were ultimately included in it (de Vries, 1976).

An apparently growing feeling within the Fund that LDCs warranted special treatment continued into the 1970s. During the dollar crisis of 1971, however, international monetary negotiations again took place largely outside the IMF and the voice of developing countries was faint. The failure of these moves to shore up the Bretton Woods system led to an attempt to make a full assessment of the international monetary system, and to produce reforms which would cover all aspects of that system. This discussion took place under the auspices of the Fund in the Committee on Reform of the International Monetary System and Related Issues (The Committee of Twenty or C-20). The interests of LDCs were well represented on the Committee, with nine out of the twenty members. Two technical groups set up by C-20 looked at issues of specific concern to LDCs, namely the SDR/aid link and the transfer of real resources. The Committee's report and 'Outline of Reform'[2] urged that future international monetary arrangements be organised so as, 'to give positive encouragement to economic development and to promote an increasing net flow of real resources to developing countries'.

The report and 'Outline of Reform' of C-20 are significant landmarks in the evolving relations between the IMF and LDCs. Although for some years eight or nine Executive Directors from LDCs had sat on the Fund's Executive Board, for the first time LDCs now participated fully in an attempt to remake the international monetary system, and the proposed changes envisaged that the international monetary system should specifically cater for the problems of development. Some distance had been travelled from Bretton Woods.

Although, subsequent to the C-20 discussions, the IMF has maintained its concerns for LDCs' problems, the move towards flexible exchange rates and the increasing significance of private financing have eroded the central position of the Fund in the international monetary system (Crockett and Heller, 1978) and LDCs have probably lost as a result.

Even so, the momentum generated by C-20 has not been totally dissipated. Indeed, concern with the problems facing LDCs was enhanced by the rising price of oil and its implications for non-oil LDCs. The economic situation of the developing countries and ways of protecting their economic growth from the effects of world inflation and recession have become recurrent themes at annual meetings, and have resulted in modifications to the operation of the IMF.

Following a suggestion of C-20, a Joint Ministerial Committee of the Boards of Governors of the Bank and the Fund on the Transfer of Real Resources to Developing Countries (Development Committee) was set up, thus institutionally linking international monetary matters to economic development. The Committee has concerned itself with the transfer of real resources to LDCs, paying particular attention to the least developed countries and those LDCs most seriously affected by payments difficulties.

Further suggestions made by C-20 resulted in the establishment, in 1974 for a two-year period, of an Oil Facility (OF), the specific purpose of which was to assist countries to cope with the payments implications of the increased cost of oil. To reduce the interest rate burden associated with OF drawings the Fund also established a Subsidy Account to make concessionary assistance available to low-income LDCs that had been most seriously affected by the oil crisis. The partial insulation from the implications of increases in import prices provided by the OF and the subsidisation of interest rates were significant changes in the relationship between the IMF and developing countries.

As a further response to the deterioration in the world economic situation the CFF was liberalised in 1975 and again in 1979; in 1981 it was integrated with a scheme to assist countries facing BoP problems as a result of excess cereal imports; furthermore the percentage of quota that could be cumulatively drawn from the Fund, exclusive of CFF and BSFF drawings, was raised to 600 per cent. Modifications to the CFF in 1983 will be discussed in Chapter 5.

Other institutional changes within the IMF were the introduction of the Extended Fund Facility (EFF) and the Trust Fund. In principle the EFF provides a significant extra dimension to Fund involvement with the formulation of economic policy in member countries, since, prior to its introduction, the Fund had appeared to be more narrowly interested in short-term financial stabilisation policies. The EFF gives some recognition to the fact that payments difficulties may constitute the monetary manifestation of structural misallocation, and specifically views the balance of payments in the context of development policy.

The main purpose of the Trust Fund was to provide eligible LDCs, basically the least developed countries, with low conditionality and concessionary balance of payments assistance. A significant feature of the Trust Fund was that its establishment demonstrated a willingness by the IMF to use international monetary reform, in this case a reduction in the role of gold, as a way of benefiting the poorest countries in the world.

Another relevant institutional change was the introduction of the Supplementary Financing Facility in 1979. Since the repayment period on SFF drawings was longer than that associated with conventional stand-bys, this might have been expected to be of particular help to developing countries in which adjustment is relatively slow. Furthermore, a concessionary element to drawings under SFF was provided to low income countries by a two-tier Subsidy Account designed to reduce the associated interest rate. Subsidy arrangements were, however, not applied to the policy on Enlarged Access to Resources which superseded the SFF.

2. THE FUND AND STABILISATION POLICY

Any informed assessment of the evolution of the Fund's approach to stabilisation is made difficult by the confidentiality with which much of the material is treated. Observations can, however, be made from published material. Certainly the whole thrust of stand-by arrangements from their inception has been to bring about a reasonably prompt improvement in the external position of the borrowing country, although there is some ambiguity surrounding just how rapid the adjustment has to be.

While the range of policies supported by the Fund does not seem to have altered all that dramatically over the years, the increasing interest in financial programming shown by the Fund since the late 1960s has brought with it an increase in the degree of precise quantitative stipulation (de Vries, 1976).[3]

In the early 1970s Executive Directors began to show a particularly keen interest in the ways in which programmes were formulated, the models on which they were based, and the effects they had on key economic variables. This led the Fund to study a number of questions:

> Was a monetarist analysis equally applicable to both developed and developing countries? Were there not important differences between countries in respect of the transmission mechanism explaining how monetary influences affect real output, employment and the price level? . . . To what extent did programmes based on credit ceilings affect domestic employment and the distribution of income? Were aggregative techniques useful for influencing the newly emerging socio-economic objectives of enhancing employment and redistributing income? (de Vries, 1976).

In the early 1970s, then, there seemed to be the beginning of a reappraisal of the Fund's involvement in economic stabilisation. The outcome of this reappraisal, which was made more necessary by events in the 1970s, was, one suspects, reflected by changes in policy, as regards both the content of programmes and the period of repayment, that were made at the end of the 1970s.

Previously the IMF had tended to respond to pressures from developing countries by enlarging the range of its facilities rather than by changing its policy conditions. However, in the late 1970s and early 1980s there were some potentially significant changes in the form of lengthening the possible programme period for stand-bys and in the form of the 1979 *Review of the Guidelines on Conditionality*. Lengthening the programme period, for instance, appeared to offer countries the chance to pursue rather longer term balance of payments policies, thus allowing the Fund to put greater emphasis on structurally oriented policies and on supply, as opposed to demand, management.

The 1979 *Review of Guidelines on Conditionality*, while endorsing the Fund's belief in conditionality, included what seemed to be certain changes from the previous position.[4] Perhaps most frequently quoted as an example of liberalisation was the statement in the *Review* that 'the Fund will pay due regard to the domestic social and political objectives, the economic priorities, and the circumstances of members, including the causes of their balance of payments problem'. However, the *Review* also emphasised the need to encourage members to adopt corrective measures at an early stage in their BoP difficulties and recognised that in many cases a longer period of adjustment is required than normally associated with a stand-by arrangement.

In fact neither the lengthening of the programme period nor the 1979 *Review* turned out to be of great practical importance. Apart from a brief interlude discussed later, the Fund's preference remained strongly for short-run programmes with the emphasis being placed on short-term policies, even though a series of programmes might be negotiated. Meanwhile, as suggested by Gold (1979), the 1979 *Review* was, in retrospect, much more an attempt to clarify and codify existing practice on conditionality than to break new ground, and the reference to social and political factors had little discernible effect on actual lending policies. The Fund clearly retained its views concerning, first, the need for countries to adjust irrespective of the origin of their BoP problems and, second, what policies were, generally speaking, most useful in bringing about such adjustment. The logic of a more supply-oriented approach to adjustment was largely rejected by the Fund for a series of theoretical and operational reasons, and sound demand management remained the centrepiece of Fund programmes.

However, while downplaying the practical significance of the 1979 *Review* as such in changing the nature of conditionality, there have undeniably been variations over recent years in the stringency with which conditionality has been exercised. For a time at the end of the 1970s and the beginning of the 1980s there was a move towards a rather more liberal approach. Programmes that in previous years might not have been were approved by the Executive Board; longer programme periods were used, loans were more heavily front-end loaded, waivers were more easily available, and borrowers were not always required to eliminate negative real interest rates or cut the fiscal deficit significantly. However, with political changes in certain important member countries, notably the US, and some feeling within the Fund that the changes had not been successful, this relaxation proved to be short-lived.

Williamson (1982) has statistically investigated this recent period in the Fund's history (i.e. 1978–81) by looking at the frequency, size and duration of programmes and the real appreciation in a borrowing country's exchange rate prior to the approval of a Fund programme. 'Tough' conditionality he takes as being represented by a precondition of adequate devaluation, whilst a failure to require devaluation even when necessary to correct a preceding real appreciation is taken to show weak conditionality.[5] Williamson discovers a surge in Fund lending under high conditionality arrangements between mid-1979 and mid-1981. Before May 1979 an average of just over one high-conditionality programme was approved each month. Between June 1979 and June 1981 this average rose to 2.5 per month before falling back to 1 per month in the subsequent nine months. Not only were more programmes approved but Williamson also finds that their average value in relation to quota increased noticeably. Indicative of this is that before 1979 only one programme amounted to over 250 per cent of quota, whereas between October 1979 and December 1980 eleven programmes were of this size. Although part of this increased lending activity may no doubt be explained by demand-side factors following the second major oil price increase, this is unlikely to be the whole story, since demand remained high after mid-1981 and yet the number of approved programmes declined. Further examination shows that, compared to previous and subsequent periods, between October 1979 and May 1981 there was a significant switch towards multi-year programmes, and an increased reluctance to require devaluation in order to reduce any prior appreciation in the real exchange rate; Williamson interprets the evidence as supporting the claim that Fund conditionality was eased in mid-1979 and retightened in mid-1981.

The reasons for the apparent changes in the conduct of conditionality and in the form of economic programme supported by the Fund are difficult to pin down in any precise fashion. One factor might have been the Fund's own liquidity position. From a situation of considerable spare lending capacity in the late 1970s, by mid-1981 a much larger proportion of Fund resources had been committed, and yet at least some powerful countries were reluctant to see quotas significantly increased or the Fund borrowing from the private capital market. The increasing stringency of conditionality might then be interpreted as a means of rationing scarce resources.

Other explanations would interpret the relaxation in conditionality as a diplomatic manoeuvre by the Fund to improve its image with LDCs, and would point to political resistance from the US and other industrial countries to a major role for the Fund as the reason for the subsequent tightening.

It is interesting to note that, whatever the reasons, the changes in the conduct of conditionality between 1979 and 1981 occurred without any changes in formally stated Fund practice. Indeed the Managing Director claimed that the same basic policies had been applied throughout the period against a changing world economic environment (de Larosiere, 1982). Such claims suggest that formal statements, such as the 1979 *Guidelines*, are sufficiently broad to accommodate considerable practical flexibility, with this flexibility depending largely on the attitudes of powerful countries or country groupings, as represented by their Executive Directors. The apparent scope for flexibility in the practical interpretation of the Articles of Agreement offers some hope for those who suggest that certain modifications in Fund conditionality are required.

The Fund does, however, continue to see its Articles of Agreement as defining its basic responsibility as being to provide balance of payments finance and adjustment advice and incentives, and not longer run development assistance, and it resists any proposals that are seen as changing this basic function. However, since the distinction between balance of payments problems and developmental problems is frequently very far from clear, the Fund's role is as a result left somewhat ill-defined. The changing world economic environment has unavoidably drawn the Fund into more dealings with developing countries and into considering issues which have significant implications for development. Indeed, from being viewed in its early years as an institution which had no special concern for the problems of developing countries some recent reviews see the Fund as having become, or at least as being well on the way to becoming, an institution whose only role is that of assisting the poorer countries for whom private financial markets do not provide a feasible alternative (Williamson, 1979). To the extent that this is the case it is a transition that the Fund has found awkward, partly because of the size of the imbalances with which it has had to deal, partly because of its lack of influence over adjustment in surplus countries, and partly because of the changing causes of deficits in developing countries, which imply that credit control, which for a number of reasons frequently appears to the Fund to be the best single performance criterion, may not always be the most cost-effective way of correcting deficits. In many ways then the relationship between the Fund and developing countries is at something of a watershed.

3. EVIDENCE ON THE GENERAL PATTERN OF DRAWINGS

Member countries may draw on the Fund, subject to quota limits, where they have a balance of payments need which complies with various eligibility criteria, and where in some cases a suitable economic programme can be negotiated. Developing countries have made considerable use of the IMF as a source of international finance. However, amongst developing countries there has been a considerable range of experience both between oil-exporting and non-oil developing countries and amongst non-oil LDCs. While some have made frequent and large drawings, others have had little or no recourse to the Fund. During the mid-1970s, however, the majority of developing countries did draw on the Fund, and 1976 was a peak year for drawings. These fell in the late 1970s before picking up again in the 1980s. Another peak was reached in 1983 with drawings declining in 1984 (see Table 3.1).

Further geographical breakdown reveals that prior to 1977 the developing countries of Latin America and the Caribbean had historically drawn most from the Fund. However, since 1977 and up to 1981 this was not the case. Indeed, after 1976 drawings from LDCs in the Western Hemisphere dropped dramatically.

As Table 3.2 reveals, Asian and African LDCs instead became the principal clients of the Fund. This distributional change proved to be only temporary and was reversed in 1983. However, care has to be exercised in interpreting the data in Table 3.2 since, although the major debtor countries of Latin America drew most from the Fund, the majority of programmes continued to relate to the poorer developing countries (see Table 3.3).

Another noteworthy trend underlying Table 3.1 is the shift over to the dominance of high conditionality finance. In 1984 87.7 per cent of all drawings by developing countries on the Fund fell into this category as compared with 75 per cent in 1983 and 62 per cent in 1982. As can be seen from Table 3.1, the traditionally low conditionality CFF and BSFF were relatively little used in 1984, whereas in

TABLE 3.1 *Fund purchases and repurchases[1] (billion SDRs)*

	1978	1979	1980	1981	1982	1983	1984
Total purchases[2]	1.2	1.7	3.4	6.8	7.4	12.6	7.3
Credit tranches	0.4	0.9	1.8	3.4	2.5	4.9	3.1
Extended Fund facility	0.2	0.2	0.6	2.1	2.1	4.6	3.3
Compensatory financing facility	0.6	0.6	1.0	1.2	2.6	2.8	0.8
Buffer stock financing facility	—[3]	—[3]	—	—	0.1	0.3	—[3]
Total repurchases	4.8	4.1	3.2	2.1	1.6	2.0	2.3
Net purchases	—[4]	—[4]	0.2	4.7	5.8	10.6	5.0

1. Almost all the above transactions relate to developing countries.
2. Excludes reserve tranche purchases and Trust Fund loan disbursements.
3. Less than SDR 50 million.
4. Repurchases exceeded total purchases.

SOURCE: *IMF Survey*, 4 February 1985.

1982 the CFF had been the single most significant source of finance from the Fund. In stark contrast the EFF, which was very little used in the latter part of the 1970s, became a very significant source of finance during 1981–4. Indeed, by 1984 it was the single largest source of Fund finance to LDCs. Significantly, however, and as revealed by Table 3.3, the greater use of the EFF reflected large credits to a small number of NICs rather than a large number of smaller credits to poorer developing countries.

3.1 Trends in drawings on the Fund: some possible explanations

While there is no obvious overall trend in terms of developing countries' drawings on the Fund, by examining the years 1965–84 a number of sub-periods do emerge. In 1965–9 drawings were relatively high, they were low between 1970 and 1973, higher during 1974–6, low again during 1977–9 and higher again between 1980–3 though falling again in 1984. Given the diversity of LDC experience, it is difficult to provide a satisfactory explanation of these variations, but world economic developments, institutional changes, and policy changes are consistent with the pattern of drawings.

TABLE 3.2 *Developing countries: use of Fund credit, 1977–83 (in billions of US dollars)*

	1977	1978	1979	1980	1981	1982	1983
Developing countries	–0.2	–0.3	0.2	1.5	6.1	7.1	11.7
Of which, major borrowers	–0.2	–0.5	–0.5	1.2	3.4	5.7	9.3
Non-oil developing countries	–0.2	–0.3	0.2	1.5	6.1	7.1	10.2
By analytical group							
Net oil exporters	0.2	—	—	–0.3	0.1	0.5	1.0
Net oil importers	–0.3	–0.3	0.3	1.7	6.0	6.6	9.2
Major exporters of manufactures	–0.1	–0.6	–0.4	0.5	1.1	2.0	4.2
Low-income countries	–0.3	–0.2	0.2	0.6	2.1	2.7	1.8
Excluding China and India	0.1	—	0.2	0.3	1.3	1.1	0.8
Other net oil importers	—	0.5	0.5	0.6	2.9	1.8	3.2
By area							
Africa (excluding South Africa)	0.1	0.3	0.4	0.5	1.6	1.2	1.4
Asia	–0.3	–0.2	—	1.0	3.2	2.3	1.7
Europe	—	0.1	0.1	0.6	1.2	1.3	1.4
Middle East	0.1	0.1	–0.1	–0.3	–0.2	—	—
Western Hemisphere	–0.1	–0.6	0.2	–0.2	0.3	1.5	5.7
Memorandum item							
Drawings outstanding at end of year[1]							
Developing countries	8.0	8.0	8.3	9.5	14.9	21.2	31.3
Non-oil developing countries	8.0	8.0	8.3	9.5	14.9	21.2	30.8

1. Year-to-year changes in drawings do not necessarily match corresponding use of Fund credit estimates because of valuation adjustments.

SOURCE: *World Economic Outlook*, IMF, Washington, 1984.

54

TABLE 3.3 *Stand-by and extended arrangements, as of 31 December 1984 (thousand SDRs)*

Member	Date of Arrangement		Expiration Date		Total Amount Agreed	Undrawn Balance
Stand-by arrangements					6,673,735	3,557,067
Argentina	28 Dec.	1984	27 Mar.	1986	1,419,000	1,419,000
Belize	3 Dec.	1984	31 Mar.	1986	7,125	5,925
Central African Republic	6 July	1984	5 July	1985	15,000	10,000
Chile	10 Jan.	1983	9 Jan.	1985	500,000	—
Dominica	18 July	1984	17 July	1985	1,400	430
Gambia, The	23 Apr.	1984	22 July	1985	12,830	10,200
Ghana	27 Aug.	1984	31 Dec.	1985	180,000	120,000
Haiti	7 Nov.	1983	30 Sept.	1985	60,000	39,000
Hungary	13 Jan.	1984	12 Jan.	1985	425,000	—
Ivory Coast	3 Aug.	1984	2 Aug.	1985	82,750	41,370
Jamaica	22 June	1984	21 June	1985	64,000	36,000
Korea	8 July	1983	31 Mar.	1985	575,775	95,925
Liberia	7 Dec.	1984	6 Jun.	1986	42,780	34,280
Madagascar	10 Apr.	1984	31 Mar.	1985	33,000	6,000
Mali	9 Dec.	1983	31 May.	1985	40,500	6,500
Morocco	16 Sept.	1983	15 Mar.	1985	300,000	90,000
Niger	5 Dec.	1984	4 Dec.	1985	16,000	12,800
Peru	26 Apr.	1984	31 July	1985	250,000	220,000
Philippines	14 Dec.	1984	13 Dec.	1986	615,000	530,000
Portugal	7 Oct.	1983	28 Feb.	1985	445,000	185,700
Sierra Leone	3 Feb.	1984	2 Feb.	1985	50,200	31,200
Sudan	25 June	1984	24 June	1985	90,000	70,000
Togo	7 May	1984	6 May	1985	19,000	3,000
Turkey	4 Apr.	1984	3 Apr.	1985	225,000	56,250
Uruguay	22 Apr.	1983	21 Apr.	1985	378,000	226,800
Western Samoa	9 July	1984	8 July	1985	3,375	1,687
Yugoslavia	18 Apr.	1984	17 Apr.	1985	370,000	90,000
Zaire	27 Dec.	1983	26 Mar.	1985	228,000	70,000
Zambia	26 July	1984	30 Apr.	1986	225,000	145,000
Extended arrangements					8,121,250	3,013,495
Brazil	1 Mar.	1983	28 Feb.	1986	4,239,375	1,496,250
Dominican Rep.	21 Jan.	1983	20 Jan.	1986	371,250	247,500
Malawi	19 Sept.	1983	18 Sept.	1986	100,000	66,000
Mexico	1 Jan.	1983	31 Dec.	1985	3,410,625	1,203,745
Totals					14,794,985	6,570,562

SOURCE: *IMF Survey*, 4 February 1985.

The drop in drawings during 1970–3, for example, coincided with a sharp decline in the number of LDCs experiencing payments deficits, as compared with 1965–9. During 1974–6, by contrast, the proportion of developing countries recording deficits increased.

The introduction of the OF also contributed to the increase in drawings during 1974–6, as did the liberalisation of the CFF in 1975. Indeed, it has been estimated that had the rules governing the CFF remained unchanged, drawings under this facility in 1975 would only have been 20 per cent of their actual amount (Goreux, 1977). This liberalisation combined with the world economic recession would then seem to provide a reasonable explanation of the sharp rise in drawings under the CFF in 1976. As the relative importance of the OF and CFF increased, so the share of drawings under the ordinary tranches diminished and, in particular, fewer drawings extended into the upper tranches. Indeed, in the period following 1973–4 approximately two-thirds of the resources provided by the Fund to member countries involved low conditionality.

For 1977–9 the problem is to explain the generally low use of Fund finance; although difficult to estimate precisely, there is little doubt that the Fund possessed considerable excess lending capacity during these years. A number of suggestions may be made. Bearing in mind the somewhat lagged response of drawings to BoP performance, part of the explanation probably lies in the fact that LDCs experienced some improvement in their overall BoP during 1976 and up to 1979. Even though the current account remained in deficit, the size of the deficit fell in 1977, and even though it increased in 1978 and 1979, there was an increase in capital inflows. The major exporters of manufactures were particularly successful in attracting private finance. Also, although not returning to the growth rates experienced in 1973–4, the value of non-oil LDCs' exports increased significantly during 1976–80 and as a result they had less claim on CFF assistance.

Apart from any reduction in the need for BoP finance, the fact that an increasing proportion of Fund resources were available only at high conditionality, with this frequently involving devaluation, may have also made countries more reluctant to turn to the Fund, especially where commercial loans were available. The trend towards greater emphasis on high conditionality was quite marked and rapid and by 1980 more than three-quarters of the Fund's financial commitments were on this basis. The change was brought about by the particular method used for enlarging members' access to Fund resources, which involved increasing the percentage of quota that could be drawn rather than increasing quotas themselves. Thus first credit tranche conditionality applied to 25 per cent of a quota even though 600 per cent of the quota could, in certain circumstances, be drawn. In such a case only 4 per cent of Fund resources were available to a member at low conditionality in contrast to the 25 per cent that would have been available if quotas had been increased six-fold. At the same time, since the SFF, and latterly the EAP, have been financed by borrowing, the concessionary element in the related Fund finance has been greatly reduced.

Finally, during the latter half of the 1970s there were changes in the Fund's clientele. Many of its traditional borrowers, such as the Latin American and Far Eastern newly industrialising countries, had less need to borrow, yet low income countries, which often had a greater need for Fund finance, were also perhaps more wary of the appropriateness of Fund conditionality to their economies. Also, since the size of their economies tends to be small, a switch of lending towards the poorer LDCs would, country for country, tend to reduce the value of Fund lending.

But why did the use of Fund credit expand in 1980 and expand quite dramatically in 1981? Certainly it was not because the richer LDCs were borrowing more again. Indeed, as of end December 1981, 66.7 per cent of IMF commitments under conditional programmes were to countries with a 1978 per capita GNP of less than $700 and 99.7 per cent to countries where it was less than $3000 (Morgan Guaranty, 1982). Instead, increased Fund activity in this period probably reflected a combination of other factors. First, as noted earlier, after 1979 the Fund attempted in various ways to make conditionality less unattractive to LDCs by, for instance, taking a less strong stand on devaluation and by moving towards multi-year programmes. Second, the further big increase in oil prices in 1979, a marked and more general deterioration in their terms of trade after 1978, and deepening recession in many industrial country markets combined to increase the size of LDCs' BoP deficits in 1981. Low income countries experienced a significant fall in the volume, unit price, and value of exports and an increase in import prices, and with poor access to private capital markets had little alternative other than to borrow from the Fund.

For 1982–4 the size of drawings does seem to reflect what was happening in the better-off LDCs, with the large drawings of 1982–3 mirroring their considerable debt problems and the shortfall in their export receipts resulting from industrial recession in much of the developed world. For 1984 the decline in drawings reflects strengthening export performance and the effects of the adjustment policies put in place in 1982–3. The lower use of the CFF, though obviously connected to export performance, might also be related to the new guidelines on the use of the facility which were introduced in 1983 (see Chapter 5 for discussion of these).

4. THE ECONOMIC CHARACTERISTICS OF USER-COUNTRIES

Given the evidence already presented, a question arises as to whether drawings by developing countries display any discernible economic pattern. If so, what are the economic characteristics, both of those countries that do draw on the Fund and of those that do not; and is it possible to predict which LDCs are likely to draw on the Fund and in what amounts?

In an attempt to shed some light on these questions Bird and Orme (1981) regressed LDC drawings on country economic characteristics such as the balance of payments position, the debt service ratio, the rate of inflation, per capita income, the level of reserves, the value of imports, and access to Eurocurrency credits. From both a statistical and an economic point of view they found that their model was satisfactory when tested against 1976 data. The estimated coefficients were consistent with a priori reasoning for all the explanatory variables except external debt, for which the coefficient was, in any case, not significantly different from zero. On the basis of their evidence it appeared that the IMF and the Eurocurrency market were providing complementary rather than competing sources of finance and that reserve use and drawings on the Fund were, if anything, complementary activities. Developing countries seemed to draw more from the Fund as their payments situation and their general economic performance deteriorated, but tended to draw less as they became richer. However, since re-estimated for 1977 the results were poor, there can be very little confidence in the stability of the implied demand function. The model was also tested separately for OF and CFF drawings. While providing a poor explanation of the former, it provided a good explanation of the latter. An attempt to distinguish between low and high conditionality drawings was frustrated by lack of data.

Bird and Orme also analysed the behaviour of those LDCs that did not draw on the Fund in 1976. On the basis of their model expected drawings were estimated for twenty-seven developing countries which did not actually draw on the Fund and for which data were available. It was discovered that only eight of these had predicted drawings of zero. The remaining nineteen would all have been expected to draw on the Fund, given their economic situation. It is interesting to note, however, that the authors' attempts to explain the reticence of these countries to draw by reference to the conditionality that would have been attached to drawings proved generally unsuccessful. It thus appears that drawings are not a purely economic phenomenon. Political, social and institutional factors also need to be taken into account and a case by case approach may therefore be more rewarding.

5. THE SIGNIFICANCE OF FUND FINANCE TO DEVELOPING COUNTRIES

In order to gain an appreciation of the quantitative importance of drawings from the Fund, Table 3.4 shows the contribution that reserve-related credit facilities, including the use of Fund credit, have made towards meeting non-oil developing countries' current account balance of payments deficits, as compared with other sources of finance. For most of the period covered, with the possible exception of 1982 and 1983, the IMF emerges as a relatively insignificant source of finance for developing countries. However, care has to be exercised in interpreting these figures.

First, in certain years and certain countries the Fund has provided a directly significant amount of finance. This is particularly true for many low income countries with limited access to private capital.

Second, even where only a small proportion of the deficit has been covered, the availability of Fund resources has often been such that a much larger amount could have been used. Further increases in quotas could mean that a potentially significant proportion of LDCs' financing needs might in principle be met by the IMF.

Third, even though the absolute amounts of finance provided by the IMF may be small, the adjustment programmes validated by the Fund may result in larger inflows from other sources, particularly the Eurocurrency market. There is some evidence for this catalytic effect. In the regression analysis undertaken by Bird and Orme, a positive correlation between Fund drawings and Eurocurrency drawings was found, and this was supported by a test which gave a Spearman's rank

TABLE 3.4 *Non-oil developing countries: financing of current account deficits and reserve accretions, 1977–84*

	1977	1978	1979	1980	1981	1982	1983	1984
	(In billions of US dollars)							
Current account deficit	30.4	42.3	62.0	87.7	109.1	82.2	56.4	50.0
Increase in official reserves	11.5	16.3	11.8	6.8	5.4	-3.8	6.1	13.3
Total	42.0	58.6	73.8	94.5	114.5	78.4	62.5	63.3
Financed by								
Non-debt-creating flows, net	14.1	17.0	23.7	24.1	27.2	23.9	21.3	23.0
Long-term borrowing from official creditors, net	13.1	13.8	17.0	20.0	22.6	21.6	22.6	23.1
Borrowing from private creditors, net	18.4	32.8	36.5	60.6	70.5	36.2	20.2	21.2
Reserve-related liabilities	2.9	2.0	-0.5	5.3	9.8	15.4	8.4	1.0
Errors and omissions	-6.5	-6.9	-3.0	-15.4	-15.5	-18.8	-10.0	-5.0
	(In per cent)							
Distribution of financing flows								
Non-debt-creating flows, net	33.6	28.9	32.2	25.5	23.8	30.6	34.1	36.3
Long-term borrowing from official creditors, net	31.3	23.5	23.0	21.1	19.7	27.5	36.1	36.5
Borrowing from private creditors, net	43.8	55.9	49.5	64.1	61.6	46.2	32.3	33.5
Reserve-related liabilities	6.9	3.4	-0.6	5.7	8.5	19.6	13.4	1.6
Errors and omissions	-15.5	-11.8	-4.1	-16.3	-13.6	-24.0	-15.9	-7.9

SOURCE: *World Economic Outlook*, IMF, Washington, 1984.

correlation coefficient between drawings on the Fund and Eurocurrency credits over the period 1971–9 of 0.64. However, it is also clear that drawings from the Fund and the acceptance of the related conditionality is, in itself, neither always a necessary nor sufficient condition for access to commercial loans. Brazil, for instance, borrowed heavily from the Eurocurrency market during the 1970s while making no use at all of the Fund; at the same time India, which in absolute terms made the largest cumulative drawings on the Fund up to end 1979, borrowed only $165m from the Eurocurrency market, even though it would seem that private banks would have been prepared to lend more; Bangladesh which ranked sixteenth in terms of drawings on the Fund, borrowed nothing from the Eurocurrency market. Examination of the nine stand-by arrangements concluded during 1975–7 where no agreement had existed during at least the previous two years confirms the variety of experience amongst LDCs. No clear pattern emerges in terms of the inflow of Eurocurrency credits following the conclusion of a stand-by. In some cases, such as Uruguay, Congo, and Costa Rica, there was an increase in the inflow of Eurocurrency credits, while in others, such as Egypt, Nepal and Tanzania, there was not. This result is consistent with evidence collected by Kapur (1977). Undertaking a cross country regression analysis of data from twenty-five LDCs that borrowed from the Eurocurrency market during 1972–4, he found substantial confirmation for the view that the flow of credit is positively related to a country's economic growth and export performance, and negatively related to projected increases in the debt burden and the degree of private banking exposure. Eaton and Gersovitz (1980) further confirm that banks do not regard the existence of an IMF programme as a sufficient guarantee of creditworthiness. It is also true, however, that bankers have frequently stated that they put great store by IMF involvement when considering their own lending strategy towards developing countries (Institute of Bankers, 1979). The situation has probably evolved through time, with the banks now putting more emphasis on their own independent country assessments but also looking crucially at the Fund's position.

6. THE FUND AND THE PRIVATE INTERNATIONAL BANKS

The relationship between the IMF and the private sector has attracted much attention in the period since 1973–4 as the commercial banks have become heavily involved in providing BoP finance to developing countries. While in aggregate terms the banks have frequently accounted for the largest share of financial inflows to developing countries, this overall picture is misleading, since the pattern of bank lending has been very heavily skewed (Bird, 1980a; Killick, 1981). The vast majority of private loans go to a narrow range of richer LDCs, with the low income countries receiving often as little as 2 per cent of gross publicised Eurocurrency credits. Indeed such countries have been net depositors with the private banks (Killick, 1981).

Certainly, as noted earlier, by the end of 1981 the IMF and private banks were essentially involved in different countries, with the Fund doing most of its lending to countries deemed uncreditworthy by the banks. This seemed to mark a significant change in a relationship between the Fund and the banks, which had previously stressed the Fund's catalytic effect.[6] However, in 1982–3 the situation further changed as a number of the larger LDCs, particularly Mexico, Argentina and Brazil, which had previously been reliant on private capital, encountered debt problems which forced them to turn to the Fund, an option that had until then been often staunchly resisted. In these countries the complex interrelationship between the Fund and the banks was again revealed as the banks deferred rescheduling until Fund programmes had been negotiated and as the Fund showed an anxiety to make certain that private finance would be forthcoming before its own resources were committed.

While the Fund can claim that its involvement with all member countries is essentially similar, the skewness of commercial lending implies that the nature of the relationship between the Fund and the private banks will vary between LDCs. While the banks will no doubt take Fund involvement into account in determining their lending, it is unlikely that they will place exclusive reliance on it – particularly given the quite high proportion of Fund programmes that are suspended for some reason or another. Thus in some low income countries which have a BoP need for finance, and which have been able to negotiate an IMF programme but which are deemed a high risk by private banks, the Fund will be on its own and the catalytic effect will in practice be non-existent. In some middle and high income countries deemed independently creditworthy by the banks it will be the banks that may be on their own, at least for protracted periods. In still other LDCs both the Fund and the banks may be simultaneously involved. It is quite possible therefore that the Fund may be supporting the private sector in one context yet acting as a substitute for it in another.

Linked to the discussion over the relationship between the IMF and the private banks has been the much broader debate over the durability and wisdom of commercial lending to LDCs for BoP financing on the scale undertaken, the danger of an international banking collapse, the appropriate division of labour between the banks and the Fund, and the ways in which their activities may be co-ordinated (Bird, 1981b, 1982b; Llewellyn, 1982a, 1982b; Maynard, 1982). These issues are taken up again in Chapter 14.

4 IMF Conditionality and Economic Development

Leading on from the discussion in Chapter 3, this chapter introduces the debate over IMF conditionality as it impinges on developing countries. The chapter focuses on the nature and impact of, and possible reforms to, 'high' conditionality. Questions relating to the appropriate blend between high and low conditionality and a more detailed assessment of key Fund facilities are held over until the next chapter.

While there is now little disagreement over the basic principle of conditionality (Dell, 1981), there is considerable disagreement concerning what conditionality should be designed to achieve and over the way in which its aims may be best realised. The debate about conditionality also involves the wider debate about what role the Fund should have in the world economy; differing views about this are unavoidably reflected in differing views about conditionality.

In principle, conditionality may be used to achieve a variety of ends. Fairly narrowly and uncontroversially, it may be seen as a way of ensuring that borrowers are able to repay loans; indeed the Articles of Agreement require adequate safeguards to ensure the 'revolving and temporary character' of the use of Fund resources. More widely it may be seen as a way of ensuring that borrowed resources are used to assist BoP adjustment, as a way of encouraging private capital inflows, as a way of rationing scarce Fund resources, or as a mechanism for counter-cyclical world economic management. From amongst these wider objectives the Fund certainly seems to accept the first two, pointing to Article V3(a) which requires the Fund to assist members to solve their BoP problems in a manner consistent with the provisions of the Agreement. However, as already noted, private borrowing is unavailable for many of the LDCs that borrow from the Fund, so that the catalytic role of conditionality is limited to a more exclusive subset of Fund members. This suggests that the concept of 'a' role for the Fund may in any case be too simplistic; it is feasible, and many would argue desirable, that the Fund should have different roles in different countries. Thus, in certain middle and higher income LDCs the Fund may be a lender of last resort called in only when the economic situation has deteriorated to crisis proportions and when creditworthiness has been seriously damaged – here the Fund may play a crucial part in restoring creditworthiness and in supporting the private sector. In many low income coutries, on the other hand, the Fund may be a lender of first and only resort, and creditworthiness, even in the fairly long run, will be a largely irrelevant issue.

Related to this notion of a dual role, the debate over conditionality involves a discussion of the balance between low and high conditionality resources within the Fund. In particular it may be argued that middle and higher income LDCs have considerably less need for low conditionality finance than do low income countries, since they can conveniently finance BoP deficits caused by exogenously generated and reversible factors without resort to the Fund.

1. CRITICISMS THAT HAVE BEEN MADE OF FUND CONDITIONALITY

One argument is that conditionality results in asymmetrical adjustment. Under the existing international monetary system little pressure is exerted on countries to adjust in order to remove surpluses, and as a result Fund conditionality has a deflationary effect on the world economy. Again, reserve-currency countries like the United States may be able to finance deficits by increasing their externally held liabilities. Other deficit countries may be in a position to finance deficits through private, often unconditional, borrowing which allows them freedom to choose domestic policies. The less economically strong nations, however, are often forced to turn to the IMF, where they become subject to the discipline of conditionality. Of course, it might be maintained that it is just these countries that most need guidance in their economic affairs, since their lack of creditworthiness illustrates a lack of expertise in economic management. While there may be something in this, it need not always be the case. Evidence suggests that over recent years many LDCs have been faced with severe payments difficulties which have been caused primarily by external factors rather than by domestic mismanagement (Dell and Lawrence, 1980). The Fund's claim that the latter is the principal cause of BoP problems has therefore also been heavily criticised.[1]

A second group of criticisms of the IMF's use of conditionality relates to the nature and appropriateness of the conditions. Over the years statements emanating from the Fund, along with the output of the Fund's Research Department (IMF, 1977) and the invariable inclusion of credit ceilings in stabilisation programmes, have resulted in the Fund being labelled as a 'monetarist' and anti-developmental institution. Certainly a preoccupation with domestic monetary stability and an unswerving belief in the efficacy and appropriateness of internal adjustment as a means of correcting payments deficits can result in a conflict with the objective of development (Bird, 1978). Critics of the Fund's philosophy have indeed adopted this theme as the essence of their case. Their view is that the IMF has put too much emphasis on internal adjustment via demand deflation as a means of obtaining balance of payments equilibrium, and too little on development (Krasner, 1978; the Colloquium on the Interests of Developing Countries in International Monetary Reform, 1970; Corea, 1971; Payer, 1974). Indeed, it is maintained that in many cases monetary restriction designed to temper inflation succeeds only at the cost of development (Morley, 1971; Payer, 1971). It is also suggested that Fund policies show little appreciation of the structural inflexibilities which exist in many LDCs and of the political and social consequences of the policies advocated. It is further argued that the conditions are far more specific and all-embracing than is necessary merely to ensure the repayment of IMF loans. Even observers who have offered broad support for the Fund feel that its policies have gone too far on occasions (Williamson, 1979). The insistence that action to restrain internal demand be initiated at the time that drawings are made has led to the complaint that little account is taken in the possibility that deficits may be self-correcting over time (Corea, 1971).

The more outspoken critics of the Fund's involvement with stabilisation programmes in developing countries have generally adopted a structuralist stance. They see inflation as a frequently unavoidable concomitant of structural change (Hirschman, 1958; Maynard, 1964). Economic development, certainly in its initial stages, usually implies substantial structural changes in the economy, and these often induce short-run supply bottlenecks which cannot be overcome without correspondingly substantial changes in relative prices. Given downward price rigidities, such changes are incompatible with a stable absolute price level. Insistence on monetary stability may, in these circumstances, inhibit the structural shifts that are required for the longer term benefit of the balance of payments (Maynard and van Rijkeghem, 1968). In addition it is maintained that LDCs' payments problems are more structural than monetary in nature. If LDCs export goods with low price and income elasticities but import goods for which their own income elasticities are high, then economic growth is liable to be inconsistent with balance of payments equilibrium. Dependence on markets in industrial countries makes variations in the level of economic activity in these countries a potentially important source of short-run price and income instability in LDCs.

Although exchange-rate policy may permit some LDCs to insulate their economies from world price instability, critics claim that devaluation may not be the answer to fundamental and structurally based payments deficits.[2] As a result, the advocacy of devaluation by the Fund has often been criticised (Dell, 1982; Taylor, 1981; Schydlowsky, 1982). Where, for structural reasons, total export supply cannot be quickly increased, devaluation may have an inflationary impact on the devaluing economy with no sustained benefit to the balance of payments. The consequences for income distribution may have political and social repercussions which, by engendering price and income responses, quickly nullify any putative benefits of devaluation. Finally, it is argued that, in the absence of discriminatory import controls, reliance on devaluation may reduce developmental imports, with damaging long-run effects on development and the balance of payments.

Coupled with measures to deflate aggregate demand, and under its terms of reference set by the Articles of Agreement, the Fund also often advocates the liberalisation of trade and payments (Johnson and Reichmann, 1978).[3] These broad categories of policy could be expected to go hand in hand, since the pursuit of a liberal system of trade and payments necessitates a means, other than exchange controls, for reducing the demand for foreign exchange, and aggregate demand deflation is one such method. But just as critics have argued that demand deflation may not always be appropriate in LDCs, so they also argue that liberalisation may involve welfare and payments costs, not least when the liberalisation is unilateral. Instead, critics maintain that trade controls and/or multiple-exchange practices are preferable (Konig, 1968; Streeten, 1971; Cooper, 1971; Jayarajah, 1969). These instruments may improve the balance of payments at a lower cost in terms of inflation than exchange-rate depreciation, or at a lower cost in terms of forgone domestic production and employment than demand deflation. Although import restriction might harm growth prospects, it does not, the argument goes, rely on a reduction in current income to bring about payments equilibrium, as does a policy of demand contraction. Furthermore, liberalisation may impede the growth of indigenous manufacturing, which may have difficulty in competing with foreign producers, who, because of their larger scale, have lower unit costs. Advocates of multiple exchange rates maintain that the gain to be had from such a system is that it allows a country to discriminate between various imports and exports which have different price elasticities of demand and supply and have different degrees of importance in development. Import substitution and export promotion can therefore be encouraged with fewer side-effects on the economy. Moreover, the system can be an important source of government revenue while providing a politically acceptable method of realising economic objectives. In some cases where under IMF insistence multiple exchange practices have been abandoned, critics maintain that the alternative measures designed to achieve the same ends have been inferior (Konig, 1968).

According to some observers (Payer, 1974), trade liberalisation and demand deflation have generated other undesirable consequences. These have included a takeover of domestic production by foreign-owned multinationals (caused by falling domestic sales and increasing costs), a simultaneously cost-inflationary and demand-deflationary situation stemming from an attempt to balance the budget by raising the price of public utility goods and services, an increase in debt service payments arising from the foreign borrowing undertaken to fill the foreign-exchange gap created by liberalisation, and the increased importation of non-essentials. In fact, it has been argued that LDCs have lost far more in these ways than they have benefited from the additional finance gained. The relatively small amounts of Fund finance available to developing countries are, in turn, seen as partly reflecting the inappropriateness of IMF quotas, which are determined by formulae which fail to measure a country's need for external assistance. The need for IMF finance will mainly depend on the variability of the balance of payments and its structural trend, the availability of alternative sources of liquidity, the terms of such assistance, and the costs of adjustment. Since many developing countries possess small amounts of owned reserves, have little access to commercial funds and have a relatively high marginal productivity of resources, it is argued that their need for finance is large relative to that of developed countries (Bird, 1978).

Critics go on to argue that the small amount of finance provided and the strict conditionality attached to it lead countries into making every effort to avoid recourse to the Fund. Even where governments accept the conditions, the commitment to the resulting package of policies is often low and the chance of success is correspondingly small. Governments may at the first opportunity abandon Fund policies in favour of their own, even assuming that, as a result of pursuing unpopular IMF policies, the governments are not themselves overthrown beforehand.

Further criticism of conditionality has related to the apparently perverse and procyclical way in which it has been used through time. In particular this criticism has related to the tightening up catalogued in Chapter 3 that occurred after mid-1981 in an environment of world recession and rising world unemployment. The deflationary effect of conditionality has, so critics maintain, been enhanced by the switch in emphasis towards high conditionality finance (Dell, 1982).

On the balance between high and low conditionality critics have suggested that the increased emphasis on high conditionality has been unwarranted either because the causes of deficits have been largely beyond the control of the countries experiencing them (Dell, 1982), or because in such circumstances countries should at least initially be given any benefit of the doubt in selecting an appropriate adjustment policy – leaving the risk of losing Fund support as sufficient incentive to repay. Furthermore, of course, to the extent that critics see individual deficits as temporary whilst the Fund sees them as permanent, there will be disagreement over the need for adjustment at all and therefore over the appropriateness of high conditionality.[4]

Other criticisms of conditionality are more political and/or organisational. Thus, it has been alleged that the Fund, dominated by industrial country interests, is used as a vehicle for the domination and exploitation of developing countries (Krasner, 1968; Payer, 1974). Fund conditionality is seen as imposing a free market, outward-looking development strategy while being incompatible with a more inward-looking strategy involving planning and protection. Certainly tensions have arisen between the Fund and some LDCs, which see it as trying to deflect them from socialism (Nyerere, 1980). Going further, Fund programmes have been characterised as a means by which Western capitalist economies endeavour to bring about the downfall of LDC governments to which they are opposed (Payer, 1974). Thus, the entire international financial system, of which the IMF is an important part, is seen as operating against the best interests of developing countries. Fund credit is viewed merely as a way of financing the importation of goods from developed countries and a means of ensuring the continuing superiority of the developed economies' productive base. This argument challenges the whole concept of developing countries' dependency on industrial countries and the international institutions associated with them (Brett, 1979 and 1982).

At the extreme, then, the Fund is characterised by critics as a doctrinaire, inflexible and unadaptable monetarist and market-orientated institution, showing little concern for the adverse effects of its programmes on output, employment and income distribution, and yet being rather unsuccessful at improving the balance of payments. This extreme view, which is the one conventionally associated with the development lobby, may, however, be sharply contrasted with the more recently heard criticism that the Fund is a largely inappropriate vehicle for the international recycling of resources as compared with the private banks. This latter group of critics accuse the Fund of failing to encourage adjustment and of effectively supporting domestic economic mismanagement. The result of this failure has been to weaken the catalytic effect of Fund programmes on private capital flows. However, still other observers have criticised the Fund for being too ready to provide a safety net for the international banks, to the detriment of its own and the banks' lending policies. How do these pictures contrast with that painted by the Fund itself or its defenders?

2. DEFENCES OF FUND CONDITIONALITY

Until recently the Fund has shown reticence in defending itself against criticism – but this is changing, as recent additions to the literature show (Nowzad, 1982). From a positive point of view defenders argue that, bearing in mind the resources at its disposal and constraints imposed by its Articles of Agreement, which influence the way in which it conducts its affairs, the Fund has made a significant contribution towards helping countries to correct deficits efficiently by providing temporary financial assistance, policy advice and incentives. Fund involvement, it is claimed, prevents a much more marked deterioration in economic performance. Defenders frequently go on to rule as illegitimate criticisms based on the size of Fund resources or on the basic rationale of the Fund. However, while exclusion of these issues may be fair when assessing the performance of Fund staff, they are clearly very important and need to be considered when discussing the Fund more widely, since it may be felt that they form a basic constraint to meaningful reform.

Turning to some of the more specific criticisms, defenders first argue that the Fund is not a development institution and that it should not therefore provide soft aid on a semi-permanent basis. Development is instead the principal concern of the Fund's sister institution, the World Bank and its affiliates. However, having said this, defenders go on to point out that the Fund has been of significant benefit to LDCs through its normal operations and its range of specialised facilities, which have often been primarily of relevance to LDCs, as well as through encouraging the growth of world trade.

Second, defenders suggest that the Fund is a flexible, eclectic and rather open-minded institution and not the dogmatically monetarist one that some critics see. They point, for instance, to the range of facilities available, with the CFF helping with exogenously caused BoP problems and the EFF helping with structurally oriented ones. They further maintain that considerable flexibility is exercised within the narrow range of performance criteria and that this flexibility is used by missions in the field to reflect the individual characteristics of borrowers. The small number of performance criteria used itself gives maximum policy discretion to borrowers, but also gives the false impression that the Fund lacks subtlety. Furthermore, defenders point to the nature of Fund programmes, which include the use of the exchange rate and other relative price policies, as evidence of a much broader theoretical underpinning. On the emphasis on monetary variables, and in particular on the very common use of credit ceilings as performance criteria, defenders suggest that it would be surprising if these were ignored; that in some cases financial policy is merely supportive while the main thrust of IMF programmes lies elsewhere; that credit ceilings meet the requirements of a good performance criterion, ie. data are available; they enable the programmes to be objectively monitored; and they are under the, albeit approximate, control of the authorities. What other variables could be used that would involve fewer problems?

More generally defenders reject the accusation that there is a Fund fixation with demand side variables. While arguing that indeed aggregate demand has to be adjusted to a level consistent with supply, they further argue that many elements within Fund programmes, such as devaluation or interest rate changes, have a beneficial effect on supply and on the underlying structure of production and trade. The use of multi-year programmes has also been used by defenders to represent the concern that the Fund has over supply side considerations and over encouraging development at the maximum rate that the maintenance of financial stability and BoP viability will permit. To the extent that IMF programmes are demand-deflationary, this is interpreted as evidence of previous internal economic mismanagement, with the Fund merely bringing economic reality to the attention of frequently over-ambitious governments. However, advising that expenditure must be cut to be consistent with output and sustainable net imports is not anti-socialist nor anti-development. Defenders go on to point to the satisfactory working relationship maintained by the Fund with a number of socialist countries. Of course, even where governments accept the economic wisdom of Fund prescriptions, it may prove politically more convenient for them to present the policies as 'Fund policies' which have been unwillingly forced on them. Defenders claim that an even greater degree of political and social unrest would eventually, possibly quite quickly, result if Fund programmes were not pursued.

The criticism that the Fund opts for overly tough measures often results, so defenders claim, from the fact that countries only turn to the Fund at a late stage in their difficulties when the situation has reached crisis proportions. Furthermore, given that in such circumstances quick results are required, it is easier to produce these by reducing demand than by increasing supply. Where earlier referral is made – as in the case of the EFF loan to India in 1981 – the Fund staff suggest that a more balanced and relaxed approach to conditionality may be adopted.

A third major issue that defenders anxiously take up with critics is the relevance of the endogeneity or exogeneity of the causes of BoP deficits. As noted earlier, some critics argue that a more lenient approach to conditionality should be adopted where countries are not responsible for the problems they are facing. However, the Fund's view is that the causes of the problem are only of secondary importance. The prime issue, which according to the Fund is clouded by the causation argument, is whether the problem is transitory or non-transitory. If transitory and self-correcting, then, although short-term financing may be required, adjustment is not. In these circumstances low conditionality finance is quite appropriate; hence the low conditionality attached to the CFF, and also to the Oil Facility at a time when it was felt that oil-related disequilibria might not persist. However, if not transitory, BoP adjustment is required irrespective of the causes of the deficit, and here high conditionality resources are appropriate. Thus, the decision not to introduce a new oil facility following the second major increase in oil prices in 1979 has been defended on the grounds that this would have reduced the incentive to undertake required adjustment. The changing balance towards high conditionality lending and the toughening up of conditionality in mid-1981 have been defended on similar grounds.

A fourth general defence of the Fund argues that too much is expected of it. With limited resources, and in the face of governments which are often reluctant to face up to economic realities and are unwilling to adopt unpopular measures, it is hardly surprising that examples of Fund successes are far from plentiful. However, defenders claim that failures are little or nothing to do with Fund conditionality *per se* but rather reflect the immense size of the problems – social, economic and political – that many LDCs face, together with the lack of commitment to adjustment from governments. Critics are seen as being out of touch with the real world in which the IMF is involved and as judging the Fund against standards which are impossible to attain. Similarly, whilst recognising the asymmetry argument put forward by critics, defenders see little that the Fund can constructively do about such problems other than undertake 'firm surveillance' of surplus countries and lobby against the protectionist measures adopted in industrial countries which make the outward-looking adjustment strategies favoured by the Fund that much more difficult to implement.

Turning finally to the issue of developed country domination of the IMF, defenders argue that this reasonably reflects the economic significance of the countries involved and that to reduce their influence would lead to rich countries by-passing the Fund to the disadvantage of LDCs. In any case it is maintained that LDCs do wield considerable, even disproportionate, influence within the Fund, and that they have been able to achieve many significant modifications to their benefit.

3. ASSESSING SOME OF THE ISSUES

Rather than attempting a full evaluation of all the various aspects of the conditionality debate itemised above let us extract three issues for further commentary: (i) the causes of payments deficits, (ii) the nature of Fund programmes, and (iii) the effects of Fund programmes.

3.1 The cause of deficits

There is considerable empirical evidence to support the view that since 1973 the deteriorating world economic environment has caused significant payments difficulties for developing countries. Data in Chapter 2 show that many LDCs have experienced a marked decline in their terms of trade. Furthermore, during the 1980s world economic recession was coupled with increasing real interest rates and these were the source of still further payments difficulties for developing countries.

In addition to such casual empiricism, more rigorous studies have also discovered that external factors have been a principal or even prime course of payments deficits. Dell and Lawrence (1980) found than an increase in import quantities was the primary factor in explaining the deterioration in the trade position of selected NOLDCs over 1973–6 in only 12 per cent of cases, whereas it was the primary factor in 21 per cent of cases between 1962 and 1972. They argue that this reflects the declining relative significance of expansionary domestic policies as the cause of payments problems. By comparison, in 68 per cent of cases the principal cause of the deterioration was increasing import prices, or decreasing export prices, or decreasing export volume, all factors which, according to Dell and Lawrence, reflect external rather than internal causation. More recently, and on the basis of an econometric study, Khan and Knight (1984) also found that external factors, primarily in the form of deteriorating terms of trade, had been an important cause of payments deficits in developing countries, though they also found that fiscal deficits had played an equally important role.

3.2 The nature of Fund programmes

Fund programmes comprise three components: preconditions, performance criteria, and various, frequently numerous, other policy elements. Whilst the performance criteria form the centrepiece of an IMF programme, and of IMF conditionality, a few words on the other components will not be misplaced.

Preconditions relate to policy actions which must be undertaken before an agreement is put up for approval by the Executive Board. Although it is difficult to get information about them, since they are not normally mentioned in 'letters of intent,' preconditions most commonly relate to measures such as devaluation and interest rate policy. Furthermore they apply to the clear majority of Fund programmes.[5]

Letters of intent do, however, often mention a wide range of nonquantified but fairly specific microeconomic policy objectives relating to various aspects of fiscal and monetary policy, pricing policy, wages policy, trade policy and economic efficiency. While failure to comply with such policy objectives may damage a borrower's credibility with the Fund, it does not interrupt the flow of credit agreed under the stand-by, which is not conditional upon such policies being adopted. For this reason this component of a Fund programme is considerably less significant than the performance criteria, though the two components are related in the sense that the policy commitments undertaken should be consistent with and reflect the means by which performance criteria are to be achieved. It is to these that we now turn.

Performance criteria are policy targets and ceilings included in the letter of intent in quantitative or objective terms. Features of the variables chosen to act as performance criteria are that information on them should be available with only a short lag, they should give an accurate picture of economic performance, and should be within the control of the domestic authorities.

Table 4.1 summarises the performance criteria used in a representative sample of thirty upper tranche IMF stand-bys over 1964–79. Standard clauses relating to avoiding new multiple currency practices and payments restrictions are not mentioned in the table but are also usually appended to IMF agreements. It clearly emerges that credit ceilings are by far the most common performance criterion used by the Fund, a finding confirmed by the Fund's own research.[6] However, the ceilings are usually on the rate of credit expansion and rarely call for zero growth or a reduction in the total quantity of credit. Furthermore, there are many variants under the general heading of credit ceiling; control may relate to total domestic credit, credit to the private sector or credit to the government. Similarly, controls may relate to the holdings of specific assets by the banking sector and/or the central bank.

The apparent preoccupation with credit ceilings suggested by Table 4.1 might at first glance be interpreted as reflecting a fixed

TABLE 4.1 *Performance criteria in upper-tranche stand-by arrangements*[1]

	Number of observations[2]		
	1964–9	*1970–3*	*1974–9*
1. Credit ceilings:			
(A) Total domestic credit	3	10	9
(B) Credit to government public sector	7	5	7
(C) Credit to private sector	5	—	1
2. Devaluation	3	—	—
3. Reduction in current payments arrears	—	1	2
4. Minimum levels for foreign exchange reserves	1	1	4
5. Restrictions on new external debt	3	7	5

1. In addition to the criteria listed there are standard provisions that borrowing countries will not introduce new multiple-currency practices; bilateral payments agreements with Fund members; restrictions on current payments and on imports. There were a number of other significant items which are not set out in the table because there were no occasions on which they were used as performance criteria. These included interest rate, pricing and wages policies.
2. For each entry the maximum number of observations is 10.

SOURCE: IMF

belief in the monetary approach to the balance of payments. However, this argument does not bear close inspection. Although the Fund's Research Department has indeed made a significant contribution to the development of the monetary approach, the Fund's version of this general approach lays considerable emphasis on short run adjustment paths which are ignored in the general equilibrium versions associated with the principal academic contributions. More recent Fund research recognises the complex but potentially adverse effects that credit control may have on output and employment, something which is inconsistent with the strict monetary approach.[7] Furthermore, the Fund is clearly aware of the restrictive and quite probably unrealistic assumptions upon which the monetary approach is based and seems prepared to accept many of the criticisms that have been made of the monetarist model. In addition, the Fund's advocacy of policies to alter relative prices, in particular devaluation, is clearly at odds with the strict monetarist model, as is the Fund's interest in the composition of the balance of payments and the performance of the current account.

If then the ubiquitous use of credit ceilings does not reflect a single-minded acceptance of the stricter versions of the monetary approach to the balance of payments, it may reflect the view that credit variables possess the features required of a good performance criterion. However, again this is an argument of dubious validity. Although data on credit creation are relatively easily and quickly available, there is little point in concentrating on credit for this reason alone. Data shortage is an argument for collecting more data not for using only the variables on which data are currently available. Furthermore, there must be considerable doubt whether one financial variable can accurately and fully summarize what is happening in the real economy. Where structural deficiencies are identified as the underlying cause of balance of payments deficits, credit control represents too indirect a way of acting on these. Even if this were not the case, there must be some doubt concerning the scope for monetary authorities precisely to control the rate of credit creation, given the various endogenous and exogenous pressures which exert an impact on this variable.

As Table 4.1 shows, other performance criteria used in Fund programmes include devaluation, reductions in payments arrears, minimum levels of foreign exchange and restrictions on new external debt. Given the amount of publicity which it has received, it is perhaps surprising that devaluation appears only infrequently. Even allowing for the fact that it is sometimes made a precondition for Fund support, devaluation seems to be associated with only between 50 or 60 per cent of Fund programmes. Towards the end of the 1970s the Fund showed a considerable reluctance to stipulate devaluation, largely because of its unpopularity with developing countries and because of concern over the reluctance of these countries to draw from the Fund. After 1981, however, devaluation became more commonly stipulated.

Setting a minimum level on foreign exchange imposes a limit on exchange market intervention and thereby on the domestic authorities' ability to prevent depreciation of the exchange rate, while the other two performance criteria serve to highlight the Fund's view of its relationship with the private capital market. Though reducing payments arrears is clearly aimed at improving a country's creditworthiness, restricting new external debt seems at first sight somewhat inconsistent with the objective of encouraging private financial inflows. Although an overcommitment to foreign borrowing in terms of what the current account can service may, of course, adversely affect such inflows over the longer run, the Fund's main concern here would seem to be that of preventing capital inflows from disrupting domestic monetary policy and from frustrating an improvement in the current account.

Given the wide range of policies in which the Fund expresses an interest, the number of performance criteria is indeed rather narrow. An important question, then, relates to the flexibility and adaptability that may be incorporated within a Fund programme.

In principle there is considerable scope for flexibility. Credit ceilings may take on various forms and may involve various quantitative targets, tight or less tight, and these variations may be used to reflect the characteristics of individual countries. Similarly, the possibility of negotiating a waiver or a modification to the programme if initial targets are not realised provides further scope for flexibility. In addition, the existence of a range of facilities in the Fund provides the possibility of tailoring the type of finance to the needs of individual countries. Furthermore, in practice, the negotiating ability of the borrower may well influence the precise details of the final programme. However, having said all this, evidence does seem to suggest that there is a reasonably conventional type of Fund programme which, in terms of its performance criteria, places almost exclusive reliance on demand side targets. Even in the instances where the Fund does not identify over-expansionary demand policies as a principal cause of the deficit, or in the rarer ones where such policies are not even given a secondary importance, there remains an apparent reluctance to break away from the conventional demand side performance criteria.[8] This is true even in the case of the EFF, which is supposed to deal specifically with longer term, structural problems.[9]

3.3 The effects of Fund programmes: how successful are they?

The success of Fund programmes may be assessed in a number of ways. One method involves comparing economic performance before and after the implementation of a Fund programme. A second involves comparing actual performance with the performance targets set in the programme, while a third involves comparing actual performance with what would have been the situation in the absence of the Fund programme.[10]

There are fundamental problems associated with each of these methodologies. In the first case there is the question of whether an economic improvement or indeed the failure to improve can legitimately be attributed to the Fund programme. In many cases there are likely to be other factors at work which will exert a dominant effect on economic performance. In the second case there is the question of whether the initial targets were realistic. In the third there is the problem of assessing what the situation would have been in the absence of a Fund programme. Two options are available here. The first assumes that without the Fund there would have been no change in economic policy, while the second assumes that policies alternative to those supported by the Fund would have been adopted. It is quite possible that a Fund programme could be judged successful when compared with the first option but simultaneously unsuccessful when judged against the second. For all three methodologies there is the additional problem of determining the time period over which a comparison is to be made; how quickly can Fund programmes be expected to generate results? While the Fund claims that its programmes have shown a broad measure of success, empirical evidence offers far from unambiguous support for this claim. Indeed the Fund's own research reveals very mixed results; considerable variation exists between individual stand-bys, time periods and specific targets. According to this research, the greatest degree of success has been achieved in improving the balance of payments; other variables such as economic growth and inflation seem to be generally little affected by Fund programmes.[11] Clearly the balance of payments is a fairly narrow criterion for evaluating success. Indeed, it would perhaps be surprising if Fund programmes primarily directed towards establishing a viable balance of payments did not demonstrate some degree of success in these terms.

Research conducted outside the Fund[12] seems to confirm that Fund programmes have relatively little apparent impact one way or the other on growth, inflation or liberalisation, though surprisingly Fund programmes if anything seem to be positively correlated to growth.[13] Again the principal impact would seem to be on improving the current account of the balance of payments or more so the basic balance. However, even this improvement is not usually found to be significant statistically and there is no guarantee that the improvement has been achieved in the most cost-effective manner.

The impact of Fund programmes on income distribution is difficult to pin down empirically. While it is unreasonable to assume that economic stabilisation involving falling real wages, reduced government spending and subsidies, increased taxation and price rises will have no effect on the distribution of income, the precise effects will depend on the economic characteristics of individual countries, such as the degree of real wage resistance, the ownership of the factors of production, and intersectoral mobility. In principle there is no necessary reason why Fund programmes should raise income inequality and their relatively slight effect on other variables, particularly economic growth, suggests again that their effect on income distribution may be rather smaller than sometimes assumed.

It is interesting to ponder as to why Fund programmes seem to exert so little impact on the economies which pursue them. Part of the answer may lie in the relatively low degree of implementation. In turn this might reflect first a low degree of commitment by governments to IMF-supported programmes. Certainly there is plenty of case study evidence to suggest that many LDC governments put a low priority on stabilisation, and this is an explanation that the Fund itself stresses. A second explanation may be the incidence of exogenous shocks which push economies off the courses mapped out in IMF-supported programmes. Finally, however, the programmes themselves may simply be incapable of generating the objectives set. Thus if the largely financial targets set as performance criteria in IMF-supported programmes do not generate changes in the real economy, it may not be surprising that they have little effect on output and trade. Lack of implementation cannot be the whole of the answer to the low degree of success achieved by Fund programmes, since economic performance does not appear to be significantly different as between those countries that do and do not observe performance criteria (Connors, 1979).

4. SOME CONCLUSIONS ON CONDITIONALITY: THE CASE FOR A CHANGE IN EMPHASIS

The strong advocacy of credit ceilings as the fulcrum of adjustment policy is internally consistent with the Fund's view that over-expansionary demand policies are more often than not the prime cause of payments problems. In circumstances where the fiscal deficit has been allowed to grow and has been financed by domestic credit creation, there can be little doubt that the imposition of financial discipline is absolutely crucial to payments correction. But in other circumstances there must be more doubt about whether credit control should be allocated the prime role or whether it should adopt only a secondary role. Imagine, for example, a situation where a developing country moves into balance of payments deficit as a result of adverse movements in its commodity terms of trade, or following a reduction in the demand for its exports caused by recession in importing countries. Now assume either that these adverse developments are not purely temporary, or that even where they are the country has insufficient reserves or access to borrowing to finance the deficit; adjustment will be needed. The domestic policy makers' objective may reasonably be expected to be the correction of the deficit with as few harmful effects on other policy objectives as possible.[14] An adjustment strategy therefore needs to meet two criteria: it needs to be effective in actually strengthening the balance of payments, but it also needs to be cost-effective, securing this improvement at minimum welfare cost.

In the circumstances outlined above, these criteria will be met by policies which shift resources from non-traded goods (such as services and construction) into traded goods (exports and import substitutes) and policies which have an output-increasing effect. Policies are needed to encourage structural adaptation in production and trade. The changes needed are real ones, and the question is whether financial policies, of the type favoured by the Fund, will achieve them.

There is little reason to be sanguine. Financial restraint exerts its impact on the current account of the balance of payments by deflating expenditure so that imports are reduced to a level consistent with a given level of exports. To the extent that there is a reduction in the domestic rate of inflation relative to the world rate, demand may switch towards import substitutes, while similarly there may be some increase in export demand where prices are quoted in domestic currency, or an increase in export supply as profitability rises where domestic producers simply take the international foreign currency price as given. However, the principal mechanism through which financial restraint works remains that of reducing the level of domestic expenditure. Any effects on structural adaptation are largely coincidental and may even be in the 'wrong' direction. With reduced aggregate demand and increased interest rates it is likely that real output and employment will fall. Furthermore, unless imports are exclusively consumption goods or 'inessentials', it is probable that development will become constrained by a shortage of vital imported inputs and this will damage future export performance. Economic development and the longer run underlying strength of the balance of payments will further be impeded where the restriction of credit has a particularly adverse effect on export-orientated infant manufacturing industry. In many developing countries this effect of rising interest rates will be more important than the extra incentive they provide for capital inflows. Thus, while the restriction of domestic credit may certainly strengthen the short run balance of payments, it is likely to involve substantial costs for development and growth and even for the balance of payments in the long run. This is of course not to argue that interest rates should be kept at artificially low levels.

These shortcomings of credit controls as a means of bringing about structural adjustment would, of course, not matter too much if, as the Fund claims, deficits are caused by over-expansionary domestic demand management policy. Although this may have been the case in the 1960s, there is ample evidence that it has not been true for the 1970s and 1980s, when adverse exogenous terms of trade movements have assumed much greater significance. Unfortunately, whilst the causes have changed radically, the Fund's prescribed cure has not.

The track record of stabilisation programmes supported by the Fund has not been impressive. Although exceptions may be cited, Fund conditionality has not been that successful in accomplishing its prime task of encouraging payments adjustment. Recent evidence from Latin America suggests that where the correction of deficits has been achieved, the costs in terms of lower economic growth and high unemployment have often been considerable. Whatever the reasons for lack of success, the case for change is supported.

Reluctance by governments to implement programmes suggests that for some reason they see the programmes as unhelpful. The vulnerability of programmes to unforeseen external events in a world which is predictably uncertain and unstable suggests that the programmes are insufficiently flexible; while, as already explained, there are reasons for believing that financial restraint will fail to bring about the necessary structural adaptation. The upshot of all this is that the Fund is not fulfilling the objectives set out for it in its existing Articles of Agreement (specifically Article 1):

(i) To promote international monetary co-operation.
(ii) To facilitate the expansion and balanced growth of international trade, and to contribute thereby to the promotion and maintenance of high levels of employment and real income and to the development of the productive resources of all members as primary objects of economic policy.

(iii) To promote exchange stability, to maintain orderly exchange arrangements among members, and to avoid competitive exchange depreciation.

(iv) To assist in the establishment of a multilateral system of payments in respect of current transactions between members and in the elimination of foreign exchange restrictions which hamper the growth of world trade.

 (v) To give confidence to members by making the Fund's resources available to them under adequate safeguards, thus providing them with opportunity to correct maladjustments in their balance of payments without resorting to measures destructive of national or international prosperity.

(vi) In accordance with the above to shorten the duration and lessen the degree of disequilibrium in the international balance of payments of members.

The policies that the Fund traditionally supports are likely to be least suitable in low income countries, yet it is to precisely these countries that the great majority of stand-by credits, as well as EFF loans, have been made in recent years. Although, since the debt crisis, the majority of Fund finance has gone to the better-off LDCs, the majority of programmes remain with the poorer developing countries. As will be argued in Chapter 5, even the EFF, which was intended to assist with structural adaptation, has had only a muted impact. Furthermore, in the poorest countries it is also likely that external factors will be aggravated by structural weaknesses of a more domestic origin. Indeed, such weaknesses may themselves be the principal source of difficulty.

5. MAKING GOOD THE WEAKNESSES: A REAL ECONOMY STRATEGY

While the Fund may be criticised for underemphasising policies which influence the real sector of the economy and overemphasising those that affect the financial sector, the 'structuralist' critique of the Fund may itself be criticised for sometimes almost totally neglecting the importance of financial management. Adjustment policy needs to take into account both aggregate supply and aggregate demand; neither side should be ignored. Over-expansionary demand policies can easily frustrate and impede what is an essentially supply orientated adjustment strategy, and aggregate demand needs to be held in check, bearing in mind the capacity of the economy to meet it in real terms. The Fund should therefore certainly not abandon its concern with credit creation. Indeed, in some cases the 'conventional' Fund programme will be both effective and cost-effective and in these cases there is little reason to change. Fund programmes should, however, be more flexible, more related to the causes of payments problems, and formulated in a framework which sets out to achieve balance of payments improvement at minimum cost in terms of development. In general, this involves placing more emphasis than in the past on measures which have a beneficial effect on output, investment and exports. The object is to achieve a satisfactory payments position at as high as possible a level and rate of growth of real output, and sustainable domestic consumption, or, in other words, to create a viable balance of payments in a manner that also promotes, or at least minimises conflicts with, that group of government objectives called 'economic development'. The key target variable should generally be the current account of the balance of payments; it is only by reducing the current deficit that a country can safeguard against the danger of generating a financing gap that cannot be filled or against building up an unsustainably large volume of external debt-servicing obligations. The emphasis should thus be on increasing the volume and value of exports, reducing net dependence on imports through efficient import substitution, and maximising net inflows (and minimising net outflows) on the 'invisibles and transfers' account, through measures such as stimulation of the tourist industry, encouragement of the repatriation of earnings from nationals working abroad, and more efficient domestic provision of insurance and shipping services.

The growth of output can be thought of as coming from two sources: from the improved utilisation of existing productive capacity and from increases in that capacity. Greater capacity utilisation may be particularly important both because it is common for developing countries experiencing a payments crisis to be operating well below the trend level of output and because greater output from existing capacity should not, in principle, be subject to long gestation lags in a situation in which time is of the essence.

Given the need to shift resources out of non-traded goods production and into traded goods production and to expand capacity, how can this be achieved? One obvious option is to use the price mechanism.

Since a greater degree of flexibility in Fund programmes is what is being suggested, it is impossible to give a precisely defined general description of what policies should be adopted. There is bound to be considerable variation between countries, depending on their different economic and political circumstances, including the causes of the deficit, the degree of openness, the composition of imports and exports, the scope for efficient import substitution, the degree of capacity utilisation, the values of demand and supply price and income elasticities, the degree of financial and fiscal sophistication, the size of the non-monetised sector, the degree of real wage resistance, the quality of the domestic infrastructure, the scope for domestic energy production, the availability of commercial international credit and aid, the level of international reserves, and the nature of other government objectives.

However, a strong case may be made for actively using a vitally important relative price, the exchange rate; using depreciation in developing countries may in many cases be a cost-effective way of strengthening the balance of payments.[15] The usual objection that supply elasticities are too low for it to have a beneficial influence seem to be largely unfounded, though elasticities do vary between traditional and non-traditional exports and between the long and short run. Furthermore, while it may be expected to have an initially expenditure-reducing effect – which is in any case required if the current account is to improve – depreciation may help to maintain or even increase exports, output and employment. To the extent that output is increased, so are the levels of domestic expenditure, domestic credit, and imports that are consistent with balance of payments equilibrium. As far as economic development is concerned therefore, exchange rate depreciation (accompanied by disciplined domestic financial policies) represents a superior alternative to exclusive reliance on financial restraint.

In some cases, where elasticities are very low or where there is strong political resistance to the redistribution of income that it causes, depreciation may not work; in any case, it is a rather unsubtle and indiscriminate tool. It therefore needs to be complemented by more specific microeconomic policies. Again, individual circumstances will dictate what these should be, but a few examples will be indicative. Where, for instance, export supply is highly price elastic, the price incentive created by depreciation may need to be partially neutralised by imposing export taxes. In the opposite situation export subsidies may be used. Indeed, the fiscal system could be more widely used to encourage the growth of exports and efficient import substitutes, to reduce the size of the non-traded sector, to provide incentives for those investments which assist economic growth and the balance of payments, and disincentives for consumption, and to offset those effects on income distribution that are regarded as widening social inequities. Furthermore, incomes policy may be used to counter the inflationary consequences of devaluation. Although these measures may be quite specific to particular sectors of the economy (agriculture, tourism, or non-traditional exports), they are likely to exert a significant impact on macroeconomic variables such as the balance of payments and economic growth.

In principle, the fiscal system could be used on its own to simulate the effects of currency depreciation.[16] However, the practical problems involved with doing this augur in favour of using fiscal policy as an adjunct to open depreciation rather than as a replacement for it. Similarly, although exchange controls may sometimes be a useful short run and temporary balance of payments policy, since they have an immediate effect on imports, they are also subject to numerous practical problems and tend to suppress rather than correct the deficit; indeed, in the long run they may have an adverse effect on both the balance of payments and economic development, since they create a bias in favour of inefficient import substitution.[17] Even credit policy could be used in a more sophisticated way and its potential for encouraging structural adaptation exploited more fully by discriminating in favour of activities that raise output and economic growth, and strengthen the balance of payments, and against consumption. While the policy instruments listed above have not been uniformly absent from Fund programmes, they have only infrequently been used as 'performance criteria' for monitoring the implementation of programmes.

While the objective of the real economy approach is to minimise the costs of payments correction, it cannot be assumed that adjustment will be costless. Payments adjustment requires a reduction in absorption relative to output. Even though the real economy approach emphasises expanding output rather than contracting absorption, it may be impossible to avoid some cuts in domestic absorption. Also, it needs to be ensured that increases in output and income do not lead to equivalent increases in absorption. Furthermore, within the overall category of absorption it may be more important from a growth point of view to protect the investment component rather than the consumption component. This is confirmed by simple models of income determination in an open economy, which show that if exports are to rise relative to imports, savings must rise relative to investment. If investment is not to fall, savings must rise and consumption fall.

As undesirable as this may be, given the low levels of consumption in low income countries, unless there is a much enlarged flow of concessional finance, there is no alternative. The advantage of a real economy approach is that it sets out to keep the consumption sacrifice to an absolute minimum; it does not dispense with the need to adjust. However, the more successful the approach is in raising aggregate supply (and the demand for money), the less will there have to be any reduction in aggregate demand (or the rate of credit creation). Other things being equal, this means that a given payments outcome will be consistent with a larger real volume of domestic credit, which, in turn, may assist a further increase in capital utilisation and formation.

An important question that arises from discussing the real economy approach is how the change in policy emphasis could be made operational given that there seems to be no reason to abandon the concept of strict conditionality in circumstances where deficits are not temporary and self-correcting. The basic idea would be to relate conditionality to a fairly wide range of instrument variables and to judge programmes in terms of these and in terms of whether the ultimate targets are achieved.[18] There would be an agreed timetable of execution for all or most of the programme elements and explicit provision for the ways in which progress would be assessed. Programmes would then still be monitored and tested, although failure to comply with policy conditions would initially trigger off consultation between the borrowing country and the Fund and a review of the programme, rather than immediately resulting in the cutting off of the further finance. During the review the reasons for failure would be examined and a decision made with regard to future financial provision. A lenient attitude would be adopted in those cases where exogenous and unforeseen factors were responsible for the programme's failure and a new programme with new conditions would be negotiated. Although with this new type of conditionality programmes would still be subject to objective and quantitative appraisal, the aim would be to shift the emphasis away from negotiating on the basis of precise financial targets and towards achieving agreement on the underlying policy approach designed to alter the structure of production. The Fund would not only provide its own finance but would endeavour to attract other forms of financial support both in the form of aid and commercial credit.

6. IMPLICATIONS OF THE CHANGES

6.1 For developing countries themselves

If governments in developing countries refuse to accept the costs, in terms of domestic absorption, that balance of payments correction involve, and endeavour to avoid these by preventing real changes in the structure of the economy from taking place, then the outcome will almost certainly be that payments problems will become more firmly embedded. The adjustment that the balance of payments constraint will eventually enforce is therefore likely to be much more costly for economic development. Similarly, developing countries need to be persuaded that a larger number of economic variables need to come under discussion with the Fund than has conventionally been the case, if conditionality is to be made more appropriate to their economic circumstances and is to have minimum adverse effects on economic development. This requires a considerable shift in their attitude towards the Fund.

Policy deficiencies in developing countries have often reflected a reluctance to come to terms with the harsh realities of the two oil shocks and the recession in the industrial world, as well as a reluctance to place sufficient weight upon economic stabilisation as a policy objective. That many of these countries' problems have been caused by convolutions in the world economy over which they had no control is true. But this does not remove the need for adjustment. While the worsened external environment has been a major cause of their payments deficits during the past decade, domestic policy weaknesses have often compounded the difficulties.

The events of the early 1980s have left many developing-country governments in little doubt that shortages of foreign exchange constitute a massive obstacle to the fulfilment of the material aspirations of their peoples. Once such shortages are recognised as a binding constraint upon development, it follows that policies designed to deal with this problem are part of the development effort. Quite apart from loosening the hold of the foreign-exchange constraints, successful stabilisation will also reduce uncertainties and risks, and this is itself likely to have a beneficial effect on economic performance. The task then becomes one of building adjustment into the country's development strategy and planning.

One source of difficulty in this context is that planning in these countries has conventionally been regarded as a once-every-five-years effort to write a medium-term development plan. Quite apart from the numerous other difficulties and disappointments to which it has led, this approach has the defect of inflexibility. It does not lend itself to accommodating the types of exogenous shocks to which the developing world has been subjected in recent years. If stabilisation policy is to be effectively co-ordinated with other aspects of the development effort, planning will have to be more flexible than it has typically been in the past.

Furthermore, developing country governments have to accept the significance of demand management in the sense of exerting general control over the level and composition of absorption. They also need to recognise the role that relative prices can play in achieving structural adjustment. Sensible use of the price mechanism combined with proper balance of payments management need not undermine social reform. Indeed, precisely the opposite may be the case. As a particular example of this, developing countries would appear to gain little from maintaining over-valued exchange rates. The practice of holding interest rates below the inflation rate – financial repression – may also be misplaced in many circumstances. In principle, interest-rate reforms that create positive (or less negative) real interest rates are likely to have a number of advantages. They will tend to encourage domestic saving and inflows (or reduced outflows) of capital from the rest of the world; they will tend to channel available investment resources into higher productivity employments; they may, by increasing the demand for money and money-substitutes, reduce the necessary degree of credit restraint and unemployment; and they are likely to enhance the effectiveness of the conventional instruments of demand management, particularly by increasing central bank control over the money base. It must be cautioned, however, that developing-country experiences with financial reforms that have raised interest rates have been far from uniform. South Korea, Taiwan and Indonesia are commonly cited as success stories in this respect but such policies also have had negative results, as exemplified by the experiences of Chile.

Especially in many of the poorer developing countries, a key determinant of success in applying an interest-rate reform is the degree of efficiency of the financial system as a means of mobilising savings and channelling them into productive investment. It should not, however, be taken for granted that a sufficient array of investment opportunities promising high rates of return will always exist, or be perceived to exist. If they do not, raising interest rates can result in a seriously reduced investment rate. Finally, if interest-rate policy is not carefully coordinated with exchange-rate policy, unwanted results can arise via the foreign asset component of the money base. The greater the degree of exchange-rate flexibility, the greater the danger of 'overkill' through higher interest rates, which invite an unwanted inflow of short-term capital that tends to push up the exchange rate and/or swell the money base. The general case against financial repression nonetheless holds, as long as due caution is exercised in the design of policies to eliminate it.

6.2 For relations with the World Bank

The conventional division of labour between the IMF and the World Bank has been blurred in recent years, and would change further if the reforms discussed above were implemented, with the Fund lending more longer-term finance related to structural deficiencies. Traditionally, the Fund has been thought of as a balance of payments institution concentrating on demand management primarily through domestic financial policy. The orientation has been towards short-term programme support. The World Bank, on the other hand, is seen as a long-term development institution which through a mainly microeconomic approach works on aggregate supply. The great majority of its support is related to specific projects rather than programmes.

However, where payments deficits have been caused by structural problems requiring long-term solutions and where development is constrained by the balance of payments, the distinction between payments problems and development problems loses much of its relevance. For a period at the end of the 1970s and the beginning of the 1980s the Fund moved in the direction of longer term lending, showing some recognition of development problems, while the Bank started providing structural adjustment loans in support of programmes designed to strengthen the underlying balance of payments. However, this evolution of the two institutions occurred in a rather ad hoc fashion and it is relevant to ask whether their responsibilities need to be formally redefined, especially to accommodate the reforms discussed in this chapter.

At the very least it should be ensured through close consultation that their activities do not conflict. More radically, it has been suggested by some commentators that they should merge. Between these two extremes there is a range of other proposals: one is that countries facing structural payments problems should be encouraged or indeed required to apply simultaneously for both an EFF loan from the Fund and a structural adjustment loan from the Bank.[19] Fund staff would then concentrate on the demand side of a jointly recommended package of policies and Bank staff on the supply side. The institutions would in effect be exploiting their areas of traditional expertise but a balanced overall programme would be the outcome.

It remains the relevance of the final programme that is ultimately important; the institutional question is simply which set of arrangements is most likely to come up with a relevant cost-effective programme, and to be most efficient in avoiding unnecessary duplication of functions. It may well be that closer co-operation with mutual representation in country missions is the most realistic option. The Fund would retain the role of providing payments assistance linked to adjustment programmes in circumstances where deficits are non-temporary, and this does not constitute a break from its traditional role.

6.3 For relations with the private international banks

How will the private banks react to the changes in Fund conditionality? Will the catalytic effect disappear? A number of points may be made. First, as noted earlier, the importance of the catalytic effect can be overstressed, especially where the Fund and the banks are involved in different countries. Second, even where the Fund and banks are both involved, particularly in certain middle/high income developing countries, it is quite possible that the appropriate Fund programme will in fact look fairly conventional, since where excessive credit creation has caused the payments problem, emphasis on credit ceilings is quite appropriate. Third, the poor record of success of Fund programmes hardly encourages continuing confidence. This is much more likely to be provided by programmes that are successful, and the success rate may be raised by the Fund adopting a more flexible approach to conditionality which permits the root cause of the problem to be attacked. Finally, the poor record of Fund programmes has, in any case, encouraged banks to formulate their own views on the likely future economic performance of potential borrowers.

6.4 For the duration of lending, and financing the Fund

An approach to conditionality that emphasises real changes implies longer term lending by the Fund than has heretofore generally been the case, since such changes are unlikely to be achieved within one or two years. Longer term lending does, however, bring with it a fundamental difficulty: if the Fund is to extend its lending in this way, it will initially require increased resources. With existing resources the only alternative would be to lend less in any individual year but to lend this over a longer time span. However, the need for more resources does not only arise from the proposed changes in conditionality, since there is a strong case for the IMF to take on a larger share of the task of recycling international finance in order to assist world economic development and increase the stability of the international banking system. A central question is, then, from where are the additional resources to come?

Broadly speaking there are five options:

(a) increased IMF quotas,
(b) ad hoc borrowing,
(c) borrowing from private capital markets,
(d) gold sales,
(e) a form of SDR link.

However, a discussion of these alternatives is deferred until Chapter 8.

6. 5 For the uniformity of treatment

The reforms discussed here may seem to imply that not all Fund members would be treated equally or uniformly. However, another way of looking at this is to argue that different countries have different capacities to adjust. Variety amongst programmes is therefore required to ensure that the adjustment effort is approximately equivalent across countries. There seems no point in advocating a standard programme if there are not standard problems. The greater diversity of programmes would enable the Fund to make a greater contribution to solving the payments problems faced by low income countries.

7. CONCLUDING REMARKS

It is far from uncommon nowadays for the IMF to be dealing with countries whose deficits reflect structural deficiencies rather than exclusively over-expansionary demand policies. In such circumstances the cost-effectiveness of conventional Fund-backed programmes is in doubt. The Fund needs to find some way of modifying its conditionality in order to be of more use to these countries. This chapter suggests that a more flexible approach to conditionality could make a significant contribution in this direction, whilst maintaining the Fund's essential purpose as a balance of payments agency. The Fund should show a greater awareness of the possibly long term nature of payments correction, and a greater degree of concern that payments correction be achieved in the most efficient fashion, minimising the adverse effects on output, employment and on desired structural change. Unavoidably this involves lengthening the Fund's operative time horizon. Conditionality should have the role of encouraging cost-effective adjustment. In many cases this will involve adjustment in the real sectors of the economy, influencing the productive and trading performance of borrowing countries. The effectiveness of the implied policies will depend on the economic characteristics of the countries, including the causes of payments problems, the extent of capacity utilisation and the elasticity of supply once spare capacity has been used up.

During 1979 and 1980 there were some indications that the Fund was beginning to modify its approach to conditionality; there was the *Review of Conditionality Guidelines*, a move towards longer term lending and more discussion of the relevance of supply side variables. Following this period of liberalisation there was a retrenchment.

However, it is not just on the IMF side that there is a need for change. Developing countries themselves have to demonstrate greater cognizance of and political commitment to the need for adjustment.

5 The Fund's Lending Facilities: Reforming the Compensatory Financing Facility and the Extended Fund Facility

Whereas the previous chapter concentrated on the nature of IMF 'high' conditionality, this chapter examines the appropriate combination of high and low conditionality. Its principal function, however, is to look at some of the lending facilities of the Fund in a little more depth and to evaluate policies for reform. In particular, the chapter investigates the Compensatory Financing Facility and the Extended Fund Facility, although certain remarks are made concerning other Fund facilities.

1. THE BLEND BETWEEN HIGH AND LOW CONDITIONALITY RESOURCES

Data in Chapter 3 show how the use of high and low conditionality resources from the Fund has varied through the years. The trend in the 1980s has been toward more emphasis on high conditionality. Underlying such changes is the question of what is the appropriate combination of the two types of finance. Two key concepts have been used in trying to answer this question. That emphasised by the Fund has been the distinction between temporary and permanent deficits. The shift towards high conditionality is defended by the Fund in the following way. Given the non-transitory nature of most deficits experienced in developing countries, adjustment is needed. The Fund is best able to encourage this through the conditions it attaches to its financial support. Left to their own devices, many governments in developing countries lack political commitment to payments adjustment, and the provision of low conditionality finance by the Fund would therefore merely postpone adjustment, with the result that payments performance would deteriorate further, leading to an even more critical need for adjustment.

The second key concept, although seen as being largely irrelevant by the Fund, is the cause or causes of deficits. The view often associated with UNCTAD is that the causes of deficits have a vital bearing on the correct balance between low and high conditionality. Where deficits are caused by exogenously generated adverse movements in a country's terms of trade, it is argued that strict conditionality is inappropriate. Countries should not be penalised through high conditionality for problems for which they are not responsible.[1]

An intermediate attitude is that while the causes of deficits cannot legitimately be regarded as insignificant to the conditionality debate, external causation is insufficient reason to attach low conditionality to Fund finance. This view stresses three things. First, that while temporary deficits should be financed rather than corrected, in order to impose minimum cost on economic and social welfare, non-transitory deficits do require correction. Second, that IMF conditionality does have a role to play in encouraging such correction. But, third, that conditionality should be appropriate to the economic characteristics of the countries concerned, with an important determinant of appropriateness being the causes of deficits. The crux issue here is the second. Should the Fund become involved with the policies of a country whose payments problems have been externally caused? There is, in principle, a case for allowing more rather than less discretion to governments that have a good track record of payments management but which have been adversely affected by exogenous factors, and the suggestion has been made that conditionality could be tapered to accommodate various degrees of responsibility (Williamson, 1982).

However, the main problem is to convert these rather vague concepts into measurable and operationally useful ones. There are immense definitional difficulties. How can one distinguish *ex ante* between deficits that are temporary and those that are permanent, and therefore between the need for finance and for adjustment. Furthermore, given the problems, on which side is it better to err? Is it possible to state categorically the extent to which any specific payments deficit has been caused by external factors? And, in any case, for what economic phenomena can a government be held justifiably responsible? Is it, for example, responsible for a country having a particular level and pattern of production and trade, or merely for controlling the level of aggregate demand? The answer is that it is impossible to be operationally precise about the concepts which are relevant to the discussion about the balance between low and high conditionality. Some degree of subjective judgment is therefore unavoidable.

However, there are still other factors that impinge on the debate, even though they are hardly helpful in allowing a more precise answer to be given.

First, there is the question of 'moral hazard'. If countries can acquire relatively concessionary finance from the Fund with few conditions attached, will they not be enticed to engineer themselves into situations where they are eligible to receive such finance by purposely getting into balance of payments difficulties? It is in this context that it becomes relevant to distinguish between the various types of low conditionality finance. Most significantly, these include lower credit tranche drawings and drawings under the CFF, although, as will be seen later, there is some debate as to whether the CFF can continue to be regarded as a low conditionality facility following an Executive Board decision in 1983. Putting this question to one side, access to CFF finance depends on the export shortfall being largely beyond the control of the country involved. In this way the CFF essentially avoids the moral hazard problem associated with the lower credit tranche.

Second, there is the whole question of the role of the Fund, the role of conditionality, and the correct balance between global adjustment and financing. If the Fund is regarded as an exclusively adjustment-orientated institution, then there is little purpose in having low conditionality facilities, if these are simply envisaged as helping to deal with temporary imbalances which do not require adjustment. The private markets might be expected to provide such finance. However, if it is further agreed that private markets will be of little use to the least developed countries, then there may be a financing function for the Fund to perform and a related role for low conditionality facilities. Generally speaking, the more the emphasis is placed on adjustment, the less will be the relevance of low conditionality facilities.[2] As discussed in Chapter 2, it was indeed different perceptions of the need for adjustment which led to different responses to the first and second oil price increases in the 1970s, with the first being met by an expansion in low conditionality finance and the second by a relative contraction in such finance. These changing perceptions have also been reflected by modifications to the CFF.

2. THE COMPENSATORY FINANCING FACILITY

The CFF provides financial assistance to countries experiencing export shortfalls which may result from a sudden decline in the price or demand for a principal export product, or from harvest failures or other causes. The shortfall must be seen as being temporary and largely beyond the control of the country concerned. Furthermore, the borrowing country has to have a payments need for assistance. Access is constrained by a formula which calculates the size of the deviation in export receipts from an average value, as well as by certain quota limitations. Since its introduction in 1963, the CFF has been periodically modified, with changes being made to the quota limitations on its use as well as to the way in which the export shortfall is calculated; on occasions these changes have had quite a dramatic impact on the extent to which the facility has been used, as, for example, occurred in 1976 following the 1975 liberalisation.[3] Furthermore, since 1966 the facility has been separate from other Fund lending, with drawings under the CFF not affecting members' capacity to draw under other tranches. In 1981 the CFF was extended to cover abnormal increases in cereal imports. This was a significant change inasmuch as it recognised that payments problems could be related to externally caused import excesses, such as those associated with a harvest failure, as well as to export shortfalls. Such recognition was also illustrated by the oil facility which operated in the mid-1970s to assist countries in dealing with the payments implications of the increasing price of oil.

Up until recently the CFF was regarded, and classified, as a low conditionality facility. While members drawing under it were expected to co-operate with the Fund in finding solutions to their payments problems, this 'condition' in practice meant little, and countries experiencing export shortfalls had reasonably automatic and rapid access to finance. The generally lenient interpretation of conditionality as it applied to the CFF also downplayed the significance of the fact that CFF finance is available in two tranches, with access to the upper one depending on the Fund's assessment of a

member's co-operation in finding, 'where required, appropriate solutions for its balance of payments difficulties'.

In 1983 a review of the CFF led to guidelines being established for
judging 'co-operation.' At the same time the access limits were
reduced from 100 per cent to 83 per cent of quota for outstanding
purchases relating separately to export shortfalls or cereal import
excesses, and from 125 per cent to 105 per cent on their joint use. As
with so many Fund statements, there is room for debate about what
the words used actually mean and how they will be interpreted. No
doubt the Fund would argue that the changes are in no way inconsistent with the logic of the CFF and merely represent a classification
and codification of past procedures. However, an alternative view
exists. Before examining this, we may find it useful to reproduce the
text of the guidelines:

2.1 Compensatory financing of export fluctuations: guidelines on co-operation

Lower tranche

The criterion – namely, that the Fund is satisfied that the member will
cooperate with the Fund in an effort to find, where required, appropriate solutions for its balance of payments difficulties – implies a
willingness to receive Fund missions and to discuss, in good faith, the
appropriateness of the member's policies and whether changes in the
member's policies are necessary to deal with its balance of payments
difficulties. Where the Fund considers that the existing policies of the
member in dealing with its balance of payments difficulties are
seriously deficient, or where the country's record of cooperation in
the recent past has been unsatisfactory, the Fund will expect the
member to take action that gives, prior to submission of the request
for the purchase, a reasonable assurance that policies corrective of
the member's balance of payments problem will be adopted.

Upper tranche

The additional criterion of the upper tranche – namely, that the Fund
is satisfied that a member has been co-operating with the Fund in an

effort to find, where required, appropriate solutions for its balance of payments difficulties – means that, in the light of the action taken by the member and the balance of payments policies being pursued, the Fund is satisfied with the member's record of co-operation. The existence of a satisfactory balance of payments position (apart from the effects of the shortfall) or the existence of and broadly satisfactory performance under an arrangement with the Fund, or the adoption of such an arrangement with the Fund, or the adoption of such an arrangement at the time the request for a CFF purchase is made, will be considered to provide evidence of co-operation. However, the existence or the adoption of an arrangement is not a prerequisite. If a member's current and prospective policies were such as would, in the Fund's view, meet the criteria of the use of resources in the credit tranches, the member would be deemed to have been satisfactorily co-operating with the Fund, even though such use was not contemplated at the time of the CFF request.

The guidelines abound with ambiguities. In the lower tranche guidelines, for example, what is meant by '*appropriate* solutions,' 'good faith,' '*seriously* deficient,' an '*unsatisfactory*' record of co-operation,' '*reasonable* assurance'? (italics added). Similarly, the definition of 'co-operation' in the guidelines for the upper tranche covers cases where the member has had no recent dealings with the Fund, but would be able to draw on the basis of current and prospective policies.

In spite of these ambiguities, it is fairly clear that drawings under the lower tranches are now more firmly tied to a visit from a Fund mission and the adoption of policies deemed appropriate by the Fund as a precondition for assistance under the CFF. The independence of the CFF from other Fund resources seems to have been broken. A country may now establish that it has experienced a temporary shortfall in export receipts for reasons beyond its control and yet fail to gain access to CFF finance if the Fund considers other unrelated aspects of its balance of payments to be unsatisfactory. In effect, high conditionality may now apply to drawings from the Fund designed to cover even that part of a country's payments deficit which is defined to be temporary and not to be caused by inappropriate domestic policy. In a fundamental way the guidelines therefore seem to be inconsistent with numerous Fund statements which maintain that temporary deficits should be financed and that adjustment measures are required only when they are permanent. With the new guidelines, adjustment is linked to the CFF, even though the CFF is defined by the Fund to assist with problems which do not necessitate adjustment. The question is whether the conventional type of Fund-supported adjustment programme, as discussed in the previous chapter, is appropriate for dealing with the kind of problem for which the CFF was designed. Both the analysis in Chapter 4 and statements by the Fund itself suggest that it is not.

A related implication of the guidelines is that they represent a further move by the Fund to switch the global balance away from financing and towards adjustment. Although this is internally consistent with other Fund decisions – for example, that not to have a new Oil Facility after 1979 – it may yet be misguided for reasons discussed in Chapter 4. What is more, the decision emphasises still further the asymmetries in the distribution of the adjustment burden by putting additional pressure on deficit countries to correct their imbalances. A principal purpose of the CFF, namely, that countries experiencing temporary shortfalls in export receipts should nonetheless be enabled to maintain their import levels, seems to have been sacrificed.

The guidelines relating to the upper tranche also serve to stress a new connection between use of CFF and credit tranche resources inasmuch as the 'satisfactory co-operation' required for CFF access is proxied by the pursuit of policies which would permit a credit tranche drawing – presumably in the higher tranches. Again, what this implies is that countries pursuing payments policies which the Fund would not support will be deemed ineligible for compensatory financing. In what sense if any then can the CFF still be regarded as a low conditionality facility? If it cannot, this is particularly concerning, since analysis in the previous section suggested that, because of the moral hazard problem, the CFF is in many ways the most desirable form of low conditionality facility. On the basis of these arguments the modifications encapsulated in the 1983 decision have gone in the wrong direction, weakening rather than strengthening what were the special features of the CFF.

In what ways should the CFF have been modified? To answer this, a brief review of the shortcomings of the facility prior to 1983 will be helpful.

An underlying weakness is that the CFF does little to solve the more fundamental causes of export instability, but merely assists countries in coping with it. However, leaving this issue to one side, we may criticise the CFF even as a short term device.

A general criticism is that the scheme is both quantitatively and qualitatively inadequate in relation to the size and nature of the problem with which it is supposed to deal. While the percentage of quota that may be drawn under the CFF had been increased between 1963 and 1983 from 25 to 100 per cent, this was more than offset by the fact that the size of quotas in relation to world trade and to the export earnings of developing countries steadily diminished. Thus, total IMF quotas, which were equal to 16 per cent of deficit developing countries' export earnings and 64 per cent of their current account deficits in 1966–8, were equal to only 6 per cent and 12 per cent respectively in 1978–81. One result of these trends was that maximum borrowing from the CFF in 1966–8 was equal to about 32 per cent of total current account imbalances, whereas 1979–81 it was equal to only about 12 per cent.

As mentioned above, access to CFF finance not only depends on the quota limits but also on the size of the estimated shortfall. This in turn depends upon the way in which the trend is measured. An important question is whether the method of trend measurement has been accurate. Basically the choice is between using an arithmetic or geometric moving average. While the CFF started off using a arithmetically calculated trend, this was changed to a geometric trend in 1979. Since then, however, and with the prolonged recession in industrial countries, the trend growth of LDC exports would probably have been more accurately represented by an arithmetic measure, and in retrospect the change was probably inappropriate in the light of subsequent events.

Another criticism of the CFF is that, apart from cereal imports, it applies only to shortfalls in export receipts. By not relating more generally to deteriorations in developing countries' terms of trade and the purchasing power or real value of their exports, increases in import prices have been neglected, even though from a balance of payments point of view they may be equally damaging and may adversely affect the financial capacity of a country to import. It is quite possible that a country's payments position will be deteriorating at the same time as export earnings are rising, or are showing an excess over trend, simply because an increase in import prices has caused the real value of exports, expressed in terms of imports, to fall. If the purpose behind the CFF is to protect countries against fluctuations in their balance of payments caused by temporary out-side factors beyond their control, there is a strong argument for covering rising import prices as well as export shortfalls. Calculations by UNCTAD for the period 1973–82 suggest that significant differences exist between the nominal and real measures of export short-falls, with the real shortfalls facing non-oil developing countries being, on average, very much larger.[4] There seems little reason not to apply economists' well established general preference for real rather than nominal values in the case of the CFF.

A final criticism of the CFF to be examined here is that it implicitly assumes that export shortfalls will be reversed and at least partially made good within three to five years. There appears to be no strong theoretical or empirical justification for this. Indeed, given the pro-tracted cyclical downturn in many industrial countries, the real situa-tion appears to be quite different. The details of the cyclical pattern of developing countries' export receipts has significant ramifications for the direction and size of financial flows between developing countries and the IMF. With a fixed repayment schedule, repayments may coincide with a period when countries are in a poor position to make these because of contemporaneous, and externally caused, balance of payments difficulties. Since countries are already expected to make earlier repayments if their payments position rapidly im-proves, there is some logic in allowing them to postpone repayments if the cyclical upturn takes longer to arrive than expected – though there is the obvious problem of the temporary nature of CFF support and the less obvious one that problems of repayment may mean that the trend value of earnings has been overestimated.

Without the scope for flexible repayments, net purchases under the CFF may be significantly less than gross new purchases, and the fraction of current shortfalls covered by net inflows from the CFF may therefore be much less than gross figures suggest.[5] Even using gross figures, it appears that, during 1976–81, on average only about 50 per cent of the export shortfalls of developing countries, as estimated by the Fund, were covered (Griffith-Jones, 1983). This suggests that the quota restrictions form an effective constraint on the use of CFF finance, as does the empirical observation that drawings have risen when the restrictions have been relaxed. It could also suggest that the greater conditionality attached to upper tranche drawings has influenced the willingness of countries to draw more. Of course, to the extent that the Fund underestimates the size of short-falls, its calculation of the rate of compensation provided by the CFF is overestimated.

2.2 Proposals for reform

A number of proposals for reform emerge from the above discus-sion. One is to divorce access to the CFF from quotas and make it depend instead exclusively on the size of export shortfalls and exter-nally caused import excesses. Alternatives would be to raise the proportion of quotas that may be drawn, in order to relax the quota constraint, or to raise quotas themselves. In principle, the removal of quota restrictions would be the most desirable change, given the stated objectives of the CFF to protect import capacity from export shortfalls caused externally.[6] What has actually happened, as re-ported earlier in the chapter, is that the percentage of quota that may be drawn has been reduced.

Emphasising the importance of actual export shortfalls makes it even more important to ensure that these are measured as accurately as possible. The nature of the trend of export earnings needs to be kept under review so that the appropriateness of geometric and arithmetic averages may be monitored. In the short term there would appear to be a strong case for returning to the use of an arithmetic average.

Although the above reforms would help to protect the real value of CFF drawings, further protection could be provided by measuring exports in terms of the imports they buy. There is a very strong case for measuring export shortfalls in real terms, given the basic objec-tives of the CFF to maintain import capacity. Where the divergence between the rate of inflation in primary product prices and manufac-tured goods prices is marked, with the latter exceeding the former, this reform becomes pressing.

A further reform that would be beneficial to many LDCs would be to relate the repayment schedule of CFF drawings more directly and closely to payments performance and the pattern of export instabil-ity, subject to some outside limit of perhaps seven years. Again this modification would enable the CFF better to realise its basic objective.

Finally, as intimated earlier, there is little logic in making the CFF a neo high conditionality facility if the intention is still for it to finance temporary imbalances caused by factors beyond the control of the countries concerned. The 1983 modifications are only logical if the Fund's intention is to reduce the demand for its resources or to encourage adjustment in all cases of payments deficit irrespective of the cause. However, if this is the explanation, the question is whether these intentions are not severely misplaced.

One feature of the CFF that has yet to be mentioned is its global counter-cyclical implications: maintaining developing countries' demand for imports in circumstances where world demand is stagnating. Global macroeconomic stabilisation has perhaps been more frequently claimed as an advantage of buffer stocking arrangements but may, in fact, be more appropriately attributed to compensatory financing, since in this case it is export earnings that are, in effect, stabilised, while in the case of buffer stocks it is commodity prices that are stabilised and this may result in greater earnings instability.[7]

Although buffer stocks have been indirectly supported by the IMF via its little-used buffer stock financing facility, there are strong arguments for favouring the principle of compensatory financing. Apart from offering a preferable method of stabilising global macroeconomic performance, compensatory financing is free from many of the microeconomic problems associated with buffer stocks. The next chapter examines the question of buffer stocks in more detail. However, in the light of the above observations, it is interesting to note at this stage that commodity price stabilisation rather than compensatory finance has been the centrepiece of developing countries' claims for a New International Economic Order. While some, almost intangible, progress has been made with setting up commodity stabilisation schemes, the modifications that have been made to the CFF may be interpreted as being significantly retrograde from the viewpoint of LDCs. Perhaps it is time for developing country lobbyists to switch the focus of their attention.

3. THE EXTENDED FUND FACILITY

The EFF, set up in 1974, was designed to be of particular benefit to LDCs.[8] Its purpose is to provide medium term assistance to those Fund members finding themselves in the sorts of payments difficulties where the required policies are of a longer term nature than those which could be supported by the ordinary credit tranches. The 'special circumstances' under which a member can make an EFF drawing are, first, when it is 'suffering serious payments imbalance relating to structural maladjustments in production and trade and where prices and cost distortions have been widespread', and, second, when it is 'characterised by slow growth and an inherently weak balance of payments position which prevents pursuit of an active development policy'. EFF drawings are supposed to support attempts which 'mobilise resources and improve the utilisation of them and . . . reduce reliance on external restrictions'. Given such statements of intent and purpose, it is hardly surprising that the EFF has often been interpreted as representing the Fund's attempt to accommodate a supply side approach to payments stabilisation. This interpretation of the facility is further encouraged by the fact that drawings are spread over three years and repayments over four to eight years.

Although differing from conventional stand-by arrangements in terms of these details, drawings under the EFF still rest on the negotiation of a satisfactory (as seen from the point of view of the Fund) economic programme. It is therefore unambiguously a high conditionality facility, and its benefits for developing countries may only be legitimately assessed by examining the nature and relevance of the conditions attached to EFF loans. However, if the criticisms of conventional Fund conditionality made in the previous chapter are accepted, one might have thought that the EFF was a move in the right direction.

Unfortunately experience raises the question of just how far the EFF represents a genuine acceptance of the significance of structurally caused payments deficits and a commitment to assist in the resolution of such problems. On the positive side EFF programmes have been associated with a rather longer term perspective on the balance of payments, and have set rather higher targets for economic growth and for import volume than conventional stand-by programmes. On the negative side the structural aspects of EFF programmes seem to have been fairly secondary and the control of credit creation has been at their core just as it is in the case of stand-bys (Killick, 1984). Indeed the credit ceilings adopted in EFF programmes have not uncommonly been stricter than those in stand-bys.

Some critics have argued that, far from being a break in tradition, EFF programmes have, in practice, simply been conventional stand-by programmes with a few supply-oriented measures tacked on. What is undeniable is that the Fund's staff have felt uncomfortable in implementing the EFF. They feel that their expertise lies with the design of short term programmes. They also feel that governments find it exceedingly difficult to commit themselves to specific courses of action for more than one year ahead. Furthermore, the agreement of a EFF loan ties up Fund resources for three years even if the programme is suspended. At times when the Fund is constrained by a shortage of finance and desires flexibility this has been seen as an unattractive feature.

However, Fund critics of the EFF 'experiment' more frequently cite the relatively poor performance of EFF programmes as the reason for their opposition. In fact, this criticism does not bear close inspection. First, there is the argument made above that EFF programmes have, in important respects, not differed significantly from conventional stand-bys. Second, the world economy has been particularly turbulent since the EFF was introduced and there have been many factors working against the success of EFF programmes. Third, it is particularly difficult to assess programmes which call for longer term structural adjustment: for example, what is the appropriate time frame? But further, and taking the frequency of breakdown as an indicator of performance, EFF programmes do not seem very much more likely to fail than the *equivalent number* of stand-bys.

Although, as noted above, it may be misplaced to assess the effects of EFF programmes in terms of a narrow range of quantified short term indicators, the information contained in Table 5.1 is not irrelevant to such an evaluation. Examination of this table reveals that, although stand-bys do appear to have been relatively more successful in some areas than have EFF programmes, for example, in the

TABLE 5.1 *Comparative performance under Stand-by and Extended Financing Facility arrangements for selected variables, 1978–80 (prior outcome in per cent; other items in percentage points)*[1]

	Stand-bys	EFF credits
1. Ratio of current account balance to GDP		
Prior outcome	-12.7	-7.3
Actual change (increase in deficit (–))	1.1	-1.3
Targeted change (increase in deficit (–))	-0.9	-1.1
Actual minus target (increase in deficit (–))	2.0	-0.2
2. Ratio of overall BoP to GDP		
Prior outcome	-9.6	-10.0
Actual change (increase in deficit (–))	0.1	-0.7
Targeted change (increase in deficit (–))	2.0	1.5
Actual minus target (increase in deficit (–))	-2.0	-2.2

Continued on page 106

TABLE 5.1— *continued*

	Stand-bys	EFF credits
3. Real growth rate		
Prior outcome	5.2	4.0
Actual change	–3.7	–1.2
Targeted change	–1.8	–0.1
Actual minus target	–1.9	–1.1
4. Rate of consumer price inflation		
Prior outcome	25.5	10.3
Actual change	–0.3	1.9
Targeted change	–8.9	–0.5
Actual minus target	8.6	2.4
5. Overall credit growth ratio[2]		
Prior outcome	36.1	21.0
Actual change	3.2	5.3
Targeted change	0.2	–1.5
Actual minus target	3.0	6.8
6. Public sector credit growth ratio[2]		
Prior outcome	25.0	20.7
Actual change	–3.9	0.4
Targeted change	–5.4	–10.4
Actual minus target	1.5	10.8

1. This table presents averages of selected varibles for countries with arrangements. The underlying data entering into the averages are from all of the programmes in the core group of arrangements (stand-by arrangements approved in 1980 and extended arrangements approved in 1978–80) for which data for both targeted and actual changes are currently available. Each year of multiyear arrangements is entered as a separate element in the averages. The prior outcome denotes the average ratio (or rate) of the indicated variable for the year prior to each arrangement. The actual and targeted changes refer to the averages in the rates and ratios, and are measured in percentage points.

   A positive change, whether targeted or actual, refers to a rise in the indicated variable: for instance the actual change of 4.4 percentage points in the oveall credit growth ratio implies faster credit growth and a targeted change of–1.0 percentage points in the current account balance implies a decrease in the surplus or increase in the deficit.
2. Expressed as the change in credit divided by the broad money outstanding at the beginning of the period.

SOURCE: Unpublished IMF document (June 1982).

current account balance of payments – though even here the difference between the actual performance and that targeted by the Fund was not large – it is not accurate to claim that EFF programmes have been markedly less successful overall. Indeed, on the basis of a comparison between targeted and actual values EFF programmes emerge as being rather more successful in the areas of growth and inflation.

3.1 Proposals for Reform

Where does this review leave us in terms of future policy on the EFF? Given the criticisms of conditionality contained in Chapter 4, the EFF would seem to be an entirely appropriate facility through which to accommodate the changes discussed there. Indeed, in one respect the required formal policy changes are minor, since the EFF is already 'on the books'. Even the existing rubric is not inconsistent with the proposed reforms.[9] However, in another respect, of course, the proposed changes are major, since what is required is a change in attitude and interpretation and this may be more difficult to achieve. Having the EFF set up may be a necessary condition for implementing change, but it is by no means sufficient.[10]

6 Commodity Price Stabilisation and International Financial Policy

As noted in the previous chapter, there are basically two approaches to the problem of export instability that are of interest from the viewpoint of international financial policy. The first is the compensatory financing approach. The second is the buffer-stock approach.

The compensatory technique attempts to deal with *earnings* instability in an ex-post fashion, by neutralising the effects of export instability on the balance of payments. The buffer-stock technique, on the other hand, endeavours, in an ex-ante way, to prevent export-*price* instability from arising. There are circumstances, however, under which buffer-stock export-price stabilisation will fail to engender stability in export earnings. Compensatory-financing and buffer-stock arrangements are then not perfect substitutes for one another.

1. BUFFER STOCKS

Although a neat theoretical case may be made for buffer stocks there are also arguments against; so decisions must rest on a careful evaluation of the associated costs and benefits.

1.1 The case for buffer stocks

Much of the appeal of buffer-stock schemes rests on their susceptibility to simple economic analysis. Just as demand and supply analysis may be used to explain why price variations occur, the same analysis may be used to explain how such variations may be eliminated. Given that an equilibrium price emerges as a result of the interaction between demand and supply factors, the effect of autonomous changes in demand on price may be neutralised by offsetting changes in supply, whilst the effect of autonomous changes in supply on price may be neutralised by offsetting changes in demand. An autonomous increase in supply would not then have any impact on price if demand increased equivalently. It is the purpose of stabilisation or buffer-stock schemes to eliminate, by means of offsetting interventions in the market, cyclical price variations caused by fluctuations in demand and supply. In a situation of excess supply the stabilisation agency would enter the market as a demander, and would accumulate a buffer stock of the commodity in question. In conditions of excess demand the stabilisation agency would offload some of its buffer stock on to the market, thereby serving to increase supply. By acting in a fashion which compensates for excesses in the market, the buffer-stock scheme stabilises the market price. It is the quantity of the commodity held in the buffer stock which varies and not the price of the commodity.

A number of benefits may be claimed to result from price stabilisation. Some of these will be derived by primary-product producers. First, the greater degree of certainty with regard to prices, and in some circumstances export earnings, that would follow on from buffer-stock arrangements would help producing countries in their domestic economic management. The availability of foreign exchange could become more predictable, and efficient development planning more feasible. Indeed, some commentators have maintained that, even where buffer stocks do not result in increased earnings stability, this is far outweighed in importance by the macroeconomic benefits (see UNCTAD, 1977). Second, the effect of buffer stocks in increasing the price stability of natural products would serve to improve the competitiveness of these products relative to synthetic substitutes, and thereby increase the long-term demand for them.

Other benefits would be derived by primary-product consumers. First, consuming countries would benefit in terms of a relatively assured supply of primary commodities, because of the supplementation of production by stock decumulation.[1] Second, a system of buffer stocks for key commodities would serve to reduce the incidence of major inflationary shocks emanating from sharp upward movements in commodity prices. Inasmuch as primary-product importing countries react to such surges of inflation by introducing demand-deflationary fiscal and monetary measures which cause output to fall and unemployment to rise, the removal of the commodity-price source of inflation generation would have real benefits in terms of raised or maintained output and employment. Commodity-price stability might then assist economic management not only in the producing countries but also in the consuming ones. This might be even more the case where primary-product price stabilisation induces greater stability in the producing countries' demand for imports of industrial goods from the primary-product consuming countries. Steadier growth and a lowered rate of inflation in industrial countries would, furthermore, exert a beneficial feedback effect on LDCs. Third, any reduction in price uncertainty induced by buffer-stock intervention could lower the costs of uncertainty, such as those imposed by inventory holding and forward transactions.[2]

More generally, a system of buffer-stock arrangements could result in a greater degree of world economic stability.[3] Evidence drawn from the early 1970s is consistent with the hypothesis that instability in commodity prices, which reflects variations in the demand for and supply of primary commodities, can play a major causal role in generating world economic instability. Since there is no reason to believe that demand and supply in commodity markets will be stagnant, especially where unstable expectations play a crucial role in influencing both demand and supply, an equilibrating mechanism is required. In principle, equilibrium may be achieved through the operation of the price mechanism. Thus, as demand emanating from the world's manufacturing sector exceeds output emanating from the primary sector, the price of primary products will tend to rise, and this will cause demand to fall and supply to expand. Similarly, as the supply of primary commodities outruns the demand for them, commodity prices will tend to fall, supply will fall and the demand for them will rise; manufacturers will experience a reduction in their costs and will expand both their output and their demand for inputs.

In practice, however, it seems as though this equilibrating device may have operated in a perverse fashion. Since primary products are inputs to manufacturing, since changes in primary-product prices represent changes in costs to manufacturers, and since prices in the manufacturing sector are largely cost-determined, an increase in commodity prices tends to be reflected in higher manufactured good prices. As a result, a rise in the price of primary products relative to that of manufactured goods tends to be temporary, as is therefore the incentive to increase the supply of primary products and to contract the demand for them. In addition to the cost-inflationary implications, however, an increase in commodity prices tends to be world demand-deflationary, the deflation resulting both from the effects of the redistribution of world income to those with a higher propensity to save, and from the policy responses induced in primary-product importing countries following the increase in cost inflation. Aggregate demand deflation in the major primary-product importing countries is likely to reduce the demand for commodity imports, with the result that export earnings in producing countries may fall, even though their commodity terms of trade have improved. Over the longer run, then, excess demand for primary products results in an acceleration in the world rate of inflation, but no relative price change as between primary products and manufactured goods. Equilibrium is achieved not by relative price changes, but by income changes, which serve to reduce the demand for primary products. Should the reduction in aggregate demand overshoot its equilibrium level, commodity prices will tend to fall. The fall in commodity prices may not, however, cause the demand for primary products to rise, even though real income in consuming countries will increase as a result. This expansionary influence on demand may be outweighed by the fact that export earnings in LDCs will tend to fall, as therefore will the LDCs' demand for manufactured goods; certainly there is no reason to believe that a fall in primary-product prices will automatically be associated with a rise in the level of activity in industrial countries.

It may be concluded from the above analysis that the market mechanism may act as an imperfect regulator for maintaining equilibrium between changes in the supply of and changes in the demand for primary products. Buffer stocks could in principle provide a superior regulator. In a situation of excess demand for primary products, supply would be augmented from buffer stocks, prices would not rise, or at least would not rise by a large and sudden amount, and therefore the cost inflation and demand deflation associated with a rise in commodity prices would be avoided. In a situation of excess supply and with buffer-stock intervention, earnings in producing countries would not fall and therefore the demand for manufactured goods would be maintained.

It would seem, then, that primary-product producing countries, primary-product consuming countries, and the world in general stand to benefit from a system of buffer stocks. There are, however, counter-arguments.

1.2 The case against buffer stocks

The case against the use of buffer stocks as a price-stabilising device comprises a combination of theoretical, empirical and practical arguments. First, from a theoretical viewpoint, stabilising price may not always stabilise earnings. Buffer-stock intervention will tend to stabilise both price and earnings where price instability in the market is caused by variations in demand, but where price instability is caused by variations in supply, this will not be the case; indeed, maintaining a stable price through market intervention may result in a larger fluctuation in earnings than would have existed in a free market. To illustrate this, imagine a commodity where the price elasticity of demand equals – 1 over the entire length of the demand curve. In this case the impact of variations in supply on earnings are perfectly neutralised by offsetting variations in price. A low level of supply is matched by a high price, and large supply is matched by a low price. In this instance, then, price instability serves to ensure earnings stability. Buffer-stock intervention in such a market could indeed stabilise price, but this would be at the cost of destabilising earnings. Following a leftward shift in the supply curve, earnings would fall; whilst, following a rightward shift in the supply curve, earnings would rise. In the case of buffer-stock intervention, variations in earnings positively reflect variations in supply, since price is fixed through the activities of the intervention agency.

With either a price-elastic or price-inelastic demand curve, shifts in supply will of course cause instabilities in export earnings, even in a free market. Buffer-stock intervention in such cases will, however, tend either to exacerbate earnings instability or change its nature. Earnings instability will be exacerbated where demand is price–elastic, although the higher is the price elasticity of demand the lower will be the degree of additional earnings instability caused by buffer-stock intervention in the market. Where demand is inelastic with respect to price, buffer-stock intervention will change the nature of the relationship between variations in supply and variations in earnings. In a free market and with demand inelasticity, a fall in supply will cause earnings to rise and an increase in supply will cause earnings to fall. With buffer-stock intervention, on the other hand, a fall in supply will also cause earnings to fall, whilst an increase in supply will cause earnings to increase. This change in the nature of the relationship between variations in supply and variations in earnings may be deemed undesirable, since the market will now fail to give producers appropriate equilibrating signals, either in terms of price or earnings. Following a supply glut, not only will price fail to fall, but earnings will rise, and producers may thereby be encouraged to increase supply in the future. Following a supply shortage, not only will price fail to rise, but earnings will fall, and this may serve to reduce future output. Furthermore, with buffer-stock intervention, the market signals facing consumers will fail to adjust to changes in the availability of supply, and this may also prevent a reduction in the discrepancy between demand and production.[4] Correction of the discrepancy may not be wanted in circumstances where the disequilibrium is of a cyclical or short-run nature, but a serious problem arises in contemporaneously distinguishing between those disequilibria that are only short run and those that are long run.

A central problem with buffer stocks is that of determining the price to be stabilised. In order to differentiate between cyclical and secular movements in price, it is necessary to be able to identify the price trend. This may be difficult to do on the basis of *ex-ante* information. A great deal of uncertainty surrounds the future demand for and supply of many primary products and this creates a forecasting problem.[5] Where the buffer-stock agency miscalculates the trend, it is quite possible that its activities will raise the degree of price instability rather than reduce it. Where the intervention agency overestimates the long-run equilibrium price, it will experience a continuous accumulation of stocks and a continuous decumulation of financial resources. The same outcome would result if the agency were behaviourally reluctant to see the market price fall.[6] Similarly, where the intervention agency underestimates the long-run equilibrium price, this will result in a continuous decumulation of stocks. In either case the long-term existence of the agency may be open to question. In the first case, it would tend to run out of funds, thus forcing it to sell its stocks of the commodity and thereby causing price to fall. The price fall would be emphasised by the fact that the activities of the agency would have served to maintain production at a level above equilibrium. In the second case, the buffer-stock agency would eventually run out of its stocks of the commodity concerned and the market price would then have to rise. The rise in price would be emphasised because of the sub-equilibrium level of production implicitly encouraged by the activities of the agency, as well, perhaps, as by any attempts by the buffer-stock agency to replenish its stocks. The instability could be enhanced by the activities of private speculators who anticipate the collapse of the buffer stock.

In circumstances where private speculation in a particular commodity market is destabilising in terms of price, the intervention of an agency with superior powers of forecasting could serve to stabilise the market price through counter-speculation.[7] In deciding whether a buffer stock will stabilise price, a key issue is whether the stocking agency can forecast demand and supply, and therefore price, better than can private speculators. Some observers have expressed doubts over this;[8] and, indeed, it may be the case that for some commodities the extent of uncertainty effectively precludes forecasting with any degree of confidence. Furthermore, the buffer-stocking agency needs to take into account the impact of its own existence on demand and supply.

There are a number of other reasons apart from any superior forecasting ability why it might be deemed better to have a system of international buffer stocks than one of privately held speculative stocks. The main reason is that the level of privately held stocks is likely to be socially sub-optimal, since not only may the private cost of stockholding exceed the social cost, but, in addition, the social benefits of stocking may exceed the private benefits, which are expressed purely in terms of the speculators' profit. One beneficial externality which may be associated with international buffer-stock schemes is that their very existence may influence speculators' expectations in such a fashion that private speculators behave in a price-stabilising way. The extent to which this externality is derived will depend upon the speculators' confidence in the ability of the buffer-stock agency to defend its chosen price or price range.

Even if it is possible to overstate the theoretical case against buffer stocks, there still remains the practical problem that stocking involves storage, and that not all primary commodities may be stored without deterioration: some of them are perishable. For these commodities buffer-stocking arrangements are clearly inappropriate. Hart (1976) maintains that a commodity is 'durable in storage' if it can be kept for at least one year with the sum of storage costs and grade loss not exceeding 5 per cent of the cost of fresh supplies. This description would fit most fibres, grains, metals, forest products and fuels.[9]

Another argument often used in the case against buffer stocks is the argument of experience. Only one commodity agreement involving an element of buffer stocking has survived during the period since 1945: the International Tin Agreement (ITA).[10] However, this agreement has only marginally reduced the instability of tin prices and of producers' incomes. More significant than the buffer-stock aspect of the ITA have been the transactions of the United States stockpile, which has been outside the tin agreement and which has served to defend ceiling prices, and the export-regulation aspects of the ITA, which have enabled floor prices to be defended through restriction of total supply. Evidence of previous failure is, of course, consistent with a number of hypotheses. On the one hand, it is consistent with the view that there is something intrinsically unworkable about buffer stocks. On the other hand, it is also consistent with the view that the circumstances necessary for the successful operation of buffer stocks have simply not been achieved. In the past it has been the conflict of interests between producers and consumers, and, indeed, between more and less efficient producers, as well as the inadequacy of finance, that has brought about the failure of most buffer stock schemes.[11]

1.3 The terms of trade

One aspect of various proposals for the introduction of a system of buffer stocks is that not only should stocking be used to stabilise price around the trend determined by the free operation of the market, but, in addition, the buying and selling behaviour of the stocking agency should be designed to encourage a secular increase in the price of primary products and thereby improve the terms of trade as between primary commodities and manufactured goods. In order to achieve an improvement in the terms of trade, it is envisaged that buffer stocks would be supported by a system of supply management, under which export quotas or taxes could be used to control the quantity supplied to the market. Without supply management, the maintenance of a price greater than the equilibrium one would cause over-production. By limiting output, producers will indeed tend to cause a rise in the market price and, where demand is price-inelastic, in export earnings as well.[12]

The first issue here relates to the effectiveness of buffer stocks and export controls in encouraging an improvement in the terms of trade of LDCs. Certainly, where synthetic substitutes are readily available, demand facing producers of natural products is likely to be price-elastic, and for this reason the ability of producers to raise price may be limited. Again, the scope for increasing earnings will be influenced by the market share of the LDC producers: where this is small, unilateral action by LDCs as a group will tend not to be very effective.

The second issue concerns the view that an increase in the prices of primary products relative to those of manufactured goods may not benefit all LDCs. Indeed, some primary-product importing LDCs may lose as a result.[13]

The third issue is whether an increase in the relative price of primary products would cause an acceleration in the world rate of inflation and world instability, as evidence collected from the period immediately following 1973 might at first sight seem to suggest. More careful examination of this period, however, reveals that it was the large and sudden increase in commodity prices which generated instability, and, possibly, moved the rate of inflation above the threshold at which expectations became elastic. It is probable that consuming countries could better adjust to the gradual and predictable increase in primary-product prices that would be associated with commodity agreements.

The final issue relates to the way in which the supply of commodities might be controlled. Broadly speaking, there are two options: export quotas and export taxes. Export quotas have proved difficult to negotiate and have tended to break down because of failure to secure full participation by all producing countries, thereby allowing non-participants to profit at the expense of participants by increasing their output at the higher price; or because of a failure by participants to control domestic output and, as a result, continually accumulate stocks; or because of failure to make the commodity agreement flexible enough to reflect changes in the pattern of production and trade in a way that does not penalise the relatively efficient producers.

Even where introduced and effective, export quotas may have undesirable consequences. Although they are likely to induce a redistribution of income from consuming to producing countries, the redistribution may be from the relatively poor in rich countries to the relatively rich in poor countries; indeed, the income gains may not be derived by residents of LDCs at all, but rather by foreign business enterprise. The population in general in LDCs may, of course, gain indirectly in terms of any investment, development and diversification that is induced by export quotas, but such effects may be deemed unlikely. The gainers from export quotas may simply increase their consumption of foreign goods, or may invest abroad, or may invest in speculative luxury projects at home. Even where productive domestic investment is undertaken, this may well be in the commodity subject to the export quota rather than in alternative diversifying projects; indeed, inasmuch as export quotas raise or maintain the price of the commodity concerned, they tend to militate against diversificaton. So, although export quotas tend to raise export earnings in LDCs, they do not ensure that these extra resources will be used for developmental purposes. This is where export taxes become relevant. Taxes may be levied in addition to quotas or instead of them. Either way, export taxes may be used to offset excess supply,[14] to bring about an acceptable distribution of the extra earnings associated with higher commodity prices, and to channel the additional export earnings into diversification-oriented investment.

2. THE ROLE OF INTERNATIONAL FINANCIAL POLICY

The direct connection between the commodity problem and the international financial system lies in the provision of finance. The system could be designed in such a way that it provides the finance necessary for the operation of compensatory and buffer-stock schemes. The precise nature of the connection may, however, vary, and it is in terms of such variation that it is possible to distinguish between various proposals. For instance, in relation to the financing of buffer stocks, some proposals envisage the IMF acting merely as a financial intermediary raising and distributing loans; other proposals go further than this and endeavour to relate commodity stabilisation to the regulation of the world's supply of international money. Schemes of the latter type see the IMF, or some similar agency, acting not merely as an intermediary but as having the power to create the international finance that is required. Under such schemes emphasis has either been put on the financing of buffer stocks, with variations in the supply of international reserves essentially constituting a side-effect (see, for example, Keynes, 1942), or on a form of commodity reserve currency which is rather more incidentally associated with the holding of stocks.

2.1 A commodity-reserve currency[15]

For more than a hundred years economists have been discussing the principle of relating the international monetary system in some way to commodities. Much of the discussion, although perhaps not primarily concerned with the issue of commodity stabilisation, has had implications for it. Illustrative of the discussion is a plan that Professors Hart, Kaldor and Tinbergen (HKT) put forward in 1964 for an international commodity-reserve currency. They correctly identified the conflict which arose from within the gold-exchange system (GES) as a result of the simultaneous need, at that time, for extra liquidity and for confidence. In attempting to remedy this weakness of the GES, they suggested that the IMF should issue commodity-backed international reserves (bancor). The main purpose of the plan was to create an internationally acceptable reserve asset other than gold and key currencies. It was thought that by monetising primary commodities the backing required to make the new asset acceptable would be provided. Other, secondary, features of the plan were, first, that by acquiring commodities from reserve-currency countries as well as from primary producers these currencies could be amortised over time; and, second, that by buying commodities in times of failing prices and selling them in times of rising prices, the overall price of commodities would be stabilised.

The plan envisaged bancor being backed by a composite bundle of commodities, units of which would be bought and sold on the market. The composition of the bundle would be relatively constant. It was not a major intention of the scheme to eradicate instabilities in the prices of individual commodities, although it is likely, given the constitution of the HKT scheme, that such instabilities would be dampened, particularly where instabilities are commonly generated by variations in world aggregate demand. Purchases and sales under the HKT scheme, and under more recent versions of it,[16] would be in terms of the composite bundle of commodities rather than just individual commodities; thus, while the price of an individual commodity would tend to be stabilised under the scheme, provided that the commodity concerned were a component of the composite bundle, the stabilisation of individual commodity prices would not be as great as if transactions were concentrated on individual commodities. Indeed, under the HKT scheme, and the Hart 1976 version of it, the intention is that the relative prices of commodities would still vary.

The commodity-reserve plan has come in for numerous criticisms. Essentially these relate to three features of the scheme. The first relates to the fact that the scheme forgoes the opportunity of deriving the social saving which would be achieved by using a fiat international money. The second relates to the cost of maintaining and servicing the large commodity stockpile that would be required.[17] A large measure of the variation in cost estimations hinges on whether the buffer stocks associated with the commodity-reserve currency constitute the only stocks held, and whether the entire growth in the supply of world money is associated with commodity purchases. Clearly, where the commodity-reserve system exclusively holds stocks, and is the sole source of reserve growth, the size of the associated buffer stocks and the related storage costs will indeed be large. But where other stocks are held outside the commodity-reserve system, and world liquidity growth is supplemented by other means, the costs of the commodity-reserve currency would be correspondingly reduced.

The third criticism relates to the problems which might arise from endeavouring to use one instrument – namely, the creation of bancor – to achieve both an adequate growth of international reserves and commodity-price stability. The validity of this criticism is perhaps questionable. Certainly, where two equivalent systems for expanding international reserves could be adopted, it is more efficient to choose the one which generates the greatest external net benefits. Where one scheme for expanding world reserves is inferior on monetary grounds but superior in terms of its external effects, the issue is less straightforward, and the desirability of the alternative schemes rests on a full evaluation of all the associated costs and benefits. In the case of the commodity-reserve currency, on purely monetary grounds this system of reserve creation is inferior to those systems based on fiat money, simply because of the social saving associated with the latter.[18] However, the external benefits for LDCs may be greater, and are certainly more explicit, in the case of a commodity-reserve currency.[19] From a world welfare point of view, which system is superior overall depends on the size of the relative costs and benefits and on their distribution. The issues raised here are involved and open to debate. Fortunately, the introduction and existence of the SDR facility overcomes many of the monetary costs associated with a commodity-reserve currency, but still permits the pursuit of certain developmental objectives. From a monetary point of view, a significant feature of the SDR is that it is unbacked; it is an 'outside' international asset which, to all intents and purposes, acts as money simply because, by international agreement, it is generally acceptable. As compared with commodity monies and, indeed, commodity-backed monies, the SDR gives rise to a social saving. The existence of the SDR provides reason to reappraise the possibility of linking the international monetary system with commodity-price stabilisation.

2.2 SDRs and the Financing of Commodity Stabilisation

Unlike plans for commodity-reserve currencies, a link between the creation of SDRs and commodity stabilisation would not need to concern itself with the problem of the global adequacy of international liquidity. This problem may be left to the normal operations of the SDR facility, under which appropriate changes in the quantity of international liquidity are made by general consent through the creation (and perhaps cancellation) of SDRs.

The aim of a link between the SDR and commodity stabilisation would simply be to prevent large, short-term variations in the market prices of certain major primary products. In the process of stabilising primary-product prices, however, the SDR/commodity stabilisation (SDR–CS) link would tend to protect the international reserves of primary-product exporting countries (PPXCs) where the price of their exports would otherwise have fallen, and the reserves of primary-product importing countries (PPMCs) where the price of their imports would otherwise have risen. The SDR–CS link would remove one source of instability and uncertainty in the world economy.

The scheme in outline might work as follows. As the price of a particular primary product falls, a Commodity Stabilisation Agency (CSA) such as the IMF enters the market as a residual buyer. Most simply, the CSA could be provided with SDRs, which would then be used to finance the purchase. Alternatively, the CSA might convert SDRs credited to it by the Special Account of the IMF into foreign exchange. Assuming for the moment, however, that SDRs are directly used in the transaction, the outcome of this procedure would be (i) that the primary product price would be stabilised, (ii) that the PPXC would acquire SDRs, and (iii) that the CSA would acquire a stockpile of the primary product in question.

Assuming a supply curve which is inelastic at least in the short run, whether the PPXC would acquire net reserves as a result of the activities of the CSA would depend on whether the initial price fall was caused by a rightward shift in the supply curve, in which case it would, or a leftward shift in the demand curve, in which case it would not. In the latter case, the only change in the reserves of the PPXC as

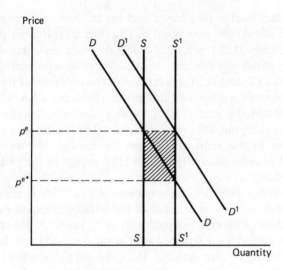

FIGURE 6.1

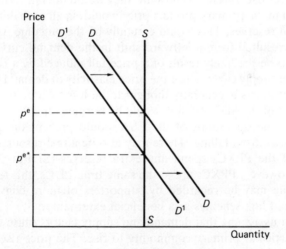

FIGURE 6.2

compared with a situation in which the price of the primary product had not fallen would be a change in the composition of reserves.

This analysis is illustrated in Figures 6.1 and 6.2. In Figure 6.1, as the supply curve shifts from $S\ S'$ the price falls from p^e to $p^{e\ *}$. If the objective of the CSA is to re-establish the old equilibrium price, it will enter the market as a buyer and act to shift the demand curve from D to D'. At the new point of equilibrium it is clear that total export earnings (total revenue) will have risen as compared with either the initial equilibrium situation or that represented by the intersection of S' and D. If, however, it is the objective of the CSA to stabilise export earnings and not prices, then the CSA will be required to enter the market as a buyer (assuming that the demand curve is inelastic) but will operate so as to shift the demand curve not as far over to the right as D', but far enough for the quantity demanded to rise sufficiently to offset the impact of the price fall on total revenue.

In Figure 6.2, whether the objective of the CSA is expressed in terms of price stability or in terms of the stability of export earnings is not significant. With either objective in view, the CSA will attempt to counteract perfectly the leftward shift in the demand curve from D to D' by increasing its own demand. Both the old equilibrium price and the old level of export earnings will simultaneously be re-established.

The benefit of the SDR–CS link to the PPXC is that its reserves would either rise or remain constant; they would not fall. Without the link, a fall in the primary-product price would, in all probability, lead to a fall in reserves. This would certainly be the outcome where the price fall resulted from a leftward shift in the demand curve; but it would also be the likely result of a price fall induced by a rightward shift in the supply curve, since the price elasticity of demand for most primary products is generally thought to be less than unity.

The cost of the SDR–CS link would be borne by the PPMCs in the sense that the operations of the CSA would prevent the primary-product price from falling. There may also be a real-resource cost to PPMCs if the PPXCs spend any extra reserves (SDRs) acquired. Where, however, PPXCs are at the same time LDCs, this feature of the scheme may be regarded by supporters of more conventional liquidity-aid link schemes as a beneficial externality.

Now let us assume that demand and supply factors cause the price of our particular primary commodity to rise. The price rise may be due to a rightward shift in the demand curve, a leftward shift in the supply curve, or both. In the absence of an SDR–CS link, what would happen? If the price rise had been caused by a rightward shift in the demand curve, then the foreign-exchange receipts of the PPXC would rise and the reserves of the PPMC would fall. On the other hand, if the price rise had been caused by a leftward shift in the supply curve, the impact on total revenue and reserves would depend on the price elasticity of demand. Where this is less than one, again the reserves of the PPXC would rise and those of the PPMC would fall.

If the CSA is in operation, however, then, as the price of the primary product rises, the CSA offloads its stocks of the commodity on to the market, thus serving to neutralise the rise in price. PPMCs buy these stocks, paying for them either in SDRs or in reserve currencies. Assuming for a moment that payment is made in SDRs, the outcome of CSA activity will be (i) that the CSA accumulates SDRs but decumulates its stocks of the primary product, and (ii) that PPMCs acquire the primary product but lose SDRs.

In the case of an upward movement in prices, the PPMCs benefit from the existence and involvement of the CSA, either by losing fewer reserves, or by gaining a greater real quantity of the primary product. The cost of CSA intervention is borne by the PPXC in terms of reserve-gain forgone.

At the end of the complete primary-product price cycle, the CSA will have recovered the full value of its initial SDR payment to PPXCs. Indeed, the CSA will recover SDRs in excess of this initial payment, since the SDR selling prices of primary products supplied by the CSA to consumers will be greater than the SDR buying prices paid by the CSA to the primary-product producers.

A number of features of the SDR–CS link scheme should perhaps be emphasised.

First, the link relates to cyclical price variations. It is suggested not that the scheme should be used to prevent long-term relative price movements, but, rather, that it should be used to avoid short-term instability around secular trends in the terms of trade. To this end it is proposed that CSA price-intervention points should be flexible, with the intervention prices being related to market trends. Thus, for example, it is envisaged that a long-term rightward shift in a supply curve, or an equally permanent leftward shift in a demand curve, would be reflected in a fall in the market price for that commodity. The CSA would endeavour to estimate the long-run equilibrium price of a primary product by reference to demand and supply trends. Where short-run variations in either demand or supply resulted in deviations from this price, the CSA would intervene, buying when the market price fell a specified percentage below the long-run equilibrium price, and selling when the price rose a specified, though not necessarily equal, percentage above the long-run price. CSA prices could be adjusted downwards or upwards in the event of undesirable stock accumulations or decumulations.

Second, the SDR–CS link could conveniently be integrated with a scheme for the amortisation of reserve currencies. Integration could be achieved at either the price floor when the CSA is buying, or at the price ceiling when the CSA is selling. The 'price-floor version' of reserve-currency amortisation would involve the exchange, at the outset, of SDRs for reserve currencies, and then the use of these currencies to purchase primary products. The PPXCs which would receive these reserve currencies could then use them in the normal way to buy goods and services, except that the PPXCs would be constrained to spend the currencies in the appropriate reserve-currency countries. Integrating the SDR–CS link with a 'price-floor version' of reserve-currency amortisation would therefore involve an unfortunate and unnecessary element of tying.

This could be avoided by integrating the link with a 'price-ceiling version' of reserve-currency amortisation. Under this version the CSA would accept reserve currencies in exchange and as payment for primary products. The CSA would then itself deposit these currencies with an amortisation account in the IMF in exchange for SDRs. Eventually the reserve-currency countries would be required to amortise the IMF's holding of their own domestic currencies.

A third important feature of the proposed SDR–CS link is that it would not preclude or interfere with SDR–aid link schemes, the rationale of which is more specifically the provision of development assistance. The SDR–CS scheme may be regarded as being additional and complementary to those other links, since it fulfils a different and non-competitive purpose.

Fourth and finally, the SDR–CS link represents a scheme from which most countries would benefit. All countries are, to some extent, PPMCs, whilst not all of them are PPXCs. At any particular stage in a primary-product price cycle, exclusive PPMCs will have an unambiguous stance, since they will either be gaining where the price is falling or losing where the price is rising. Given a universal movement in primary-product prices, countries which are at one and the same time both PPMCs and PPXCs may have an ambivalent attitude, since they may simultaneously be gaining from a rise in export prices and losing from a rise in import prices, or losing from a fall in export prices and gaining from a fall in import prices. Depending on the structure of trade and the direction and configuration of primary-product price movements, individual countries may either gain or lose. If countries are risk or uncertainty averters with regard to future reserve levels, they are likely to prefer stable and reasonably predictable prices, with neither the chance of gain nor the risk of loss. Although at points in the price cycle of a primary commodity certain countries may stand to gain from selling a highly priced good or buying a lowly priced one, gains enjoyed at some stages of the cycle will, assuming reserves yield a diminishing marginal rate of utility, fail to compensate for losses incurred at other stages. All countries are likely to find it easier to plan for growth and development in an environment in which primary-product prices are not subject to large and violent fluctuations.

Since all countries stand to gain from commodity stabilisation, it seems appropriate that the financing of stabilisation schemes should be provided centrally and multilaterally by an international agency such as the IMF. We have seen that SDRs could be used quite conveniently to finance market intervention, even though they are not yet accepted as a medium of exchange; so, to begin with at least, the stabilisation agency would have to convert them through the IMF into acceptable currency, which would then be used to purchase the buffer stock. As soon as there were a cyclical upturn in the price of the primary commodity, the agency would begin to sell its buffer stock and could then use the resulting accumulation of foreign exchange to buy back SDRs. A significant advantage of this system of financing buffer stocks is that it is consistent with the attempt to make SDRs the central reserve asset in any reformed international monetary system. The scheme could easily be modified to permit SDRs to be used directly in transactions, and could, as noted already, be integrated with reserve-currency amortisation.

Alternatively or additionally, the profits which result from selling gold at a market price above the official price could be used to finance buffer stock schemes, in part at least.

2.3 The size of the financing problem

There are a range of costs associated with operating a system of buffer stocks; these may be divided into private and social costs. Private costs include both the initial cost of stock acquisition and provision of storage facilities,[20] and the running costs of the buffer stock once it has been acquired. Gross private running costs include interest charges, where the buffer stock is financed by borrowing; the maintenance of an administrative and marketing structure; and losses associated with turnover transactions, where the buffer stock agency is selling commodities which have deteriorated in quality through storage, such that there is a continuing cost associated with maintaining any given quantity of them in store. Net private running costs are likely to be lower than gross private running costs, since the buffer stock will by nature make a profit in its commodity transactions. The wider the spread of the intervention prices, the greater will these trading profits tend to be; on the other hand, a high ceiling price will be associated with larger storage costs, whilst a low floor price and high ceiling price will generally reduce the effectiveness of the scheme in terms of its stabilising objectives. The gross social cost of buffer stocks may deviate from their gross private cost, since storage will involve an additional social cost in terms of the sacrifice of current consumption. Meanwhile, net social cost will also differ from net private cost. The reasons for this discrepancy are, first, the existence of centrally administered buffer stocks may obviate the need for other stocks; second, confidence in the long-term viability of the buffer stock may encourage private speculators to operate in a price-stabilising way; and, third, the world economy will tend to benefit from commodity stabilisation in terms of more stable development, more efficient use of resources, a lower rate of inflation and a higher level of employment.

The size of resources needed to finance buffer stocks will essentially depend on the private net costs of setting up the scheme. These private net costs will in turn depend on the specific details of the buffer-stock arrangements. The first factor to be taken into account is the required degree of price stability, or, in other words, the acceptable amount of price variation. The lower that prices are allowed to fall before the stabilisation agency intervenes, the fewer will be the initial resources required. A second factor is the commodity coverage of the buffer-stock scheme. This concerns the number of commodities included in the scheme and the relationships between them. The fewer the commodities included, the smaller will tend to be the initial financing problem;[21] while, if the prices of all commodities covered by the scheme fall together, the size of the initial financing problem will be greater than if the prices of just a few of the commodities fall. The size of the financing problem will be minimised as the negative correlation between the price movements of commodities included in the scheme is maximised. If the prices of the various primary products incorporated in the scheme do move in different directions, it is quite possible that, once the scheme has been established, finance freed by selling stocks of one commodity may be used to finance the buying of stocks of another commodity.[22] However, the more closely and positively related are the prices of the commodities included in the scheme, the greater will be the initial financing requirements. Primary-product prices are more likely to move together the more significant are demand factors, as compared with supply factors, in generating price changes. This is because it is perhaps rather more probable that primary commodities will experience broadly similar shifts in demand than in supply.

A third factor bearing on the size of required finance is the relevant price elasticities of demand and supply, since these will affect the extent of commodity-price variation. The lower the elasticities, the greater will be the degree of price variability, and therefore the greater the initial amount of finance will need to be.

A fourth factor is the nature of private speculation. Where private speculators behave in a market-stabilising fashion, the size of agency buffer stocks will be reduced. The confidence of private speculators in the ability of the buffer-stock agency to stabilise the market may itself depend on the size of the financial resources available to the agency. Indeed, it could be that, the larger are the resources available to the buffer-stock agency, the lower will be the likelihood that these resources will be needed.

Clearly, then, it is not easy to define the amount of finance that would be needed to operate a buffer-stock scheme. Everything depends on the precise nature of the scheme itself.

To some extent, arguments concerning the size of the initial financing problem may also be interpreted as dealing with the time period over which any system of buffer stocks is to be established. Provided that storage and administrative costs are not excessive, a stabilisation agency should be able to make a trading profit, which may then be used to expand the size and coverage of the buffer-stock scheme over a number of years. In any case, it may be advisable to begin a system of buffer-stock schemes on a relatively small scale, in order to gain experience, and this would naturally reduce the size of the initial financing problem.

2.4 Implications for world economic stability

It has been a common theme amongst advocates of the notion of linking the international monetary system in some way with commodities that such a link would encourage a greater degree of world economic stability. Clearly, one of the pricipal functions of the international monetary system is to act as stabilising factor in world economic development.

In what ways, then, might a connection between the international monetary system and commodities generate stability? First, by stabilising short-run prices, a buffer stock scheme will increase the ability of primary-product producing countries to plan development and may thereby generate a secular increase in supply. An increase in supply relative to demand will tend to reduce prices and hence lower the secular rate of world inflation.

Second, although the introduction of buffer stocks, which is, of course, most properly conducted at a time of excess commodity supply, is associated with an increase in the international supply of money, it should be remembered that an increase in money supply tends to be inflationary only when the money supply expands at a faster rate than real output. Under a buffer-stock scheme such as the one outlined in the previous section the supply of international money would tend to rise most during a period of generally low prices. Where low prices reflect below-trend demand, the increase in international reserves caused by buffer-stock intervention and the preservation of income levels in primary-product producing countries may help to sustain full employment in the world economy rather than cause inflation. The activities of the buffer stock could then prevent the transmission and exacerbation of recession. It is unlikely that increases in the quantity of international money generated as a result of an expansion in the supply of particular goods would be of a sufficiently universal significance to pose a serious inflationary threat; and, in any case, in a situation of general excess commodity supply the buffer-stock scheme may again be stabilising. In the absence of market intervention and in conditions of excess supply, commodity prices will tend to fall and adjustment in commodity markets will be effected by means of a cutback in supply. Demand may not rise, since developed countries will tend to experience a reduction in the demand for their exports, because of the lower incomes in primary-product producing countries. If, instead, a buffer-stock agency acts to increase incomes in primary-product producing countries by absorbing the extra production, effective demand for manufactured goods will rise. There will be an expansion in the exports of developed countries and this will generate a multiplier effect, which will cause the rate of absorption of primary commodities to increase until it balances the rate of production.[23]

During a period of cyclically high demand, when the problem of inflation is most potent, the buffer-stock scheme would be withdrawing more than the initial allocation of SDRs from circulation and would be increasing the real supply of primary products to world markets; the scheme would serve to negate the effect which high levels of demand would otherwise have on prices. The effect of rising commodity prices on income in producing countries, and the associated increase in demand for imports from developed countries, would also be offset by the operations of the buffer stock.

The monetary implications of the buffer-stock scheme emerge as being counter-cyclical, serving to expand monetary demand and the supply of international money during cyclical troughs, and to contract the supply of international money (as well as increase the level of real supply) during cyclical peaks. Furthermore, to the extent that the commodity-stabilisation scheme might be used to hasten the replacement of reserve currencies by one reserve asset, namely the SDR, the scheme would help to eradicate one of the major intermediate sources of world monetary instability.

3. CONCLUDING REMARKS

Commodity instability has significant implications for LDCs, being a determinant of many of the balance of payments difficulties which they experience. Compensatory-financing and buffer-stocking arrangements may be used in an attempt to deal with certain aspects of the problem. The international monetary system has for a number of years provided compensation for export shortfalls, and it has also provided some indirect support for buffer-stock schemes. LDC lobbyists have made the establishment of commodity buffer stocks a central element in their claim for a new international economic order. There are arguments both for and against buffer stocks. In certain circumstances they could operate to the advantage of developing countries. More imaginative use of the SDR could provide the finance for such activities. However, it also needs to be recognised that the many problems associated with buffer stocks, apart from the provision of finance, make compensatory financing a generally preferable approach. Many of the benefits for LDCs from an SDR-financed commodity stabilisation scheme could be derived through compensatory financing or through modifications to the SDR which are un-connected with commodity stabilisation. The lack of progress with attempts to set up an integrated programme for commodities, and the lack of support that is likely to be forthcoming from developed countries in circumstances where primary product prices are falling relative to those of manufactures, suggest that developing country negotiators would be better advised to focus their attention in areas other than buffer stocks.

7 Interest-Rate Policy and International Finance

We have seen in earlier chapters, that the international financial system has been used both explicitly and implicitly to assist developing countries. Within the IMF, for instance, the General Account and the Special Drawing Account have provided significant amounts of finance for such countries. Indeed, special facilities within the Fund – the Compensatory Financing Facility, the Buffer Stock Financing Facility and the Extended Fund Facility – have been of perhaps principal benefit to developing countries.

Some proposals envisage extending this function, using the international financial system to provide developing countries with larger amounts of finance. Best known amongst these is the idea of an SDR link. Many proposals, including the link, rely on there being quite significant changes in the basic structure of the international financial system, with a diminution in the importance of reserve currencies and gold and an increase in the importance of SDRs. These policies are examined in subsequent chapters. This chapter examines a policy which in many respects is much more modest; the use of subsidies to reduce the cost of credit for developing countries.

A potential advantage of subsidies is that they may be used to help resolve another apparently intractable problem, namely, the disadvantageous position of low-income developing countries within the international financial system. Unlike middle- and high-income LDCs, low-income countries enjoy little access to private international finance and therefore rely heavily on bilateral and multilateral aid as well as on credit from the IMF. However, a significant proportion of IMF credit is financed by borrowing and is available to ultimate borrowers only at near commercial rates; even the Fund's normal charges are far from gratuitous.[1] Subsidies offer a way of reducing these charges and of thereby raising the concessionary element of Fund finance. Subsidies therefore hold the prospect of

131

providing benefits to low-income countries within the context of the existing international financial framework.

However, the debt crisis has served to focus attention on the use of interest-rate caps as a way of alleviating the problems encountered by the principal debtors, the better-off LDCs. This chapter therefore also examines the use of interest rate subsidies to assist the indebted middle- and high-income developing countries.

1. INTEREST-RATE SUBSIDISATION AS A MEANS OF ASSISTING LOW-INCOME COUNTRIES

1.1 The use of subsidies in the Fund

The Fund, as a Trustee, has administered two subsidy accounts: the first relating to drawings under the oil facility and the second to drawings under the supplementary financing facility. The purpose of both accounts has effectively been to reduce the cost of drawing from these relatively high cost facilities to a group of relatively poor countries.

1.1.1 The oil facility subsidy account

This was established in 1975, with subsidy payments being calculated, 'as a percentage per annum of the average daily balances, subject to charges, of the Fund's holdings of eligible members' currency outstanding under the 1975 oil facility'. The rate of subsidy was set at 5 per cent. Eligibility was originally limited to those thirty-nine Fund members listed by the United Nations as being most seriously affected by the increase in the price of oil, although only eighteen of these actually made a purchase under the oil facility. However, in 1978 eligibility was modified to permit any surplus in the account to be used to assist seven more countries, thus making the subsidy available to all those members of the Fund that were eligible to receive assistance from the Trust Fund and that had also used the oil facility.

Table 7.1 provides a list of the beneficiaries and gives the status of subsidy payments both for 1981 and cumulatively. As of June 1981, total subsidy payments approaching SDR 165 million had been made.

The account was financed by currency contributions from the 24 Fund members (plus Switzerland) listed in Table 7.2, with the contributed funds being invested in US government obligations until required for the payment of the subsidy.

1.1.2 The supplementary financing facility subsidy account

This was established in 1980 with the aim of having total resources of SDR 1 billion. Although in part to be financed by contributions from industrial and oil-exporting countries, it was intended that about 75 per cent of the finance would eventually come from repayments of, and interest on, Trust Fund loans. A formula equivalent to that used for determining the size of subsidy payments for the oil facility subsidy account was again used, though of course based on purchases under the SFF. However, a significant change from earlier practice was that the subsidy was made available on a two-tier basis, the full rate – 3 per cent – being paid to those members with per capita

TABLE 7.1 *Oil facility subsidy account: total use of 1975 oil facility by beneficiaries, and subsidy payments for financial year ended 30 April 1981*[1] *(in millions of SDRs)*

	Total use of 1975 oil facility	Subsidy at 5%	
		Amount	Cumulative to date
Original beneficiaries: subsidy for financial year ended 30 April 1981			
Bangladesh	40.47	1.17	9.52
Cameroon	11.79	0.35	2.75
Central African Republic	2.66	0.07	0.63
Egypt	31.68	1.00	7.30
Haiti	4.14	0.12	0.98
India	201.34	—	26.95
Ivory Coast	10.35	—	1.42
Kenya	27.93	0.75	6.68
Mali	3.99	0.13	0.92
Mauritania	5.32	0.16	1.24
Pakistan	111.01	2.98	26.47

continued on page 134

TABLE 7.1—*continued*

	Total use of 1975 oil facility	Subsidy at 5%	
		Amount	Cumulative to date
Senegal	9.91	0.25	2.40
Sierra Leone	4.97	0.16	1.15
Sri Lanka	34.13	1.00	8.01
Sudan	18.30	0.51	4.36
Tanzania	20.61	0.50	5.00
Western Samoa	0.42	0.01	0.10
Yemen, People's Democratic Republic of	12.02	0.35	2.82
Subtotal	551.03	9.51	108.68
Additional beneficiaries: subsidy for financial years ended 30 April 1978–1981			
Grenada	0.49	0.08	0.12
Malawi	3.73	0.64	0.87
Morocco	18.00	3.21	4.10
Papua New Guinea	14.80	1.93	2.73
Philippines	152.03	25.49	35.93
Zaire	32.53	5.81	7.40
Zambia[2]	29.72	3.37	3.37
Subtotal	251.30	40.54	54.52
Total	802.33	50.05	163.20

1. Purchases began in July 1975 and continued until May 1976. The subsidy amounts shown are calculated as a percentage per annum of the average daily balances, subject to charges, of the Fund's holdings of each eligible member's currency outstanding under the 1975 oil facility during the year.
2. Zambia received a subsidy only for the period 1 July 1978 to 30 April 1981.

SOURCE: *Annual Report*, IMF, 1981.

income equal to or less than that used for determining access to International Development Association (IDA) resources, but only half the full rate being paid to those remaining countries with per capita incomes which, although above the IDA level, were not greater than that of the member that had the highest per capita income in 1979 and was eligible to receive assistance from the Trust Fund. Furthermore, a constraint was imposed that the payment of

TABLE 7.2 *Oil facility subsidy account: contributions (in millions of SDRs)*

Contributors	Anticipated total contributions [1]	Contributions received as of 30 April 1981
Australia	5,700	5,700
Austria	2,300	2,300
Belgium	5,600	5,040
Brazil	1,850	1,850
Canada	9,500	9,500
Denmark	2,200	1,577
Finland	1,600	1,600
France	12,900	12,373
Germany, Fed. Rep. of	13,700	13,720
Greece	600	597
Iran	6,000	6,000
Italy	8,600	8,600
Japan	10,300	9,537
Luxembourg	110	108
Netherlands	6,000	6,000
New Zealand	1,700	1,407
Norway	2,100	2,100
Saudi Arabia	40,000	40,000
South Africa	1,350	1,350
Spain	3,400	2,450
Sweden	2,800	2,800
Switzerland	3,285	3,285
United Kingdom	12,050	11,641
Venezuela	6,000	6,000
Yugoslavia	900	900
Total	160,545	156,436

1. In some cases where contributions are being made in instalments, budgetary approval will be required in each year that a contribution is to be made. SDR amounts may be subject to small adjustments owing to exchange-rate changes.

SOURCE: *Annual Report*, IMF, 1981.

subsidies should not reduce the cost of using the SFF below that of using the Fund's ordinary resources.

As of end of April 1981, the eighty-three developing countries listed in Table 7.3 were eligible, on the basis of their per capita income, to receive a subsidy (though of course countries joining the Fund and meeting the per capita criterion would also be eligible), but of these only twenty had outstanding purchases under the SFF.

TABLE 7.3 *Fund members that would be eligible to receive a subsidy on basis of per capita income data*

Members eligible for full rate of subsidy

Afghanistan	Malawi
Bangladesh	Maldives
Benin	Mali
Bolivia	Mauritania
Burma	Nepal
Burundi	Nicaragua
Cameroon	Niger
Cape Verde	Nigeria
Central African Republic	Pakistan
Chad	Papua New Guinea
China, People's Republic of	Philippines
Comoros	Rwanda
Congo	St Lucia
Djibouti	St Vincent
Dominica	São Tomé and Principe
Egypt	Senegal
El Salvador	Sierra Leone
Equatorial Guinea	Solomon Islands
Ethiopia	Somalia
Gambia, The	Sri Lanka
Ghana	Sudan
Grenada	Swaziland
Guinea	Tanzania
Guinea-Bissau	Thailand
Guyana	Togo
Haiti	Uganda
Honduras	Upper Volta
India	Vietnam
Indonesia	Western Samoa
Kampuchea, Democratic	Yemen Arab Republic
Kenya	Yemen, People's Democratic
Lao People's Democratic Republic	Republic of
Lesotho	Zaire
Liberia	Zambia
Madagascar	Zimbabwe

Members eligible for reduced rate of subsidy

Botswana	Lebanon
Colombia	Mauritius
Dominican Republic	Morocco

Ecuador	Paraguay
Guatemala	Peru
Ivory Coast	Syrian Arab Republic
Jordan	Tunisia

SOURCE: *Annual Report*, IMF, 1981.

1.2 The use of subsidies: the principal issues

The use of subsidies raises various issues. While clearly the main motivation for them is to raise the effective flow of concessional resources to poor countries in the pursuit of international equity, it is also important to consider their likely impact on the efficiency of the international financial system. If they are an inefficient type of reform, this consideration would have to be balanced against any equity gains. In fact, the argument may be made that subsidies in the context discussed here represent potentially an economically efficient, as well as an equitable, form of international financial reform.

Subsidies within the IMF constitute tied aid. However, the tying is not in the conventional form of procurement or project tying but rather in the form of specific programme tying. Thus access to an IMF subsidy rests on the previous agreement and implementation of Fund-endorsed economic policies. In this way subsidies as aid escape the more common criticisms of tying. For those who argue that conventional forms of aid are overly concentrated on projects as opposed to programmes, subsidies offer one way of redressing the balance. At the same time they also offer some protection against the conventional criticism of programme aid, namely, that donors can exert little influence over the way in which resources are used and are therefore unable to ensure that resources are used productively rather than to raise consumption or to finance military expenditure. In the case of IMF subsidies, access to additional subsidised finance depends, initially at least, on the achievement of precise performance criteria. Failure to fulfil these criteria may be expected to lead to the curtailment of further instalments of Fund finance and therefore to the attached subsidies.

Provided that Fund programmes are themselves appropriate to the countries in which they are pursued, then it may be seen as an advantage that subsidies provide an additional incentive for countries to turn to the Fund for finance and to expose themselves to Fund conditionality. In this way subsidies may not only provide extra finance for low-income countries but may also encourage the pursuit of required adjustment strategies. As a result, world economic efficiency may be raised.

Clearly vital to this argumentation is the assumption concerning the appropriateness of Fund conditionality. If this is in fact ineffective and/or cost-ineffective, then the related case for subsidies evaporates. It is for reasons such as these that developing countries themselves might opt for more straight untied aid in preference to an aid-cum-subsidy scheme. However, if they can be convinced of the relevance of Fund conditionality, then it might be anticipated that both recipients and donors would see advantage in subsidies as compared with some more traditional forms of aid.

Another attractive feature of subsidies is that they give recipients access to much larger amounts of finance than just the size of the subsidy itself; there is a form of multiplier associated with subsidies, the size of which may be expressed as the reciprocal of the rate of subsidy. Donors may therefore feel that they are indirectly providing more finance for any given amount of aid, and recipients may also regard this as an attractive feature.

Three further issues remain to be discussed: (i) the coverage of the subsidy scheme, (ii) the size of subsidy payments and the rate of subsidy, and (iii) the method of financing. These issues are of course related, for with a given amount of finance available for a subsidy scheme, a fundamental choice exists between wide coverage and a higher rate of subsidy. In principle, a third option is to make the amount of finance the dependent variable, letting this be determined by the chosen coverage and rate of subsidy. However, in any practical sense it is likely that the scheme will be resource-constrained. In order to maximise the impact of the subsidy on adjustment and therefore on economic efficiency, there would seem to be a case for choosing the option involving fairly widely defined eligibility and a fairly low rate of subsidy. Again, however, this case rests crucially on the appropriateness of Fund conditionality. It also implicitly assumes that drawings on the Fund are elastic with respect to the rate of interest of Fund finance. It would only be in circumstances where drawings were inelastic with respect to the rate of interest that a case for narrower coverage and a higher rate of subsidy could be supported on grounds of efficiency.

1.2.1 Coverage

With regard to the coverage of the subsidy, and given the equity objective of the scheme, there would seem to be little practical alternative to using per capita income as a proxy for need, even given the well-known difficulties involved with using such a measure. More fanciful indicators of basic needs would almost certainly prove difficult to operate. Since most low-income countries are heavily reliant on the Fund for finance, this would ensure that the majority of them would have access to this form of aid, and the distribution of subsidy aid might therefore be expected to be more equitable than that of some other forms of aid. However, it should be recognised that access to subsidy aid of the form discussed here does in turn and in the first instance depend on a country drawing from the Fund for balance of payments reasons. Low-income countries not drawing from the Fund will not derive the aid related to the subsidy. Potentially this constitutes a significant weakness and causes a 'moral hazard' type of problem, since countries may be under an incentive to pursue over-expansionary policies which result in BoP problems in order to take advantage of the concessionary resources only available to them under the subsidy scheme. Other low-income countries that have been prepared to accept higher domestic costs in order to protect their external position would in effect be sacrificing potential aid. As a result, the distribution of subsidy aid could be regressive and could have an adverse effect on economic efficiency; though similarly, in principle, it would be possible to use other conventional aid flows to compensate for the problem of distribution by directing a larger share of these to those countries that had not availed themselves of subsidy aid.

1.2.2 Subsidy Payments

With regard to the size of subsidy payments (S) these could be calculated in either of two ways. Under the first method they might be expressed as a percentage, the subsidy rate(s), of total drawings (D) from the Fund under any specified facility, such that:

$$S = s(D) \tag{7.1}$$

Whereas under the second they might be determined such that:

$$S = sr(D) \qquad (7.2)$$

where r is the unsubsidised rate of interest on specified drawings from the Fund.

The first method, which has been the one adopted by the Fund, clearly results in much larger subsidy payments. For example, with:

$$D = \text{SDR } 1000$$
$$r = 10 \text{ per cent}$$
$$\text{and} \quad s = 5 \text{ per cent}$$

method (7.1) gives an effective interest rate of 5.0 per cent and an effective subsidy (s*) of 5.0 per cent, whereas method (7.2) gives an effective interest rate of 9.5 per cent and an effective rate of subsidy of only 0.5 per cent. Thus under method (2):

$$s^* < s$$

Given the use of method (7.1), the oil facility subsidy account had the effect of reducing the average cost of using resources related to that facility from about 7.75 to about 2.75 per cent, while the SFF subsidy account has reduced the effective rate of interest 3 percentage points (at full rate) or 1.5 percentage points (at half rate) below the rate of interest paid by the Fund for SFF resources (plus 0.2 per cent for loans of over $3\frac{1}{2}$ years).

The question of the actual rate of subsidy and the related value of subsidy payments may in practice be answered by the coverage of the scheme and the size of resources that are made available to support it, with the rate adjusting to be consistent with these constraints. However, it should be noted that, because access to subsidies in the IMF depends on the unknown size of BoP deficits, it is very difficult to predict *ex ante* and precisely the total value of subsidy payments associated with any given rate of subsidy unless some overall constraint is imposed. Nevertheless, the total value of payments will clearly vary positively with the rate of subsidy and the coverage of the scheme. Asking what is the optimum rate of subsidy is akin to asking what is the optimum volume of aid. Even so, the efficiency criterion alluded to earlier does suggest that the rate of subsidy should be high enough to induce countries to draw from the Fund and to be able to support the related interest and repayments, without, it might normatively be added, having to sacrifice domestic expenditure unduly. Furthermore, there may be a case on the grounds of equity and efficiency for having the rate of subsidy set on a sliding scale, perhaps varying between countries inversely with their per capita incomes. In principle, such a system could be very subtle, involving a multitude of rates or, less complex, with just a few rates, though these would unavoidably involve arbitrary cut-off points. As already noted, the Fund has encompassed multiple rates in the SFF subsidy account by having a two-tier subsidy.

1.2.3 Financing

As with many aspects of aid, the above analysis suggests that the availability of finance might constitute an effective constraint on the further development of interest-rate subsidy schemes within the Fund. A key question is how subsidies might be financed. Three alternatives suggest themselves. The first is contributions. As noted earlier, there is reason to believe that donors may find interest-rate subsidies a relatively attractive way in which to give aid. At the same time this form of financing would be largely outside the scope and control of the Fund. A second and complementary alternative is to sell the Fund's remaining stock of gold, and use the investment income from this. Such a course of action may be presented as being quite consistent with both the efficiency and equity objectives of the international financial system, since it could contribute to reducing the monetary role of gold and would serve to enhance resource flows to developing countries.[2] In effect, the Fund has incorporated both means of financing with its existing subsidy accounts. In the case of the SFF subsidy account the intention, as noted earlier, was to provide SDR 750 million by using the repayments to the Trust Fund, the resources for which, let it be recalled, initially came from the auctioning and restitution of gold.

The third financing option would be to increase the rate of interest charged by the Fund to relatively rich members. Aid would then in effect be provided formally through the IMF rather than having it act as an informal intermediary. However, such a plan may be rather too radical to stand much chance of being accepted, moving the Fund, as it does, significantly in the direction of becoming an aid agency. Furthermore, it might deter richer countries from turning to the Fund, and part of the international social benefit potentially associated with Fund finance could be lost. In practice, on the basis of recent evidence, the scheme would not raise much finance, given that very few industrial or oil-exporting countries have drawn finance from the Fund. Even so, there is a case for reducing the concessional element of Fund finance that goes to richer developing countries and industrial countries which have access to other means of finance. Given that some Fund finance does have a grant element, it is quite legitimate to be concerned about the most appropriate distribution of this.

1.3 Some proposed modifications to existing subsidy arrangements and their effects

From the foregoing discussion it would appear that there is considerable scope for making greater use of interest-rate subsidies in the context of the IMF. From the various options available the following modifications would seem worthy of further consideration:

(i) The wider application of subsidies to cover all types of Fund finance. Combined with certain reforms in the nature of conditionality, this modification would enable the Fund to make a significant concessionary contribution towards alleviating the economic problems faced by low-income countries.

(ii) The use of multiple rates of subsidy as between countries based on per capita income to enable greatest assistance to be offered to those countries in greatest need, and possibly as between drawings under various Fund facilities to equalise the effective rate of interest paid under each.

(iii) Further gold sales by the Fund with the proceeds invested in SDR-denominated assets to provide a continuing supplement to the finance provided by contributions, if not to take over the sole financing role.

Table 7.4 provides some 'orders of magnitude' estimates of the size of concessionary resource flows that would be made available by one such subsidy scheme. The calculations rest on the assumption that the subsidy reduces the rate of interest on all Fund resources to 3 per cent for low-income countries, using the current Fund criterion for determining eligibility. Other underlying assumptions are specified in the notes to the table. Actual purchases for the financial year ended April 1981 are taken and that period in fact involved a very clear preponderance of low-income countries. It may be seen that total subsidy payments would have been about SDR 128 million. The effective subsidy expressed as a percentage of unsubsidised payments shows some variation between countries, ranging from a minimum of 44.1 per cent for Lao People's Democratic Republic to a maximum of 72.7 per cent for Pakistan, and depends on which Fund facilities had been used most intensely, thus reflecting the differential rate of subsidy on the various facilities. The total subsidy payments estimated in Table 7.4 could easily have been financed by investment returns from the sale of IMF gold. At a market price of SDR 300 per fine ounce the sale of the entire IMF gold stock would have raised about SDR 31,000 million and therefore an annual return of at least SDR 3000 million. Clearly, with finance of this amount the scope of the subsidy scheme could be extended beyond that envisaged in Table 7.4. However, it must be recognised that a once-for-all, or even slightly staggered, gold sale of this size would cause a significant reduction in the market price of gold. The figures quoted above therefore clearly overstate the finance that would be raised by such a sale. The more modest alternative scheme that could be financed with only a fractional sale of IMF gold is, for this reason, more attractive.[3] Although the concessionary flows shown in Table 7.4 are small by comparison with other aid flows and the size of balance of payments and debt problems in low-income countries, they would still be significant for the recipients and would, of course, expand in line with any general increase in the quantity of resources available from the Fund.

2. INTEREST-RATE POLICY TO ASSIST THE MAJOR BORROWERS

Up to now this chapter has discussed the use of interest-rate subsidies as a means of assisting low-income countries. A related, although in many ways significantly different, proposal is to establish an interest-rate facility within the Fund which would provide short to medium term finance to help cover unexpectedly high or above-normal interest payments. Countries availing themselves of loans from the facility would therefore continue to meet the full interest charges on their previously negotiated commercial loans. There would be no direct subsidy element; the purpose would be to ease short-term liquidity difficulties associated with rising interest rates. Again, unlike the

144

TABLE 7.4 Estimated payments associated with a subsidy scheme[1] (In millions of SDRs)

	Interest payments related to purchases within the ordinary credit tranches	Interest payments related to purchases under the credit tranche/SFF	Interest payments related to other purchases within the credit tranche	Interest payments related to purchases under the ordinary EFF	Interest payments related to purchases under the EFF/SFF	Interest payments related to purchases under the CFF	Total purchases (excluding those within the reserve tranche)	Total interest payments without subsidy	Total interest payments with subsidy	Subsidy payment[2]	Subsidy payment as percentage of total interest payment without subsidy
Bangladesh	1.51	—	—	5.34	8.35	—	195.00	15.20	5.85	9.35	61.51
Bolivia	0.66	1.47	—	—	—	—	27.00	2.13	0.81	1.32	61.20
Central African Republic	0.22	—	—	—	—	0.49	13.00	0.71	0.39	0.32	45.07
Chad	—	—	—	—	—	0.38	7.10	0.38	0.21	0.17	44.74
China, People's Republic of	24.30	—	—	—	—	—	450.00	24.30	13.50	10.80	44.44
Dominica	0.00	—	—	0.02	0.04	0.11	2.69	0.17	0.08	0.09	52.94
El Salvador	0.58	—	—	—	—	—	10.75	0.58	0.32	0.26	44.83
Equatorial Guinea	0.16	—	—	—	—	0.60	14.10	0.76	0.42	0.34	44.74
Grenada	—	—	—	—	—	0.11	2.30	0.11	0.06	0.05	45.45
Guyana	—	—	—	1.37	1.42	—	35.63	2.79	1.07	1.72	61.65
Haiti	—	—	0.57	0.69	—	—	16.55	1.26	0.50	0.76	60.32
India	—	—	—	—	—	14.36	266.00	14.36	7.98	6.38	44.43
Ivory Coast	2.15	—	2.85	1.41	—	—	72.68	6.47	2.18	4.29	66.31
Kenya	—	5.01	—	—	2.21	—	90.00	7.16	2.70	4.46	62.29
Lao People's Democratic Republic	0.59	—	—	—	—	—	11.32	0.59	0.33	0.26	44.07
Liberia	0.71	1.89	—	—	—	—	32.00	2.60	0.96	1.64	63.08
Madagascar	1.02	1.27	—	—	—	1.58	60.70	3.87	1.82	2.05	52.97

Malawi	0.54	1.20	—	—	—	—	22.00	1.74	0.66	1.08	62.07
Mauritania	0.15	0.61	—	—	—	—	8.90	0.76	0.27	0.49	64.47
Mauritius	0.66	3.78	9.38	8.94	—	2.70	90.50	7.14	2.72	4.42	61.90
Morocco	—	—	—	—	7.56	—	309.10	25.88	9.27	16.61	64.18
Nepal	—	—	6.89	7.17	—	0.57	10.49	0.57	0.31	0.26	45.61
Pakistan	1.15	5.26	—	—	11.20	—	292.87	32.15	8.79	23.36	72.69
Peru	4.16	16.30	—	—	—	—	74.00	6.41	2.22	4.19	65.37
Philippines	—	—	—	—	—	—	240.00	20.46	7.20	13.26	64.80
St Lucia	—	—	0.18	—	—	0.15	4.50	0.33	0.14	0.19	57.58
St Vincent	—	—	0.04	—	—	0.07	2.04	0.11	0.05	0.06	54.54
Senegal	0.27	—	0.22	1.32	2.08	—	43.25	3.60	1.30	2.30	63.89
Sierra Leone	—	—	—	0.61	1.05	—	25.10	1.93	0.75	1.18	61.14
Sri Lanka	—	—	—	1.92	—	—	30.00	1.92	0.90	1.02	53.13
Sudan	0.47	1.63	1.99	2.75	4.30	3.65	173.35	12.69	5.20	7.49	59.02
Tanzania	0.72	0.73	—	—	—	0.81	40.00	2.91	1.20	1.71	58.76
Togo	—	—	—	—	—	—	20.50	1.45	0.62	0.83	57.24
Vietnam	—	—	2.84	—	—	—	28.40	2.84	0.85	1.99	70.07
Western Samoa	—	—	0.08	—	—	0.11	2.75	0.19	0.08	0.11	57.89
Zaire	5.29	—	—	—	—	—	98.00	5.29	2.94	2.35	44.42
Zimbabwe	2.03	—	—	—	—	—	37.50	2.03	1.13	0.90	44.33

1. Based on purchases from the Fund, financial year ended 30 April 1981, assuming that (i) the subsidy reduces the effective rate of interest on Fund purchases to 3 per cent; (ii) an actual rate of interest on drawings under the credit tranches, compensatory financing facility and buffer stock financing facility of 5.4 per cent on drawings under the ordinary extended fund facility of 6.4 per cent, and on drawings under the supplementary financing facility of 10 per cent. The Table excludes the following low income countries which, while drawing on the Fund, drew exclusively within the reserve tranche: Comoros, Papua New Guinea and Yemen Peoples' Democratic Republic. It also excludes the following countries which are not classified by the Fund as eligible for subsidies: Cyprus, Israel, Jamaica, Korea, Panama, Romania, Turkey, and Yugoslavia.

2. Difference between payment with and without subsidy.

SOURCE: IMF *Annual Reports*.

subsidy arrangements reviewed above, the interest-rate facility is intended to be of principal benefit to the main debtor nations.

By means of such a facility designed to help deal with the liquidity aspects of the debt problem related to rising interest rates, countries would be able to draw an amount from the Fund depending in part on the extent of the unanticipated increase in interest rates and in part on the size of their quotas. The rationale for a new facility of this type is often presented by drawing an analogy with the CFF, since it is claimed that in both cases balance-of-payments problems emerge as a result of temporary and externally caused factors, and that measures are required in order to protect import capacity.

In fact, the analogy is not perfect. Unlike the CFF, the interest-rate facility would help to deal with problems that might be related to inappropriate domestic economic policy. Moreover, governments might be encouraged to overborrow in relation to their calculations of the debt capacity of their economies – particularly if they felt that interest rates were relatively low – knowing that a facility existed by which financial assistance would be available should they rise. There would therefore be a 'moral hazard' problem from which the CFF is exempt. What is more, the moral hazard would also affect the banks making the loans, since their perceived risk would fall. The facility might also be seen as reducing the need to keep interest rates down, and this could have global costs.

In a sense the facility could be interpreted as being primarily a way of protecting and insuring the earnings of the banks. This, of course, need not in itself be a bad thing. It might, for example, encourage a larger flow of commercial finance to the developing world than would otherwise occur, but, even so, these implications need to be explicitly recognised.

The existence of the moral hazard problem means that, unlike the CFF, high conditionality might be appropriate in the case of the interest-rate facility. In which case, one might ask, how would the facility differ from the ordinary upper credit tranches or the EFF which may already be drawn upon by countries encountering payments problems in connection with rising interest rates? The difference would be largely quantitative rather than qualitative. Countries would simply have access to more finance in such circumstances. However, given limited Fund resources, expansion in the direction of an interest-rate facility could reduce the amount of assistance the Fund could offer in other directions. The distributional aspects of the facility are therefore an important consideration. Some countries could benefit from it but others might lose.

The distributional aspects would be affected by the way in which the facility was financed. If it were financed from quota-based subscriptions and existing Fund resources, the distributional problems as just described exist. But if financed by additional borrowing, which could in principle come from those governments held responsible for the rise in interest rates because of their domestic policies, the distributional costs could be neutralised. Indeed, by means of freeing some of the Fund's own resources, the distributional consequences could favour the poorer LDCs.

Another problem with the facility relates to the way in which interest rates would be measured. This is not so much a question of which particular interest rate or average of world interest rates to use, since the facility applies to *changes* in the rate and not its absolute level, but more one of choosing between the use of nominal or real rates. This is clearly important when it is noted that in the extreme case the two measures may move in opposite directions. If it is decided to use real rates, an additional problem is which price series to use in order to convert nominal rates. Should a global deflator be used or a country-specific one? If a country-specific approach is adopted, should this be based on export prices or the terms of trade? But in these circumstances would not the rubric of the new facility begin to encroach on the CFF?

Given the shortcomings of an interest-rate facility, are there any alternative ways in which the problem of rising interest rates might be handled? One mechanism would be to reschedule interest payments as well as principal, thereby capturing the variability of interest rates in the maturity structure of the loan rather than in the contemporaneous level of interest payments. An increase in interest *rates* beyond a specified level would increase the maturity of the loan. The increase in interest *payments* would thereby be 'capped'. Such a scheme is worthy of consideration, although it is not without problems. It would, for example, reduce the banks' cash flow, unless the cash flow cost of the rearrangement of the loan could in some way be passed back to the ultimate lenders. Furthermore, there is the question of whether the scheme would be symmetrical; would falling interest rates result in shorter maturities and unchanged interest payments?

Another approach distinguishes between dealing with the cause of the problem rather than its consequences. This is similar to the question of whether it is better to try and eliminate commodity price instability or to provide compensatory finance to cope with its payments ramifications. In the case of rising interest rates an alternative to setting up an IMF facility would be to encourage countries to desist from policies which force up world interest rates. Although a case can be made that the external costs of such policies warrant such an international response, it has to be recognised that countries run their economic affairs on the basis of perceived private costs and benefits. It will be difficult to persuade governments to alter policies for external reasons if they are seen as being the best ones on domestic grounds. *Some* scheme for offsetting the external costs may therefore be required.

3. CONCLUDING REMARKS

The first part of this chapter investigated the actual and possible use of interest-rate subsidies within the context of the IMF. It is concluded that subsidies offer a potentially useful supplement to other forms of aid both in quantitative and qualitative terms. They could be particularly attractive to donors, given their connection with IMF conditionality, and could provide an economically efficient and equitable method of granting aid. At the same time subsidy aid would be free from the more conventional types of tying, and for this reason could be quite attractive to recipients, particularly if Fund conditionality is accepted by them as being appropriate to their own economies. Three worries are, first, that subsidies might not result in additional aid but merely replace other forms of aid, in which case there would probably be distributional consequences; second, that the criteria for access to subsidies would involve not only a per capita income test but also a BoP test; and, third, that IMF conditionality may not be appropriate to low-income countries. With regard to the first, the quantities involved would seem to make additionality likely. With regard to the second, those low-income countries not in BoP difficulties would indeed be ineligible for subsidies because of their ineligibility for Fund finance. Similarly, countries unwilling to turn to the Fund would not receive subsidies. Furthermore, it is perhaps unlikely that other forms of aid provision are sufficiently flexible to compensate for this deficiency. With regard to the third, this issue has been discussed at length in Chapter 4.

However, no system of aid provision is problem free and low-income countries exist in an other than ideal world. In such an environment interest rate subsidies offer a useful additional type of aid; they serve to enhance the role of the Fund and raise the scope for the Fund to help low-income countries.

Furthermore, if the Fund begins to finance its activities by commercial borrowing, interest-rate subsidies will become even more important, since they will offer about the only way in which the cost of finance may be reduced below commercial levels for low-income countries. In such circumstances the effective subsidy will, *ceteris paribus*, clearly rise.

The absolute value of subsidy payments will also rise if IMF quotas are increased in an attempt to expand the Fund's activities. At the same time subsidies seem less vulnerable to the resistance encountered with other schemes designed to use the international monetary system as a channel for directing additional resources to developing countries, and therefore constitute a practical as well as a theoretical option.

The final section of the chapter examined the idea of an interest-rate facility in the Fund. Although rising interest rates have created difficulties for some developing countries, it is difficult to know the extent to which this is likely to be an enduring problem. Furthermore, consideration of both efficiency and equity suggests that there may be better ways of dealing with the problem.

8 Financing the Fund and Reforming Quotas

Although the International Monetary Fund has had a high profile over recent years, particularly in relation to its role in helping to alleviate debt problems, it is frequently overlooked that the Fund's activities are constrained by its own resources. These in turn, and in large measure, depend on the value of IMF quotas. Since quotas also affect the extent to which members are eligible for assistance from the Fund, it is clear that they are of considerable importance. Furthermore since developing countries have been the principal clients of the Fund over recent years, they clearly have a particular interest in the availability of Fund finance.

However, increases in quotas cannot be taken for granted. Quota reviews have been seized upon as providing an opportunity for examining many aspects of the Fund's role not only as an economic but also as a political institution. The issue of quotas cannot then be dissociated from that of the Fund's role in the world economy. With only a small role to play, the financing of its limited activities might constitute a relatively minor problem and IMF quotas would hardly be a significant issue. However, if the Fund is envisaged as having a large role to play, the adequacy of its resources becomes that much more important.

Yet adequacy depends not just on the *size* of the Fund's activities but also on their *nature*. If envisaged primarily as an adjustment institution, vetting and validating the macroeconomic programmes of member countries and thereby encouraging private capital inflows, the Fund will require relatively few resources of its own. On the other hand, if intended to be a significant independent source of balance of payments finance, then clearly the Fund will require many more own resources.

These observations suggest that a fairly detailed and quantified definition of the Fund's role is a prerequisite for estimating the value of resources that will be needed to carry the tasks through. It may be

150

noted, for example, that reforms discussed in Chapter 4 and designed to modify the nature of Fund conditionality to allow for longer term programmes call for a significant expansion in the Fund's resources. If these are unforthcoming, the scope for modifying conditionality is immediately and significantly reduced. In practice, it may well be that the value of the Fund's resources is determined first, with the nature of the Fund's activities then being effectively constrained to comply with this. Either way, what the Fund can do depends on the resources it has at its disposal and, in large measure, these at present depend on the value of IMF quotas. The Fund clearly accepts the importance of quotas in determining its activities.

> It is generally agreed that the resources available to the Fund should be sufficient for the Fund to play its important role in the adjustment and the financing of balance of payments deficits. . . While the Fund has had to supplement the resources obtained through quota subscriptions by borrowing from members, particularly in the circumstances prevailing since the middle of the 1970s, it is generally accepted that its activities should be financed primarily from quota resources.
>
> IMF *Annual Report*, 1982, p. 73.

1. IMF QUOTAS: FUNCTIONS, DETERMINATION AND EVOLUTION

Quotas are significant to members of the Fund, since they effect (a) voting rights, (b) the size of ordinary drawing rights and access to other special facilities, such as the Compensatory Financing Facility (CFF), Buffer Stock Financing Facility (BSFF) and Extended Fund Facility (EFF), (c) the size of SDR allocations and (d) the size of subscriptions to the Fund. Table 8.1 shows the current upper limits placed upon drawings from the Fund under its various facilities, expressed as a percentage of members' quotas.

The quotas initially used by the IMF were based on a formula worked out by the United States Treasury. Quotas were fixed at approximately 90 per cent of:

2 per cent of national income in 1940
plus 5 per cent of gold and dollar balances on 1 July 1943

TABLE 8.1 *Financial facilities of the Fund, their conditionality – Possible cumulative purchases (per cent of quota)*

| | Present position | | With supplementary financing facility | |
	Tranche policy	Extended facility	Tranche policy	Extended facility
Before Second Amendment took effect				
Gold tranche	25.0	25.0	25.0	25.0
Credit tranches				
4 × 36.25	145.0	—	145.0	—
1 × 36.25	—	36.25	—	36.25
Extended facility	—	140.00	—	140.00
Supplementary financing[1]				
3 × 34.0	—	—	102.0	—
With extended facility	—	—	—	140.00
Subtotal	170.0	201.25	272.0	341.25
Compensatory financing	75.0	75.0	75.0	75.0
Buffer-stock financing	50.0	50.0	50.0	50.0
Cumulative total[2]	295.0	326.25	397.0	466.25
After Second Amendment took effect				
Reserve tranche	25.0	25.0	25.0	25.0
Credit tranches				
4 × 25	100.0	—	100.0	—
1 × 25	—	25.0	—	25.0
Extended facility	—	140.0	—	140.0
Supplementary financing[1]				
1 × 12.5; 3 × 30	—	—	102.5	—
With extended facility	—	—	—	140.0
Subtotal	125.0	190.0	227.5	330.0
Compensatory financing	75.0	75.0	75.0	75.0
Buffer-stock financing	50.0	50.0	50.0	50.0
Cumulative total[2]	250.0	315.0	352.5	455.0

1. In special circumstances a stand-by arrangement may be approved for purchase beyond these limits and the normal limitations under tranche policy; in such cases purchases will be made with supplementary financing. The amount of such additional finance will be quantified in relation to a member's need and the adequacy of its program.
2. In addition, some member's have used Oil Facility drawings. The average use by those members was equal to 75 per cent of quota.

SOURCE: IMF Treasurer's Department.

plus 10 per cent of the maximum variation in exports between 1934
   and 1938

plus 10 per cent of average imports between 1934 and 1938,

the resulting total being increased in the same ratio as that which the
country's average annual exports in the periods between 1934 and
1938 bore to its national income. The reason for calculating quotas at
90 per cent of a certain figure was to leave some leeway for an
addition to any quota which did not adequately reflect the economic
and political weight of any particular country.

To a considerable extent the quota formula was spurious, since it
had previously been agreed between the US and the UK Treasuries
that the total amount of quotas should be about $8000m, that the US
quota should be about $2500m and that the UK quota should be
about half that of the US one. Furthermore, it had been agreed that
the USSR and China should have the third and fourth largest quotas
respectively. A trial-and-error process was then used to derive a
quota formula which would generate the desired results. As it turned
out, quotas were not rigidly based on this formula, but instead the
formula was taken as a point of departure for negotiations.[1]

The Articles of Agreement provided for five-yearly, and latterly
more frequent, review of quotas, and also allowed individual quotas
to be reviewed at any time merely at the request of the member
concerned. Apart from being the most recent, the Eighth Review of
Quotas adopted by the Fund's Board of Governors in March 1983
had a number of notable features.[2] First, 'extensive discussions' took
place in the Executive Board of the Fund concerning various aspects
of quotas, including simplyfying the existing method of quota calculation. The outcome of these discussions was that the economic criteria
used in the past were retained, but some modifications designed to
'broaden the definition of certain economic variables that represent
these economic criteria' were made. Furthermore, the number of
individual formula calculations was reduced from ten to five by
eliminating those including merchandise trade as a proxy for the
current account.

Second, having already increased Saudi Arabia's quota from SDR
1041.1 million to SDR 2100.0 million in September 1981, following a
request from Saudi Arabia for a substantial increase in its quota, the
Eighth General Review was taken as an opportunity to raise the
quotas of seventeen members of the Fund with existing quotas of less

than SDR 10 million by an amount slightly more than proportionate to the overall increase.

Third, there was a very public delay in getting many members – in particular the United States – to confirm the proposed 47.5 per cent increase in aggregate Fund quotas.[3] The new quotas, which are shown in Table 8.2, were arrived at in what is a fairly conventional way by distributing 40 per cent of the overall quota increase to members of the Fund in proportion to their existing individual quotas (also shown in Table 8.2), and 60 per cent '. . . in the form of selective adjustment in proportion to each member's share in the total of "calculated" quotas, which (as described above) are derived from formulas considered to broadly reflect members' relative positions in the world economy' (IMF *Annual Report*, 1983, p. 86).

While the distribution of a given global or aggregate quota increase is at least approximately based on certain objective criteria, the size of the increase seems to rest much more on what the Executive Board feels is necessary to support the Fund's activities. For example, the Fund's *Annual Report*, 1983 (p. 86), states that, 'the overall magnitude of the increase in Fund quotas under the Eighth General Review was agreed in the light of the financing and adjustment role *envisaged* for the Fund in the world economic conditions *likely to prevail over the next several years*' (italics added).

2. THE PRINCIPAL ISSUES

2.1 Multipurpose quotas

The first, and in some respects fundamental issue, is that quotas are used for more than one purpose. This would not constitute a problem if these purposes were perfectly positively correlated. However, in fact, the purposes may be in direct conflict. Countries in the strongest economic position to provide the resources necessary to run the Fund are, almost by definition, unlikely to be the ones in greatest need of the Fund's financial assistance. Similarly, the criteria for evaluating a country's position in the General Account of the Fund may not be the same as those relevant for assessing its need for SDRs.

Quotas, as currently used, may then be insufficiently subtle and flexible to perform the various jobs that they have been given to do. More than this, it is doubtful whether any single set of individual

TABLE 8.2 *Fund quotas, present and proposed, 1983*

Member	Quotas (in millions of SDRs) Present	Proposed	Quota shares (as per cent of total) Present	Proposed
Afghanistan	67.5	86.7	0.111	0.096
Algeria	427.5	623.1	0.700	0.692
Antigua and Barbuda	3.6	5.0	0.006	0.006
Argentina	802.5	1,113.0	1.314	1.236
Australia	1,185.0	1,619.2	1.941	1.798
Austria	495.0	775.6	0.811	0.861
Bahamas	49.5	66.4	0.081	0.074
Bahrain	30.0	48.9	0.049	0.054
Bangladesh	228.0	287.5	0.373	0.319
Barbados	25.5	34.1	0.042	0.038
Belgium	1,335.0	2,080.4	2.186	2.311
Belize	7.2	9.5	0.012	0.011
Benin	24.0	31.3	0.039	0.035
Bhutan	1.7	2.5	0.003	0.003
Bolivia	67.5	90.7	0.111	0.101
Botswana	13.5	22.1	0.022	0.025
Brazil	997.5	1,461.3	1.634	1.623
Burma	109.5	137.0	0.179	0.152
Burundi	34.5	42.7	0.057	0.047
Cameroon	67.5	92.7	0.111	0.103
Canada	2,035.5	2,941.0	3.334	3.267
Cape Verde	3.0	4.5	0.005	0.005
Central African Republic	24.0	30.4	0.039	0.034
Chad	24.0	30.6	0.039	0.034
Chile	325.5	440.5	0.533	0.489
China	1,800.0	2,390.9	2.948	2.656
Colombia	289.5	394.2	0.474	0.438
Comoros	3.5	4.5	0.006	0.005
Congo	25.5	37.3	0.042	0.041
Costa Rica	61.5	84.1	0.101	0.093
Cyprus	51.0	69.7	0.084	0.077
Denmark	465.0	711.0	0.762	0.790
Djibouti	5.7	8.0	0.009	0.009
Dominica	2.9	4.0	0.005	0.004
Dominican Republic	82.5	112.1	0.135	0.125
Ecuador	105.0	150.7	0.172	0.167
Egypt	342.0	463.4	0.560	0.515
El Salvador	64.5	89.0	0.106	0.099

continued on page 156

TABLE 8.2—*continued*

Member	Quotas (in millions of SDRs) Present	Proposed	Quota shares (as per cent of total) Present	Proposed
Equatorial Guinea	15.0	18.4	0.025	0.020
Ethiopia	54.0	70.6	0.088	0.078
Fiji	27.0	36.5	0.044	0.041
Finland	393.0	574.9	0.644	0.639
France	2,878.5	4,482.8	4.714	4.979
Gabon	45.0	73.1	0.074	0.081
Gambia, The	13.5	17.1	0.022	0.019
Germany, Federal Republic of	3,234.0	5,403.7	5.296	6.002
Ghana	159.0	204.5	0.260	0.227
Greece	277.5	399.9	0.454	0.444
Grenada	4.5	6.0	0.007	0.007
Guatemala	76.5	108.0	0.125	0.120
Guinea	45.0	57.9	0.074	0.064
Guinea-Bissau	5.9	7.5	0.010	0.008
Guyana	37.5	49.2	0.061	0.055
Haiti	34.5	44.1	0.057	0.049
Honduras	51.0	67.8	0.084	0.075
Hungary	375.0	530.7	0.614	0.589
Iceland	43.5	59.6	0.071	0.066
India	1,717.5	2,207.7	2.813	2.452
Indonesia	720.0	1,009.7	1.179	1.121
Iran, Islamic Republic of	660.0	1,117.4	1.081	1.241
Iraq	234.1	504.0	0.383	0.560
Ireland	232.5	343.4	0.381	0.381
Israel	307.5	446.6	0.504	0.496
Italy	1,860.0	2,909.1	3.046	3.231
Ivory Coast	114.0	165.5	0.187	0.184
Jamaica	111.0	145.5	0.182	0.162
Japan	2,488.5	4,223.3	4.076	4.691
Jordan	45.0	73.9	0.074	0.082
Kampuchea, Democratic	25.0	25.0	0.041	0.028
Kenya	103.5	142.0	0.170	0.158
Korea	255.9	462.8	0.419	0.514
Kuwait	393.3	635.3	0.644	0.706
Lao People's Democratic Republic	24.0	29.3	0.039	0.033
Lebanon	27.9	78.7	0.046	0.087
Lesotho	10.5	15.1	0.017	0.017
Liberia	55.5	71.3	0.091	0.079

Member	Quotas (in millions of SDRs)		Quota shares (as per cent of total)	
	Present	Proposed	Present	Proposed
Libyan Arab Jamahiriya	298.4	515.7	0.489	0.573
Luxembourg	46.5	77.0	0.076	0.086
Madagascar	51.0	66.4	0.084	0.074
Malawi	28.5	37.2	0.047	0.041
Malaysia	379.5	550.6	0.622	0.612
Maldives	1.4	2.0	0.002	0.002
Mali	40.5	50.8	0.066	0.056
Malta	30.0	45.1	0.049	0.050
Mauritania	25.5	33.9	0.042	0.038
Mauritius	40.5	53.6	0.066	0.060
Mexico	802.5	1,165.5	1.314	1.294
Morocco	225.0	306.6	0.368	0.341
Nepal	28.5	37.3	0.047	0.041
Netherlands	1,422.0	2,264.8	2.329	2.515
New Zealand	348.0	461.6	0.570	0.513
Nicaragua	51.0	68.2	0.084	0.076
Niger	24.0	33.7	0.039	0.037
Nigeria	540.0	849.5	0.884	0.944
Norway	442.5	699.0	0.725	0.776
Oman	30.0	63.1	0.049	0.070
Pakistan	427.5	546.3	0.700	0.607
Panama	67.5	102.2	0.111	0.114
Papua New Guinea	45.0	65.9	0.074	0.073
Paraguay	34.5	48.4	0.057	0.054
Peru	246.0	330.9	0.403	0.368
Philippines	315.0	440.4	0.516	0.489
Portugal	258.0	376.6	0.423	0.418
Qatar	66.2	114.9	0.108	0.128
Romania	367.5	523.4	0.602	0.581
Rwanda	34.5	43.8	0.057	0.049
St. Lucia	5.4	7.5	0.009	0.008
St. Vincent	2.6	4.0	0.004	0.004
São Tomé and Principe	3.0	4.0	0.005	0.004
Saudi Arabia	2,100.0	3,202.4	3.439	3.557
Senegal	63.0	85.1	0.103	0.095
Seychelles	2.0	3.0	0.003	0.003
Sierra Leone	46.5	57.9	0.076	0.064
Singapore	92.4	250.2	0.151	0.278

continued on page 158

158

TABLE 8.2—*continued*

Member	Quotas (in millions of SDRs)		Quota shares (as per cent of total)	
	Present	Proposed	Present	Proposed
Solomon Islands	3.2	5.0	0.005	0.006
Somalia	34.5	44.2	0.057	0.049
South Africa	636.0	915.7	1.042	1.017
Spain	835.5	1,286.0	1.368	1.428
Sri Lanka	178.5	223.1	0.292	0.248
Sudan	132.0	169.7	0.216	0.188
Suriname	37.5	49.3	0.061	0.055
Swaziland	18.0	24.7	0.029	0.027
Sweden	675.0	1,064.3	1.105	1.182
Syrian Arab Republic	94.5	139.1	0.155	0.154
Tanzania	82.5	107.0	0.135	0.119
Thailand	271.5	386.6	0.445	0.429
Togo	28.5	38.4	0.047	0.043
Trinidad and Tobago	123.0	170.1	0.201	0.189
Tunisia	94.5	138.2	0.155	0.153
Turkey	300.0	429.1	0.491	0.477
Uganda	75.0	99.6	0.123	0.111
United Arab Emirates	202.6	385.9	0.332	0.429
United Kingdom	4,387.5	6,194.0	7.186	6.880
United States	12,607.5	17,918.3	20.648	19.902
Upper Volta	24.0	31.6	0.039	0.035
Uruguay	126.0	163.8	0.206	0.182
Vanuatu	6.9	9.0	0.011	0.010
Venezuela	990.0	1,371.5	1.621	1.523
Vietnam	135.0	176.8	0.221	0.196
Western Samoa	4.5	6.0	0.007	0.007
Yemen Arab Republic	19.5	43.3	0.032	0.048
Yemen, People's Democratic Republic of	61.5	77.2	0.101	0.086
Yugoslavia	415.5	613.0	0.680	0.681
Zaire	228.0	291.0	0.373	0.323
Zambia	211.5	270.3	0.346	0.300
Zimbabwe	150.0	191.0	0.246	0.212
Total	61,059.8	90,034.8	100.002[1]	100.001[1]

1. The sum of the individual percentage shares differs from 100,000 because of rounding.

SOURCE: *Annual Report*, IMF, 1983.

country quotas could successfully fulfil such a multipurpose role. Rather than a country having one multipurpose Fund quota there may be a case for having what are, in effect, multiple quotas.

2.2 The global quota

Broadly speaking, it is the size of the overall global quota, determining subscriptions, that constrains the Fund's activities. Yet the precise mechanism by which the global quota is determined remains unclear to those not involved in the decision-making. Although statements from the Fund, examples of which were quoted earlier, refer to vague concepts such as 'the financing and adjustment role envisaged for the Fund', the details of how such concepts are translated into a specific global quota are not explained. What is clear is how the global quota is *not* calculated. It is not simply an aggregation of the individual country quotas calculated cn the basis of the various formulas mentioned above.

If the economic underpinning of the global quota is ill-defined, the process by which its value is changed, by means of (usually five-yearly) reviews, has become increasingly unsatisfactory in a world where global economic variables can and do change rapidly.

Quotas seem to be altered in *lagged* response to events rather than in anticipation of them. This is not surprising, since global forecasting is insufficiently precise and accurate to allow a consensus to be reached about the future. However, the system used for changing quotas lengthens the lag and limits the ability of the Fund to respond swiftly to a changing global economic environment. Instead the Fund is forced into using *ad hoc* measures to increase its resources and therefore raise the amount of financial assistance it can offer deficit countries. Although such measures allow the Fund to be more flexible than it could otherwise be, they do have a number of deficiencies. As a later section will suggest, there may be a case for increasing flexibility by modifying the arrangements through which the global quota is changed.

A further problem is that, while it is sensible to monitor and re-assess the role of the Fund, it is unlikely that this is best achieved under the current system of general quota reviews, especially if, as might be suspected, this system allows subjective and concurrent political factors to dominate objective economic ones.

These points may be seen as arguing for a more objective basis for determining the global quota and for some form of indexing which allows quotas to be altered more frequently and more automatically than is the case at present.

2.3 Individual country quotas

While the global quota affects the amount of resources the Fund has at its disposal, individual country quotas *determine* the distribution of subscriptions to the Fund, voting rights, and SDR allocations. They also *set an upper limit* on the quantity of General Account finance that members can borrow. That quotas *do not determine countries' actual* drawings from the Fund is because these are also affected by various eligibility criteria. Members without a 'balance of payments need' cannot borrow from the Fund irrespective of their quota. Similarly, members' access to finance through the Fund's various special facilities depends both qualitatively and quantitatively on the nature of their payments deficits. For example, members not experiencing a temporary shortfall in export receipts are ineligible to draw from the Fund under the CFF. Furthermore, in the case of upper credit tranche drawings or drawings under the EFF, the Fund's financial assistance depends on the ability of a member's government satisfactorily to negotiate a programme of economic measures with the Fund. Again members unable to do this will not receive financial support beyond the lower credit (low conditionality) tranche whatever their quota.

This is not to deny that quotas are of considerable significance. The key issue is whether the way in which individual quotas are arrived at accurately summarises the various facets of a member's relationship with the Fund. One part of this question is the extent to which actual quotas differ from those calculated using the various formulas. Another related part of the question is the extent to which the 'calculated quotas' provide a satisfactory objective means of determining individual quotas; are all relevant economic variables considered, and are they given appropriate weights?

However, it is very important not to become fixated by quotas and to lose sight of the fact that quotas are only one factor determining an individual member's access to Fund finance. Nor should the political influences over the determination of quotas be forgotten.

2.4 Problems with multipurpose quotas

As noted above, a fundamental problem with quotas springs from their use for what are often conflicting purposes. As a country's quota increases, so do its voting rights and its subscription (though relative voting power depends on a country's relative quota). It may be assumed that countries contributing more of the Fund's *supply* of resources will in any case demand a larger say in its decision-making.[4] This was no doubt one reason why Saudi Arabia requested an increase in its quota in the early 1980s.

However, it may also be assumed that, in general, it will not be these countries that have the highest *demand* for Fund resources either in the form of drawings on the General Account or SDRs. For this reason total drawings on the Fund have represented only a small proportion of total quotas. As of end December 1981, total drawings represented only 34 per cent of total quotas. The situation changed somewhat in subsequent years as some of the larger developing countries encountered debt problems and turned to the Fund for financial help.

It seems then that while there may need to be a positive correlation between voting rights and subscriptions (in relative terms) and while there may be a positive correlation between the demand from members for General Account finance and for SDRs, the correlation between the former pair of factors and latter pair is less clear and may be negative. If this is the case, one set of quotas will be unable simultaneously to provide a satisfactory distribution of subscriptions, voting rights, and drawing rights amongst members of the Fund.

The issues are still more complex than the above discussion suggests. Drawings on the Fund may be made under a range of facilities. Although these are differentiated from one another in terms of their eligibility criteria, they are all constrained by reference to the percentage of quota that may be drawn. However, a country's quota does not, and indeed one quota cannot, accentuate or weight the particular variables relevant to *each* of the special facilities. The result is that countries experiencing particularly acute balance of payments problems caused by a specific factor, such as an export shortfall, may be able to finance only a relatively small proportion of the deficit by drawing on the Fund.

There are a number of ways round this problem. One is simply to remove the percentage of quota constraint on drawings, leaving the size of access to be determined, in the case of the CFF for example, exclusively by the size of the export shortfall. A second is to modify the quota formula specifically to incorporate, again in the case of the CFF, export shortfalls. A third is to increase the percentage of quota that may be drawn under any specific facility,[5] while a fourth is to raise quotas, thereby effectively relaxing the constraint on drawings in absolute terms.

However, each of these potential 'solutions' involves difficulties. If the size of access to the Fund's resources is divorced from quotas (or the percentage of quota that may be drawn is increased) while quotas continue to determine subscriptions and the size of the Fund's resources, there is no guarantee that the demand for resources will not exceed their supply. The problem then becomes one of either reducing demand or of increasing supply by some means other than using quotas, such as by borrowing.

If quotas are retained but modified to reflect *more* precisely the purposes of one particular facility (say the CFF), they may become *less* appropriate for determining the access to other facilities (say the EFF).[6] Meanwhile, raising quotas overall raises a series of problems to be discussed later.

A further complexity with multipurpose quotas is that even if it is decided to use them exclusively to indicate members' demands for Fund resources rather than their ability to pay subscriptions or their demand for votes, there still remain significant distinctions between those resources available under the General Account and those available through the Special Drawing Rights Account. This is an important issue which has become highlighted in the context of the developing countries' claim for a link between SDR allocation and developmental assistance; discussion of the link is deferred until Chapter 10.

So far this section has illustrated some of the problems associated with the multipurpose role of Fund quotas. Broadly speaking, there are two policy options available to try and deal with these. The first is to retain a multipurpose role for quotas but to change the value of individual country quotas. The central problem with this option is that changes which move a quota towards its optimal value in terms of one function are likely to move it away from its optimum value in terms of another.

The second option is to introduce what are *in effect* multiple quotas. Under such a scheme access to the Fund's General Account resources would be determined by one set of factors, possibly distinguishing still further between different facilities, SDR allocation would be determined by another set of factors, and subscriptions and voting rights by yet another set. Apart from the political difficulties that a scheme of this type might encounter, arising from the fact that borrowers would probably end up borrowing more from the Fund and 'creditors' subscribing more to the Fund, the only constraint would be that of ensuring that the demand for resources did not exceed the supply. This problem, along with others related to the global quota, is examined in the next section.

3 THE GLOBAL QUOTA

As described earlier, quotas have been raised by a series of quinquennial and general reviews, of which the Eighth General Review is the most recent.[7] However, the details of the ways in which the increases are determined have not been made freely available by the Fund. Instead the increases have been explained in general terms by referring to the Fund's need for resources to carry through its various activities.[8] A suspicion is therefore created that the final outcome of the reviews rests on political factors and on bargaining within the Executive Board.

One way of testing this hypothesis is to see whether it is possible to explain retrospectively the variations in the sizes of quota increases (ranging from 25 per cent in the case of the Fourth General Review to 50 per cent in the cases of the Third and Seventh Reviews), in terms of key international economic variables. Such an exercise is carried out later in this section.

However, initially it is worth noting that the general review method of changing quotas may itself be unsatisfactory. Although, in principle, individual countries may request that their quotas be changed at any time, the system of infrequent reviews imposes a degree of rigidity on the structure and operations of the Fund. It becomes more difficult for the Fund to respond swiftly, and in a quantitatively significant way, to changes in the world economy, since there is no automatic and direct way in which the Fund's resources may be made to reflect such changes. In these circumstances either the Fund's contribution to dealing with global economic problems has to be constrained or other methods for increasing its resources have to be found.

In practice, both these outcomes have been observed. During the period 1973–4 to 1981–2 the Fund made only a somewhat muted contribution towards financing global payments deficits. Instead it was the private international banks that played the principal role in recycling international finance.

Of course, care needs to be used in accepting such general statements uncritically. For some countries the Fund remained a very important source of finance while the banks were of little relevance, and in some years, notably 1976, the Fund financed a not insignificant proportion of global current account deficits (largely, in this particular case, as a result of reforms to the CFF in 1975). Furthermore, during 1977–8 there is evidence to suggest that the Fund was not resource-constrained at all but, rather, possessed a significant amount of spare lending capacity; it was the demand for Fund assistance which, for various reasons, was low at this time.[9] Still, in general terms, it seems legitimate to argue that an excess demand for Fund resources has been the more normal state of affairs, with quotas imposing an effective constraint on the amount of financial assistance it can offer its members. Variations in IMF conditionality may then have been used as a means of rationing scarce Fund resources.

In an attempt to overcome this constraint the Fund has sought temporarily to extend the percentage of quota that countries may draw both through the Supplementary Financing Facility and latterly through its Policy on Enlarged Access.[10] The Fund has also over the years introduced special facilities either on a permanent basis (the CFF, the BSFF and the EFF) or on a temporary one (the Oil Facility) to deal with special problems that it was felt would not be adequately dealt with by stand–by drawings under the credit tranches.

While such initiatives have helped to increase members' access to Fund finance, they have also created a need for the Fund to increase its own resources. Raising quotas constitutes one way of doing this. However, as explained earlier, raising quotas not only increases the *supply* of Fund resources but may also increase the *demand* for them. If demand has increased for some reason unconnected with quotas, such as a fall in primary product prices relative to those of manufactures, or a relaxation in, or modification to, conditionality, raising quotas may prove to be a not fully satisfactory way of meeting the extra demand for Fund resources.

In any case quota increases may be difficult to negotiate quickly, and therefore, when faced with potential or actual shortages of resources, the Fund has frequently resorted to borrowing as a means of increasing its capacity to lend.

The Fund summarises its borrowing activity in the following way:

Borrowing provides an important temporary supplement to the Fund's ordinary resources. To date the Fund has borrowed from official sources, which include its members, Switzerland, and central banks and other official institutions in these countries. These borrowing arrangements and agreements have been as follows: the General Arrangements to Borrow (GAB), initially established in 1962; the oil facility agreements entered into in 1974 and 1975, with drawings terminating in 1976; the supplementary financing facility, which took effect in 1979 with borrowings to terminate in 1984; and the bilateral borrowing arrangements with the Saudi Arabian Monetary Agency and with the central banks and official agencies of certain industrial countries to finance the Fund's commitments under the policy on enlarged access.

The Fund's guidelines for borrowing provide that the Fund will not allow the total of outstanding borrowing, plus unused credit lines, to exceed the range of 50 to 60 per cent of the total of Fund quotas. Since at present all GAB lines of credit may not be called upon at the same time, the total of borrowing is defined to include either outstanding borrowing by the Fund under the GAB or one half of the total credit lines under the GAB, whichever is the greater. On April 30, 1983, the Fund's total outstanding borrowing and unused lines of credit, calculated in accordance with these guidelines, amounted to SDR 20.21 billion, equivalent to 33.1 per cent of quotas (34.4 per cent on April 30, 1982).

IMF *Annual Report*, 1983, p. 93.

In certain respects the Oil Facility, the Supplementary Financing Facility and the Policy on Enlarged Access and the borrowing associated with them represent a significant step in the direction of breaking away from the rigidity imposed by quotas and discussed in the previous section of this chapter. While still equating the *aggregate* demand for and supply of Fund resources, these measures have served to alter the *distribution* of demand and supply. As a result of them some countries have become eligible to draw more resources *from* the Fund while subscribing no more resources *to* it; at the same time other countries have lent more resources *to* the Fund while not demanding any more resources *from* it. In this way the Fund has acted as an intermediary in the process of international financial recycling, and the connection between quotas and both the demand for and supply of Fund resources has been relaxed.

However, there are arguments to suggest that the mechanisms used by the Fund for escaping from the rigidity of the quota system are unsatisfactory and that greater reliance on suitably reformed quotas would be preferable. On the *demand* side these arguments relate both to the *cost* of those purchases from the Fund which are financed by borrowing, as well as to their *nature*. As regards cost, the charges on resources drawn under the Oil Facility or under the SFF or the EAP are higher than those applying to purchases under the Fund's other facilities; though, as discussed in the previous chapter, Subsidy Accounts have been used in the case of the Oil Facility and the SFF in an attempt to assist the Fund's poorer members meet the higher charges.

With regard to their nature, because the SFF and EAP have been used to 'top up' upper credit tranche stand-bys and EFF loans, they have meant that a higher proportion of Fund lending has been of a high conditionality type than would have been the case had quota increases been used to generate an equivalent amount of additional resources. This of course need not constitute a problem if Fund conditionality is perceived as being appropriate to those countries borrowing from the Fund, but this is not universally the case. The implications of the means of financing the Fund for the balance between high and low conditionality resources should not therefore be neglected.

On the *supply* side the main problem is the uncertainty associated with *ad hoc* measures. Can economically strong countries, and those in substantial balance of payments surplus – the identity of which may well change and become more dispersed – be relied upon always to provide the resources necessary for the Fund to maintain its programme of loans? While, given the institutional constraints and the immediacy of the problems, borrowing may have been the only way of dealing with the Fund's own liquidity problems in the late 1970s and early 1980s, it may not represent the best long term solution for financing the Fund.

Yet similarly, and under the existing system of negotiated infrequent reviews, can quota increases of sizes which permit the Fund to play a central role in international economic affairs be guaranteed? If not, considerable costs are likely to ensue. If the resources are not forthcoming, there will be global costs in terms of higher levels of unemployment and lower levels of output and trade, as well as in terms of the extra pressure put on other means of international financing, in particular through the private sector. Furthermore, there will be costs on individual countries arising from a shortage of finance and therefore from the extra emphasis that has to be placed on adjustment. But even if extra resources are eventually made available, the *uncertainty* regarding the outcome of negotiated quota reviews may cause significant instability in the international banking system, disrupting flows of finance throughout the world and having adverse consequences for real economic variables both in debtor and creditor countries.

One way of ensuring that the Fund has sufficient resources is to index quotas against indicators of the need for Fund resources, bearing in mind that there are arguments for basing the distribution of potential access to Fund finance on a different set of criteria than that used for determining the distribution of subscriptions – an issue to be discussed in the next section. By introducing a more automatic and direct link between the need for Fund resources and their supply, many of the costs associated with infrequent reviews could be avoided.

Moreover, the effects of global inflation on the real value of quotas could be more easily neutralised. As things stand, quotas are expressed in nominal SDRs; inflation therefore means that from the very moment a new set of quotas is ratified their real value begins to fall. Clearly the quantitative relevance of this depends on the rate of inflation; an acute problem in the mid-1970s the problem has become less significant in the 1980s, even though other reasons for questioning the adequacy of quotas associated with different aspects of global economic performance have become more marked. Index linking is, of course, a fairly conventional means of trying to reduce some of the costs of inflation. But if the global quota is to be linked to broader indicators of global economic performance, what should these indicators be?

One option that has been mentioned by some commentators is to use the value of world trade. The ratio of quotas to world trade has fallen significantly from 14.2 in 1950, to 11.5 in 1960, to 8.2 in 1971 and to 3.8 in 1981. Although the precise value of the ratio depends on whether the year chosen is just before or just after quotas have been raised, the downward trend is well established. However, although the quota-to-trade ratio is convenient to calculate, there is reason to believe that it is a poor proxy for the adequacy of Fund resources, since the demand for these is related to the incidence and size of payments deficits, which may not be perfectly positively correlated with the *level* of world trade. Indeed, the use of the quota-to-trade ratio may be criticised for basically the same reasons as those assembled against using the reserves-to-imports ratio as a measure of reserve adequacy, the most telling of which is that the simple use of ratios fails to provide a rigorous explanation of what constitutes the optimum value for the particular ratio chosen, or indeed what factors most significantly influence this value. This leads on to the question of whether it is possible to gain any insight into assessing the adequacy of Fund resources and therefore quotas from other approaches to the adequacy of international reserves.

In the case of Fund quotas there are in fact additional problems on top of those normally associated with judging reserve adequacy. In part these relate to the cost of producing extra Fund resources, which require countries to swap foreign exchange and SDRs for Reserve Positions in the Fund and to subscribe more of their own currency to the Fund at a potential future real resource cost. But they also relate to the benefits of Fund resources, since these are affected by the fact that a large proportion of Fund resources are conditional – the benefits therefore depend on the appropriateness of the conditions attached to Fund loans. Moreover, the benefits of extra Fund resources also depend on the global advantages of expanded Fund activity. While it is possible to talk about these in general terms, it is difficult to convert them into a satisfactory and objective specific value. In relation to this latter point only a small part of Fund resources may be counted as 'reserves'; the rest represents credit.

A conclusion from the above discussion is that Fund resources have distinctive features as compared with other forms of reserve assets and international liquidity. Their conditionality, along with the fact that Fund operations may involve positive externalities, needs to be borne in mind when assessing the adequacy of Fund resources.

Faced with the problems of quantification, analysis of the adequacy of international reserves has also drawn on a qualitative or symptomatic approach. The basic idea behind this is as follows: a shortage or excess of reserves will exert an impact on certain key economic variables either directly, through, for instance, affecting the domestic money supply, or more indirectly by encouraging the pursuit of particular policies. By observing the *policies* that are pursued and the performance of certain key *economic variables*, one may reach tentative conclusions about reserve adequacy. This approach has also been subjected to considerable criticism,[11] and again its deficiencies are multiplied if adopted as a means of assessing the adequacy of Fund resources. The question is not simply one of whether there are enough reserves or whether there is enough international liquidity but also one of whether there is the right balance *between* the various reserve assets and components of international liquidity; does the system need more Fund-based resources *relative* to the other types of international finance? Although it is possible, in principle, to derive a symptomatic guide to answering this question – for example, by examining the appropriateness of macroeconomic policies in individual countries or by looking at the implications of private bank financing – it is difficult to convert such generalities into specific values for Fund quotas.

While this brief review suggests no easy answers to the problem of determining the adequacy of the global quota, it does help to identify some of the factors that should be taken into account. It has, in other words, identified some of the arguments in the implicit demand function for Fund resources.

Returning to the idea of automatically altering the global quota by indexing it to a number of variables, the discussion provides some ideas as to what these variables might be. To begin with, however, the purposes envisaged for the Fund need to be defined. In the existing Articles of Agreement, these purposes are clearly expressed (see Chapter 4).

Under its Articles the Fund emerges as being both a balance of payments financing and adjustment institution. The need for Fund resources therefore depends on:

(i) the size and location of current account balance of payments deficits,
(ii) the size and distribution of actual and desirable private financial and other financial flows.
(iii) the size and distribution of non IMF-based reserves, and
(iv) the efficiency of and cost of balance of payments adjustment.

Having used these variables to indicate the need for Fund finance overall, one must consider other variables which indicate how this finance should be broken down between high and low conditionality facilities within the Fund; these include the causes of deficits and the likelihood of appropriate adjustment measures being undertaken.

As far as the global quota is concerned, and using the above factors, a formula of the following type may be suggested:

$$Qg = \frac{\alpha(D - p^f - O^f - R^e)}{\beta}$$

where:

Q^g is the global quota.

D is the aggregated global balance of payments deficit on current account,

p^f is the 'desirable' value of private bank financing, given the country distribution of current account deficits, which may be *greater* or *less* than the actual value,

O^f is the value of other sustainable payments-related financial flows,

R^e is the 'excess' reserves of non-reserve currency deficit countries,

α depends on an assessment of the need for financing as opposed to adjustment (which will in turn depend on the costs of adjustment) with the need for complete financing being reflected by $\alpha = 1$ and the need for complete adjustment by $\alpha = 0$, and

β reflects the fact that, for various technical reasons the Fund is, at any one time, able to lend out only a proportion of its total resources.

Assuming that β may be treated as invariant, the size of the required global quota will change as α, D, P^f, and O^f R^e change. It will be positively related to α and D and negatively related to p^f, O^f and R^e.

Of course this formula gives a false sense of precision. In reality there can be little precision in estimating α or P^f or even O^f. With regard to α, there is the additional problem that IMF-supported adjustment programmes are linked to the provision of finance, so that the relationship between adjustment and financing may be positive with greater Fund finance going hand in hand with more adjustment. As regards P^f, there are many difficulties associated with defining its value, since it raises the whole question of the relationship between and relative roles of the IMF and private banks in financing payments deficits. Furthermore, if actual bank loans are below their 'desirable' level, it may be that the Fund will have to respond to actuality unless pressure can be brought to bear on the banks to increase their lending.

However, to the extent that certain elements in the formula could be objectively measured, changes in these would focus attention on whether the values of the less objective variables had changed in an offsetting fashion. Some measure of objectivity could be introduced even for these variables by drawing on the symptomatic approach to assessing reserve adequacy described earlier. A falling growth in world trade, falling import coefficients, an increasing global level of spare capacity, and falling world expenditure, could be used to indicate that the actual value of α had fallen, with greater emphasis being placed on adjustment.

While it is difficult to see how the need for judgement could be completely eradicated from global quota decisions, there would seem to be considerable scope for introducing a much higher degree of automaticity than currently exists. Given the unavoidable elements of subjectivity involved, direct and automatic indexation would seem to be out of the question. However, by changing quotas more regularly, their real value could be more effectively maintained.

Bearing in mind the administrative costs of changing quotas, not least that they would have to be agreed by the Executive Board and by national governments, one could alter them annually or bi-annually, depending on the global rate of inflation (somehow measured). For example, with inflation running in excess of 7.5 per cent, the quota level could be reviewed each year. Either way the global quota would be inappropriate in terms of its basic determinants for less time than is the case at present. Also, by responding more swiftly to world economic conditions, there would be less need to engage in the uncertain business of global forecasting. Table 8.3 presents some calculations based on the global quota formula discussed above.

The results are clearly sensitive to the assumed values for α, P^f, and R^e. On the assumptions that about 80 per cent of the observed deficit in 1982 needed to be financed in the short run, that private financial inflows stood at about their desirable level, and that deficit countries held significantly deficient reserves, the required global quota is calculated as SDR 96.6 billion. This suggests that an increase of 58.4 per cent in the global quota following the Eighth General Review would have been more appropriate than the 47.5 per cent increase that was actually adopted. Allowing for more financing relative to adjustment and for a smaller role for private capital raises the required value for the global quota. For example, with $\alpha = .9$ and P^f $15 billion, the required global quota is estimated at SDR 116.5 billion. This would have involved a 91 per cent increase in its actual value in 1983.

Of course, as noted above, such calculations give a false impression by implying an element of precision in an area where it is very difficult to be precise. How can one be precise about the correct division between financing and adjustment, or the desirable level of

TABLE 8.3 *Estimation of global quota[1]*

	α	β	D	P^f	O^f	R^e	$Q^{g\$}$	$Q^{g\mathrm{SDR}}$ (*billions*)
1982*	.8	.5	89	20	20	−20	110.4	96.6
1982**	.9	.5	89	15	20	−20	133.2	116.5
1982***	1.0	.5	89	15	20	−20	148	129.5
1978	.8	.5	51	11.5	13.8	19	10.7	9.4

1. Based on the formula $Q^g = \alpha \dfrac{(D - P^f - O^f - R^e)}{\beta}$.

SOURCE: *World Economic Outlook*, IMF, 1983.

private capital flows, or about the optimum level of liquidity? Even the use of the observed deficit may be misplaced in calculating the size of the required global quota, since it is quite feasible that 'inadequate' Fund resources might constrain the deficit below its 'optimum' level.

Yet, bearing in mind such limitations, the formula provides some insight into the question posed at the beginning of this section. Taking the Seventh General Review, it suggests that the Fund required relatively few resources at this time, given the values of D, P^f, O^f and R^e. This coincides with the earlier observation that the Fund had excess lending capacity. But quotas were still increased by 50.25 per cent. It would appear that global quota increases do not significantly reflect the needs of the international economy. It is difficult to explain the actual differences in quota increases that have occurred in terms of the key economic variables used here, which suggests that, as supposed, political factors have been significant.[12]

A slightly different approach to calculating the size of a required increase in the size of the global quota has been canvassed by Williamson (1982). This approach still commences by pointing out that the global quota has to be related to the role envisaged for the Fund. Williamson argues that,

Quotas . . . need to be large enough to enable the Fund to fulfil its traditional role as a major source of temporary balance of payments finance to those countries that have not achieved significant access to the international capital market, preferably by extension of low conditionality financing where a deficit arises due to circumstances outside a country's own control.

He goes on to draw attention to the fact that the terms of trade of the countries of sub-Saharan Africa have deteriorated by over 20 per cent 'in recent years' and that their foreign trade is of the order of 20 per cent of their GDP, meaning that 'the type of payments shock that the Fund is in business to finance can easily reach 4 per cent of (their) GDP'. By imagining Fund programmes that finance a tapering proportion of exogenously caused deficits, he suggests that the Fund should be able to finance a deficit equal to $(4 + 3 + 2 + 1) = 10$ per cent of one year's GDP.

Taking those countries listed as 'low income' in the World Bank's *World Development Report* as providing a minimum estimate of the countries without access to the international capital market, Williamson calculates that 10 per cent of their GNP (excluding China and India) amounts to $17 billion in 1981 dollars. To this figure he adds $10 billion to cover loans to China and India and another $5 billion for loans to other countries that, even though not low-income countries, lack extensive access to private capital. This gives a total *potential* call on Fund resources of $32 billion from countries with a low private credit rating.

Of course not all such countries would necessarily be drawing from the Fund at the same time, though to a significant extent their problems may be positively correlated. Williamson argues that the Fund should be in a position to respond to 75 per cent of this potential total demand, i.e. $24 billion in 1981 figures. By the late 1980s and after allowing for inflation, this is estimated to be equal to $48 billion or SDR 42 billion.

Williamson then allows for occasional but simultaneous drawings from two or three of those developing countries that have previously enjoyed extensive access to private capital as well as from developed countries, arguing that 8 per cent of total quotas should cover these. Further allowing for the fact that only about 50 per cent of the total of Fund quotas is available for lending at any one time, Williamson estimates the required size of total quotas (Q) as follows:

$$42 + 0.080 = 0.5Q$$

with the left-hand side of this expression showing the demand for Fund resources and the right-hand side showing their supply. The implied global quota is SDR 100 billion.

Williamson's approach is reassuring inasmuch as it also relates the size of the required global quota to (a) the underlying role of the Fund, (b) a proxy for the size of payments deficits and (c) the availability of non-Fund finance. Nor is the value that emerges that far from the estimates made above. However, the final figure that it comes up with is sensitive to the assumptions made. If instead of those used above one allows for Fund finance to cover other payments deficits in addition to those caused by adverse terms of trade movements, and allows for a larger percentage of the potential demand on Fund resources to be actually made effective, and also allows for a higher demand from those countries that have previously relied on the private international capital market, then the final figure for the global quota can be significantly different. For example, if the following figures are used:

$$80 + 0.12Q = 0.5Q$$

it may be seen that

$$Q = 210.5$$

i.e. the size of the required global quota more than doubles.

The very sensitivity of the final outcome to the assumptions made suggests that it may be wise to keep such projections to a minimum and instead to change the global quota more frequently in response to real occurrences.

A number of conclusions emerge from this discussion of the global quota. Calculating the size of the 'optimum' global quota is, in principle, best carried out from the *demand side*. In other words, one needs to begin by clearly defining the Fund's role both as a balance of payments financing and adjustment institution and in relation to the role of the private international capital markets and other forms of international financing. The existing Articles of Agreement provide what many might regard as a satisfactory statement of this role.

Once the Fund's role has been defined it is then necessary to calculate the level of resources needed to carry this out, and for this purpose one has to convert the descriptive elements of the Fund's role into objective and quantifiable indicators. This task could involve using a global quota formula.

Use of such a formula would introduce an element of automaticity into changing the value of the global quota. However, it is more realistic to think in terms of more frequent reviews of the quota based on an 'objective' formula rather than complete automaticity, which could even limit the degree of flexibility that the Fund could show in extreme circumstances.

The current method of determining the global quota is unclear and unsatisfactory. Failure to increase quotas by amounts that might be deemed adequate on the basis of objective indicators has meant that the ability of the Fund to play an important role in international economic affairs has been effectively constrained, and this has imposed significant costs on the world economy. If the existing system of general but infrequent reviews is retained, there is no reason to believe that these costs will not be continued into the future.

In influencing the size of the Fund's activities, the global quota, as described here, is related both to the aggregate of individual country quotas and to the total of Fund subscriptions. The distribution of Fund resources amongst members and the means of financing the Fund's activities warrant further investigation. It is to these issues that the following sections are devoted.

4 THE CALCULATION OF INDIVIDUAL COUNTRY QUOTAS

From the establishment of the Fund up until the early 1960s individual country quotas were based on the Bretton Woods formula:

$$Q = (0.02Y + 0.05R + 0.10M + 0.10V) (1 + X/Y)$$

where:
Y is national income in 1940,
R is gold and dollar balance on 1 July 1943,
M is average imports during 1934–8,
V is maximum variation in exports during 1934–8, and
X is average exports during 1934–8.

However, there was growing dissatisfaction with the formula, first, because of the small quotas it awarded some countries and, second, because using more contemporaneous data awarded new members large quotas by comparison with existing members. Therefore after 1958 more emphasis was placed on comparability as the basis for determining quotas. Eventually, in 1962–3, the formula was revised by redefining the variability component[13] and by reducing its coefficient as well as by scaling down the weights of the other components by half in order to make the sum of the calculations correspond more closely to the actual size of Fund quotas. Four other formulas, in addition to the revised Bretton Woods formula, were also introduced at this time, containing the same basic variables but different coefficients – the weights for trade and variability were increased while those for national income and reserves were reduced. In two of these formulas the ratio of exports to national income was eliminated. Furthermore, in addition to making calculations using data on national income, reserves, exports, imports, and the variability of exports (known as Set I data), extra calculations were made using Set II data in which current receipts, current payments, and the variability of current receipts were substituted for exports, imports, and the variability of exports – previously data on these variables had not always been easily available. The results of these various calculations were used in devising the initial quotas of new members from the mid-1960s through until the early 1980s. The choice of the four modified formulas was based on the closeness of their fit to the then structure of the Fund. More precisely the four formulas were:

Scheme III:
$(0.0065Y + 0.078M + 0.5065V) (1 + X/Y)$

Scheme IV:
$(0.0045Y + 0.07M + 0.9622V) (1 + X/Y)$

Scheme M4:
$0.005Y + 0.044M + 0.044X + 1.044V$

Scheme M7:
$0.0045Y + 0.039M + 0.039X + 1.304W$

After the 1962–3 review, quota calculations were made for all Fund members, using the revised Bretton Woods formula, the four other formulas, and both Set I and Set II data. Then, to quote from the Fund, 'the calculations based on the Bretton Woods formula using Set I and Set II data are averaged. The lowest two calculations of the four modified formulas, using Set I data, are averaged and the lowest two, using Set II data are averaged; these two averages are then averaged. The higher of the average derived from the Bretton Woods formula and the final average derived from the modified formulas is the calculated quota' (*IMF Survey*, 5 June 1978, p. 167). As a result of this procedure, the calculated quotas of industrial countries tended to be based on the Bretton Woods formula because of their high reserves and low ratios of trade to national income, while those of developing countries tended to be based on the modified formulas. The Fund claimed that 'the multiformula approach provides more flexibility to take into account the diversity of structure among the economies of Fund members' (*IMF Survey*, ibid.).

Under the Eighth General Review the method for calculating quotas was re-examined. The definitions of some of the economic data entering into quota calculations were modified, national income being replaced by GDP and year-end gold and foreign exchange reserves by a wider concept of average external reserves, including SDRs and RPF. Furthermore, Set I calculations using trade data were eliminated, and the role of the variability component was reduced by 20 per cent in all the formulas except the Bretton Woods one. The five formulas used under the Eighth Review were as follows:

Revised Bretton Woods formula
$$(0.01Y + 0.025R + 0.05P + 0.2276VC) (1 + C/Y)$$

Other modified formulas
Scheme III:
$$(0.0065Y + 0.0205125R + 0.078P + 0.4052VC) (1 + C/Y)$$

Scheme IV:
$$(0.0045Y + 0.03896768R + 0.07P + 0.76976VC) (1 + C/Y)$$

Scheme M4:
$$(0.005Y + 0.042280464R + 0.044 (P + C) + 0.8352VC$$

Scheme M7:
$$(0.0045Y + 0.05281008R + 0.039 (P + C) + 1.D432VC$$

where
Y = GDP (1980),
R = average monthly reserves (1980),
P = annual average current payments,
C = annual average current receipts in 1976–80, and
VC = variability of current receipts defined as one standard deviation from the five-year moving average in 1968–80.

For the purposes of the Eighth Review, the calculated quota was the higher of (i) the Bretton Woods calculation and (ii) the average of the lowest two of the remaining four calculations, though 'before a calculated quota for each member as defined above can be derived, the results of each of the four modified formulas are first uniformly adjusted so that for each formula, the sum of the calculations for all members equal that derived from the revised Bretton Woods formula'.

Although the use of formulas, whatever their precise construction, suggests that the calculation of quotas is objective, this impression is somewhat misleading. Quotas calculated on the basis of the formulas are in aggregate greater than actual quotas, while, for individual countries, comparability as well as some allowance for their overall economic significance plays an important part in determining actual quotas. As the Fund points out, 'in practice the calculated quotas serve as a basis for discussion and smaller or larger adjustments are made to them taking into account the important functions of quotas in the Fund, before actual quotas are finally agreed'.

One possible interpretation of the evolution of Fund quotas outlined above is that, having commenced from a specific set of constraints, namely target quotas for particular countries, the formulas used have continued to be underscored by other factors. Thus, when the Bretton Woods formula applied to contemporary data suggested quotas for new members in excess of those for existing members of comparable size, it was the comparability criterion that was adopted and new quotas that were adjusted downwards. Similarly, when modified formulas were introduced, these were adjusted to ensure that the sum of calculated quotas did not exceed the sum emerging from using the Bretton Woods formula. The quota calculations have therefore offered only a form of constrained objectivity.

In thinking of ways in which the system of deriving actual quotas might be improved, it may therefore be helpful to go back to first principles and to re-examine why countries need to borrow resources from the Fund. Again, as in the discussion of the previous section, the role of the Fund underpins the analysis of individual country quotas.

Since the purpose of the Fund is to provide financial assistance to countries encountering balance of payments difficulties, clearly the state of the balance of payments will be a crucial influence on whether countries need to turn to it. There are of course numerous ways of defining the balance of payments and various views on which sub-account is the most relevant. In assessing a country's need for Fund help there are in fact various aspects of the balance of payments that warrant examination. First, there is the current account and its composition; merely to look at trade in goods or even trade in goods and services will ignore components, such as interest payments, which are likely to be very important in debtor countries. Second, there is the capital account and its composition. Here it is important to examine the extent to which a current account deficit may be sustained in the sense that there are offsetting (reliable) long term capital inflows.

Faced with a deficit on its basic balance, a country may, even so, not need to borrow from the Fund if it has a high level of international reserves which can be decumulated or if it can borrow from the private international capital market to finance the deficit. Indeed, even with low reserves and limited access to private capital, recourse to the Fund may be unnecessary if the deficit may be quickly eliminated through appropriate adjustment policy.

At first glance this discussion seems to imply that individual country quotas should be based on a formula which includes a measure for payments imbalance, a measure for access to private capital, a measure for the costs of adjustment, and the level of reserves. Quotas would vary positively with the size of payments deficits and with the costs of adjustment and negatively with the size of access to private capital and with the level of reserves. However, further thought reveals that there are some important implications and problems associated with a quota formula of this type.

First, it would mean that countries in payments surplus would have a zero quota; similarly, it would mean that one implication of a country adopting and following through a successful IMF-supported adjustment strategy would be that its quota would fall. This problem can be overstressed; as things stand, countries without a balance of payments need are ineligible to draw from the Fund whatever their quotas.[14] But another aspect of surplus countries having zero quotas is of more concern. If subscriptions to the Fund are based on quotas, a zero quota for many of the economically strong nations would clearly starve the Fund of resources. This is an issue that was discussed earlier and will be further discussed when the Fund's own financing is considered. Second, the simple formula mentioned above implies that drawing from the Fund and borrowing from the banks are substitutes for one another. In addition, it implies a particular type of relationship between the two institutions.[15] Third, the relationship between quotas and reserves would be negative, whereas under the present quota formulas it is positive. Finally, with large swings in payments imbalances as well as in the availability of private bank financing individual countries' calculated quotas could be volatile.

These various implications need not necessarily cause too many difficulties. Provided that quotas are modified frequently and reflect members' current needs for Fund finance, potential volatility should be of little concern, since quotas will only fall or fail to increase in circumstances where, according to an objective measure, countries require less help from the Fund, and will only rise where the need for help increases. Similarly, the problem of providing the Fund with resources merely illustrates the intrinsic problems of the multipurpose quota and suggests that individual countries may warrant a *demand quota* which determines their access to Fund finance and a *supply quota* which determines their subscriptions to the Fund. To a certain extent the change in the sign of the coefficient on reserves further illustrates this problem. The logic in most circumstances would suggest that countries with relatively few owned reserves will have a relatively large demand for Fund credit.

More difficult problems are to form a view on what is a desirable value for short term capital inflows from the banks to individual countries, and to estimate the costs of adjustment. In the light of these problems, the individual country quota formula might be:

$$Q^i = \alpha^* \, (D - P^f - O^f - R^e)^i$$

where:

Q^i is the individual country's calculated quota,
D is the current account deficit,
P^f is the 'desirable' value of private bank lending/borrowing,
O^f is the sustainable capital account surplus,
R^e is the level of 'excess' reserves, and
α^* reflects the costs of adjustment, with countries with higher adjustment costs having larger α^*s and therefore larger quotas.

A formula such as this emphasises a country's demand for Fund resources to spend rather than its demand for international reserves to hold.

By comparison with it, existing Fund formulas are based largely on intermediate variables such as income and trade levels. While these variables may influence a country's demand for reserves, incidence of deficits, and international credit rating, they are not variables that stand as direct proxies for its demand for Fund resources.

One problem with the formula proposed above is that it may not always be easy to base it on contemporary data (averages for recent years would no doubt have to be used, as they are in existing formulas) and unavoidably it will therefore be backward-looking. If the Fund is to offer immediate help to members facing problems, without using projections, some inclusion within the formula of factors influencing a country's vulnerability to payments shocks, such as export concentration or export instability, as well as some forms of import instability, could be included. There could then, for example, be an additional term reflecting the structural characteristics of a country's balance of payments.[16] An advantage of the formula as it stands, however, is that it is closely related to the global quota formula discussed in the previous section. However, as with the global quota, it may be unwise to rely too heavily or exclusively on an objective formula. It remains sensible to permit countries to make out a case for why their quota should be different from that calculated by the formula.

4.1 The distribution of Fund resources

Having established a set of individual country quotas, it may seem logical to argue that Fund resources should be distributed on the basis of them. However, a number of issues are hidden by this basic statement. First, should Fund resources be distributed on the basis of calculated quotas or actual quotas? Second, will the sum of individual calculated quotas equal the global quota and will this in turn equal the total of Fund resources?

With regards to the first of these questions, if calculated quotas accurately reflect countries' needs for Fund resources, they offer a useful basis for distribution. However, if calculated quotas are modified to act as a proxy for members' ability to pay subscriptions, then they are unlikely to be the best basis upon which to distribute resources. Furthermore, if on occasions actual quotas are allowed to depart from calculated quotas because it is felt that in some circumstances the latter may not fully reflect a country's need for Fund assistance, then clearly it would be inconsistent to distribute resources solely on the basis of calculated quotas. However, the existence of large and consistent discrepancies would suggest that the formula used for calculating quotas is inappropriate and should be modified.

In practice, the distribution of quota increases has not been based purely on calculated quotas. The Fund has recognised 'the need for an improvement in the Fund's quota structure by laying more emphasis . . . on member's relative positions in the world economy'. The solution to this problem used by the Fund has been to distribute a part (60 per cent in the case of the Eighth Review) of the overall increase in proportion to each member's share in the total of calculated quotas, with the rest being distributed in proportion to their existing quotas. It is instructive to ponder on the logic of this. In effect, what it is saying is that it would be unsatisfactory to distribute quota increases purely on the basis of existing quotas and that *relative* calculated quotas provide a superior basis. If this is true, why not distribute the quota increase purely on the basis of calculated quotas? Individual quotas would then change according to the following formula:

$$\Delta Qa^i = \frac{Qc^i}{Qc^t} \Delta Qa^t$$

where:

ΔQa^i is an individual country's actual increase,

Qc^i is a country's individual calculated quota,

Qc^t is the sum of calculated quotas, and

ΔQa^t is the actual increase in the total quota.

But this raises the question of why the actual increase in quotas, and therefore the actual global quota, should be less than the sum of calculated quotas?

If individual calculated quotas accurately measure the need for Fund resources and the sum of these therefore measures the global need for Fund resources, then, on the basis of the formulas proposed in this chapter, the sum of individual calculated quotas should at least approximately equal the global quota. To keep the actual global quota below this level is therefore to constrain the Fund's activities.

Also relevant in this context is the problem of changing *existing* quotas. As mentioned earlier, it is difficult to imagine some strong countries accepting a reduction in the value of their existing quota. Such political constraints imply that new calculated quotas may be of most practical use in determining the distribution of future increases in the global quota. These would be determined on the basis of global need and would be distributed on the basis of the share of individual member's calculated quotas in the sum of calculated quotas. Countries not needing access to Fund finance according to the new quota formula would therefore receive no increase in their existing quota. But what are the implications of this for financing the Funds activities?

5 FINANCING THE FUND

5.1 Quota-based subscriptions

Up to now most of the discussion of quotas in this chapter has related to their function in determining members' access to Fund resources. But once the need for Fund resources has been calculated, the question arises of how these resources are to be raised. At present approaching 70 per cent of the Fund's resources comes from members' subscriptions, which are determined by their quotas, with additional resources coming from Fund borrowing from members. Other Fund-based loans through the Trust Fund have been financed by sales of Fund gold, while there has also been some discussion of the Fund borrowing directly from private capital markets.

Although there are arguments both for and against the Fund engaging in borrowing to supplement its resources, there is a broad consensus that subscriptions should continue to represent the main source of Fund finance. However, if quotas are modified better to reflect the need for Fund finance, both in aggregate and distributionally, then apart from indicating the total quantity of Fund resources required, the same quotas may not be the best way of determining which members provide the resources and in what amounts. Again, the problem is that one set of quotas are being asked to fulfil too many purposes.

The solution may therefore be to determine subscriptions on the basis of a different set of quotas to the one used for determining country access. What objective criteria might enter into such a quota formula? One might relate to the distribution of the benefits from the Fund's activities. At first sight there might seem to be difficulties with this criterion, since the main users of Fund resources might be expected to be relatively poor countries with few spare reserves. Yet since subscriptions are paid mainly in domestic currency and only in part in reserve assets, which in any case are translated into a Reserve

Position in the Fund and a reserve tranche, it may not be unreasonable to expect such members to make subscriptions even with the real resource costs that they imply. However, the Fund will certainly continue to need inflows of hard currencies that it primarily gains from the subscriptions of the reserve currency countries. Can these countries be expected to subscribe their currencies to the Fund if their drawing rights have been curtailed? The likely answer is that the industrial countries do not subscribe to the Fund only in anticipation of making drawings – in fact such drawings are few and far between. They subscribe in order to finance an institution whose activities are regarded as globally beneficial and beneficial to the industrial countries by enhancing international economic stability. The benefit criterion should not therefore exclude industrial countries. But it could be complemented by an ability-to-pay criterion, under which the richer industrial countries would be required, as at present, to provide most of the Fund's resources. This discussion suggests the following type of formula:

$$Q^s = a\,Y + b\,R + c\,(B)$$

where:
  Q^s is a member's subscription quota,
  Y is per capita national income,
  R is reserve holdings (including gold valued at its market price),
  B indicates the member's benefit from the Fund's activities either as a recipient of its resources or as a beneficiary of its stabilising role (the latter could be proxied by a country's level of trade), and a, b, and c are the coefficients with $a>b>c$.

The relationship between the total supply quota and the global demand quota would depend on the extent to which it was felt desirable to raise resources for the Fund by other means. If it was decided to keep Fund borrowing to a minimum and to aim to finance the Fund's activities as far as possible from subscriptions, the subscription formula would have to generate resources approximately equivalent to the size of the global quota. As the global quota is increased, so members would be called upon to make additional subscriptions such that their share of the extra total subscriptions would equal the share of their calculated supply quota relative to the sum of calculated supply quotas. Thus:

$$\Delta S = \frac{Q^{si}}{Q^{st}} \, Qa^t$$

where:

ΔS is the additional subscription,

Qs^i/Qs^t is the ratio of an individual country's calculated supply quota to the sum of such quotas, and

ΔQa^t is the increase in the actual total demand quota.

5.2 Borrowing from members

The Fund could, however, be financed in other ways. Borrowing from members is one method that has been used in the case of the GAB, the Oil Facilities, the SFF and the EAP. Although this has been a useful device, as noted earlier in this chapter, it also has shortcomings. Apart from the associated uncertainties and the fact that it may be easier to organise when current account surpluses are fairly narrowly concentrated, some commentators have criticised it for changing the nature of the Fund from that originally envisaged, making it more of an intermediary and less of a credit union. Furthermore, it disturbs the distribution of rights and obligations amongst the Fund's membership.[17]

5.3 Borrowing from private markets

Just as the World Bank finances some of its activities by private borrowing, could the IMF not avail itself of this source of finance? Although this again would alter many of the basic features of the Fund, direct borrowing from commercial banks does, in principle, offer a way of recycling resources from surplus countries to deficit ones; there would simply be two intermediaries involved in the transaction. The incentive for banks to lend to the Fund would have to arise from the rate of return offered to them by the Fund and their own assessment of the risk involved in lending to the Fund, which could, of course, be influenced by the way in which the Fund planned to use the extra resources. If the banks assessed the risks associated with lending to the Fund as being less than those involved with direct lending to the eventual recipients of Fund credit, they might be prepared to accept a relatively low rate of return. By diversifying their portfolio of assets, the prospect of lending to the Fund could be quite attractive to banks, since it would enable them to combine high return/high risk lending directly to developing countries with low return/low risk lending indirectly through the IMF.

However, it might encourage them to pull out of direct payments financing. Indeed, the most common criticism of Fund borrowing from private markets is that it would crowd out other borrowers, including developing countries, and possibly the World Bank. In this context it needs to be recognised that debt crises have in a sense done this anyway, and the counter-argument can be made that in aggregate terms Fund borrowing might well crowd in additional financial flows; even so, the concern has to be taken seriously.

Another problem with direct borrowing relates to its cost. Would the Fund simply on-lend at the price and for the time period on which it borrowed or would it attempt to transform the maturity and reduce the interest rate. Where the Fund charged a lower rate on its lending than it paid on its borrowing, an additional financing problem would clearly arise. However, if it did not do so, direct borrowing from private markets would be of more limited benefit to many developing countries.

Finally, too heavy a concentration on private borrowing as a means of financing the Fund would expose its activities to the vagaries of the capital market. A continuing flow of finance could not be relied upon. Moreover, resort to borrowing from the markets might persuade some governments to reduce their own financial support for the Fund, with the result that it might become even more difficult to get agreement on quota increases.

In conclusion, and bearing in mind the public-good nature of many of the Fund's activities, it seems more appropriate that these should be supported by government subscriptions.[18]

5.4 SDR allocation

A third alternative, which is in certain ways more attractive than either of the above, is for the Fund to finance its activities by the creation of SDRs which would then be transferred to the General Account.[19] The attractions are associated with increasing the significances of the SDR and of allowing the Fund to use its own asset more fully. Furthermore, quotas in their role of determining individual country subscriptions could be dispensed with. Such a move would of course mean that some SDRs would be issued to Fund members in the form of conditional and repayable credit – under the auspices of the General Account – and others unconditionally as non-payable reserve assets – under the auspices of the SDR Account. It would also rely heavily on the SDR becoming a more useful asset. Finally, there is the implicit presupposition that it would be easier to get governments to agree to extra SDR allocations to the General Account than to quota increases. This may be the case, since countries would not be asked to give up financial resources directly. But they might still see a potential real resource cost. More to the point, if they oppose any expansion in the Fund's activities, they may be expected to resist this by whatever means it is to be financed.

6. CONCLUDING REMARKS

Quotas perform important and central functions within the Fund and effectively underpin its activities. However, the decline in the size of quotas relative to almost every other global economic variable, and the relative decline in the size of the Fund, has focused attention on the way in which quotas are determined and changed. Problem areas relate to the multipurpose role of quotas, and the global quota, the calculation of individual quotas and the distribution of Fund resources and subscriptions. Upon inspection many of these problems are found to be interrelated, with the multipurpose role of quotas being fundamental.

The analysis here suggests that the Fund should break away from the idea of a multipurpose quota and should instead base the allocation of SDRs, access to Fund resources under the General Account, and subscriptions on different formulas. The first two should emphasise the need for such resources, while the latter should emphasise the ability of members to pay.

The 'objective' formulas discussed here would, however, lead to an enhancement in the Fund's lending capacity. Whether such proposals will be accepted depends crucially on what role is seen for the Fund by the governments of influential countries. Quota policy cannot be divorced from politics. If they are uncommitted to the idea of the Fund or a financing institution, they are unlikely to vote for proposals that will enhance it. Yet, with fears about international financial instability, the environment may be more conducive to such reforms than it was at the beginning of the 1980s.

An aspect of quotas not discussed thus far but relevant to getting reforms through the Executive Board relates to voting rights. These are currently determined by the sum of basic votes, which are 250 for each member, and the votes proportional to a member's quota, one vote for every SDR 100,000 of quota. Membership of the Executive Board is as follows: the members with the highest five quotas each appoint one Executive Director, with the other Directors being elected by groups of countries. The two members with the largest net creditor positions may also appoint Directors if they are not already represented amongst the members with the largest five votes.

If quotas were to be modified along the lines suggested here, clearly the way of determining votes would need to be modified. By basing voting power on demand (or user-based) and supply (or subscription-based) quotas, both users and suppliers of the Fund's resources could be represented in its decision-making, and the potential influence of developing countries perhaps raised. However, it needs to be recognised that to get changes made, even in terms of voting power, these have to be accepted by the Executive Board as currently constituted; a prerequisite remains that of persuading people of the usefulness of the Fund.

9 Reserve Currency Consolidation, Gold Policy and Financial Flows to Developing Countries

Many of the problems associated with the Bretton Woods system and subsequent arrangements have stemmed from a lack of central control over both the total quantity of reserve assets in the system as well as their composition. The IMF does, however, exercise control over the creation of SDRs and, in principle, the quantity of SDRs created may be related to the requirements of the international monetary system so as to ensure that there are neither too many nor too few international reserves, though it is, of course, notoriously difficult to define the optimum quantity of reserves.[1] Furthermore, in a situation where all central banks are holding their reserve assets in the form of SDRs, the problem of instability, which is caused by switching the currency composition of reserves, evaporates.

On the basis of these arguments a case may be made for encouraging the SDR to become the principal reserve asset in the international financial system. An SDR-based system should prove to be generally more stable than an alternative one based on multiple reserve currencies. Under the latter system the IMF would exercise control over the quantity of reserves only to the very limited extent that SDRs and other unconditional drawing rights at the Fund represented a component of the total. The quantity of reserves would to a much greater extent reflect the BoP positions of the reserve currency centres. The instability resulting from central banks changing the composition of their reserves would remain and might even be enhanced. Mature reserve centres that experienced unsatisfactory performance might

189

find themselves under more pressure if alternative reserve currencies were available and, furthermore, the new reserve centres would become exposed to the sorts of speculative movements in and out of their currencies that create problems for both monetary and exchange-rate policy. To help deal with these problems it seems likely that a multiple reserve currency system would have to incorporate some arrangement whereby central banks agreed to hold their reserves in certain minimum currency proportions.

A further problem with a multiple reserve currency system is that the compositional multiplicity of currencies could in practice turn out to be rather limited. Under such a system reserve growth would depend on running payments deficits in reserve currency centres; it would, therefore, by definition take place in the form of relatively weak currencies. It seems to be one of the fundamental inconsistencies of the multiple currency reserve system that there would be a shortage of strong currencies into which it might be anticipated that central banks would wish to move, and a superfluity of weak currencies from which it might be anticipated that there would be an outward movement.

From between the alternative systems outlined earlier there is much to be said in favour of the one based on SDRs. It was this alternative that was advocated by the Committee of Twenty and that is envisaged in the Second Amendment to the Articles of Agreement of the International Monetary Fund.[2] Many of the modifications that have been made to the rules that underpin the operation of the international monetary system, albeit rather loosely in an environment of flexible exchange rates, may be interpreted as endeavouring to facilitate a change in this direction. Examples include the decision to sell a proportion of the Fund's holding of gold, to extend both the uses to which SDRs may be put and the range of institutions that may acquire them, to modify the means of valuation, and increase the rate of interest.

When one examines the operation of the international financial system in practice, however, there is evidence to suggest some resistance to move to an SDR-based system. Certainly in the years since it was introduced in 1970 the SDR has failed to acquire a quantitatively important role in the working of the international financial system. Quite possibly this reflects shortcomings in the SDR itself. In an environment of flexible exchange rates it is difficult to see how the risk associated with holding SDRs could in general terms be reduced other than by using the asymmetrical basket method of valuation that was discussed, but rejected, by the Committee of Twenty. Under the current method of valuation, an individual country whose trading or debt pattern is not reflected by the weighting scheme used in valuing SDRs may be under an incentive to hold a blend of currencies different from the one indirectly implied by holding SDRs. However, to change the composition of currencies in the SDR basket or to modify their weighting to be more suitable for one country may, simultaneously, make it less suitable for another. Although holding SDRs involves less risk than holding any single currency, it may easily involve more risk than holding a custom-made combination of currencies. In such circumstances the argument that, because of its low degree of risk, the SDR can afford to offer a lower than market rate of interest becomes less compelling.

Other reasons why the SDR may not be regarded as a close substitute for foreign exchange relate to its usefulness, rather than the risk and return that are associated with it. While foreign exchange may be regarded as money, it may be more appropriate to regard SDRs as a form of credit, even though SDR use is no longer subject to reconstitution. SDRs may not be used directly in the purchase of goods or financial assets, prices are not normally quoted in SDRs, dealings in SDRs exclude the private sector, and even in the official sector SDRs may not be used for intervention in the foreign exchange market. It might be imagined that while these limitations remain, it will be difficult for the SDR to gain a position of dominance relative to reserve currencies.

Instead of examining the aforementioned issues in detail, this chapter concentrates on a related aspect of the transition to an SDR system. Assuming that there is agreement to move to an SDR system, a question arises as to how such a move may be engineered. One method would involve meeting any increase in the demand for international reserves by making additional allocations of SDRs. Under such a plan, however, it would take a long time to establish an SDR-based system. With a rate of growth of international reserves of 10 per cent per annum and with this being met exclusively by additional allocations of SDRs, it would take 15 years before SDRs represented more than 75 per cent of total reserves. If reserve growth is to occur in other ways as well, such as through the revaluation of official holdings of gold, this figure if anything underestimates the time that it would actually take to establish the SDR in a position of dominance.

If, as seems likely therefore, the time period implied by this first method is thought to be unacceptable, then attention shifts to a second method that involves swapping SDRs for foreign exchange, and possibly gold.

1. KEY PROBLEMS WITH A SUBSTITUTION ACCOUNT

By examining the various proposals for a Substitution Account that have been put forward at different times, it is possible to extricate the main issues that have to be resolved. The first concerns the identity of the assets to be deposited with the Account. While most schemes have concentrated on the substitution of currencies, the scheme could, in principle, also operate for gold.

The second problem concerns the nature of the asset to be issued by the Account in exchange for deposits. In some early versions it was assumed that this would be the SDR proper. In later versions emphasis switched to a separate SDR-denominated asset. To be an acceptable substitute for foreign exchange, the asset would need to be attractive both in terms of the range of institutions that would be permitted to deal in it and its marketability. While it may be more expedient to introduce a new asset strictly for the purpose rather than to try and make appropriate modifications to the SDR, the ramifications of this decision for the distribution of the costs and benefits associated with the Account are central.

The third problem relates to the degree of compulsion that would be used to encourage participation in the scheme. The choice ranges from a completely mandatory scheme, under which countries would be required to surrender a fixed proportion of their holdings of reserve currencies in exchange for SDRs, to a completely voluntary scheme, under which participation would be left to the discretion of individual countries. The argument against compulsion is that it reduces freedom of choice with regard to the composition of a country's reserves. The argument against voluntary schemes is that there is no guarantee that they will achieve the objective of bringing about a reduction in reserve currency balances. While it may be easier to reach agreement on a voluntary basis, this may simply mean that effectively no Account is introduced. If this is the case, the price of having a voluntary Account may well be the need for restrictions on central banks' freedom of choice in selecting the composition of their reserves. If it is accepted that the international community in general will benefit from the activities of the Account, there may be a case for not leaving its success to the discretion of individual countries. While for the international community as a whole the social benefits of the scheme may exceed the social costs, for individual countries private benefits may be less than private costs. If the non-participation of important individual countries means that the Account will be ineffective, then there may be a case for compulsion. Another argument in favour of compulsion is that under a voluntary scheme there would tend to be purely speculative movements into the Account from reserve currencies. The irreversibility of transactions, which seems to be an agreed principle in all versions of the Account, would, however, reduce the likelihood of this becoming a major difficulty and, even if it did, it would be fairly easy to deal with, simply by requiring countries to give a period of notice prior to substitution. Voluntary participation need not then imply that participation would be left completely open. It could involve participants voluntarily accepting a programme of substitution extending over a number of years. In any case, provided SDRs are made sufficiently attractive to potential holders, the degree of compulsion would become largely irrelevant, since countries would be anxious to substitute SDRs for reserve currencies.[3]

A fourth problem relates to the time period over which the Account is to be implemented. At one extreme the scheme could be introduced on a once-for-all basis. The implication would be a sudden and large conversion of foreign exchange holdings for SDRs. While there would be no change in the total quantity of reserves, there would be a dramatic change in their composition. The alternative would be to substitute SDRs for foreign exchange holdings gradually and progressively. Under this variant there would be no large creation of SDRs at any particular time and the problem of damaging confidence in the SDR as an asset that might be associated with a large allocation would thereby be avoided. The longevity of the Account would clearly depend on the annual rate of substitution. It would also depend on whether there was a simultaneous movement, within the international monetary system, towards an asset settlement method of international payment. One implication of failing to achieve a movement of this kind would be that the Substitution Account might be called upon to convert new foreign currency balances as well as old ones. It would therefore need to exist on a continuing basis.

How long the Substitution Account would exist also depends on the fifth issue, namely, what happens to the currencies that are deposited with the Account. The question here is whether they should be amortised or not. Amortisation could occur at a fixed annual rate or it could be related to either SDR acquisition or the balance-of-payments position in reserve currency countries. The relationship to SDR acquisition or the balance of payments could in turn either be symmetrical, having capacity to slow down as well as speed up amortisation, or asymmetrical, with there being a fixed minimum rate of amortisation. However, discussions of the Substitution Account within the IMF seem to have moved away from the concept of amortisation altogether, and it is envisaged that the Account would simply invest its stock of currencies.

Attention has instead focused on the financial arrangements that would underpin the Account; this is the sixth principal problem area. A key issue relates to the financial objectives of the Account, whether it is to make a profit, break even or make a loss – in which case there is the question of how the loss would be covered. Whereas the prime purpose of a Substitution Account is to change the composition of reserves, its activities would have incidental ramifications for the total quantity of reserves. Assuming, for example, that currencies deposited with the Account were to be invested in the issuing country and that interest were to be paid to the Account in the same currency, and assuming further that interest were to be paid on SDRs issued by the Account in the form of SDRs, the total quantity of reserves would rise at a rate equivalent to the interest rate on SDRs expressed as a fraction of total reserves. If, on the other hand, interest on the Account's holdings of currencies were to be paid in SDRs, then this would have the effect of reducing the total quantity of reserves as compared with a system where interest was paid in the issuer's own currency. Whether total reserves would actually fall would depend on the rate of interest paid to the Account by reserve centres as compared with that paid by the Account to recipients of SDRs. A profit for the Account would imply a reduction in total reserves, and a breakeven situation would imply no change in total reserves. Apart from the effect on total reserves, the profitability of an SDR-based Account would, in principle, seem to be largely irrelevant, since payments in excess of receipts could be covered by an additional creation of SDRs. The likelihood of a loss being incurred by the Account would depend significantly upon whether reserve currency amortisation were to be incorporated within the scheme. With a once-for-all scheme which involved amortisation, the income of the Account would diminish through time as the Account's stock of reserve currencies fell. Since the level of interest payments by the Account would remain constant, it would experience increasing deficits over time. On the other hand, with a progressive scheme interest payments would gradually rise while interest receipts would remain relatively constant over the lifetime of the Account. The end result, however, would be the same and the size of the Account's deficit would tend to rise. Without amortisation the likelihood of a loss would be considerably reduced, since under a once-for-all scheme the Account's capital stock would remain intact, while under a progressive scheme it would rise in conjunction with liabilities.

The foregoing discussion of the issues to which the concept of reserve currency consolidation gives rise reveals that, while the basic notion is fairly straightforward, the exact details can vary widely. The effects may, therefore, depend importantly on the precise mechanism by which consolidation is induced. A version of the Substitution Account which involves the introduction of a new SDR-denominated asset, an infinite lifetime, and no amortisation of reserve currencies, might have a harmful effect on certain strategic objectives of international monetary reform, such as the establishment of the SDR as the principal international reserve asset, and the achievement of a more symmetrical distribution of the adjustment burden involving an asset settlement as opposed to liability creation method of international payment.[4] Focusing initially, therefore, on a version that involves the direct use of SDRs and the amortisation of reserve currencies, the next section examines ways in which such an Account could be arranged so as to generate financial flows to developing countries.

2. SUBSTITUTION ACCOUNTS AND FINANCIAL FLOWS TO DEVELOPING COUNTRIES

As established earlier, a Substitution Account which involved the amortisation of reserve currencies would imply a fall in the quantity of international reserves, and this could have a deflationary effect on the world economy. In order to prevent such a fall from occurring, a special and additional allocation of SDRs could be made, equal to the annual amortisation and interest obligations accepted by reserve currency centres. The additional SDRs could be channelled towards developing countries either through direct allocation or through the intermediation of a development agency. Not only would the deflationary aspects of the Account be neutralised, but an additional flow of financial resources to developing countries would be induced.[5]

A central problem with any version of the Substitution Account which involves amortisation is that of determining the rate at which amortisation occurs. Since amortisation implies that reserve centres will liquidate their currency by transferring SDRs to the Account, the rate of liquidation will largely depend on the rate at which SDRs are being accumulated by reserve countries through balance-of-payments surpluses or new allocations. If SDRs constituted an international medium of exchange, the connection between a BoP surplus and the acquisition of SDRs would be straightforward. By running surpluses, reserve centres would earn the SDRs required to liquidate their currencies. Under the present system, however, users first have to swap their SDRs into foreign exchange. Thus, under the aforementioned plan, a developing country receiving additional SDRs would use them by swapping them for foreign exchange. If the SDRs were swapped for (say) dollars, the countries supplying the dollars would experience a change in the composition of their reserves: dollar holdings would fall and SDR holdings would rise. The developing country receiving the dollars might then use the dollars acquired to buy goods from the US. In this case the US would run the surplus that would be the counterpart to the deficit in the developing country; although the total quantity of externally held dollar liabilities would fall, the total quantity of international reserves would remain constant. The improvement in the balance of payments of reserve centres could be guaranteed by tying the expenditure associated with additional SDR allocations to purchases from the relevant reserve centre, though clearly this would tend to reduce the quality of the aid enjoyed by the recipients of the SDRs.

A reduction in the quantity of reseve currencies in the international financial system could, however, occur independently of the state of the balance of payments in reserve centres. First, reserve centres could be requested to exchange a proportion of their accumulated SDRs for the Account's holding of currency. Second, a proportion of future normal SDR allocations could be set aside to cover currency amortisation. Third, the IMF could call upon reserve centres to receive the additional SDRs from developing countries and to provide the necessary foreign exchange. Under any one of these schemes the quantity of reserve assets held by the reserve currency countries would fall at the same time as the fall in the quantity of reserve currencies.

While a Substitution Account which incorporates reserve currency amortisation offers the most convenient way of engineering an extra financial flow to developing countries, a similar result could be achieved even under versions of the Account which do not involve amortisation. Under one such scheme reserve currency countries would be required to pay in the form of SDRs a rate of interest on the Account's stock of their currency in excess of the rate of interest that would be paid to holders of the SDRs issued by the Account. The effect of this interest rate differential would be to reduce the total quantity of SDRs in the system. To restore the quantity of SDRs to its previous level, a special allocation of SDRs could then be made to developing countries.[6]

2.1 Estimating the financial flows to developing countries

Taking first of all the version of the Substitution Account that involves amortisation, we see that the size of the related financial flows to developing countries (F) depends on the amount of externally held reserve currencies (E), the proportion of these externally held currencies that countries wished or were required to retain (t), and the intended life span of the Account (L). Thus

$$F = \frac{E - tE}{L} \tag{9.1}$$

If we concentrate on dollars and use the following illustrative figures, $E = \$200$ billion, $t = 0.25$, and $L = 50$ years, the annual flow to developing countries would be \$3 billion. Table 9.1 illustrates the way in which the size of the flow would vary as the values of L and t vary. If interest payments made to the Account exceeded those made by the Account, international reserves would fall unless additional SDRs were created, and in these circumstances the financial flow to developing countries would tend to be larger. Over time, however, the size of flow would fall, as interest payments by the Account rose and as receipts fell, in line with the increasing stock of SDRs issued and the declining stock of currencies held respectively.

Under the version of the Account which involves an interest rate differential, the size of the financial flow depends on the Account's stock of currencies $(E - tE)$ and the size of the differential between the interest paid by reserve centres (r^c) and that paid by the Account to depositors (r^d). Thus

$$F = (r^c - r^d) \cdot (E - tE). \tag{9.2}$$

Assuming that reserve centres agree to pay a rate of interest, which is 10 per cent higher than that paid to depositors, then with the following illustrative figures, $E = \$200$ billion, $t = 0.25$, $r^c = 11$ per

TABLE 9.1 *Financial flows to developing countries from an aid-augmented Substitution Account, assuming reserve currency amortisation ($ billion)*

E	t	K	F
200	0.25	50	3.0
200	0.25	40	3.75
200	0.25	30	5.0
200	0.25	25	6.0
200	0.25	20	7.5
200	0.25	15	10.0
200	0.25	10	15.0
200	0.50	50	2.0
200	0.40	50	2.4
200	0.30	50	2.8
200	0.20	50	3.2
200	0.10	50	3.6
200	0.50	25	4.0
200	0.40	25	4.8
200	0.30	25	5.6
200	0.25	25	6.0
200	0.20	25	6.4
200	0.10	25	7.2

For definition of terms, see text.

cent, and $r^d = 10$ per cent, the financial flow to developing countries would be $1.5 billion.

On the basis of the assumptions made, Table 9.2 suggests that the financial flow would rise gradually over the first ten years of the scheme and level off thereafter.

A question that now arises is whether the reserve centres would have the required capacity to meet the annual amortisation and/or interest payments (A) that are implied by the financial flows estimated earlier. These would not be able to exceed the sum of current account balance-of-payments surpluses (B), net capital inflows (C), annual SDR allocations received (S), and the annual reduction in the cumulated stock of SDRs (R/L), thus:

$$F \leq A, \tag{9.3}$$

and

$$A \leq B + C + S + R/L \tag{9.4}$$

Applying this formula to US data, confirms that there should be little difficulty in meeting the obligations that would be imposed by amortisation. However, this conclusion rests heavily on the value of S that is assumed. In the estimation made earlier the value attributed to

TABLE 9.2 *Financial flows to developing countries from an aid-augmented Substitution Account involving interest-rate differentials ($ billion)*

	(1)	(2)	(3)	(4) (1) × (2)	(5) (1) × (3)	(6) (4) − (5)
Year 1	15	11/100	10/100	1.65	1.5	0.15
Year 2	30	11/100	10/100	3.30	3.0	0.30
Year 3	45	11/100	10/100	4.95	4.5	0.45
Year 4	60	11/100	10/100	6.60	6.0	0.60
Year 5	75	11/100	10/100	8.25	7.5	0.75
Year 6	90	11/100	10/100	9.90	9.0	0.90
Year 7	105	11/100	10/100	11.55	10.5	1.05
Year 8	120	11/100	10/100	13.20	12.0	1.20
Year 9	135	11/100	· 10/100	14.85	13.5	1.35
Year 10	150	11/100	10/100	16.5	15.0	1.50
Year 11	150	11/100	10/100	16.5	15.0	1.50

Column (1): Stock of reserve currencies held and SDRs issued by the Substitution Account.
Column (2): The rate of interest paid by reserve currency countries to the Substitution Account on its holdings of their currency.
Column (3): The rate of interest paid by the Account on SDRs issued by it.
Column (4): Interest payments by reserve currency countries to the Account.
Column (5): Interest payments by the Account to holders of the SDRs issued by it.
Column (6): Financial flow to developing countries in the form of linked SDRs.

S is based on the assumptions that, first, the annual rate of growth of international reserves is 10 per cent, second, reserve growth is met exclusively by additional SDRs, and, third, the US retains its current cumulative share in new SDR emissions. If instead of this the 1979 allocation of SDRs is taken as an indicator of future allocations, then the value of A falls to $2.2 billion, $0.8 billion below the estimated financial flow associated with the scheme involving amortisation. In this case the capacity of the US to meet amortisation and interest payments would present an effective constraint on the size of financial flows. In the version of the Account involving an interest rate differential, however, the capacity of reserve centres to meet their obligations would not seem to constitute a problem.

3. GOLD DEMONETISATION AND FINANCIAL FLOWS TO DEVELOPING COUNTRIES

The objective of making the SDR the principal reserve asset in the international monetary system not only implies a reduced role for reserve currencies but also a reduced role for and perhaps the eventual demonetisation of gold. This could be aided by the activities of a Substitution Account, which could also within the context of gold demonetisation be used to enhance the flow of resources to developing countries. The basic mechanism by which the Gold Account would operate would be similar to that involved with reserve currencies. Broadly speaking, gold would be exchanged for SDRs through the Substitution Account. The implications of such a substitution for the total quantity of reserves depends on the SDR price paid for the gold deposited and the price at which gold is valued for the purpose of calculating reserves. Clearly, if gold is valued for reserve purposes at its now defunct, relatively low, official price, and the Substitution Account pays the market price, then the effect of the substitution will be to raise the level of international reserves. Where, however, reserve gold is valued at the market price, then an increase in reserves would only occur if the Account were to pay a price above the market one. If the Account paid the market price for the gold deposited, the effect on total reserves would be zero, whereas if the Account paid a price below the market one, the effect would be to reduce total reserves. In this latter case an additional allocation of SDRs could be made to developing countries in order to make good the shortfall in reserves.

Many similar problems occur with the substitution of gold as do with the substitution of reserve currencies. Central amongst these is whether the scheme is to be mandatory or voluntary. With a voluntary scheme, the need to provide an incentive for central banks to substitute SDRs for gold through offering a sufficiently high price would limit, if not rule out, the possibility of inducing an additional flow of resources to developing countries. Compulsory schemes do, however, offer such an opportunity, even though they may prove correspondingly less acceptable.

One such scheme would require central banks to deposit a proportion of their holdings of gold with a Substitution Account in exchange for SDRs, receiving an initial price below the market price but above the old official price. Payment would be made on an instalment basis, with depositors receiving only the first instalment immediately upon substitution. The Account would gradually acquire most if not all of the monetary gold within the international monetary system and would gradually sell it off for commercial use, with the pattern of sales being determined by the state of the private market rather than by some predetermined time schedule. The profit made by the Account as a result of these activities, i.e. the difference between the first instalment paid for the gold and the price received for it on the open market, could then be distributed between the depositing country by way of the final instalment and developing countries. Those developing countries that deposited gold with the Account could receive a larger share of the profit than would developed-country depositors.

The size of the financial flow to developing countries (F) would depend on the quantity of gold affected by the scheme (G), the difference between the market price of gold (MP) and the purchase price adopted by the Account (PP) which could move in fixed relation to the market price, and the proportion of the profits directed towards developing countries (Z), thus:

$$F = G(MP - PP)Z \tag{9.5}$$

Assuming the following illustrative values: G = 1,000 million oz, MP = SDR200/oz, PP = SDR100/oz, and Z = 0.5, the accumulated flow of finance to developing countries would be SDR50 billion. The process of demonetising gold in this way would in practice have to be spread over a number of years, not least to protect the market price of gold and thereby the size of financial flows to developing countries.

In this context a key question relates to the extent to which the present historically high price of gold is essentially a speculative price which depends on gold's monetary role. Certainly expectations that the rise in price will be greater than the opportunity cost of holding gold will encourage speculators to increase demand and thereby bid up the actual price. If a scheme of demonetisation and gold substitution were to be announced, speculation could equally cause a self-fulfilling fall in price. However, assuming gold is valued at its market price for the purpose of calculating reserves and provided the Gold Account receives a price above the one it pays, the scheme would provide scope for directing additional financial flows to developing countries without raising the total value of reserves.

For the Gold Account to maximise its profits, it would clearly need to maximise this difference between the selling and buying price. Implied by this might well be a rather prolonged selling programme. As soon as the time dimension enters the analysis, future profits need to be discounted and the object of the Account becomes that of maximising the discounted present value of the profits from gold substitution.[7] It follows that from the point of view of maximising the benefit of the scheme to developing countries much would depend on the price elasticity of demand for commercial gold and on the discount rate that developing countries apply to those resources generated in the future. With a low price elasticity and a low discount rate, developing countries will tend to favour a relatively slow rate of demonetisation, whilst with a high price elasticity and a high discount rate a more rapid rate of demonetisation will tend to be favoured.

Assuming that the stock of gold held by monetary authorities is substituted for SDRs at an annual rate of 2 per cent, and that the Account sells the gold at the same rate then, on the basis of the figures used earlier, the annual financial flow to developing countries over a fifty-year life span would be SDR1 billion.

4. DEVELOPING COUNTRY ATTITUDES TO RESERVE ASSET SUBSTITUTION

The long term objective of a substitution account is, as stated above, that of improving the structural operation of the international monetary system by replacing reserve currencies, and perhaps also gold, with SDRs. In this way, the account would make a contribution toward establishing the SDR as the principal international reserve asset and would not only help in bringing the quantity of international reserves under more central and purposeful control but would also help in eradicating instabilities generated by central banks that switch the composition of their reserves.

From this definition it might be anticipated that developing countries would be strongly in favour of such an account, since they would benefit both from increased exchange-rate stability and from the possibility of adapting an SDR system in order to include a link. Clearly, the establishment of a link will be of little benefit to developing countries unless the creation of SDRs occurs at frequent intervals and in substantial amounts. From the viewpoint of the developing countries, what is needed is a system in which the incremental demand for reserves is met by an additional supply of SDRs. The link and the proposed substitution account therefore seem to be complementary. While a link establishes a structural connection between the creation of SDRs and the provision of financial flows to developing countries, a substitution account attempts to ensure some structural connection between reserve growth and SDR creation. Both of these connections are needed if reserve growth is to lead to more financing for developing countries.[8] It is not surprising, then, that the reservations of developing countries during recent discussions about the establishment of a substitution account have related primarily to the specifics of the actual account proposed rather than to the general principle of substitution.

Criticisms of a substitution account by developing countries have related to the following factors:[9]

(a) its effect on the SDR,
(b) its effect on the process of international adjustment and the distribution of the adjustment burden,
(c) its effect on exchange-rate instability and the management of global liquidity,
(d) its effect on developing countries as holders of reserves, and
(e) its financial arrangements.

4.1 Effect on the SDR

The concern of developing countries in this context has two dimensions: first, that the issuance by a substitution account of a viable and high-yielding SDR-denominated asset may damage the prospects that the SDR will become the international monetary system's principal reserve asset; and, second, that the existence of a competitive rate of interest on assets issued by the account will raise the rate of interest on SDRs and thereby the charges on the use of Fund resources in general. Indeed, this second concern has been presented as perhaps the major deterrent to the support of a substitution account by the developing countries (UNCTAD, 1972). However, given the increase in the rate of interest on SDRs, this is no longer a valid objection. Attention of developing countries should perhaps now be more appropriately focused on ways in which an SDR system based on competitive interest rates may be used or adapted to direct financial flows to them and on ways in which the concessionary element of such flows may be raised for the low-income countries. As described earlier in this chapter, one method would involve charging reserve centres a higher rate of interest on the account's holdings of their currency than is paid to depositors, using the differential for development financing.

4.2 Effect on international adjustment

In principle, a substitution account provides an opportunity for encouraging reserve currency countries to adjust their balance of payments. This may be achieved by requiring such countries, particularly the United States, to amortise the account's holdings of their currencies over time by buying back previously issued liabilities with SDRs that have been either allocated to them or earned through the net exportation of real resources. Amortisation was a constituent element of versions of the substitution account discussed by the Committee of Twenty, but it was abandoned in later versions, which, as a result, were seen by developing countries as having the prime objective of supporting the US dollar. As noted earlier, it is a central part of the criticism by developing countries of the postwar international financial system that there have been asymmetrical pressures on countries to adjust, with the non-reserve currency deficit countries carrying a relatively large proportion of the burden.

As illustrated earlier in this chapter, amortisation of reserve currencies also provides an opportunity to introduce a version of the link that does not rely on net additions to international reserves or that permits the additional financial flow to developing countries to exceed any overall increase in the quantity of international reserves, as dollars held outside the United States, where they are counted as reserves, are returned to the United States, where they are not so counted. Indeed, without this compensating increase in linked SDRs, developing countries as a group could easily lose from the world deflationary impact of balance-of-payments correction in the United States. Individually, developing countries might still lose, even with a compensating link, if the distribution formula for SDRs differs from the pattern of US imports among developing countries. From the point of view of the world demand for their exports, developing countries might therefore be expected to prefer redistribution of the adjustment burden to take the form of expansionary policies in surplus countries rather than deflationary policies in the United States. In view of this, it is only by moving toward an asset settlement system based on SDRs, and away from a liability system that relies on deficits in the United States for additional reserves, that developing countries will be able to gain a larger share of the benefits from reserve creation.

4.3 Effect on exchange-rate stability and global liquidity management

The concern of developing countries is that a substitution account will do little to help stabilise exchange rates through a reduction in the incidence of currency switching, since it will convert only the relatively involatile currency holdings of central banks, and not the more volatile privately held balances.

With regard to the management of global liquidity, it has been argued (Kadam, 1979) that the account will create reserves simply as a reflex to the reserves already created by individual national authorities and will do nothing to induce the more democratic control of reserve creation from which developing countries stand a chance of benefiting. In a narrow sense this is true but, as implied earlier, the consolidation of reserve currencies that a substitution account would involve may be seen as a first step toward an SDR system based on asset settlement and could therefore eventually lead to the better management of global liquidity.

4.4 Developing countries as holders of reserves

Concern has been expressed that developing countries could lose from the introduction of a substitution account in their role as holders of reserves. This could be brought about if a market in SDR-denominated assets failed to develop, if such assets had a low degree of usefulness, if they carried a low rate of interest relative to that available in the Eurocurrency market, where a number of developing countries have placed reserves, or if the possible sterilisation of reserves forced developing countries to turn to the Eurocurrency market for funds at a time when it was both difficult and expensive to borrow from that market. The conclusion is that developing countries might prefer to hold their reserves in the form of dollars rather than in SDR-denominated assets.

Of course, if participation in the account were to be voluntary, there would be no reason for developing countries to convert dollars into SDRs unless they considered this to be to their own advantage. On the other hand, voluntary participation may be less effective for bringing about a move toward establishing the SDR as the principal reserve asset, and developing countries may thus benefit from a higher degree of compulsion. With a compulsory substitution account, developing countries would simply have to regard the loss of freedom with respect to reserve management as a price they have to pay. The question, then, is not so much a matter of whether there are costs but rather whether these exceed the benefits. For the majority of developing countries this is unlikely to be the case, although it may well be, at least initially, for those richer developing countries with significant reserve holdings and Eurocurrency deposits that would be by-passed as recipients of SDRs in some versions of the link. To argue that developing countries as a group benefit more from the free operation of the Eurocurrency market and from a largely unmanaged international financial system[10] ignores the position of a large number of them, in particular the low-income countries, that have few dealings with the private market. Again, however, it seems that developing countries will not have an unambiguous view.

4.5 Financial arrangements of the account

As already noted, the financial arrangements of the substitution account could exert an influence over the total quantity of reserves – and this could be significant for developing countries.

A more specific concern of developing countries in the discussions about a substitution account in the early 1980s was over the proposal that the Fund's gold should be used to provide backing for it and to guarantee its financial viability. Developing countries, not surprisingly, viewed this suggestion as being inconsistent with the whole concept of the Trust Fund and saw it as implying a 'reverse link'. In conjunction with their view that the version of the account then being discussed made the United States the principal beneficiary, the use of the Fund's gold to support the account rather than to provide concessional assistance for the poorer developing countries was particularly unacceptable.

Since the general objectives of a substitution account, as presented at the beginning of this section, are to the advantage of developing countries and since the account could be organised so as to be of direct benefit to developing countries in terms of generating additional financial inflows, it is not in their interests to resist all attempts to introduce such an account but to argue for a version of the account that directs at least a share of the direct benefits to them.

5. RECENT POLICY ON GOLD AND IMPLICATIONS FOR DEVELOPING COUNTRIES

A central problem with all reforms that try to use the operation of the international monetary system for the benefit of developing countries is that changes that are technically feasible may not be acceptable in practice to industrial countries, whose compliance under existing institutional arrangements is necessary for their activation. The potential conflict between what is equitable and what is acceptable is highlighted by what happened with respect to gold during the 1970s. Events in this sphere of international finance have also clearly shown how the stated intentions of the Fund and the aspirations of its developing member countries may be frustrated in what are largely unforeseen ways. Since the Jamaican Accord of 1976, a stated objective of international monetary reform has been to reduce the monetary role of gold – an objective that developing countries have seen as in their own interests. In an attempt to help realise this objective, the Fund abandoned the official price of gold and undertook to dispose of a third of its gold stock. It was agreed that 25 million ounces of gold would be sold back to Fund members in proportion to their quotas at a price of SDR 35 an ounce and that a further 25 million ounces would be sold at a series of public auctions over a period of four years, with the profits going to a Trust Fund that would make disbursements on concessional terms to eligible developing countries, essentially the poorer developing countries. Thus, developing countries scored an apparently significant advance, inasmuch as an element of international monetary reform became structurally related to the provision of additional financial assistance to developing countries. There is no doubt that the Trust Fund has provided eligible countries with both an absolute and relatively important source of low-conditionality financing. However, neither can there be doubt that developing countries have actually lost as a result of the abandonment of the official gold price and the dramatic increase in the market price of gold that this change probably facilitated. Furthermore, to the extent that concern over the future stability and form of the international monetary system has caused the demand for gold and therefore its price to rise, the failure to restore confidence in the system and to find credible solutions to international financial problems has acted against the interests of developing countries. Inasmuch as the instabilities of the 1970s were a reflection of the rise in the price of oil, non-oil developing countries have been affected by this phenomenon twice over.

The general move toward revaluing reserve gold at its market price has meant that countries have experienced an increase in their reserves in proportion to their gold holdings. Such revaluation has generated both a wealth effect, in the form of potential resource transfers, and a liquidity effect. As regards the wealth effect, the prime beneficiaries have been the gold-holding and gold-producing countries. It has been estimated that 90 per cent of reserve asset gold is held by industrial countries, with five of them holding more gold individually than all the non-oil developing countries together. It has also been estimated that the net gain for industrial countries from gold revaluation during the 1970s was well in excess of $400 billion, compared with under $30 billion for non-oil developing countries.[11] The inequitable distribution of the gains from the sale of gold by the Fund is further emphasised if they are calculated on a per capita basis and if allowance is made for the fact that a large proportion of the gold that developing countries hold as a group is held by India and Afghanistan.

The liquidity effect of the revaluation of gold has been to prevent any de facto demonetisation of gold. To the contrary, with gold valued at its market price, it reasserts itself as the principal reserve asset and as the major source of reserve growth during the 1970s. Far from there being a move toward the greater control of reserves as envisaged in the Second Amendment of the Fund's Articles, the aggregate value of reserves depends to a very significant degree on the vagaries of the gold price, which at best is likely to be only loosely related to the requirements of the system for international liquidity. Some insight into the significance of these changes for developing countries may be gained by calculating how much more the reserves of developing countries would have risen if the aggregate reserve growth during the 1970s had been brought about through the creation of SDRs. The answer seems to be about $100 billion. Reserve growth through gold revaluation, as opposed to SDR creation, is clearly to the relative advantage of industrial countries (and, in particular, the major gold-holders among them) and to the relative disadvantage of developing countries.

The neutrality of reserve growth, so much a theme of the case against the link, has not been achieved in recent years, and the potential resource transfer has been in favour of the wealthiest industrial countries. Developing countries may therefore express legitimate interest in proposals designed to redirect this potential resource transfer. Technically there are a number of ways for achieving this. One, as outlined above, would be through a gold substitution account. A second would be to impose some form of tax on the windfall profits of gold-holders. A perhaps more realistic proposal would be to use the remaining stock of gold held by the Fund to provide financing for developing countries.[12] This general notion itself incorporates a number of possibilities, and developing countries may disagree among themselves over the most appropriate arrangements by which the transfer would be achieved.

The financing could, for example, be used to enable the Fund to expand its activities or to widen them by introducing new lending facilities or by changing the conditions under which resources are lent. Alternatively, it could be used to subsidise interest payments or to provide some kind of guarantee fund to support commercial lending to developing countries. As regards the provision of subsidies, the views of individual developing countries would no doubt depend on whether they would be eligible for them or not. Low-income countries might prefer this variant, compared with a guarantee fund that they might feel would not be of principal benefit to them unless the guarantees were to be offered only on their commercial borrowing. At the same time, countries that had previously had access to private financing without a guarantee might also be apprehensive about the effects that a guarantee system would have on their relative creditworthiness.

The financing could, of course, be channelled directly and unconditionally to developing countries according to some distribution formula. Again, the views of individual developing countries would depend heavily on the formula adopted – whether, for example, it was related to Fund quotas or to some other measure of need. Another option would be to distribute the financing through international development agencies, such as the World Bank or regional development banks. Again, the attitudes of individual countries would depend on their potential access to such institutions. Countries that preferred programme aid rather than project aid or that did not feel able to meet commercial interest rates might, for example, be opposed to distribution through the World Bank.

However, there is another problem. If the Fund sold its stock of gold, a further appreciation in the price of gold could again confer greater benefits on the purchasers of gold – almost certainly the industrial countries – than on the developing countries. This implies either that some form of international capital gains tax would be needed or that the Fund should use its stock of gold only as collateral for raising loans from private capital markets. In this case, however, the low-income and less creditworthy countries may feel that they would be excluded from the additional commercial financing that would result.

6. CONCLUDING REMARKS

This chapter has endeavoured to examine the potential role of a Substitution Account within the IMF. The long-term objective of such an Account is to improve the structural operation of the international monetary system by replacing reserve currencies, and perhaps also gold, with SDRs. Problems are created by having domestic currencies doubling as reserve assets and the Substitution Account aims to help overcome these.

The Substitution Account may also be used to encourage additional financial flows to LDCs. Although other mechanisms exist within the context of international monetary reform that would also achieve this end, the Substitution Account offers what is in certain ways a logical first step. If and when a system which is based on the SDR has been established, the role of the Substitution Account might be superseded by more conventional schemes which aim to link the creation of SDRs with the provision of finance to developing countries. The removal of reserve currencies and gold from international monetary reserves would mean that any increase in the demand for international reserves would have to be met through extra allocations of SDRs and the SDR-aid link would establish a structural connection between reserve growth and financial flows to developing countries (see Chapter 10).

The distribution of the costs and benefits associated with the Substitution Account differ with the different versions that might be operated. Thus a version which does not incorporate amortisation grants an apparently high proportion of the benefits to reserve centres, since they would gain from the funding of their short-term externally held liabilities. Developing countries have been suspicious of the motivation behind the advocacy of the Substitution Account, feeling that whilst it may well be of direct benefit to others, it will be of little direct benefit to them and may indeed affect them adversely. Instead they have continued to press for the introduction of an

SDR-aid link. The link would, of course, be of far greater significance to them if the SDR could be made the principal reserve asset, and a Substitution Account could offer one way in which this might be encouraged. The question then becomes one of finding a version of the Account which would protect or enhance their interests while still being attractive to reserve currency countries.

From amongst the schemes discussed in this chapter, one based on interest-rate differentials might well be the most generally acceptable. It would involve an additional financial flow to developing countries of reasonable magnitude in the sense of being significant for developing countries but not unacceptably large for reserve currency countries. Depositors might be prepared to accept the rather lower rate of return on SDRs than on reserve currencies, given the greater stability in the value of SDRs as compared with individual currencies. Similarly, reserve currency centres might be prepared to pay for the effective funding and stabilisation of their short-run liabilities. In any case reserve countries already pay market-related interest to official holders of their currencies, and the ability of the international community to alter in a relatively costless fashion the asset characteristics of international reserve assets in the aggregate provides an opportunity to redirect some of these interest payments into international uses such as the alleviation of poverty.

10   The Link

The basic notion behind the SDR link is very straightforward. It is that, since international financial systems confer benefits on the participating countries, decisions need to be consciously or subconsciously made about the distribution of these benefits. The link is a means by which it is intended to distribute a significant proportion of the benefits, or seigniorage, to developing countries. This argument is further endorsed by the claim that historically international financial systems have not involved distributional neutrality and that, in fact, most of the seigniorage has gone to the relatively rich countries in the world. The purpose of the link is to remove this apparent inequity.

However, while the basic idea of the link is clear a more detailed examination reveals a range of problems relating both to equity and efficiency. It is to an investigation of some of these that this chapter is addressed.

1. DIFFERENT LINKS AND DEVELOPING COUNTRY PREFERENCES

Although it is usually described as 'the link', there are in fact numerous versions of the link, which share the basic idea of raising the proportion of any given SDR allocation to developing countries. One set of proposals involves an 'inorganic link', through which developed countries would make voluntary contributions in the form of currencies or SDRs to development agencies or developing countries at the time of each SDR allocation. Some versions of this inorganic link imply that contributions could only be spent in the contributing country. The only difference between an inorganic link and conventional aid is that such a link would be related to the receipt of SDRs. Not surprisingly, then, developing countries may regard any form of inorganic link as inferior to an organic version. The only reason they might support its introduction is that they see it as better than nothing and as standing more chance of being accepted and implemented because it requires no change in the Fund's Articles of Agreement. An inorganic link might be a stepping-stone toward an organic link, which involves a formal connection between the creation of SDRs and the provision of development financing and which requires amendments to the Articles of Agreement.

There are a number of variants of the organic link, including,

(a) an increase in the proportion of SDRs allocated directly to developing countries,
(b) a direct allocation of SDRs to development agencies, and
(c) an agreed contribution of SDRs to development agencies or developing countries by industrial countries.

Version (a) could be based on existing Fund quotas, or it could involve a change in the distribution of quotas in favour of developing countries that would also raise their access to Fund resources in general and their voting rights, or it could involve severing the connection between the distribution of SDRs and Fund quotas. It can be argued that quotas do not provide an appropriate basis on which to distribute linked SDRs. Quotas are supposed to reflect countries' demand for reserves to hold. A principal objective of the link is, however, that SDRs should be spent by developing country recipients. It might be more appropriate therefore to distribute SDRs on the basis of per capita income, reflecting the link's aim of redistributing wealth. Furthermore, the distribution formula could be amended to take more account of balance of payments instability and the costs of adjustment. On both of these criteria, a larger proportion of SDRs would go to developing countries.[1]

Under version (b) development agencies could either exchange the SDRs allocated to them for currencies to be used to finance loans to developing countries or transfer the SDRs to the accounts of countries supplying developmental goods, allowing these recipients to pay exporters in domestic currency. From the point of view of developing countries, a drawback of this version, compared with version (a), is that the additional financing might be tied to projects or might be conditional on the acceptance of specified macroeconomic policy objectives in such a way that the quality of the aid is reduced. The development agencies that were involved could also therefore exert an important influence over the attitudes of developing countries toward version (b) (Helleiner, 1974). For similar reasons, developing countries might be expected to disfavour the intermediation of industrial countries that would be involved in version (c). Clearly, the only reason why any developing country is likely to favour some form of intermediation, as opposed to direct country allocation, is if it stands to receive more SDRs as a result. Since, for any given allocation of SDRs, more for some developing countries means less for others, it is clear that the precise form of link is a potentially contentious issue among developing countries.[2] While they are likely to show a uniform preference for an organic and untied version of the link, beyond that their interests may be expected to diverge.

More recently, two further types of link that have been proposed and discussed within the Fund would integrate the link with the activities of the Fund. Version (d) would involve SDRs being used to provide the financing for some form of subsidy account. Under this version, SDRs could either be directly allocated to such an account, or contributions could be made by initial recipients voluntarily or according to a prearranged formula. The account would then redirect the SDRs at its command to developing countries or only to low-income countries either as grants (in which case contributors would themselves have to retain the obligations associated with the SDRs contributed) or as a line of interest-bearing credit (in which case the developing countries receiving the SDRs would be asked to meet the related interest obligations). In this latter case there would be no 'subsidy' as such, although developing countries would still receive more SDRs than they would under a distribution based on quotas. In many ways this version differs little from versions (b) and (c). One significant difference, however, is that, as proposed, the SDRs would be used by developing countries to help meet Fund charges. In this way version (d) of the link is, to an extent, tied to Fund conditionality and may therefore be less attractive to developing countries, though clearly the idea of subsidised interest rates would appeal to them.

Under version (e) SDRs would either be directly allocated or contributed to a special account, which would use them to support stabilisation programmes approved by the Fund. In effect, developing countries agreeing on a programme with the Fund would gain access to more resources than was previously the case. The SDRs could be used either to expand drawings under existing tranches and facilities or to finance a new Fund lending facility. In one sense, developing countries might find such a scheme attractive, since they would receive more financing for accepting a programme to which they had already agreed in order to secure a Fund stand-by arrangement or extended facility drawing. Version (e) would therefore provide an extra incentive for developing countries to turn to the

Fund. However, there is little doubt that they would prefer a scheme of direct and unconditional allocation to one that involves the intermediation of the Fund, as the appropriateness of the Fund's conditionality for developing countries is in some debate (see Chapter 4). Version (e) would become more attractive to developing countries if the SDRs allocated to them by the special account did not have to be repaid and if the interest rate on their use of the SDRs was subsidised by, for instance, contributors retaining all or part of the related obligations.

2. BENEFITS TO DEVELOPING COUNTRIES FROM A LINK

The total benefits to developing countries from a link depend, first, on the number of SDRs allocated to them, and, second, on the benefits per SDR. From a user's point of view, the benefits vary positively with the social marginal productivity of real resources and inversely with the social discount rate, the interest rate on SDR net use, and the size of any reconstitution requirements. The benefits to users exceed the grant element associated with SDRs to the extent that the excess of the rate of return to real resources over the rate of discount exeeds the commercial interest rate. For countries holding 100 per cent of their cumulative SDR allocation, the benefit from an allocation of SDRs is essentially the liquidity yield on them. For countries making a net acquisition of SDRs while holding a given portfolio of foreign exchange, the marginal liquidity yield is reduced by the real resource cost of earning the additional SDRs. While a high rate of interest on SDRs favours countries acquiring them, a low rate of interest favours net users. Only a handful of developing countries have held their entire cumulative allocation of SDRs, and even fewer have actually acquired them. The vast majority have been net users and for this reason have benefited in the past from the relatively low rate of interest on SDRs.

While there are a number of difficulties involved in imputing real resource flows from data on net use and acquisition, attempts to estimate the effect of the unlinked SDR scheme on real resource transfers strongly suggest that the initial flow of real resources has been toward developing countries, implying that an 'informal link' has operated.[3] Since the potential permanent real resource inflow available to net users of SDRs rises as the reconstitution requirement diminishes and falls as the rate of interest on SDRs rises, it might be expected that developing countries have a somewhat ambivalent view on changes in regard to the SDR that have lowered the reconstitution requirement from 30 per cent to 15 per cent and then to zero and at the same time raised the interest rate from 60 per cent of the combined market rate to 80 per cent and, from 1981, to 100 per cent. In fact, in terms of short-run potential real resource inflows, developing countries have probably gained more from the abrogation of the reconstitution requirement than they have lost from the interest rate increase. However, in the medium to long term this situation will be reversed.[4]

The benefits to developing countries from SDRs, however, are considerably greater than figures on resource flows suggest, since such flows fail to take into account either the marginal productivity of the resources received, which may be particularly high in the case of developmental imports, or the fact that significant benefits are derived from holding SDRs, as well as from spending them.[5] Furthermore, developing countries may have benefited indirectly from SDR allocations to industrial countries through induced policy changes in the recipient countries, which may have resulted in an increased capacity for developing countries both to earn foreign exchange by exporting to industrial countries and to acquire it through increased investment in and aid to developing countries by industrial countries.

While the introduction of a formal link would increase the direct benefits to developing countries, it would reduce or remove this indirect benefit.[6] The problem here is one of quantification. Certainly, the indirect benefit to developing countries has not been immediately apparent following allocations of SDRs in the early 1980s.

Also difficult to quantify is the extent to which conventional aid is likely to be seen by donors as being independent of the link. If aid donors regard the link as a substitute for other forms of aid, developing countries may lose overall from its introduction. Certainly if, as seems likely, the distribution of linked aid is different from that of conventional aid, the pattern of overall aid disbursment will change as a result of introducing the link and the change may well be regressive. However, the quantity of aid is not the whole story; a link may still be advantageous from the viewpoint of developing countries, even if it leads to a small net reduction in overall aid, if at the same time it raises the quality of aid in terms of raising the grant element, modifying conditionality, and relaxing the associated tying arrangements. Because the increase in the rate of interest clearly emerges as having reduced the benefit of SDRs to developing country users, an important question is whether this increase was necessary and whether it was in their interests in other ways.

3. THE CASE FOR A MARKET-EQUIVALENT INTEREST RATE

From the viewpoint of the efficiency of the international monetary system, there is a strong case for SDRs to carry a market-equivalent interest rate. This stems from the theory of the optimum quantity of money. Applied to SDRs, the argument runs as follows.[7] The optimum stock of SDRs is reached when their marginal benefit in the form of the liquidity yield equals their marginal cost of production. As the latter is almost zero, SDRs should be created up to a point where the marginal liquidity yield is also almost zero. The international community will benefit from having such an optimum stock of SDRs in terms of the balance of payments strategies permitted, which will involve more financing, a slower rate of adjustment, and a lower welfare cost in terms of lost output and unemployment. To encourage this optimum stock of SDRs to be held over the long run, however, the opportunity cost of holding SDRs needs to be reduced to practically zero. This reduction may be achieved by paying a rate of interest equivalent to the rate of return on other assets. Even though the 'basket' method of SDR valuation makes the capital value of SDRs more stable than that of the individual currencies comprising the basket, central banks will find SDRs an unattractive asset if the rate of interest they carry is significantly below that available on convertible currencies.

The motivation for raising the interest rate on SDRs has clearly been to encourage their acceptance as the principal reserve asset in the international financial system. Developing countries have therefore found themselves in an awkward dilemma. To make the link an effective and significant source of aid, they want SDRs to be the principal source of reserve creation. To ensure this role, SDRs need to carry a commercial interest rate. But a commercial interest rate seems to lower the grant element on SDRs to zero and means that the seigniorage goes to holders of SDRs in proportion to their holdings, rather than to net users.

Some antagonists have, in any case, criticised the objective of non-neutrality as embodied in the link. Indeed, as originally established, the SDR was intended to be neutral with respect to resource transfers. To this end, as noted earlier, SDRs are allocated on the basis of Fund quotas that are assumed to reflect countries' long-run demand for reserves to hold. The real resource flows that have actually taken place were, therefore, not an intentional part of the SDR scheme. Moving over to a 'market' method (Grubel, 1972) of allocating seigniorage will reduce the size of the informal link, and the majority of the developing countries will lose.

Support for neutrality is based on two arguments: first, that the existing distribution of resources throughout the world is acceptable, or indeed optimal (largely a normative issue); second, that it is inappropriate to induce real resource transfers through international monetary reform. This argument is valid only to the extent that the inclusion of a link in SDR allocation imposes costs in terms of inefficiency. Raising the interest rate to a commercial level would seem to defend the SDR's integrity, while by encouraging recipients to hold their allocations it would seem to nullify any inflationary repercussions. So where does this leave the developing countries?

If it is accepted that efficiency dictates a commercial interest rate, the question immediately arises as to whether this is completely inconsistent with any form of SDR link.

3.1 The link and market interest rates

Although a competitive SDR interest rate certainly reduces the benefits of the link to net users, it is invalid to conclude as a result that these benefits fall to zero. First, most of the developing countries that are able to raise commercial credit must pay a rate above the combined market rate used for calculating the rate of interest on SDRs (in percentage terms, as much as 15 per cent higher). Furthermore, the rate on SDRs represents a weighted average of rates across countries, and these may be subject to considerable disparity. To a certain extent, then, the grant element on SDRs depends on the currency in which commercial borrowing would otherwise have been undertaken.[8] These two factors combine to suggest that SDRs may continue to incorporate a significant grant element for developing countries, even with a so-called market-equivalent interest rate.

Second, some developing countries find it impossible to borrow even at commercial interest rates; these countries face an availability constraint. The allocation of SDRs to them, even at a commercial interest rate, will help to overcome this. Indeed, to the extent that capital market imperfections prevent resources from moving to where their marginal productivity is highest (in developing countries?), the link serves to raise international economic efficiency by encouraging world output to rise.

Third, from a theoretical point of view, it is the interest rate on the marginal acquisition of SDRs that needs to be at a commercial level. In terms of efficiency there is no reason why the rate paid by developing country users should not be subsidised, thereby raising the grant element. The problem here is the practical one of how the subsidy would be financed. In principle, financing could be arranged by transfer of SDRs from industrial countries to developing countries, with the former retaining the interest obligations, or by allocation of additional SDRs to developing countries in perpetuity, or by a charge imposed by the Special Drawing Rights Department of the Fund at a lower rate for developing countries on their net use than the rate paid to countries acquiring SDRs.[9]

Finally, aside from the interest rate on them, SDRs are a form of unconditional credit; they involve no fixed repayment schedule and require no statement of need by users. Developing countries, wary of borrowing from the Fund because of the conditionality, may find SDRs very attractive. Furthermore, since net users only have to pay interest and do not have to repay capital, in the short run payments on SDR net use therefore tend to be lower than they would be for an equivalent commercial loan.[10] On the other hand, developing countries are concerned that an increasing interest rate on SDRs brings with it an increase in general Fund charges. There is also the possibility that a higher rate may induce a greater reluctance on the part of surplus countries to adjust by spending reserves. In each of these cases a higher interest rate on SDRs imposes costs on developing countries.

Based on a comparison between the interest rate on SDR net use and on what LDCs would have to pay to attract funds from the banks, Bird (1981) calculates that many of them would continue to receive an aid content of 33–43 per cent from linked SDRs involving a market related rate. With a subsidy on interest payments, the aid content can clearly be raised still higher. It is of course difficult to quantify the aid content of relaxing the availability constraint or of removing conditionality, but recipients would no doubt regard these as significant.

4. ARGUMENTS FOR AND AGAINST THE LINK

The relevance of particular arguments for or against the link tend to vary with the type of link being discussed. For instance, some arguments relevant to a link which allocates SDRs directly to LDCs might not apply, or would apply with less force, to a link which allocates SDRs indirectly to LDCs through the intermediation of a development agency. Having acknowledged this factor, however, it is possible to draw up a list of facets of the link which have generally been suggested as being either favourable or unfavourable.

4.1 Arguments in favour of the link

First, the link provides a mechanism through which the international community can organise an increase in the flow of real resources to LDCs. The growth of aid through conventional channels has failed to keep up with the growth of world output and trade, and what aid has been provided has frequently been tied. The link could be so arranged as to supply untied, and perhaps concessionary, multilateral aid, which would tend to expand automatically with world economic growth. An often-stated constraint on the granting of aid by developed countries has been its implications for the balance of payments.

Second, the link could have favourable implications for the balance of payments of developed countries. These countries would earn SDRs through exporting goods and services to LDCs. The cost of the scheme to developed countries would be a real-resource one rather than a balance-of-payments one. Indeed, where developed countries show a preference for earning reserves through surpluses and LDCs show a preference for real resources, the link would indeed be Pareto efficient.

The desire of developed countries to run surpluses will tend to be frustrated if no country or group of countries is prepared to run the implied deficits. If LDCs are prepared to run deficits and an SDR link enables them to finance these deficits, surpluses may be achieved by developed countries without incurring a cost in terms of unemployment. In a situation where the choice is between a linked and an unlinked SDR system, the linked system may have an equivalent beneficial impact on price stability, since with a link in operation developed countries will be forced to earn SDRs. Developed countries wanting extra reserves will thus have to adjust their economies in order to maintain competitiveness.

Third, SDRs are a fiat money, and fiat money gives rise to a social saving. Furthermore, there is the seigniorage associated with reserve creation. Although Pareto efficiency in the international monetary system does not dictate a particular distribution of SDRs, considerations of equity suggest that the social saving and seigniorage should be directed towards poor rather than rich countries.

It is probably fair to conclude that the case in favour of the link hinges fundamentally on the three points raised above, namely, the quantity and quality of aid, the reconciliation of developed countries' trading targets, and the equitable distribution of the social saving and seigniorage. However, the compulsion of the case for the link is not independent of world economic conditions, and is likely to be strongest where developed countries are experiencing difficulties in avoiding both unemployment and balance-of-trade deficits. Deflationary actions taken by individual developed countries in order to improve their balance of payments at the BoP cost of other developed countries may lead to competitive deflations and a rise in the level of unemployment in the developed world as a whole, with little or no change in relative BoP positions. The problem facing developed countries combines two elements: an inadequate level of aggregate demand and an inadequate level of exports relative to imports. In these circumstances the link may provide the solution. Exports represent a component of aggregate demand. An increase in the exports of developed countries would then not only serve to improve the balance-of-payments positions of these countries but would also absorb unutilised capacity. An increase in the exports of developed countries could be brought about by a link, since LDCs with excess SDRs would tend to spend them on imports from developed countries. By means of the link the notional demand in LDCs for the products of developed countries could be made effective, and the unemployment caused in the developed countries by inadequate aggregate demand could thereby be removed. In conditions of unemployment the real-resource cost of the link to developed countries is less apparent; indeed, the opportunity cost of the link to these countries becomes zero. This is because the link itself serves to create an incentive to produce the extra real resources, which are exported. As compared with a situation in which there is no link, developed countries experience a net gain in terms of the employment generated, and may even experience a resource gain through the multiplied increase in aggregate output.[11] In conditions of unemployment, then, there appears to be a fourth argument in favour of the link.

4.2 Arguments against the link

It is suggested by opponents of the link, first, that the link would generate additional inflation. Effectively this argument is based on an international version of the quantity theory of money. A net increase in world aggregate monetary demand with no matching increase in real supply will be reflected in an upward movement in prices. Where aid is expressed in money terms, and the inflation is such that the terms of trade move against the LDCs, then LDCs least of all will benefit from the link.

A second argument is that any aid equivalent gained by LDCs as a result of the link will be offset by reductions in other forms of aid. Third, the allocation of aid would tend to be rather random if SDR creation is related solely to the needs of the international monetary system. This point involves the belief that international money creation and development assistance are independent activities, motivated and determined by different factors, that should not be pursued through the use of one common instrument. The fear appears to be that (from the point of view of the international monetary system) too many or (from the point of view of development) too few SDRs would be created.

Fourth, but leading on from this, it is maintained by critics that the link would distribute the aid burden in an inappropriate way.

A fifth argument against the link is that it would tend to reduce confidence in the SDR as a reserve asset. Other arguments are, sixth, that the link scheme would somehow reduce or remove parliamentary control over the provision of aid, with this exacerbating the threat of inflation; seventh, that balance-of-payments disequilibria between developed countries would be enhanced, as surplus countries would tend to win most of the LDCs' SDR-financed export orders; and, eighth, that the link represents inefficient international monetary reform, inasmuch as the SDR system could be organised in a way which would generate no permanent real-resource transfers. By distributing SDRs in line with countries' long-run demand for reserves to hold, or by charging a competitive rate of interest on SDR use equivalent to the rate of return on real resources, it would be possible to make all countries better off in terms of the liquidity yield from SDRs, and no country worse off in terms of the loss of real resources.

4.3 An assessment of the arguments for and against the link

Space does not permit a full evaluation of all the arguments and counter-arguments which have been raised in discussions over the link. Instead of attempting to present an all-embracing appraisal therefore, this section concentrates on certain broad areas of concern.

4.3.1 Aid

There are a number of aspects of aid over which the SDR link might exert an influence. Crucial amongst these are (i) the total quantity of aid, (ii) the quality of aid, and (iii) the distribution of the benefits and burdens of aid.

Although an *ex-ante* answer to the question of whether additional aid will be generated by the link is impossible, it seems probable that extra aid would result. Linked aid would be multilateral in character and it might be expected that the aid burden would be more evenly spread between donors than is the case with unilateral aid. Additionality might be particularly likely if the link adopted involved direct country allocations. Allocations to a development agency might, to a greater extent, be associated with conventional aid, and might encourage the view amongst donors that agency aid is provided through the international monetary system, thus removing the need for them to make direct contributions.

In any case the amount of aid associated with the link may be relatively small. Over the first basic period of SDR allocation, the overall increase in concessionary aid, even if developed countries had contributed 50 per cent of their allocated SDRs to aid, *ceteris paribus*, would have been little more than 10 per cent. Part of the benefit to LDCs from the link may of course come from the improved quality of aid rather than from an increase in its quantity. The quality of aid generated through the link depends essentially on two factors, namely, (i) whether the aid comes through an agency, and, if so, which agency, and (ii) the rate of interest on SDR net use. Individual

LDCs will tend to value direct allocations more highly than indirect agency allocations.

With regard to the distribution of the benefits, the type of link adopted is very significant. With a system of direct allocations based on IMF quotas, a high percentage of the development assistance associated with the link would go to the relatively well off LDCs. If conventional aid fell as a result of its implementation, then the link could turn out to have a regressive impact on aid. It might be anticipated that the least-developed countries will favour a link which embodies agency allocation and concessionary interest rates. Richer LDCs, on the other hand, will, if they are substantial holders of SDRs, tend to favour a direct link, which incorporates a higher interest rate.

4.3.2 Inflation[12]

The real value of aid could, of course, fall if the link were to cause inflation. Assuming the existence of certain conditions, the theoretical logic of the argument that the link is inflationary cannot be challenged. The necessary conditions are, first, that the linked SDRs which are allocated to LDCs are spent; second, that aggregate real supply does not expand sufficiently to offset the increase in aggregate monetary demand which is financed by the allocation of SDRs; third, that compensatory expenditure-reducing policies which would serve to free the real resources to be transferred to LDCs are not undertaken; and, fourth, that the world economy does not possess spare capacity which may be used to increase real output. But, even assuming that the conditions are met, three further issues are important.

The first of these concerns aid. If the international community agrees that its richer members should provide development assistance to its poorer members, the inflation case against the link rests on the assumption that SDR-linked aid is more inflationary than other forms of aid. The crux of the argument that this is indeed the case relies on the view that conventional aid is visible and is matched at a national level by compensating fiscal actions, whilst SDR-linked aid is less visible and will not be so compensated. The strength of this argument is, however, by no means self-evident.

The second issue concerns the desire to increase the quantity of international liquidity. If it is felt appropriate that liquidity should be expanded, then the significant question is whether the SDR-aid link is a more inflationary mechanism for bringing this expansion about than alternative mechanisms. Three alternative mechanisms may be mentioned: increasing the price of gold, expanding the reserve currency system, and increasing the allocation of unlinked SDRs. Each of these mechanisms might also be inflationary. Indeed, it may be suggested that the link is the least inflationary method of creating extra international reserves. Compared, for instance, with the unlinked SDR scheme, the linked scheme forces developed countries to earn reserves and thus encourages the competitive pursuit of low rates of inflation. Direct, unearned SDR allocations are initially distributed to all participants, irrespective of the state of their domestic economies. The unlinked method of SDR distribution thereby forgoes the opportunity to incorporate an anti-inflationary bias in the initial allocation of reserves.[13] Furthermore, if, in terms of real resources, reserves are more productive in LDCs than in developed countries, from a supply point of view the linked method of SDR allocation may be less inflationary.

The third issue concerns the size of the inflationary threat. This in turn depends on a number of factors, including the size of the SDR emission, the proportion of SDRs that are linked, the propensity of LDCs to spend SDRs, the geographical location of SDR-financed expenditure, the level of employment and capacity utilisation in the countries receiving SDR-financed export orders, and the saving and trading propensities and patterns in these export-order receiving countries, along with the desire of these countries to increase their holdings of international reserves.

To some extent it is possible to estimate the size of the inflationary impetus emanating from the link. This is conventionally done in an *ex-post* fashion by calculating the percentage addition to aggregate demand through extra export demand that would have resulted if various forms of the link had been in operation. Every estimation that has been made shares the common conclusion that the size of the increased demand generated by the link, whatever its precise form, would be very small. Dell (1969), for instance, calculates that, even with an SDR allocation of SDR 5000 million, the addition to demand for output in the OECD countries would be less than 0.3 per cent. Such calculations view the inflationary impact of the link in global terms. For individual surplus developed countries, which, because of their greater competitiveness, might expect to receive most of the extra export demand, the threat of inflation may, at first sight, seem more severe. Once again, however, estimation of the inflationary impact, even allowing for the concentration of expenditure on the exports of these countries, reveals that the threat is insignificant. Cline (1976) estimates that the first-round net impact of a link on export demand (with an SDR emission of SDR 3000 million) would be no more than 0.70 per cent, even in the most competitive economies. It is difficult to see how such a small increase in aggregate demand could generate significant additional inflationary pressure, even assuming that aggregate supply is inelastic. Given the generally small import propensities of the major surplus developed countries, the second-round inflationary impact in other developed countries would be even smaller.

What evidence is available, then, unanimously demonstrates that, although the inflation argument against the link is qualitatively correct, it is quantitatively unimportant.

The evidence is, however, not comprehensive. One concern that has been expressed by opponents of the link is that, once it has been adopted, considerable pressure would be exerted by LDCs to increase the allocation of SDRs beyond the amount required for global liquidity purposes. It may be countered, of course, that developed countries, which bear the real-resource cost of the link, may be reluctant to increase SDR allocations at anything but a fairly moderate rate. The voting requirements of the SDR scheme would seem to ensure that a substantial degree of consensus over the appropriate allocation of SDRs is required before allocations are made. The inflationary threat from this aspect of the link would therefore appear to be somewhat overstated.

4.3.3 Relevance to contemporaneous economic conditions

In conditions where developed countries are experiencing unemployment the inflation argument against the link reappears as an expansion argument in its favour. Similarly, however, many of the arguments mustered to challenge the claim that the link would be inflationary in conditions of full employment may be used to question the view that it would induce expansion in conditions of unemployment. Perhaps the most significant of these is the argument that the actual size of the link would be relatively small. Whilst this point may be valid, the argument that unemployment is temporary whilst the link is permanent is less well founded, since the link could in principle be activated counter-cyclically.[14]

4.3.4 Efficiency and equity

International financial systems may distribute social saving and seigniorage in various ways and to various recipients. Seigniorage under the gold-exchange standard is distributed to gold producers, gold-holders and reserve-currency countries. The only new question raised by the link is that of the optimal distribution of seigniorage. It cannot be denied that distributing financial claims on real resources to LDCs at a cost lower than the value of the real resources to LDCs would help to bring about a more equal distribution of world income. As compared with the GES, LDCs would gain in terms of extra real resources, non reserve-currency countries would neither gain nor lose from the link (although, as compared with the unlinked SDR scheme, they would forgo the opportunity of deriving an unearned increase in reserves), and reserve-currency countries would lose real resources, having to earn reserves instead of gaining real resources by spending internationally acceptable but domestically produced reserves (of course, they would gain to the extent that there are costs as well benefits associated with being the world's banker).[15]

But would the pursuit of greater international equity via the introduction of the link damage the efficiency of international financial arrangements and the chances of efficient reform? An important observation here is that reform depends not on actual costs and benefits but on perceived costs and benefit. If decision-takers perceive the link as being inefficient, they will base decisions on this belief. Indeed, this belief may impede advance in other areas, such as that of endeavouring to establish the SDR as the principal reserve asset.

Having noted that perceptions are very important, economic analysis suggests that there is little reason to feel that the link represents inefficient international financial reform. With market related rates on net use and acquisition, IMF control of SDR creation, and a low risk of default on interest obligations, the integrity of the SDR should not be damaged by the link. Indeed, on the contrary, there are strong reasons for claiming that the link scheme is efficient via its effects on global output, employment and payments disequilibria.

The more relevant worry for LDCs is that, should they succeed in incorporating a link into the SDR scheme, fear of the inflationary effects would mean that SDR allocations would become less likely. LDCs gain nothing from a link which is not activated, and they would lose if SDR allocations that would otherwise have been made are not.

5. CONCLUDING REMARKS

The main strength of the link proposal lies in its objective of assisting LDCs. Its principal rationale is as a wealth redistributive measure. However, many of the arguments both for and against the link are difficult to verify *ex ante*. Examples include the argument that a link will lead to a reduction in other forms of aid and that it will sabotage confidence in the SDR. Where quantification can be attempted, it seems that the implications of the link are uniformly minor. Yet the exact impact of the link significantly depends on its precise nature: for example, on the distribution formula and the rate of interest paid by net users.

Variations of this sort account for the different views about the link among developing countries. Creditworthy NICs stand to gain relatively little from the link, even though they might be expected to prefer receiving extra SDRs to borrowing from private capital markets. The main beneficiaries would tend to be the LICs which do not have access to private finance. Indeed, the more restrictive the list of countries to which linked SDRs are allocated, the more the benefits that these countries might derive. Alternatively, by introducing only a partial link such that (say) LICs received 50 per cent more SDRs than they would expect under the quota formula, the perceived costs of the link could be minimised, since in aggregate terms its impact would be small.

Although the major borrowers will not be indifferent to SDR allocations which increase their reserves and improve their creditworthiness, LICs in particular might therefore be unwise to abandon the notion of a link. However, their representatives and negotiators need to change the perceptions of many industrial countries. From this viewpoint there might be an argument for dropping the name 'the link' and for substituting a new one. More significantly, they need to emphasise the low costs that would be associated with a more restricted scheme for the allocation of supplementary SDRs to LICs. The precedent for treating LICs as a special case has already been set with the Trust Fund and the subsidy accounts.

Another way in which the chances of a link being accepted could be increased would be to consider channelling extra SDRs through the General Account as a form of IMF credit. Via this mechanism, linked SDRs would of course become conditional. A problem here is that IMF credit only goes to countries in balance of payments need. The implied distribution of the associated 'aid' might therefore not be equitable. Furthermore, there would be a related moral hazard problem as countries might be encouraged to pursue policies designed to gain them access to Fund finance. LICs would no doubt prefer unconditional SDRs, and could argue that the theory of the demand for international reserves supports the claim that their reserves are inadequate. Of course they would probably not hold extra SDRs as reserves but rather spend them. Their principal concern is to gain access to greater quantities of international finance, whether in the form of reserves, credit or aid. In this sense the question of the precise nature of the link in terms of reserves versus credit is of secondary significance. LICs' preferences would also depend on the nature of Fund conditionality and whether it was viewed as appropriate (see Chapter 4). Again LIC negotiators need to weigh up what is ideal against what is achievable. It may be better to go for a scheme which yields some benefits and a good chance of being implemented than to stick out for one which, while if adopted would yield greater benefits, at the same time has a much lower chance of being implemented.

11 Private Bank Lending to Developing Countries

Apart from the move to flexible exchange rates, one of the most noticeable aspects of international finance since 1973 has been the changing role of the private international banks. During the 1970s they were central in recycling finance from oil producing countries to the non-oil developing world. However, in the 1980s they became more reluctant to lend and often had to be coerced to do so by central banks and the IMF.

Yet even though their role has aroused much interest and concern, the analysis underlying their activities remains poorly developed.[1] The purpose of this chapter is not to provide a sophisticated model of international bank lending which is then tested against the data. Much less ambitiously, it sets out to provide a very basic theoretical insight into the forces which influence bank lending.

Having discussed the underlying theory, the chapter concludes by identifying weaknesses of international bank lending to developing countries. Proposals for reform are discussed in Chapter 13.

1. EXPLAINING THE PATTERN OF BANK LENDING

There are basically two alternative approaches to explaining the pattern of private international financial flows to developing countries. The first distinguishes between the significance of demand and supply factors. The central question here is whether flows are determined largely by the demands of borrowers, with supply being relatively elastic and responding quite passively to demand; or whether flows are supply-constrained, with borrowers unable to raise additional finance and the banks rationing credit.

In the former case the concept of a foreign exchange constraint is relatively meaningless. Instead, constrained by factors other than the availability of foreign exchange, countries decide on an optimum combination of economic growth and external debt and then simply borrow what they require.

In the latter case the availability of foreign exchange is the binding constraint, with countries modifying their domestic aspirations and policies to be consistent with the quantity of funds that they can attract. Here it is the banks that are active participants, with the borrowers adjusting to whatever volume of finance is provided.

The second approach is closely related to the first, though it differs in emphasis. It focuses instead on whether the flow of funds is rationed through price or in some other way. Is the rate of interest at which countries borrow from the banks the market clearing rate, or is there excess demand at the prevailing interest rate? If loans are not rationed by price, how are they rationed? Moreover, is it rational for banks to ration credit by means other than price? Why should banks be reluctant to do more business at a higher price?

The issues raised above may be illustrated schematically by using a series of diagrams. In Figure 11.1 the banks' supply of funds is shown as being infinitely elastic (S), and they are prepared to supply as much finance at a given interest rate as borrowers are prepared to borrow. In these circumstances it is clearly the demand side of the market (D) that determines the level of business.

Similarly, in Figure 11.2 demand is again the active determinant although now it is assumed that the supply of funds is no longer infinitely elastic. The result is that an increase in the demand for funds leads to an increase both in the rate of interest and in the flow of funds. The rate of interest is here performing a rationing role.

Figure 11.3 illustrates a situation where the supply of funds schedule first becomes completely inelastic and then bends backwards, with the banks supplying less finance as the rate of interest rises. Figure 11.3 has some interesting properties. Depending on the location of demand and supply schedules, it can generate a stable local equilibrium (in the sense that, if disturbed, market forces will encourage the system to return to the initial equilibrium) such as point A, or an unstable one (in the sense that, once disturbed, the system moves away from the initial equilibrium) such as point B. But is it anything other than a diagrammatic quirk that the supply schedule is infinitely inelastic or backward bending, or can this possibility be defended in terms of economic logic? A number of explanations may be offered.

First, let us assume that banks set out to maximise their *expected*

Rate of interest

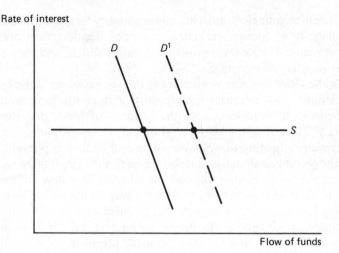

FIGURE 11.1

Rate of interest

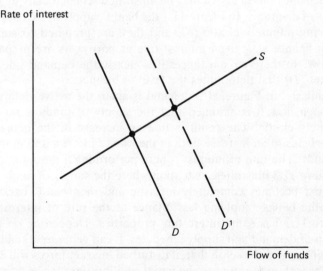

Flow of funds

FIGURE 11.2

profits. This is not an unreasonable assumption, although legitimate questions may be raised about the objectives of banks; are they maximisers or satisficers, and, if the former, what will they set out to maximise? After all, banks have many features of the large multinational companies, for which alternative theories of the firm have been

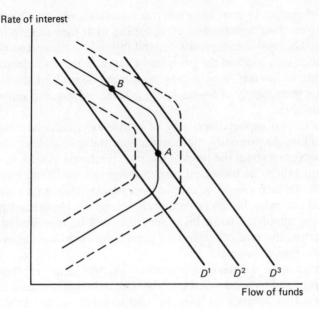

FIGURE 11.3

developed. However, on the assumption of profit maximisation, the lending process will be affected not just by the unit profit on each deal struck and the level of business but also by the probability of the borrower repaying the loan – or, in other words, by the risk of default. If this risk increases significantly as the rate of interest rises, it will be quite rational and quite consistent with their objectives for the banks to *reduce* their supply of loans to this category of borrowers. Given the possibility of default, there is likely to be an interest rate which uniquely maximises the banks' expected returns. If, at this rate, the demand for funds by potential borrowers exceeds the supply of funds made available by the banks, credit will have to be rationed by a non-price means. The interest rate will be a pseudo-equilibrium one in the sense that no market forces would encourage the banks to lend more. Increasing the rate of interest merely raises the banks' perception of the probability of default by increasing the benefits of default to the borrower.[2] The supply of funds will also change if the banks' assessment of the default risk changes for other reasons. Thus, the supply schedule will shift to the right as the perceived risk declines and to the left as it increases.

A second explanation of supply inelasticity follows on from the fact that it is not the rate of interest as such that determines the banks'

234   *International Financial Policy and Development*

rate of profit. An increasing interest rate raises what the banks have to pay on their deposits as well as raising what they receive for their loans. The banks' unit profits depend instead on the spread between the price they pay and the price they charge. If the spread narrows as the rate of interest rises, it may again seem logical for the banks to reduce their supply of loans. There is some evidence to support this relationship.[3]

These two explanations may of course be combined. While the banks may be primarily concerned about the spread, borrowers will be concerned about the level of the rate of interest as well, since they are unlikely to be protected from a rising rate by having equivalent assets. An increase in the rate of interest may then both narrow the spread and raise the risk of default. It emerges as being quite possible that the supply of bank loans schedule will become inelastic with respect to the rate of interest or even bend backwards above some specific rate of interest.

Up to now we have concentrated on the shape of the supply schedule and have assumed that the demand schedule has a 'normal' shape. This assumption may be unwarranted, since, although an increasing interest rate may be expected to encourage risk-averting borrowers to reduce their borrowing and to put more emphasis on correcting their balance of payments deficits, it will increase the size of repayments (interest plus amortisation) on existing debt. Borrowers may need to borrow more in order to finance these payments. In this case the two forces will pull in opposite directions and it may end up that the demand for loans at some point would increase along with the rate of interest. The demand schedule will then have the shape shown in Figure 11.4, and it again becomes possible to encounter an equilibrium that is unstable (point A in Figure 11.4).

2. APPLYING THE ANALYSIS: A SUPPLY AND DEMAND INTERPRETATION OF RECENT BANK LENDING TO DEVELOPING COUNTRIES

The interesting question is whether simple demand and supply analysis may be applied to help explain observed flows of private capital to developing countries in the late 1970s and the early 1980s. Different answers emerge, depending on the way in which interest rates are defined.

For the period 1978–82 there was generally a positive correlation

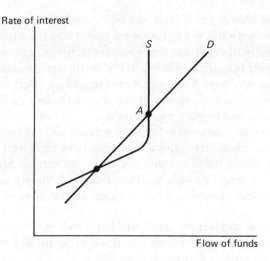

FIGURE 11.4

between nominal interest rates and the flow of private bank loans (apart from 1980–1)[4] and this in turn suggests that demand side factors had the dominant influence in determining international bank lending.[5]

However, care has to be exercised in reaching such a conclusion. What if, as discussed above, the supply of bank lending is more appropriately related to the spread than to the interest rate. If the absolute value of the spread falls as nominal interest rates rise, then the positive correlation noted above may be interpreted as revealing a negative correlation between the 'price' (i.e., spread) and 'quantity' variables, and this would suggest that supply side factors are more important.

Furthermore, it needs to be recognised that, as already stated, the international banks are intermediaries, the volume of funds they can lend is constrained by what they can attract from ultimate lenders, and the supply of deposits is likely to respond positively to the rate of interest. Indeed, this may provide an explanation of why spreads narrow as rates rise, since, following an inflow of deposits, banks compete to make loans and are willing to cut their profit margins in order to increase total profits. Again, in these circumstances there would seem to be supply domination.

But what if it is the *real* rather than the nominal rate of interest which is the more relevant concept? For a time in the early 1980s the correlation between real rates and bank loans was negative or zero. During this period it yet again seems that it was the supply of funds through the banks that was the dominant factor in explaining lending to developing countries rather than the borrowers' demand for funds, though this may have had a significant secondary effect and, indeed, seems to have been of primary importance in the late 1970s when real interest rates and lending rose together.

If the inverse relationship between spreads and the rate of interest relates to nominal rates, and if real rates have increased as nominal rates have fallen, it follows that real rates and spreads are positively related. This would provide further evidence of supply side domination in the determination of international capital flows to developing countries.

A demand and supply configuration which is consistent with a negative relationship between the flows of loans and real interest rates is presented in Figures 11.5 and 11.6. Here it is suggested that during the 1970s and early 1980s both the demand for loans schedule and the supply schedule shifted to the right, but that the supply shift was greater, since, in addition to borrowing, deficit countries decumulated reserves and adjusted to deal with their payments problems. During the later phase after 1981–2, while the demand schedule shifted to the right more gradually, the supply schedule shifted significantly to the left.

Hypothesising of this type raises a number of questions. Let us examine two in particular. First, what determines the demand for and supply of loans, is the real interest rate more relevant than the nominal rate and what factors will cause demand and supply schedules to shift? Second, what about the credit rationing approach, which denies the existence of a conventional market equilibrium solution as an explanation of events in the late 1970s and 1980s? Does this have anything to contribute to our understanding?

The real *ex-post* price of borrowing, reflecting the real resource costs of repayments, depends not only on the nominal rate of interest but also on what happens to the price of a borrower's exports and to exchange rates. Where borrowing is to finance future imports, it will also depend on future import prices or more generally on expected movements in the terms of trade.

Having implied that the real rate of interest may be relevant, we must face the problem of choosing the appropriate price index with which to deflate nominal rates. For individual borrowers there is a case, as suggested above, for using export prices. For developing

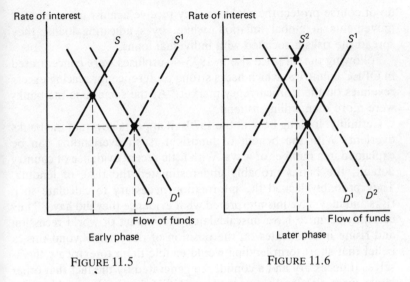

FIGURE 11.5

FIGURE 11.6

countries as a group the argument that their exports are highly concentrated on primary products would suggest that commodity prices might be used. Yet for the major developing country borrowers the degree of export concentration on primary products is less marked than for other developing countries, and this deflator may therefore be less appropriate.

In addition to the real interest rate, the demand for loans depends on the size of current account deficits in borrowing countries, or the excess of national investment over saving, the willingness of monetary authorities to run down international reserves, the scope for and cost of domestic adjustment designed to eliminate deficits, and the rate of time preference between current and future absorption. Given the size of payments deficits encountered by non-oil developing countries after 1973, it seems reasonable to assume that the demand schedule has shifted persistently, though latterly less rapidly, to the right.[6]

As noted earlier, the supply of loans from the banks depends not only on the expected return on lending but also on the supply of funds deposited with the banks. This in turn depends on the size and location of balance of payments surpluses and the rate of interest on offer. Lenders are also likely to base their lending decisions on real rates and these will be influenced by movements in their import prices and exchange rates. By using flexible nominal rates, the banks do of course protect the real rate they receive against unanticipated movements in global inflation, while, by syndicating loans, they spread the risks associated with individual loans.

Following the oil price rise in 1973–4 surpluses were concentrated in OPEC countries, which had a strong preference for placing excess revenues on the Eurocurrency market.[7] At the same time the banks were more than willing to lend.

Certainly, looking back at the 1970s, it appears now that the banks overlent. With the benefit of hindsight, such overlending can be explained in a number of ways. With little recent evidence of country default, the banks probably underestimated the risks of lending. They probably lacked the information necessary to calculate such risks and may have misinterpreted what evidence they did have. They certainly seem to have miscalculated the impact of world recession and rising interest rates on the position of debtors. Beyond this, a belief that short term lending would enable them to extricate themselves if necessary and a confidence generated by the fact that other banks were also lending, as well as a belief that banks would not be allowed to go bust by national and international regulatory authorities, all had the effect of reducing their perceived risks.

By the early 1980s the OPEC surplus had fallen dramatically and the banks had become more sensitive to risk; indeed, they were probably by now overstating the probability of default on the basis of the debt crisis in 1982. Furthermore, many of the other causes of previous confidence had evaporated. The banks accepted that mistakes could be made, and recognised that their ability to get out of lending to LDCs was constrained largely because implicit guarantees turned out to be only partial. Meanwhile, increasing bank regulation and supervision as well as growing opportunities elsewhere also served to limit bank lending to developing countries. On the basis of these factors it is not unreasonable to suppose that the supply schedule of bank loans to developing countries shifted leftwards.

3. CREDIT RATIONING AND CREDITWORTHINESS

If we turn to the credit-rationing approach, this might also suggest that in the period since the end of the 1970s the banks have become more aware of the risks of lending to developing countries, with the result that the supply schedule of loans has not only shifted to the left but has become increasingly inelastic. According to this approach,

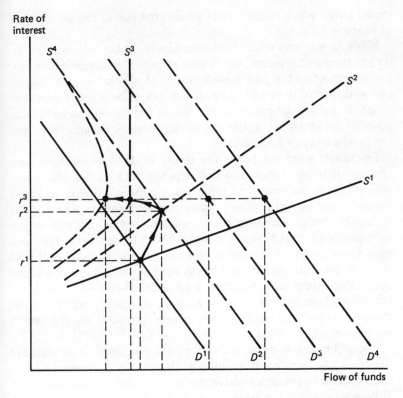

Note: This figure illustrates the credit-rationing approach described in the text, with the interest rate not rising above r^3 even under conditions of excess demand. At r^3 the banks are maximising their expected profit, bearing in mind the risks of default. Other ways of credit rationing are then used.

FIGURE 11.7

however, events in the late 1970s and 1980s are more appropriately illustrated by Figure 11.7, with the rate of interest being set at a maximum level where the demand for loans exceeds their supply and with the banks rationing loans on the basis of their assessment of creditworthiness.

The course of events in the 1980s is consistent with just such a credit-rationing interpretation. Indeed, with the real rate of interest levelling off and the volume of loans declining during 1982–3, reality is perhaps more consistent with this explanation than with a market model under which interest rates would continue to rise as the level of business falls.

Many factors will affect creditworthiness. These include a country's natural endowments, the degree of export and import diversification, export and import growth, the level of reserves, the volume and structure of debt and the past conduct of debt repayment, the scope for balance of payments correction and the willingness of the government to exploit it, the size of the domestic savings ratio, and the productivity of investment.

Essentially what the banks are trying to do is to estimate their chances of being repaid, and this depends both on the *ability* and *willingness* of borrowers to repay. A borrower's ability to repay depends on how productively loans are used and on whether the necessary foreign exchange can be earned. It also depends on the time profile of repayments as compared with foreign exchange earnings. Even where a borrower is basically solvent, liquidity problems may still be encountered; and banks may be even more concerned about this aspect of a borrower's position. Banks will search for variables which provide an early warning of liquidity crises, such as changes in the borrower's net foreign asset position, and the rate of domestic credit creation.

The willingness to repay depends on the borrower's assessment of the costs and benefits of defaulting. Banks may in general be less keen to lend to countries where the benefits from default are large, although usually if the benefits are large, the costs will be as well, with the result that the risks of default do not rise. In general, borrowers have shown a strong revealed preference to avoid default if at all possible. This suggests that borrowers as well as banks may be risk-averters.

4. THE SHORTCOMINGS OF BANK LENDING

Although it must be conceded that bank lending made a vital contribution to balance of payments financing after 1973, experience has also revealed a number of shortcomings associated with it. These relate both to efficiency and equity.

However, a prior question is whether the banks themselves will decide to remain in the business of balance of payments financing or whether, subject to the constraints imposed on them by the IMF and their desire to protect previous loans, they will try to pull out. A number of related factors are at work here. The first is the country risk.

The question is how the banks will assess risk in the future and whether the system may be modified so as to reduce risk. The IMF may have a role to play here. The second relates to banks' own risk and is affected by their degree of exposure in developing countries and their own capital-asset ratios. Commercial bank shareholders have become increasingly concerned that the banks have overlent to developing countries in general and to specific developing countries in particular.

Almost certainly the falling capital–asset ratios of the banks that occurred during the 1970s and early 1980s were seen by their shareholders and the various regulatory agencies as a weakening in their balance sheets. The banks therefore began to regard it as imprudent to allow the ratio to fall further if they were to retain confidence.

While the net exposure of the banks in developing countries has been small overall, net claims have been high in relation to developing country exports. Furthermore, the growth in net exposure was rapid at the turn of the decade, rising by more than 600 per cent between 1977 and 1982. Moreover, aggregation can be misleading. Most international lending has been concentrated in a relatively small number of banks and has been made to relatively few countries; for some American banks their loans to Brazil and Mexico alone have exceeded their total equity, and this has clearly made them reluctant to extend additional loans. For as long as other banks were prepared to enter the business of lending to developing countries, bank lending in aggregate was able to increase, but when such opportunities for expansion had been exploited, further growth relied on the elasticity of supply, and, as noted above, this may be low or negative.[8]

Considerations such as these lead back to the question of the efficiency of bank lending. World economic inefficiency will result if bank lending is unstable, if it is unrelated to the underlying productivity of resources throughout the world, and if there are external costs associated with it.

It is certainly unstable. The banks moved rapidly into balance of payments financing following the rise in the price of oil in 1973–4 and then endeavoured to extricate themselves in the 1980s. In general terms they were quick to lend to developing countries following the (temporary) upsurge in commodity prices, and anxious to reduce their lending as borrowers encountered declining terms of trade and debt difficulties. Such instability is enhanced by the tendency towards 'herd behaviour' that characterises the banking community.

242   *International Financial Policy and Development*

Withdrawal by one bank can quickly encourage other banks to follow suit rather than to offset the withdrawal by lending more themselves, or at least to maintain the level of their involvement. Indeed, there is a problem in the sense that all banks will have an incentive to reduce exposure at the first whiff of repayment problems, yet not all of them will be able to do so, since such behaviour would certainly induce default.

As the above discussion implies, lending may be only loosely related to the underlying strength of an economy or the marginal productivity of resources. Banks may have imperfect information and may misinterpret what information they do have; they may be unduly influenced by transient and often largely cosmetic factors, or, in syndicated loans, by the views and prestige of the 'lead' bank. This can of course work both ways. On some occasions banks may over-lend yet on others they may underlend. Either way, they are unlikely to allocate capital efficiently.

Furthermore, factors which alter the creditworthiness of one developing country can have an influence on the willingness of banks to lend to other countries, which is quite unrelated to their economic performance and prospects – the so-called contagion effect. For example, a fall in the price of oil will create debt problems for oil producers such as Mexico and Venezuela and will damage their credit rating with the banks. But as a result of debt problems in these countries the banks may become more risk-averse and less prepared to lend to other countries whose economic prospects actually improve as oil prices fall, because the price of a major import has fallen and because a falling oil price tends to increase world aggregate demand and therefore the demand for their exports. The lack of simultaneity in the debt servicing capacity of borrowers suggests that such a response is irrational, though to the extent that the withdrawal of funds itself creates a liquidity, and perhaps with rising interest rates, even a solvency problem in the affected countries, it may seem rational after the event. Of course, some causes of debt difficulties, such as rising interest rates, may affect all debtors simultaneously and, in these circumstances a more uniform cross-country response would seem more logical; although even here, the ability of borrowers to deal with rising interest rates may well vary.

Another externality associated with bank lending relates to its global consequences. If banks pull out from providing balance of payments finance and nobody else steps in to take their place, the result will be that borrowers will have to correct their deficits more rapidly. Rapid correction can be brought about by deflating domestic aggregate demand, and thus the demand for imports, or by introducing import controls. Either way, the countries that provide the imports will experience a reduction in their exports and a deterioration in their balance of payments, which they, in turn, may have to correct. A vicious circle of deflation, recession, protectionism, and falling world trade can become entrenched from which most countries stand to lose. Furthermore, the mere uncertainty of bank lending may give rise to external costs.

At the same time, is it really the banks' responsibility to ensure that things do not go wrong in this way? They will undoubtedly see their principal responsibility as being to their shareholders, and they are likely to take the view that these interests are best served in an uncertain world environment by trying to maximise short-run private profits; it may be unreasonable to expect them to assume the global role of maximising world economic welfare.

The concept of welfare moves us on to the question of the distribution of bank lending. In aggregate terms, and as shown in Chapter 2, this is heavily skewed, being concentrated in industrial countries and a narrow range of middle and high income developing countries. The banks have usually deemed low-income countries uncreditworthy.

Again, however, it is unreasonable to criticise the banks for the inequitable distribution of their lending. After all, they are not charitable institutions. Indeed, on the contrary, they would be more open to criticism were they to lend to countries that seemed to have little chance of repaying the loans. At the same time, the elements of market failure remain, not only with respect to equity but also in terms of efficiency. If bank lending fails to meet the requirements of an efficient and equitable market solution, should so much of the recycling of world capital be left in their hands or should international agencies be more heavily involved?

5. CONCLUDING REMARKS

The policy implications of the discussion in this chapter may now be spelled out. Bank lending has been an important source of finance to some developing countries but has involved a number of problems. Factors influencing the size of banks' lending come from both the demand side and the supply side, although there is evidence to suggest that, particularly over recent years, supply-side factors have been more important. Policies need to be directed towards dealing with the problems associated with bank lending and need to address both the demand for and the supply of loans. Both efficiency and equity need to be taken into account. It is to a fuller discussion of the specifics of policy that Chapters 12 and 13 are devoted.

12 Developing Country Debt: a Review of the Policy Alternatives

This chapter sets out to provide a broad overview of many elements of the debt problem which has been so much a feature of the international financial system in recent years. Although there is a brief introduction to various policy alternatives, a more detailed examination of a more limited range of policies is held over until the next chapter.

1. THE ECONOMICS OF DEBT

By relaxing the constraints imposed by domestic saving and foreign exchange, external borrowing allows countries to increase their current standard of living by comparison with what it would otherwise be. The size and duration of this positive effect depends essentially on how the extra resources are used and on the marginal productivity of capital.

In the case of grants, i.e. financial inflows with a grant element of 100 per cent, there are no further problems. Although there will be debate over how the money should be used, the question of repaying the debt does not arise.

But most international financial flows are not grants. They are loans that have to be repaid with interest. By borrowing, countries are, in effect, trading off future domestic absorption (i.e. consumption and investment expenditures) in favour of current absorption. They are relaxing current constraints at the cost of imposing future ones.

Borrowing initially allows investment to exceed domestic saving, and imports to exceed exports. However, the crux of the debt problem is that in order to service loans these inequalities have to be reversed to an extent and within a period of time determined by the conditions of the loans.

In order to avoid a debt problem it is therefore necessary for a borrower to close the domestic savings gap and to go on to generate excess saving. However, since loans normally have to be repaid in foreign exchange rather than in domestic currency, it is also necessary to convert this excess saving into foreign exchange, and, to do this, exports have to increase relative to imports.

Let us concentrate first of all on savings, and take the simplest possible savings function, where aggregate saving depends on the level of income, savings will increase if either the propensity to save or national income increases. Both changes may occur simultaneously if the marginal propensity to save exceeds the average propensity to save and if the loan causes national income to rise. Assuming for a moment that the repayment of the principal of the loan can be financed by further borrowing, national income will rise provided the marginal productivity of the resources borrowed exceeds the rate of interest on the loan.

With regard to the foreign exchange aspect of the problem, a borrower's holdings of foreign exchange will increase either if exports expand or if there is substitution away from imports. What is required then is a shift of domestic resources into the tradeables sector of the economy. Relevant in this context is a whole range of both demand and supply side factors. Is it possible for the borrower to induce an increase in exports by altering the structure of prices via exchange rate policy or the use of subsidies and taxes, or is there a constraint on export growth imposed by the income elasticity of demand for exports and the growth of income in export markets? Does the borrower's marginal productivity to import lie below the average propensity to import, in which case the import coefficient will fall with economic growth, or is there scope for encouraging import substitution again through the exchange rate or fiscal system? And, furthermore, will measures to increase the tradeables sector reduce economic growth, as essential imports are forgone and essential domestic resources exported?

It is the interrelationship between these various issues that makes debt a complex problem. Generally speaking, however, borrowers with a rising savings ratio, a low and falling incremental capital-output ratio, rapid export growth potential relative to import growth, and paying relatively low interest rates, should encounter few debt problems. On the other hand, borrowers with falling saving ratios, high and rising ICORs, low export growth, little scope for import substitution other than of the type that adversely affects economic growth, and paying relatively high interest rates, are likely to find difficulties – difficulties that will be compounded by the fact that debtors will then find it much more difficult to refinance their existing stock of debt.

A further aspect that complicates debt management relates to the time pattern of repayments. A borrower, while fulfilling the basic solvency criterion that the marginal productivity of the resources borrowed exceeds the rate of interest on the loan, may still encounter liquidity problems in particular years because of temporary shortages of foreign exchange. An additional difficulty here, however, is that what starts off as a liquidity problem may end up as a solvency problem, largely because of its effect on the expectations of lenders, who may become less keen on refinancing debt or may decide to increase the spread on loans. Furthermore, debtors may have to repay the debt in specific foreign currencies, yet their foreign exchange earnings may be in other currencies. Variations in exchange rates can therefore sometimes create debt difficulties if the earning power of exports falls when expressed in the particular currency required.

From this discussion it is possible to identify a number of broad reasons why debt problems emerge. First, there may be factors that are exogenous to the debtors, such as falling export demand resulting from a world economic recession, or rising real world interest rates, or unfavourable changes in exchange rates between other currencies. Second, debt may have been poorly managed, with the borrower borrowing too much, given the capacity of the economy to repay, failing to choose the most appropriate sources of finance (possibly borrowing over a shorter term and at a higher cost than necessary), and failing to collect adequate information about the debt position. Third, and in addition to poor debt management, the economy itself may have been poorly managed. Failure by governments to undertake measures to increase domestic savings, by, for example, repressing financial markets and preventing domestic real interest rates from rising above very low or even negative levels, or by resisting the opportunity of raising saving compulsorily through the fiscal system, are likely to mean that the savings gap will not be closed. Furthermore, reluctance to reduce exchange rates that are greatly overvalued or to encourage export promotion in other ways will mean that the foreign exchange gap will not be closed.

However, other factors may also be at work in causing debt problems. As noted in Chapter 11, these may be as much to do with creditors overlending as with debtors overborrowing.

In practice, of course, any specific country's debt problem will probably have arisen as a result of a combination of these reasons, even though one or other of them may dominate. More on this later.

Once debt management problems emerge, they frequently become increasingly difficult to control. Failure to service existing debt means that new debts need to be contracted in order to finance old ones; consequently debt accumulates and the chances of being able to service it recede. Lenders, seeing the deteriorating debt position, regard the borrowers as less creditworthy and as a result it becomes yet harder for them to refinance outstanding loans.

Given the problems associated with overborrowing, the concept of 'debt capacity' is clearly important. Unfortunately, it is a somewhat complex concept, since it can be affected by changes in a number of factors, such as the terms of trade, the exchange rate and inflation. However, assuming that these variables do not change, a borrower's rate of debt accumulation will vary positively with the size of the savings gap and the interest rate on loans and negatively with the rate of economic growth and thus the productivity of capital. If an initial savings gap is not closed, or indeed if saving exceeds investment by less than is required to make interest payments on existing loans, new borrowing will be needed if the target growth rate is to be achieved. Indebtedness will therefore increase. If, on the other hand, saving increases so that it exceeds investment by an amount equal to interest payments, then net indebtedness will level off, and, if by more, net indebtedness will fall.[1] By trying to calculate the difference between investment and saving in the future, borrowers can get some idea of their future capacity to service debt and thereby avoid the slide into further debt.

However, as noted above, such forecasts need to be complemented by considering what may happen to imports and exports, the terms of trade, interest rates and exchange rates. There is therefore no simple formula that allows debt capacity to be estimated with precision and full confidence. And in any case a borrower's capacity to service debt is very closely related to the macroeconomic and microeconomic policies that are pursued, since many of the relevant variables can be influenced by governmental policy as well as by structural and behavioural change in the economy.

This analysis suggests that evaluating debt capacity is far from simple. Each case needs to be examined on its own merits, with many aspects of a country's economic and political structure being taken into account.

1.1 Global Aspects of Debt

Up to now we have looked at the debt problem from the perspective of the individual borrower, implying thereby that debt problems are in some way self-contained. This is far from the truth. To illustrate the point, consider two possibilities. The first is that when faced with an unmanageable debt problem, a major borrower decides to default. Given the structure of bank lending, this could result in failure for those banks whose lending is heavily concentrated in that country. Banking systems rely crucially on confidence, and the loss of confidence that default would bring would have ramifications for both the countries in which the lenders were located as well as for other borrowers. It is difficult to estimate precisely the effects of such defaults but it is clear that the consequences would be global and not country-specific.

The second possibility is that the borrower pursues a programme of economic policies designed to reduce imports and shift the current account of the balance of payments into surplus. But again the outside world would not be unaffected by such measures. A fall in one country's imports means a fall in other countries' exports. Given a simple income–expenditure model, this implies a multiplied decline in income in the exporting countries and in turn a fall in imports. This means a further fall in other countries' exports. World trade shrinks, economic growth slows down, unemployment rises. Again the debt problem is shown to be a global phenomenon. Precisely how significant these trading interrelationships are depends on a range of import, export and saving coefficients, and a sophisticated model would be needed to calculate them.

However, the overall conclusion that may be drawn from this is that there is a mutuality of interests in avoiding severe debt problems.

2. THE SIZE OF THE DEBT PROBLEM: SOME FACTS AND FIGURES

The foregoing discussion identifies a number of variables that might help to indicate the size and nature of the debt problem. From our analysis of debt capacity it emerges that the chances of being able to service debt rise with the growth of output and exports. It is to be expected then that in an environment of slow growth and stagnating export performance, debt will become more difficult to manage, especially if, at the same time, the terms of lending harden, with rising interest rates and falling maturities. However, it also needs to be stressed that mechanically referring to a series of debt indicators can easily lead to misinterpretation, since whether a given debt situation constitutes a problem depends crucially on the economic and political circumstances of individual countries. Debt is but one aspect of the much broader problem of economic management and should not be viewed in isolation.

Examination of data on debt reveals a number of developments since the early 1970s. The most important of these can be listed and discussed quite briefly. First, there has been a big increase in the nominal amount of external debt. During 1972–82, for instance, the volume of outstanding medium term and long term debt held by developing countries increased some five-fold as these countries endeavoured to maintain their rates of economic growth in spite of a deteriorating external environment. However, much of this increase reflected the rapid inflation that occurred during the 1970s. Indeed, when measured in real terms, or in relation to other economic magnitudes such as exports, the debt situation at the end of the 1970s was not substantially different from that at the beginning of the decade. But in the early 1980s the debt situation deteriorated. Not only did real debt continue to increase, but even where there was a decline in the rate at which indebtedness was growing, this was more than offset by a reduced rate of export growth. As a result, both debt/export and debt service ratios increased significantly for most important debtors. Thus the debt/export ratio for the twenty-one major LDC borrowers rose from less than 125 per cent in 1980 to nearly 180 per cent in 1982.

Second, within this overall picture there was a large shift away from public debt towards private debt. Between 1976 and 1981, for instance, about two-thirds of the increase in long term and medium term debt was to private banks, mostly as a result of syndicated lending, and by 1983 more than a quarter of total external debt was short term. With short term debt included, the increasing share of the private sector has probably been much sharper. Whereas the convention had been to exclude short term debt from the discussion of debt problems – since it was usually assumed to be trade-related and rolled over automatically – this was no longer the case by the beginning of the 1980s. Many borrowers resorted to short term borrowing in order to finance longer term payments deficits, and an implication of this was that the roll over of such short term credits was no longer automatic. Indeed, the need to refinance or reschedule short term debt became a pressing aspect of the entire debt problem. The move towards borrowing from the banks brought with it a hardening in the terms of overall debt, as the average maturity of the debt shortened and interest payments on it increased. These developments in the structure of debt meant that for any given amount of debt there was a more severe debt problem, especially in terms of illiquidity. The use of floating interest rates and their volatility also meant that the size of the debt problem could suddenly increase as interest rates increased. Between 1980 and 1982, consequently, net interest payments more than doubled. Of course, where borrowers also hold substantial overseas deposits, there will be a benefit from higher interest rates and the adverse effect on debt will be neutralized.

Third, the shift over to the private sector served to increase the concentration of debt. One's perception of the global debt problem has therefore become increasingly influenced by what happens in a relatively small number of countries. However, debt is not only concentrated on the side of borrowers. The private debts of developing countries have also been quite heavily concentrated in the hands of relatively few banks, and this again has increased the fragility of the entire system of international capital flows.

Fourth, the contagion effect came more into play in the 1980s. Problems of debt management in some countries reduced the confidence of the banks and their willingness to expand lending. At the same time lending from other sources failed to expand to fill the gap that this left. The difficulties of refinancing or rolling over to which this gave rise itself created further debt problems.

One indicator of the deteriorating debt situation is the number of reschedulings that occur: agreements between debtors and creditors to rearrange and effectively postpone debt repayments, particularly repayments of principal but occasionally payments of interest as well. Table 12.1 shows the increasing frequency of debt renegotiations in the 1980s as compared with the 1970s.

Although it is difficult to forecast the evolution of debt – witness the fact that even at the turn of the decade the debt problems of 1982 and 1983 were not being generally predicted – there are a number of pointers that provide little cause for optimism. Not least amongst these is that by 1983 the rate of growth of ouput in the major borrowing countries had fallen below the rate of interest on loans. If

TABLE 12.1 Multilateral Debt Renegotiations, 1975–84 (millions of US dollars)

Country	Number of renegotiations, 1975–84	1975–1980 Paris Club	1975–1980 Commercial bank	1981 Paris Club	1981 Commercial bank	1982 Paris Club	1982 Commercial bank	1983 Paris Club	1983 Commercial bank	1984 Paris Club	1984 Commercial bank signed or agreed in principle
1. Argentina	2		970								(23,241)
2. Bolivia	2										(536)
3. Brazil	3				444		(3,478)	(4,532)			(5,350)
4. Central African Rep.	2			55				(13)			
5. Chile	2	216							(3,400)		
6. Costa Rica	2							97	1,240		
7. Dominican Republic	1								497		
8. Ecuador	4							(200)	(1,835)		(5,065)[2]
9. Gabon	1	105[1]									
10. Guyana	3		29				14				(24)
11. Honduras	1										(122)
12. India	3	436[3]									
13. Ivory Coast	2									(153)	(306)
14. Jamaica	4		126		103					(106)	(148)
15. Liberia	6	30		25			27	18		(17)	(71)
16. Madagascar	4			142		103			59		
17. Malawi	3					24		(30)	59		
18. Mexico	3							1,550[4]	(23,625)	475	(48,725)[3]
19. Morocco	3								1,225	(200)	(530)
20. Mozambique	1										
21. Nicaragua	3		582		188		102				
22. Niger	3							33		(22)	
23. Nigeria	1							(1,920)			
24. Pakistan	1			263[3]							28

	No.										
25. Peru	6	478	821					(450)	(380)	(1,000)	(1,415)
26. Philippines	2							(195)	(567)	(685)	(4,904)
27. Romania	4					(234)		64			(97)
28. Senegal	4			77		84					(25)
29. Sierra Leone	4	68						502		88	
30. Sudan	5	373				174		114		(245)	
31. Togo	6	170			638				74	(55)	
32. Turkey	5	4,696[3]		(92)			(1,589)				
33. Uganda	2	2,640			3,100						
34. Uruguay	1			(56)		22					
35. Venezuela	1								(815)		
36. Yugoslavia	4							(988)[4]	(1,586)	(500)[4]	(20,750)
37. Zaire	6	1,594		574				(1,317)	(150)	(1,246)	
38. Zambia	3	402						(285)			(75)
Total	113	8,166	5,638	1,284	4,473	641	1,741	10,559	41,005	3,341	112,853

Note: Data cover arrangements expected to be signed by the end of 1984 plus commercial bank reschedulings agreed in principle but not signed through 31 December 1984. Figures indicate renegotiated amounts as reported by the countries or, if in parenthesis, as estimated by staff members. Cuba and Poland, which also renegotiated debt-service payments with official creditors and commercial banks, are not members of the World Bank and therefore are excluded from this table.

1. Denotes an agreement of a special task force.
2. Includes one agreement (for $590 million) signed, and another agreed in principle.
3. Denotes an Aid Consortium Agreement.
4. Technically this was an agreement of a creditor group meeting, not a Paris Club.
5. Includes debt of $23,625 million previously rescheduled in 1983.

SOURCE: *Coping with External Debt in the 1980's*, World Bank, 1985.

this situation persists, the debt problem is unlikely simply to go away.

Two questions arise. First, how can the debt problem be dealt with in the short run? Second, are there any longer term or more fundamental reforms that would alleviate it?

However, before getting on to examine these questions, let us examine a different one. Does empirical evidence enable us to draw some conclusions about what were the main causes of the debt problems of the early 1980s? The information contained in Tables 12.2, 12.3 and 12.4 is of some help in this regard. Table 12.2 illustrates the shortfall in export receipts that occurred in 1982. Table 12.3 confirms the impact that this had on both the ratio of debt to exports and the debt service ratio that had risen from 18 per cent in 1980 to 25 per cent by 1982. Table 12.4 illustrates the dramatic turn around in real interest rates, rising from −4.6 in 1980 to +24.2 per cent in 1981. It would appear from these data that a rapidly deteriorating external environment was a principal cause of the debt crisis of the early 1980s.

But are things that simple? The short answer is 'no', for while these external or global factors affected many borrowers, not all of them encountered crises. Thus, while according to Table 12.5 Korea held the third largest amount of debt with the banks, it was able to escape debt rescheduling. Other developing countries with less debt, even in relation to the size of their economies, however, had to seek debt renegotiations. One potential explanation is that global factors may affect different countries in different ways, depending, for example, on the structure of their trade. Another potential answer, and one that seems to have some empirical support, is that some countries were better able to adjust their economies in such a way as to accommodate global changes without encountering debt crises. If this is true, it means that although external factors were the underlying cause of debt-related problems in the 1980s, the extent to which these problems led to a debt crisis depended on domestic economic management. This conclusion emphasises two points relevant to the assessment of default risk. The first is the vulnerability of an economy to external factors, such as falling export demand or rising real interest rates. The second is the scope for domestic adjustment in response to a deteriorating global economic environment.

The next sections now return to address the two policy questions raised earlier: how to deal with debt problems both in the short and long run.

TABLE 12.2 Imports, exports and trade balances of developing countries, 1981–4

| | Export values | | | | Import values | | | | Trade balances | | | |
	1981	1982	1983	1984	1981	1982	1983	1984	1981	1982	1983	1984
	(——————— % change ———————)								(——— Billions US$ ———)			
Major bank groups												
1. Sub-Saharan Africa[1]	-22.2	-8.5	-7.2	6.5	5.9	-11.8	-15.3	-14.8	-2.1	-5.1	-1.5	5.6
2. East Asia	8.5	-0.6	2.8	7.1	10.1	-3.0	3.5	4.5	-9.8	-5.8	-7.1	-3.3
3. South Asia	3.8	-3.1	-3.5	6.7	-2.0	-4.3	-2.6	0.9	-10.3	-9.7	-8.7	-8.0
4. EMENA	3.4	-6.1	-1.8	6.3	8.0	-3.9	-2.8	-2.3	-36.0	-35.9	-34.3	-29.0
5. Latin American & Carribean	3.1	-4.8	4.6	7.4	7.1	-20.7	-28.1	10.9	-10.9	6.2	33.7	34.0
Analytical groups												
1. Low-Income Countries	3.0	1.1	-1.4	7.9	-3.9	-8.6	4.8	3.5	-15.2	-9.8	-12.9	-11.5
Africa	-23.0	8.0	-1.5	10.6	-13.2	-10.0	-4.6	1.0	-4.9	-3.2	-2.8	-2.2
Asia	10.2	-0.2	-1.3	7.4	-1.2	-8.2	7.2	3.8	-10.3	-6.6	-10.1	-9.3
2. Middle-Income Countries	0.4	-3.3	1.7	6.4	9.9	-7.8	-8.4	1.7	-57.7	-38.2	-2.2	13.2
2.1 Oil Importers	4.9	-2.5	5.6	7.0	6.1	-7.0	-3.7	-2.2	-61.2	-47.4	-26.8	-16.8
Major Exporters of Manufactures	7.1	-2.6	5.7	7.0	5.8	-6.2	-3.1	2.8	-35.8	-27.4	-11.5	-4.5
Other Non-Oil	-5.1	-1.6	4.9	7.5	7.3	-10.1	-5.6	-0.4	-25.4	-20.0	-15.3	-12.4
2.3 Oil Exporters	-6.3	-4.6	-4.9	5.1	19.3	-9.5	-19.3	0.6	3.5	9.2	24.6	29.9
All developing countries[2]	0.7	-2.8	1.4	6.6	7.9	-7.9	-6.8	1.9	-72.9	-48.0	-15.2	1.7

1. Excluding South Africa.
2. Figures refer to a sample of ninety developing countries.

SOURCE: World Bank, Economic Analysis and Projections Department.

TABLE 12.3 *Non-oil developing countries: external debt, 1973–84*

(In billions of US dollars)

	1973	1974	1975	1976	1977	1978	1979	1980	1981	1982	1983	1984 Est.
Total[1]	130	161	191	228	291	343	406	489	578	655	693	730
By maturity												
Short-term[2]	18	23	27	33	53	60	66	93	114	132	113	104
Long-term	112	138	164	195	238	283	340	396	464	523	580	626
By creditor												
Official	51	60	70	82	100	119	136	158	177	198	221	241
Private	61	78	95	115	138	164	204	239	287	325	359	385
By region												
Africa	14	18	22	27	50	55	63	70	78	89	91	95
Asia	30	35	40	46	68	77	94	116	135	154	167	179
Europe	15	17	20	23	38	47	55	67	72	73	75	79
Middle East	9	10	13	16	26	31	36	42	47	52	56	60
Western Hemisphere	44	58	69	82	109	132	158	194	247	288	304	318

(*In per cent*)

Debt to exports of goods and services	115	105	122	126	132	132	121	115	128	151	158	152
Debt service payments[3] to exports of goods and services	16	14	16	15	16	19	20	18	22	25	22	22
International reserves/debt	32	27	21	23	23	25	23	20	17	14	15	16
International reserves/short-term debt	224	189	148	159	128	142	143	103	85	70	89	115
Net private financing/net financing requirement[4]	40	46	48	45	47	53	56	58	63	44	27	22

1. Covers public and publicly guaranteed debt and, where available, private nonguaranteed debt.
2. Debt with an original maturity of one year or less; series excludes data for a number of nonreporting countries.
3. Principal and interest on long-term debt and interest on short-term debt.
4. Net external borrowing from private creditors divided by the sum of current account deficits, reserve accumulation/use, and recorded errors and omissions, which are presumed to reflect unrecorded capital flows.

SOURCE: IMF.

TABLE 12.4 *Interest rates and spreads on lending to non-oil developing countries, 1979–84*

	1979	1980	1981	1982	1983	1984
Six-month dollar LIBOR	12.1	14.3	16.6	13.3	9.9	11.2
Real rate[1]	–3.8	–4.6	24.2	20.3	11.8	12.4
Spread over LIBOR (basis points)[2]	85	91	104	114	170	152

1. Defined as six-month dollar LIBOR deflated by the export price index for oil importers.
2. A basis point is 1/100 of a percentage point.

SOURCE: OECD, *Financial Market Trends*, World Bank.

TABLE 12.5 *Developing countries listed by debt to banks, September 1984[1] (in billions of US dollars)*

1. Mexico	90.02	41. Tunisia[2]	1.35
2. Brazil[2]	87.51	42. Sudan	1.34
3. Korea	31.86	43. Guatemala	1.29
4. Argentina	24.92	44. Madagascar[2]	1.16
5. Venezuela[3]	23.89	45. Cameroon[2]	1.03
6. Chile	15.84	46. Jamaica	1.03
7. Yugoslavia	14.87	47. Dominican Republic[2]	1.01
8. Philippines	14.54	48. Zambia[2]	1.01
9. Indonesia	13.80	49. Sri Lanka	0.98
10. South Africa	12.07	50. Oman	0.96
11. Malaysia	11.88	51. Jordan	0.90
12. Turkey	11.36	52. Congo[2]	0.89
13. Egypt	10.64	53. Senegal	0.86
14. Algeria[4]	10.29	54. Zimbabwe	0.86
15. Saudi Arabia	10.14	55. Burma[8]	0.85
16. Portugal	9.40	56. Trinidad & Tobago	0.83
17. Romania[5]	9.13	57. Barbados[8]	0.77
18. Hungary	8.68	58. Paraguay[2]	0.68
19. Kuwait	8.36	59. Zaire[2]	0.67
20. Liberia	8.17	60. Cyprus	0.65
21. Colombia[6]	7.61	61. Kenya	0.65
22. Nigeria[2]	7.54	62. Papua New Guinea	0.60
23. United Arab Emirates	7.49	63. Honduras[5]	0.59
24. Greece[2]	6.33	64. Gabon[2]	0.58
25. Thailand	6.16	65. Qatar[5]	0.52
26. Israel	5.63	66. Guyana	0.48
27. Peru[2]	4.79	67. Libya[11]	0.43
28. China, People's Republic of	4.60	68. Bangladesh	0.37
29. Morocco[6]	4.15	69. Ghana	0.33
30. Iran, I. R. of[7]	3.44	70. Tanzania[9]	0.33

31.	Iraq	2.90	71.	Benin[12]	0.26
32.	India	2.51	72.	El Salvador	0.26
33.	Nicaragua[8]	2.37	73.	Niger	0.26
34.	Syria[9]	2.31	74.	Sierra Leone	0.24
35.	Ivory Coast	2.29	75.	Mauritania[2]	0.23
36.	Uruguay[5]	1.98	76.	Haiti[13]	0.19
37.	Lebanon	1.82	77.	Yemen Arab Republic	0.19
38.	Bolivia	1.72	78.	Vanuatu	0.15
39.	Costa Rica[10]	1.66	79.	Somalia[2]	0.14
40.	Pakistan	1.56	80.	Malawi	0.13

1. Figures are the sum of cross-border interbank accounts by residence of borrowing bank and international bank credit to nonbanks by residence of borrower. As of the end of September 1984, unless otherwise noted.
2. Latest published data for cross-border interbank accounts (CBIA) are as of end of June 1984.
3. Latest published data for CBIA are a Fund staff estimate.
4. Latest published data for CBIA are as of end of September 1982.
5. Latest published data for CBIA are as of end of March 1984.
6. Latest published data for CBIA are as of end of December 1982.
7. Latest published data for CBIA are as of end of March 1982.
8. Latest published data for CBIA are as of end of December 1983.
9. Latest published data for CBIA are as of end of September 1983.
10. Latest published data for CBIA are as of end of December 1981.
11. Latest published data for CBIA are as of end of March 1983.
12. No CBIA data are available.
13. Latest published data for CBIA are as of end of December 1978.

SOURCE: *International Financial Statistics*, IMF.

3. SHORT-TERM POLICY: RESCHEDULING[2]

Faced with a large amount of debt that is difficult to manage, the debtor has a number of options. The first, as mentioned earlier, is to default on the loan and simply fail to make payments. This is the so-called 'market solution'. One advantage of it is that countries that have 'overborrowed' and banks that have 'overlent' learn the folly of their ways. A form of natural selection is allowed to work. Yet it remains a rather extreme and undesirable solution for a series of reasons. For the debtor, default will have a number of long term consequences, since it will become very unlikely that a defaulter will be able to attract further credit. For the banking system, the failure of banks that might result from default could be very damaging and the knock-on effects on lending countries and other borrowing countries would almost certainly be significant.

⌜Again, as mentioned earlier, the second option is to pursue a programme of demand deflation and import contraction. While this may improve the current account balance of payments in the short run, the costs in terms of economic development are likely to be high and could set off political and social unrest. Furthermore, according to the models of debt capacity, the long term solution to the problem rests on raising output and exports rather than on contracting output and imports. While such deflationary programmes may increase the confidence of lenders in the short run if they are interpreted as suggesting that the borrower is making an effort to solve its problems, they will probably fail to raise confidence in the long run unless the growth of output and exports picks up.⌟

The third option, not open to borrowers themselves, is that creditor and other countries expand their economies. This will improve the external environment in which borrowers find themselves, particularly by increasing the demand for their exports. However, care needs to be exercised with this solution. Expansion in industrial countries will not necessarily have exclusively beneficial effects. It may, for example, be accompanied by rising interest rates, which, as we have seen, create an extra debt burden. Furthermore, it may fail to encourage the disciplined economic management that is required if future debt problems are to be avoided.

The fourth option, which Table 12.1 shows has been increasingly adopted, is to reschedule debts. Official debt is usually rescheduled through the Paris Club, which was established in 1956 when a number of European countries met to renegotiate their bilateral loans to Argentina. The Paris Club brings debtors together with their creditors and observers from the IMF, the World Bank, UNCTAD and the OECD. There are no formal rules governing its operations, although certain basic features have emerged over the years. Thus, agreements reached *normally* involve only official or officially guaranteed or insured medium or long term debt not previously rescheduled, and cover payments in arrears and those coming due within a specified twelve-month period, reschedule 85–90 per cent of this debt, allowing a grace period of up to five years and a further five years to repay, request the debtor not to grant better terms to other creditors, and require the debtor country to negotiate with the IMF and put in place a stabilisation programme before the rescheduling is considered.

Rescheduling of commercial debt, which with the move to private borrowing has become increasingly significant, lies outside the scope of the Paris Club and has been handled in a rather more *ad hoc* way. In many respects the rescheduling of private debt is more complex than that of official debt, not least because of the number of banks involved. This is not to say that all the lending banks would be directly involved in the negotiations, which are usually conducted by the 'lead banks' and committees representing national groups of creditor banks, but even so it is not surprising that commercial rescheduling can take many months to arrange.

Two basic principles underlie commercial bank rescheduling. First, the banks involved agree to adopt a common approach. If one bank breaks ranks, then, because of a cross default clause, other banks do not remain bound to the agreement. Second, rescheduling is, with rare exceptions, limited to the principal of the loan. Interest payments continue and in general any arrears in the payment of interest have to be made good before the agreement is signed.

A feature of commercial bank rescheduling is the variety of terms agreed. However, typical terms involve coverage being limited to about 80 per cent of loans coming due within two years, floating interest rates linked to LIBOR or the US prime rate, a rescheduling fee, and, since 1978, the agreement of a programme of economic stabilisation with the IMF.

More recently, in 1984, renegotiations of Mexico's and Venezuela's debt involved a reduction in spreads, the use of lower reference rates – LIBOR as opposed to the US prime rate – upon which to base the rate of interest, lower fees, multi-year rescheduling, longer maturities, and the opportunity for currency conversion, as well as a commitment to return to the Fund should the majority of banks feel that ill-designed economic policies were causing payments problems.

Packages such as these have been generally heralded as representing a significant advance on earlier reschedulings. By rewarding efforts to adjust, they are seen as providing a further incentive to adjust in the future. Moreover, it has been calculated that the risk-adjusted costs to the lenders from relaxing rescheduling terms are, in fact, relatively small. Multi-year rescheduling creates more certainty about the future and assists economic planning. Longer maturities ameliorate liquidity problems, while currency conversion enables non-US banks to remove the uncertainty that variations in the value of the dollar imply for their own balance sheets.

However, the main point to grasp about rescheduling remains the same, and is that it provides debtors with time to come up with a solution. Apart from alleviating immediate liquidity problems, it is not a solution in itself. If debtors fail to undertake appropriate action in order to strengthen their balance of payments, or if outside factors do not become more favourable, rescheduling merely postpones the full impact of the debt problem. It is noteworthy that it does not reduce the overall debt/export ratio.

However, the advantages of rescheduling should not be underestimated. With high discount rates, the present value of debt service payments as perceived by debtors may fall. Moreover, there are reasons to believe that a more gradualist approach to balance-of-payments adjustment will be less costly in terms of its impact on other objectives of domestic economic policy, such as economic growth and employment, than shock treatment would be.

If this is true, rescheduling will permit more cost-efficient solutions to be adopted. Furthermore, by at least temporarily avoiding default, the deleterious effects that this would have on both borrowers and lenders are also avoided.

4. ALTERNATIVE POLICIES: AN OVERVIEW

While rescheduling offers an expedient way of taking the pressure off, there are a range of other reforms which have been suggested as providing a better long term solution. However, the formulation of a universally agreed approach is not straightforward, largely because it has to offer something to both the debtor countries, primarily interesting in ensuring a continuing inflow of finance, and the lenders, either governments or banks, primarily concerned about avoiding default and the associated losses. An appropriate balance needs to be struck between adjustment and financing, with the emphasis falling neither too heavily on adjustment in the debtors nor too heavily on financing by the creditors. It seems likely that this balance will involve a blend of reforms covering five basic issues.

4.1 Internal adjustment within the debtor country

The first of these relates to measures that will encourage borrowers to adopt those policies most likely to induce the macroeconomic and structural changes that are needed to reduce the severity of the debt problem and to ensure their ongoing creditworthiness. Models of debt capacity reveal clearly the sorts of changes that have to take place – changes to increase saving and the productivity of investment, to economise on inessential imports and expand exports. The threat of default and the jeopardy into which this would put future development provides an incentive for debtors to make such changes, but casual empiricism suggests that outside encouragement under the auspices of the IMF may also be required. The essential thing here is to try and ensure that the programmes that the Fund supports are up to the task and have the desired effects. These issues are discussed at length in Chapter 4.

4.2 External adjustment outside the debtor country

The models of debt capacity also show how sensitive the debt problem is to changes in the demand for exports, the terms of trade and interest rates. Demand expansion in the industrial countries which form the principal market for the exports of the major debtors would reduce the emphasis that would otherwise have to be placed on internal adjustment, and would enable it to take place through expanding output and exports rather than through contracting income and imports. It is hardly coincidental that the debt problem has become most pronounced at a time when the world economy has been in recession.

4.3 Reform to support bank lending

At least until more fundamental reform in the nature of development financing can be arranged, bank lending will remain important. Yet banks have become increasingly reluctant to lend to developing countries. Without going so far as to provide them with a risk-free environment, reforms could be introduced that would at least reduce the degree of uncertainty associated with such lending. These reforms include safety nets, rediscounting, refinancing, and guarantees, some of which are discussed in Chapter 13.

Co-financing with the World Bank has also been used as a way of trying to encourage the banks to continue lending. The specifics of co-financing vary. Until 1983 the World Bank and the commercial banks entered into separate loan agreements with borrowing countries, but since then there has been some joint participation in loans, with the Bank agreeing to have the repayment of its principal deferred

264   *International Financial Policy and Development*

until after commercial banks have been repaid, financing any balance
of principal left at the end of the scheduled term of commercial loans
resulting from higher than anticipated interest rates – thereby allowing borrowers' annual debt service payments to be fixed and the
maturity of the loan extended – and, in effect, guaranteeing the
repayment of the later part of loans in which it did not initially
participate. There may be scope for extending such arrangements,
utilising the conditionality that the Bank can bring to bear via
structural adjustment lending and raising the degree of control over
the way in which borrowed resources are used. Similarly, there is
scope for improving the organisation of commercial rescheduling and
for increasing the degree of co-operation between the banks, the
multilateral institutions such as the Fund and the World Bank, and the
governments of both lender and borrower countries.

Although all of the above schemes involve some degree of official
intervention, proposals have also been put forward that rely more
heavily on creating a private secondary market in developing country
debt. However, the object of such ideas remains that of providing
banks with the opportunity of selling off the debt they are owed at a
discount, which, in this case, would be determined by market forces.[3]
There is a further discussion of secondary markets in the next
chapter.

4.4 A shift away from bank lending: new instruments

While in the short run the debt position would be made more acute
by the banks pulling out of balance of payments financing, the deficiencies of short term bank lending argue for reducing its relative
contribution in the longer run. Crucial aspects of the debt position
relate to the maturity of the debt and unexpected changes in both
interest rates and exchange rates. There is, then, a case for moving
towards longer term lending in the form of bonds. This idea is again
discussed more fully in the next chapter.

Other plans of this genre also involve trying to change the basic
nature of the instruments through which creditors lend to debtors.
They include equity investments which would give lenders a 'stake' in
the borrower's future economic performance, and the index linking
of repayments to the capacity of a borrower to pay, as measured, for
example, by export growth.

Although there is a certain logic in relating debt payments to the capacity of the economy to make them, such schemes are, however, not without problems. They would clearly generate uncertainty for lenders in terms of their anticipated income stream and might there-fore not prove popular. Under a scheme where a ceiling for overall payments, expressed as a percentage of exports, was imposed, new lending might also be discouraged, with the result that the supposed alleviation in the foreign exchange constraint, which the schemes are designed to achieve, could be illusory. At the same time, however, criticisms of exchange participation notes – that they erode the sovereignty of the borrower and could result in debt payments in excess of the original loan obligation – are less valid. Debt, in any form, constrains the formulation of domestic policy, and measures could be included within the schemes to ensure that any excess payments are limited. Even so, in practical terms, the general obser-vation that equity rather than debt would be a more appropriate way of financing developing countries probably has more implications for foreign direct investment than for the redesign of lending instru-ments.

4.5 Other forms of debt relief

While the reforms discussed in sub-sections 4.3 and 4.4 above relate to banks and the private sector, there are a range of other, sometimes rather radical, proposals for solving the debt problem which apply primarily to official debt. These include most simply a general mora-torium on debt service payments, or even debt cancellation. More subtle are proposals for reciprocal tying, interest-rate subsidies, deferred repayment or extra creation of SDRs.

Reciprocal tying involves debtors repaying creditors in local cur-rency, thereby effectively tying the repayments to purchases of ex-ports from the debtor. Although having a certain appeal, particularly given donors' proclivities to tie aid, there are a number of weaknesses with the scheme, not least of which is that lenders would find it unattractive, since it limits their choice of imported commodities and sources of supply.

Interest-rate subsidies could be used to alleviate that aspect of the debt problem associated with high and rising interest rates. Subsidisa-tion could be offered in a number of ways. Donors could, for instance, provide assistance by paying a subsidy directly to commercial lenders. This would maintain the lenders' interest receipts, avoid any burden on the donor's balance of payments, and reduce the demand for foreign exchange in the borrowing countries, since interest payments would be lowered. Alternatively, donors could pay in contributions to an internationally organised subsidy fund. Payments out of the fund could then be made on a discretionary basis or on the basis of some agreed formula which would account for the deviation of interest rates from their expected trend.[4] For a further, critical discussion of these ideas see Chapter 7.

The deferral of repayment could be achieved by debtors making payments in local currency to a multilateral institution which would then on-lend the money to another developing country to buy exports from the initial debtor. This country would in effect take over the debt with the initial creditor. The debt would gradually be paid off as it came into the hands of countries with surplus foreign exchange. It would probably not be paid off in one go by one country. In the interim the debt would have served to encourage export expansion amongst developing countries.[5] While attractive as a way of encouraging intra-South trade, such a scheme suffers from a number of weaknesses. First, it involves an element of tying, while most developing countries would probably prefer to buy goods from industrial countries rather than from other developing countries. Second, although the original debtors do not default, the creditors would not know when they would be repaid. Since also the distribution of finance is highly political and this scheme spreads the benefits of finance around amongst a number of developing countries, creditors are unlikely to accept it.

An extra creation of SDRs and a modification to the formula on which they are distributed could be used to provide debtors with access to additional foreign exchange and thus alleviate their liquidity problems.[6] Although the use of SDRs involves paying a rate of interest equivalent to the market rate, they provide a permanent source of credit for the user. Since they do not have to be repaid, the cost of using them is initially cheaper than the cost of an equivalent loan which involves amortisation. The SDRs can be repurchased at any time chosen freely by the user. There is therefore no problem arising from maturity structure. What is more, the addition to a borrower's reserves that the receipt of SDRs would bring about might serve to raise the country's creditworthiness with the banks.

5. SOME GENERAL CRITICISMS

Just as there is no shortage of proposals for dealing with the debt problem, there is also no shortage of criticisms of such proposals. However, these tend to fall into two categories. The first is that the size of the debt problem has been overestimated and that by using existing techniques of rescheduling, backed up by adjustment programmes supported by the IMF, the problem may be satisfactorily handled. Of course, adopting this attitude involves a high risk. What if things do not turn out this way? The costs of being wrong could be very significant. There is also the question of whether this option is really feasible, given its emphasis on coercion.

The second criticism is that schemes for rediscounting and for setting up safety nets etc. would themselves be problematic. By reducing the expected return on loans and by effectively writing down the value of bank capital the incentive for banks to make loans would be reduced. New loans are, however, vitally important to the debtor countries. Rediscounting schemes would, so critics maintain, thereby create precisely the crisis they are supposed to help avoid. Moreover, to set up such schemes would require more public capital than seems likely to be made available, given other official capital flows. Furthermore, the schemes involve a 'moral hazard' problem, since they would encourage debtor countries to get into a situation where they warrant relief. They would discourage debtors from trying to deal domestically with their difficulties. Schemes for debt relief therefore need to avoid simply condoning excesses by borrowers, or indeed by lenders. Furthermore, in the sense that debt relief is a form of aid, the question arises as to whether such schemes represent an equitable distribution of aid. The poorest countries with little access to private capital would tend not to benefit from them.

6. CONCLUDING REMARKS

Before going on to examine some proposals in more detail in the next chapter, it may be worthwhile to draw out a few conclusions from the above discussion. First, although current arrangements involving rescheduling and the IMF may have the advantage of producing an environment that is not risk-free for the banks (and of not permitting the banks to get a 'free ride' on the back of the IMF) and yet of not giving debtors a soft option, it is unsatisfactory on a number of counts. Most significantly, the uncertainty it involves in terms of the risks of default, the emphasis on coercion, and the short term nature of rescue packages, are destabilising for the international financial system. There is a case for trying to devise a better and more structured system for handling international debt problems, and for ensuring a continuing inflow of private capital to developing countries, or at least the better-off LDCs.

Second, debt is a complex issue and proposals which treat it as if it was unidimensional are unlikely to be fully satisfactory. Undoubtedly there are problems in striking a balance between what is simultaneously offered to creditors and to debtors. Critics are therefore right to point to the potential problems associated with many proposals that have been put forward for solving the debt problem. However, this is no reason to abandon any attempt at reform – it simply makes the problem more challenging. Three issues need to be examined in any reform exercise. The first relates to the ways by which the capacity of debtors to service their existing debts may be increased. The second relates to the ways in which illiquidity crises – temporary mismatches between receipts and payments – may be handled while causing minimum economic and political disturbances. And the third relates to the ways in which the likelihood of such crises occurring in the future may be reduced.

With regard to the first issue, the role of the IMF, and to a lesser extent the World Bank, as adjustment institutions is central. This issue has already been discussed earlier in the book.

The second issue involves modifying rescheduling to allow for the stretching out of existing debt, possibly to include interest payments as well as principal. However, debt problems of the illiquidity type may be dealt with not only by reducing current payments, which rescheduling attempts to achieve, but also by increasing short term financial inflows. A question here is how such additional flows may be best achieved. Again, with respect to the official sector, this issue has already been discussed.

The third issue involves measures to deal with the overhang of relatively short term debt and more particularly to encourage future inflows of private capital. It is here that proposals for rediscounting, either through official agencies or private secondary markets, insurance schemes and guarantees, become relevant. Yet the arguments for moving away from the heavy reliance that has been placed on short term lending by the banks remain strong. This raises questions relating to the instruments through which creditors may lend to debtors and the appropriate division of functions between the banks and the international agencies.

It is to a more detailed discussion of these issues that subsequent chapters are addressed.

13 Policies to Enhance Private Lending to Developing Countries

Leading on from the discussion in the previous chapter, it may be noted that the long term problem is not so much a matter of surviving any particular debt crisis but rather of modifying financial arrangements in such a way that private capital is encouraged to flow to developing countries. Here again, the use of the phrase 'developing countries' implies too high a level of aggregation. For many developing countries the prospects for attracting significant amounts of private capital are not good. In the foreseeable future 'developing countries' in the context of private flows means a narrow range of better-off LDCs. The poorer developing countries are likely to have to continue to rely on official foreign aid or on some of the other modifications to international financial arrangements discussed in this book. For particular projects in low income countries, however, private capital may still be relevant.

Although this chapter focuses on changing international institutional arrangements, developing countries should not underestimate the extent to which they themselves can influence the amount of private capital they can attract. Borrowers can affect their own creditworthiness by the sorts of economic policies they pursue. Policies which result in large fiscal deficits and rapid rates of credit creation, or an overvalued exchange rate, can do little other than damage a country's ability to attract loans.[1] If, as the analysis in Chapter 11 suggests, banks do ration credit, countries need to be aware of the basis on which this is done. They then have the option of organising domestic economic policy in a way which maximises commercial inflows, although, of course, this is not necessarily the same thing as saying that these will be the best policies when judged by other criteria.

To some extent the impact that domestic policy has on commercial

270

flows is formalised through the intermediation of the IMF either through the 'active' or 'passive' catalytic effect – the former being where the Fund puts pressure on banks to lend further, and the latter being where there is no coercion, but nonetheless the banks view the negotiation of a programme of policies with the Fund as a sign of future good housekeeping. It may be noted here, however, that a country's involvement with the Fund may cut both ways in the eyes of commercial lenders, for while it may enhance creditworthiness for the above reasons, it also means that the country is facing payments problems which are sufficiently severe to warrant recourse to the Fund, and for this reason heavy involvement with the Fund may be interpreted as a reason for little confidence, particularly given the rather poor track record of many of the economic programmes supported by the IMF (see Chapter 4).

Still, as mentioned above, this chapter concentrates not on internal policies but on measures which may facilitate the flow of private finance to developing countries. In particular, the chapter examines ideas relating to an international lender of last resort or discounting agency, the development of secondary markets in developing country loans, guarantees, and the scope for, and nature of, new financial instruments.

1. BASIC PRINCIPLES

Although the detailed discussion of certain proposals can become quite complex, the basic issues involved in private lending to developing countries are relatively straightforward. Lenders wish to maximise their return and to minimise risk. However, given that return and risk are likely to be positively correlated, lenders have to make choices between these two features of lending. One might conceptualise of these underlying preferences in terms of indifference curves showing the various combinations of return and risk between which lenders are indifferent, the usual assumption being that lenders will be risk-averters. From the range of assets available in the market, giving various combinations of return and risk, lenders endeavour to construct a portfolio which optimises their own objective functions.

This is nothing more than the well-established theory of portfolio selection or portfolio balance. However, even though being fairly common ground, it does have interesting implications for the analysis of private lending to developing countries. Clearly to encourage such lending it is necessary either to raise the rate of return or reduce the risk. In either event the *expected* risk-adjusted real return will rise.

Most proposed reforms in this area are directed towards reducing the risk element. However, a problem is that the reduction of risk may not always represent an unambiguous gain, for, while it will encourage lending, there may be an optimal amount of lending. If lending goes beyond this level, there will be costs associated with risk reduction. Measures going too far in the direction of reducing risk may cause overlending and, indeed, overborrowing. Furthermore, to the extent that measures to reduce risk have to be paid for, they will bring with them a decline in return.

A problem, of course, is to define both in quantitative and in qualitative terms what this optimum amount of lending is. It is doubtful whether a satisfactory answer can be given to this question except to note that it depends basically on the ability of the borrower to service the related debt and therefore upon debt capacity. However, even this is only a partial answer. The concept of overborrowing really needs to be related to the social, political and economic objectives of the borrower, with optimal borrowing being that which maximises this welfare function, which itself will involve intertemporal elements. Furthermore, to the extent that borrowing has external effects, there are global aspects of the concept of overborrowing; it is not purely a country-specific issue.

Similarly, with regard to overlending, this concept may be examined from the viewpoint of the individual lender in relation to some objective function. Yet using *only* this approach would rule out the possibility of some reforms causing overlending except to the extent that lenders behave irrationally. Again, there would seem to be externalities at work here for the larger international financial community and for the world economy. Of course, in one sense, any lending that permits overborrowing to take place could be defined as *over*lending. In this sense risk-reducing measures which encourage lenders to make unsound loans could be interpreted as undesirable. It is in this context that the question of 'moral hazard' is normally raised, with reforms designed to deal with current debt difficulties in fact generating future ones.

The global aspects of overlending and underlending may be viewed in a slightly different fashion. If overlending results in the pursuit of inflationary policies while underlending leads to adoption of contractionary ones (or even in default), it follows that the optimum amount of lending occurs where the benefits from a marginal reduction in unemployment equal the costs of a marginal acceleration in inflation. However, this is not the end of it. If the intra-marginal costs of unemployment are high in relation to the intra-marginal benefits from reduced inflation, it also follows that we should not be indifferent between equal amounts of overlending and underlending. This means that, even if there is an optimum degree of positive risk needed to maintain sound lending, it may not be equally damaging to the world economy to have either too little or too much risk. In conditions of recession and of a drying up of private flows to developing countries it may be better to err on the side of reducing risks too far rather than too little.

It is probably unhelpful to pursue this line of argument much further. What transpires is that to encourage future lending, policies designed to reduce risk are relevant but that there are also risks in taking such policies too far.

In principle, lenders' risks may be reduced in a number of ways. The first is to reduce the risk associated with any specific loan. The second is to reduce overall risk through diversification of the lenders' portfolio. Both techniques are of practical relevance in discussing lending to developing countries.

A further related question is who should bear the risk if it is to be reduced for lenders, and indeed who should meet the cost of reducing risk? Should this be borne by the lenders, the borrowers, or, given the global externalities involved, some international agency? Although, again, it is impossible to provide the 'correct' answer to such a question, it needs to be recognised that any practical policy implicitly incorporates a de facto answer.

How then are these basic principles reflected in the various schemes that have or might be suggested?[2]

2. DIVERSIFICATION, SECONDARY MARKETS AND INTERNATIONAL DISCOUNTING

Diversification is a standard way of reducing risk. With respect to lending to developing countries, the principle of diversification could be applied in a number of ways. First, it could be applied to the range of instruments through which lending might be organised, with these comprising different combinations of risk and return and thereby exploiting the different preferences of different lenders. Second, it could be applied to the range of borrowers to whom loans are made.

However, for a reduced concentration of lending to reduce risk, the performances of debtor countries would need to be imperfectly correlated. Diversification here then relates not to the number of countries to which loans are made but to the range of economic characteristics reflected by the borrowing countries.

A third application of the principle of diversification relates to the number of borrowers involved in any particular loan. Euromarkets were quick to evolve the syndicated loan in order to exploit the benefits of diversification, but it is doubtful whether all the potential gains have been derived.

While syndication is a form of *ex-ante* diversification, there are other forms of *ex-post* diversification that are in the process of evolving. These include informally arranged swaps between banks to change the country concentration of their loans. Another development is the evolution of revolving underwriting facilities (RUFs). These combine the characteristics of a traditional syndicated credit with those of a bond. An underwriting syndicate agrees to supply a long term loan upon which the borrower draws by issuing short term securities that the underwriter then either holds or sells. The borrower has access to long term funds while the underwriter holds liquid marketable securities.[3]

In the above case *ex-post* diversification also incorporates elements of a secondary market.[4] The basic idea behind more fully fledged proposals for such a market in LDC debt is to raise its liquidity. By doing so, the risks associated with lending to developing countries could be reduced and the flow of funds enhanced. Of course, given that the price of LDC debt–related assets in the secondary market would be below their face value in circumstances where there was some doubt about the borrower's ability and willingness to repay, there would be a discount on the debt. Initial lenders would be paying a price in terms of lower return for eliminating risk. The size of the discount would reflect the market's judgement on the borrower's creditworthiness.

The principal advantages claimed for secondary markets are those implied by the discussion above. First, they would provide a wider choice of combination of risk and return. By giving lenders the opportunity to sell off some of their debt – albeit at a price – they would encourage lending by lenders who might otherwise be put off by the illiquidity of their loans. Second, secondary markets would, via the price of LDC debt, provide a market indicator of perceived risk. This could help lenders contemplating new loans. It would also help borrowers, since it would provide them with an objective assessment of their own creditworthiness and this would be an important factor in designing economic policy.

Secondary markets would discount LDC debt privately. However, proposals have been put forward which suggest that because of the public good nature of such discounting, in terms of stabilising the international financial system, it should be provided by an official agency or at least be officially backed. Thus, there have been claims for the establishment of an international lender of last resort.[5] Again the details of the plans vary but the general idea is straightforward and very easily explained. It is that an international agency would stand ready to purchase claims on LDC debt from banks at a discount. The agency would then negotiate with the borrower to recover the debt over a lengthened maturity and at a rate above the discounted price paid by the agency but below the original rate. Negotiation might involve conditionality relating to the policies to be pursued by the debtor.

Advocates of such a scheme argue that it has certain fundamental advantages. First, it would stabilise bank lending to developing countries, in conjunction with greater supervision, and it would neutralise periods of underlending and overlending. Second, but in relation to the first point, it would eliminate the current state of uncertainty regarding the availability and nature of lender of last resort arrangements. Decisions based on an informational vacuum are unlikely to be efficient. Third, while uncertainty may be one way of dealing with the moral hazard issue – that the availability of a lender of last resort would encourage banks not to be concerned about making unsound loans – there would seem to be preferable ways of dealing with this problem. Specifically, modification of the discount rate could be used to discourage the banks from overlending while the prospect of conditionality would dissuade the debtors from pursuing policies which resulted in the agency having to buy their debt. Fourth, advocates stress that the purpose of the agency would not be to bail out the banks at zero cost, or protect depositors, but rather would be to ensure that banks continue to lend to LDCs in 'appropriate circumstances.'

Critics argue that such schemes have numerous weaknesses.[6] From amongst these the most significant ones are as follows. First, by providing banks with the opportunity to sell their existing LDC debts, the incentive to lend further in order to protect previous loans would be removed and the flow of funds to developing countries would therefore fall.[7] In the short run this might well happen; in the longer run, however, the reduction in risks associated with a lender of last resort facility should have a positive effect. The short term problem might be overcome via various transitional arrangements which limit the extent to which existing debt could be offloaded. This criticism therefore has more merit when related to discounting as a way of solving a debt crisis than as a way of strengthening the underlying structure of lending to LDCs in the long run.

A second criticism is the moral hazard one discussed above. The issue here, however, is not whether there is a potential moral hazard problem; there is. The relevant question is how best to deal with it. Again, the argument that the price mechanism offers a better way of dealing with moral hazard than does the generation of uncertainty, which itself creates additional costs, is a strong one.

A third criticism of official discounting schemes is that they treat all debt difficulties as if they reflected insolvency on the part of the borrower rather than illiquidity. Noting, as we have done in previous chapters, the problem in distinguishing between these two concepts, this is a valid criticism if the purpose of the scheme is to reduce the rate of interest to the borrower. If, however, the principal purpose is to encourage a larger longer term inflow of funds to developing countries, then this will have implications both for liquidity as well as for solvency, even if the agency merely restructures the debt it purchases.

The fourth criticism, which on the basis of the above discussion would seem to be the most relevant one, relates to the financing of an international lender of last resort. Where is the money to come from? There are two general approaches to this sort of problem. The first is to set up the 'ideal' scheme without worrying about financial constraints, calculate the required funding, and then think of ways in which the finance might be raised. The second is to start with the amount of finance that is likely to be available and devise a scheme subject to this constraint. Some of the grander schemes that fall into the former category are almost certainly not feasible in practice. However, schemes that fall into the latter category may be insufficiently significant to be worth having.

Another important question moves the analysis one step further. Even if adequate official finance could be raised to support the activities of an international discount agency, does this represent the best use of such finance? The answer to this question depends on considerations of both efficiency and equity. If there is effectively a pool of official finance available to support developing countries, using this one way will have opportunity costs in terms of not being able to use it in others. Distributional aspects now become central. Although low income countries could benefit from the increased financial stability associated with international discounting, from the faster rates of world economic and trade growth, and from the alleviation of payments problems in the principal debtor nations which otherwise absorb significant amounts of official and quasi-official finance, they may still feel that the main beneficiaries of the scheme would be a small elite of relatively rich developing countries and that official finance would be channelled to these countries and away from them. While this may not be an adequate reason to abandon attempts to establish a discounting agency, it is something that has to be borne in mind when international financial policy as it relates to the developing world is considered more generally.

3. NEW INSTRUMENTS

The discussion in this chapter and in the previous one has suggested that there may be scope of introducing new instruments through which lenders (not just the banks) can lend and be encouraged to lend to developing countries. Financial markets are constantly evolving such instruments. This section examines one specific and rather more radical proposal. Space precludes the discussion of a second and in some ways even more radical proposal, namely, exchange participation notes (EPNs), under which lenders would essentially take an equity stake in a country's future economic performance and would share in its successes and its failures. Such equity investment could be related to exchange earnings in general, or exchange earnings from a particular commodity.[8] Although radical, the failure to discuss this idea here does not imply that such schemes are not worthy of fuller investigation. However, the new instrument to be discussed here is rather more traditional.

3.1 The time dimension and exchange risk in lending

Given the long-term and structural nature of their balance of payments and development problems, developing countries would no doubt prefer to borrow on a long term programme basis rather than the short term one on which most of their recent borrowing has been undertaken. Apart from this, many of the debt problems faced by certain non-oil developing countries are more a function of the short term maturity of the debt, and the frequently variable interest rate, rather than the level of debt itself. Short maturity need not necessarily constitute a problem if the debt may be rolled over on constant terms, but a roll over exercise is frequently taken as an opportunity to make the terms of a loan harsher, either by raising the rate of interest or the degree of effective policy conditionality, or both. Short maturities by their very nature also increase the extent of uncertainty to which borrowing countries are exposed, both with respect to the availability and the cost of finance. Increasing uncertainty can hardly fail to exert an adverse effect on the ability of potential borrowers to plan economic development. From the borrower's point of view, then, a system based on short term credits is inherently unstable.

In an environment of high and, more significantly, variable inflation it is easy to see the attraction of short term contracts to lenders. Broadly speaking, short term loans enable the nominal interest rate to be adjusted to compensate for the effects of unexpected inflation. Considerations of both return and risk mean that lenders will favour short term lending over long term lending for as long as the nominal interest rate is invariant throughout the duration of the contract. With a fixed nominal interest rate and an accelerating rate of inflation, the real rate of interest will clearly fall, whereas with a variable rate of inflation it will vary. The problem is how to encourage lenders to lend over the long term.

Another aspect of lenders' risk in international deals involves possible variations in the relative price of the currency in which the deal is denominated. A lender will tend to lose if the currency of denomination is subject to depreciation. An individual lender may endeavour to cover this risk by ensuring that total lending is denominated in a range of currencies, though this may involve the acceptance of a lower overall rate of return. Alternatively, any bias in the currency denomination of loans may be made to match a similar bias in the pattern of payments obligations. The problem of exchange risk will evaporate if all lending and importing is conducted in the same currency or similar specific currency amounts, except to the extent that receipts and payments are unsynchronised inter-temporally. To bring about such a situation in circumstances where, for reasons other than the minimisation of exchange risk, it would not be chosen, would involve lenders in a loss.

3.2 Features of a new instrument

Alternatively, lenders may be encouraged to lend over the long term by some form of index linking. This could be achieved by tying the nominal rate of return to an index of world inflation.[9] Guaranteeing a fixed real rate of return to lenders may be the price that borrowers have to pay in order to induce the long term lending that would be more appropriate for them. The question is whether deficit countries would regard this as a price worth paying. There are reasons to believe that they may do, not least because it is a price that they may effectively already be paying for short term loans which in other respects they regard as inferior. Of course, as the inflation rate falls, index linking will become more attractive to borrowers and less attractive to lenders. What the actual real rate of interest would need to be would depend on the strength of demand for finance in deficit countries as well as the supply of finance made available by lenders, although it might be expected to be considerably below the real marginal productivity of capital in developing countries.

Turning to the problem of exchange risk, in principle this can be remedied in two ways. The first is to express individual contracts in individual currencies but to hold a blend of loans denominated in different currencies. Lenders would thereby effectively have lending denominated in a basket of currencies and, as a result, the exchange risk of total lending would fall below the average exchange risk associated with each individual loan. The simpler alternative is initially to express all loans in terms of the average value of a basket of currencies. The international community already possesses the Special Drawing Right, which has its value determined by the average value of five currencies – the dollar, the pound sterling, the franc, the mark and the yen – and which is more stable in value than any individual currency. An alternative to the SDRs as a unit of account might be the European currency unit (ECU).

The above analysis has in effect defined the key features of a new recycling instrument; it is a long term bond with a maturity of perhaps fifty years, denominated in SDRs and yielding a guaranteed real rate of return. However, a number of questions remain to be answered. First, what would be the institutional arrangements under which the bond would be issued? Second, how could the problems facing low-income and uncreditworthy countries be remedied? It is to these and other questions that the following sections are addressed.

3.3 Method of issue

While developing countries would prefer to borrow over the long term than the short term, they have had singularly little success in realising this objective. Bond issues by LDCs totalled only $2.5 billion in 1983 and these were highly concentrated in a very narrow range of higher income LDCs. International capital markets abound in regulations, and developing countries have encountered immense problems in gaining access to them.[10] There seems little reason to suppose that the international capital markets will provide long term recycling in the future unless changes are made. Part of the problem no doubt results from the risk as perceived by lenders in lending on a long term basis to one individual developing country. In order to reduce this aspect of risk, a case may be made for bonds to be issued by groups of developing countries.[11] Acting in groups, developing countries may find it both easier and cheaper to borrow, since the risk facing lenders would tend to be reduced.

There are a number of criteria upon which the grouping of borrowing countries could be organised. In principle, if the aim is to reduce lenders' risk, the grouping should be arranged so as to maximise the degree of negative correlation between instabilities in individual members of the group. Alternatively, the participation of individual developing countries in a joint bond issue could be left rather more open. However, it seems likely that some constraints on participation would be required. For instance, the objective of risk spreading would require that the extent of participation by any individual country in any specific bond issue should be limited. Limitation could be achieved by not permitting any borrower a larger share of an individual bond issue than some multiple of its share of the combined national incomes of all *potential* participating countries.

Overborrowing by any individual country could be limited by not permitting the participation of countries with high debt service obligations in relation to either GDP or exports, unless for the specific purpose of funding short term debt, which in itself could be a very useful exercise. An individual deficit country's potential borrowing capacity under the new scheme would therefore vary inversely with its existing debt service ratio and its existing level of debt, and positively with its growth rate of exports or GDP. Since such limitations on participation would have the effect of reducing the supply of and increasing the demand for bonds, they would unambiguously lower the rate of interest as compared with a situation where no limitations were imposed. Their effects on the quantity of bonds issued would be indeterminate and would depend on whether the supply or demand effect were greater. If the expansionary effect on demand exceeded the contractionary effect on supply, the quantity of bonds issued would rise.

3.4 Guarantees

A similar combined effect of lowering the rate of interest and increasing the quantity of bonds issued might be achieved through offering lenders an additional guarantee against default, since this would tend to raise the demand for bonds.[12] However, guarantees raise a number of issues. What form would they take? How would they be financed and would they generate extra finance or simply use up finance that would otherwise have been lent directly? If guarantees were used to provide full backing for all loans, it might be found that finance that would have gone into direct lending would instead go into financing the guarantees; assuming that not all guarantees are called on, the short-term impact would then be to reduce the total flow of finance to developing countries. The picture would be different if guarantees were only to be partial and if finance were to be held to cover only a proportion of total guarantee obligations.

The finance required to meet guarantee obligations could be provided by contributions as a form of aid, or through international policy such as selling IMF gold. Alternatively, guarantees could be financed by lenders effectively receiving a lower interest rate than borrowers are effectively paying. This latter option could involve either lenders financing a guarantee fund, in which case they would in essence be purchasing a reduction in risk and more narrowly fixing the parameters of their loans in exchange for a lower rate of return, or it could involve borrowers providing the finance, such as in the form of paying an insurance premium in exchange for insurance cover.[13]

Whatever the case, a prior and open question is whether any form of guarantee would be necessary to ensure the success of an LDC bond issue; after all, the principal purpose behind a group issue is precisely to reduce lenders' perceived risk. Certainly guarantees would reduce the risk still further, and if risk proves to be the effective constraint on lending, they may be necessary. Whether they are or not may, of course, depend on the nature and perceived creditworthiness of the countries forming the borrowing group. There are a number of possibilities. First, lenders may simply not be prepared to lend to countries they regard as uncreditworthy, either individually or as part of a group. In these circumstances the group borrowing scheme, though still useful to creditworthy or marginally creditworthy borrowers as well as to lenders, would be of little use to uncreditworthy countries. Second, lenders may be prepared to lend, without requiring guarantees, to some countries as part of a group that they would not have been prepared to lend to individually, provided that those countries regarded as uncreditworthy do not constitute more than a certain proportion of the group. Third, lenders might only be prepared to lend to such countries even as part of a group, if guarantees were to be provided. Even if guarantees are unnecessary in the sense that lenders would be prepared to lend without them, their existence may still induce a larger flow of loans than would otherwise occur.

3.5 Distributional aspects

The above discussion introduces certain distributional aspects of an LDC group bond issue and it is worth examining these in further detail. Assume, for simplicity, that non-oil developing countries may be divided into those that are seen as commercially creditworthy and those that are not, although, of course, such a division is not so clear cut in reality. Assume further that non-creditworthy countries may be subdivided into those where a relatively high prospective rate of return is combined with an unacceptably high level of risk and those where the prospective rate of return is low. Any scheme which involves a commercial interest rate will be of little assistance to the last category of countries, since their need is for concessionary finance. Participation by these countries in a joint bond issue would therefore depend, first, on the willingness of lenders to lend to a group of which they were members, and, second, on the willingness of other borrowers to subsidise their debt service payments. Even excluding these low return countries, however, a joint bond issue would tend to involve cross subsidisation from the more creditworthy to the less creditworthy members of the borrowing group, since participation by the less creditworthy, higher risk countries would push the rate of interest above what it would have been had the group consisted solely of the more creditworthy developing countries. Considerations of this nature imply that borrowing groups may have to consist of countries possessing a similar degree of creditworthiness, unless the more creditworthy are prepared, for humanitarian, political or economic reasons, to aid the less creditworthy by effectively transferring some of their own creditworthiness. One reason why they may be prepared to do so would be in an attempt to expand export markets. Furthermore, if the joint borrowing scheme was the only form of lending that offered guarantees, even the more creditworthy borrowers could find it easier and/or cheaper to borrow as a member of a group comprising less creditworthy countries than as individuals.

3.6 The problem of default

Even though the constraints on participation will limit it, the possibility of default by borrowing countries remains. Although the lenders' risk in the case of default may be covered by guarantees, the question of how the borrowing group of countries would deal with it still has to be answered. There are a number of possibilities. First, defaulters could be barred from future participation in bond issues until they settled their obligations with the guarantee fund. However, this would have the effect of shutting off one important source of finance for countries that would tend to be in great financial need, for reasons of liquidity if nothing else. A more attractive alternative may then be to make future participation conditional on the acceptance of certain domestic policies.

A final alternative would be available if the guarantee fund were to be financed by contributions from the borrowing countries themselves. Since borrowers are in essence taking out insurance against their own default, this could be discouraged by raising the insurance premium of a defaulting member. Providing that the scheme does not create a positive incentive to default, which would clearly ruin its long term viability, there seems little reason to believe that default cannot be adequately handled.

However, a more intransigent default problem may exist with regards to low productivity countries although, as already noted, such countries may in any case be unsuitable participants in a scheme which is based on commercial criteria.

3.7 Institutional arrangements

A final point relates to the institutional arrangements under which a joint LDC bond issue might be organised. It seems unlikely that informal and *ad hoc* negotiations between individual developing countries would constitute the ideal solution, since there is little reason to believe that the resultant grouping would be consistent with the theoretical guidelines for their composition. The identification of groups and the selection of the countries to be involved in any particular bond issue might therefore be more appropriately undertaken by some form of central agency, to which interested parties would apply.

What form should this central agency take? In principle the functions of the agency could be performed by an existing institution such as the IMF or the World Bank. But it may turn out that these institutions are insufficiently flexible to accommodate an essentially new and different role, and therefore a new institution may be required. This new institution could include or exclude developed countries. An institution with exclusive LDC membership may be more attractive to developing countries but may also make the associated bonds less attractive to potential lenders, even though the institution would not be directly responsible for the related payments and obligations and would simply be co-ordinating the activities of individual participating countries as well as organising the guarantee fund if this were to be included in the scheme.

The issuing agency would also need to organise a market in the bonds, once issued, in order to increase the degree of liquidity associated with them. With little doubt it has been the liquidity characteristics of the Eurocurrency market that have made it attractive to lenders in the past.

4. CONCLUDING REMARKS

This chapter has examined various issues associated with enhancing private lending to developing countries. It is concluded that while there are problems associated with measures designed to support private lending, there is, on balance, a strong case for doing something in this direction. Lack of funds may mean that the scope for official action is strictly limited, although many of the other arguments against international discounting agencies may be somewhat misplaced. The evolution of private secondary markets would appear to be beneficial and there are signs that such arrangements are indeed evolving.

Many debt problems have been associated with the inappropriate manner in which financing has been undertaken, namely, through short term bank credits. A strong argument may be made for trying to devise new instruments which provide a more appropriate vehicle for the transfer of financial resources. In principle these are various contenders. The one examined in this chapter involves the introduction of index-linked long term bonds denominated in SDRs and issued jointly by groups of developing countries under the auspices of an international agency. Such an instrument would reduce many of the elements of risk associated with lending to developing countries. Lenders would therefore benefit. Borrowers would also benefit from the increased and more assured supply of long term programme capital. The world as a whole would benefit from the greater international stability associated with long term lending and from avoiding the crisis measures associated with debt crises. Even the non-creditworthy LDCs might benefit indirectly from the trade effects induced by an increased aggregate flow of finance to developing countries as well as through any redistribution of concessionary finance that might occur.

14 The Banks and the IMF: the Nature of, and Scope for, Co-operation

Elementary economic theory gives us some insight into the principles underlying the relationship between the banks and the Fund, since it establishes the circumstances under which private markets fail to generate an efficient solution. Apart from distributional issues, to be considered in the next section, economies of scale and externalities are amongst the principal causes of market failure. Further examination of these causes, as applied to private international financial markets, provides an initial outline of the delineation of activities between the banks and the Fund.

Rational decisions that are vital in the pursuit of efficiency are assisted by the provision of relevant and accurate information. It might be expected that more information would enable lenders, and indeed borrowers, to reach more efficient decisions. However, information is not a 'free good'. There are costs associated with both its collection and its interpretation. The Fund can collect information more cheaply than the banks because duplication can be avoided and economies of scale exploited. Moreover, with longer experience in balance-of-payments financing, the Fund may have 'learned by doing' what data to collect, while the banks still have relatively little experience in this area.

Economies of scale apply not only to the collection of information. The Fund also has more expertise, and encounters lower costs, in assessing and monitoring macroeconomic performance and policy. The principle of comparative advantage then suggests that the Fund should concentrate on the functions of collecting information and encouraging payments adjustment. At the same time, the banks should concentrate more on supplying finance.

As regards the concept of *externalities*, decisions taken by one bank based on trying to maximise its own short term profits or minimise its losses may have adverse effects on the international banking and financial system as a whole, and, in the long run, may actually have a negative feedback on the initiator. In international banking externalities pose a potentially very serious problem.[1]

Efficiency requires that external benefits are maximised and external costs minimised. These externalities may be internalised, and therefore made to have an impact on decision-taking, through the activities of the Fund. One particular externality relates to expectations and confidence, which have a very important bearing on the willingness of banks to lend. The banks clearly lend in the expectation that they will make a profit by so doing. Where their confidence is damaged, expected profits decline and lending is reduced. Indeed, the phenomenon of self-fulfilling expectations can also easily occur, where, for example, banks become less willing to lend to a country in the expectation of deteriorating economic performance, and the reduction in the availability of finance may then contribute to just such a deterioration.

Where expectations are volatile, and there are large swings in confidence not based on the underlying economic situation, the outcome will be instability in lending and associated economic instability. Finance that is easily available when confidence is high may disappear rapidly when it is low. Such instability imposes costs on borrowers, lenders, and the international financial system alike, not least because it raises the degree of uncertainty. Participants would benefit from greater continuity in lending. In principle, the Fund has an important role to play here, since by neutralising excessive swings in confidence it increases the long term volume of financing by the private sector. However, the Fund has to be able to 'read' the situation better than the banks. While, in principle, the superior availability of information should permit it to do so, the Fund also needs to demonstrate that its own advice, as represented by conditionality, is effective in the sense of raising the global level of both output and trade.

1. PRINCIPLES AND PRACTICE

The concepts introduced above provide some insight into the relationship between the banks and the IMF and help to pinpoint a number of problems.

The political economy of the world's financial system is not merely concerned with efficiency but also with equity. It is important to consider the position of individual countries or groups of countries. For instance, solutions which rank quite highly as being reasonably efficient might be unsatisfactory on equity grounds if they fail to provide assistance to the poorest countries in the world.

Recent experience illustrates this point. Attention has been focused on the problems of a small group of relatively rich developing countries. The talk has been about collaboration between the banks and the IMF to help solve *their* difficulties. The majority of low-income countries, in which a much larger proportion of the world's population lives and which, in many ways, face much more fundamental and difficult financial problems, have tended to be overlooked, partly because they have not in the past been considered sufficiently creditworthy to borrow much from the banks.

Given the Fund's limited resources, involvement with the richer developing countries ties up finance which might otherwise be lent to poorer countries. If there is to be a division of labour between the IMF and the banks, perhaps it should be in terms of the countries to which they lend, with the Fund filling those gaps in financial provision left by the banks.

Yet specialisation on the basis of this criterion precludes complete specialisation in terms of *function*. The IMF provides finance as well as encouraging adjustment. Even in the richer developing countries the Fund is nowadays increasingly required to lend its own resources, if only to increase the confidence of the banks. Complete specialisation either in terms of function or country would seem to be ruled out.

Furthermore, there is the important question of whether the banks can rely on the effectiveness of the adjustment policies supported by the Fund to increase the ability of debtors to repay loans; and whether, in turn, the Fund can rely on the banks to provide the necessary finance once an adjustment programme has been negotiated.

A problem is also associated with the provision of information by the Fund to the banks. Although the availability of more information may improve the decision-making of banks, their decisions are going to be based on endeavouring to maximise their own private performance; they may not be socially optimal if there are other considerations which, while deemed important by the international community, are ignored by individual banks. Furthermore, specific information may be open to more than one interpretation, and the decisions reached by the IMF and banks on the basis of the same information may differ.

But what if the banks take the wrong decisions? In the cut and thrust of most free markets a bad decision is reflected by a reduction in profits or a loss. The cost of the error is, however, largely contained within the original decision-making unit. On the other hand, the effect of (say) overlending by some banks is most unlikely to be so contained. It may result in a debt crisis and ultimately perhaps default. If this occurs, confidence is damaged and other banks become more reluctant to lend. Financing will be reduced, with adverse effects on both individual borrowing countries and the world economy.

To restore and maintain confidence, the Fund could, of course, act as some sort of guarantor, but this has the danger of making banks over-confident. A middle path needs to be found between providing the banks with a completely risk-free environment and making lending so risky that what is a socially optimal level of financing by the banks becomes unattractive. Externalities which exaggerate the effect of any volatility in lending argue for trying to maintain continuity.

2. BANK FINANCING IN THE 1970s AND 1980s

Amongst developing countries, those in Latin America had been the principal clients of both the Fund and the banks up until the early 1970s, even though the banks had not been heavily engaged in BoP financing. The relationship between the banks and the IMF became caricatured as one in which the Fund had a 'catalytic effect' on private capital inflows, with the banks interpreting the negotiation of a Fund programme and the granting of the Fund's 'seal of approval' as almost a sufficient indication of creditworthiness.

In the second half of the 1970s, following the first oil shock of 1973–4, the position began to change. The banks, with substantial OPEC deposits, lent large amounts to a limited number of better-off developing countries without the Fund being involved. The 'seal of approval' was no longer necessary. Meanwhile, the poorer developing countries, which were also encountering severe payments problems largely as a result of adverse movements in their terms of trade, increasingly turned to the Fund.

The mid- to late 1970s witnessed a significant overall move to the private market place and away from the official sector. Quantitatively the banks became the principal channel through which recycling occured. Within this overall pattern, the relationship between the banks and the IMF dramatically altered. By 1981 almost all the Fund's outstanding credits were to countries with relatively low per capita incomes. It appeared that a division of responsibilities with respect to country groups had de facto been achieved: the banks lending to the NICs and the Fund bailing out those countries deemed uncreditworthy by the banks.

The new found specialisation proved to be only temporary. By 1982 the major commercial borrowers, such as Mexico, Brazil and Argentina, were encountering debt problems. Perceiving the reduced creditworthiness of these countries, the banks became less anxious to lend; in crisis circumstances the Fund once again became involved, partly as a provider of finance, but perhaps mainly as an adjustment institution vetting stabilisation programmes, and thereby attempting to discourage the banks from reducing their exposure. However, the banks themselves, while again viewing the implementation of a Fund-backed programme as a necessary condition, were no longer happy to accept it as sufficient. Even so, the mutual involvement of the Fund and the banks in these heavily indebted countries almost unavoidably resulted in an increased degree of informal co-operation.

It is not difficult to identify deficiencies in the recycling mechanisms as they operated in the 1970s and early 1980s, even though at the time the contribution of the banks, and, in particular, their flexibility and adaptability in dealing with such a massive task of intermediation, was frequently discussed in terms bordering on the euphoric. Clearly, the euphoria was premature.

In summary, the deficiencies are as follows. Debt crises have not been avoided. Once encountered, they have been handled in an ad hoc and unstructured way. The system has not provided low-income countries with sufficient finance to enable them to avoid severe adjustment, which has in many cases resulted in falling living standards.[2]

It now appears that the banks overlent, and countries overborrowed, when judged against their revealed capacity to repay.[3] In part, this capacity was affected by internal factors, such as the way in which borrowed finance was used, but it was also significantly affected by world economic developments, such as the deepening recession and rising real interest rates.

In a sense, the *ex-post* observation that the banks overlent is tautologically true; the more relevant question is what makes a specific amount of lending excessive? Should the banks have seen *ex ante* that they were lending too much to certain countries? One needs to fight the temptation to be wise after the event. In many respects, the countries to which the banks lent seemed economically to be relatively strong, and there is even some evidence to suggest that borrowed resources were wisely used.

Certainly, the saving and investment ratios in the principal recipients of commercial finance were relatively high, suggesting that borrowed funds were not used exclusively to finance unproductive consumption.[4]

Although a fall in the savings ratio has been found to provide a relatively good forward indicator of debt crises,[5] a high level of domestic saving clearly does not guarantee that debt problems will be avoided. The key question is whether savings can be converted into an export surplus and thereby foreign exchange – the so-called transfer problem. In the case of countries that have encountered debt problems, the banks showed insufficient appreciation of their vulnerability to falling export demand, declining terms of trade (in the Mexican case, primarily the falling price of oil), and rising real interest rates.[6] Some form of sensitivity analysis would help to reveal the implications of different scenarios and would help banks to minimise their risks. In retrospect, during the 1970s probably too much emphasis was put on return and too little on risk.

Consideration of return and risk enables a further distinction to be drawn between the Fund and the banks, since the Fund is not concerned with maximising its rate of return. After all, it lends a significant proportion of its resources at sub-market interest rates. Instead, it attempts to maximise the likelihood that its loans will be repaid by attaching conditionality to the majority of them.

Perhaps the main lesson to be learned from the experience of the 1970s is that greater emphasis needs to be placed on the appropriateness of the uses to which finance provided by the banks is put, appropriateness in this context meaning the contribution towards strengthening the underlying balance of payments. In this way the incidence of debt crises can be reduced. In other words, in the long run, the debt problem needs to be handled through prevention rather than cure.

It should be noted at this stage that such prevention would not necessarily reduce commercial inflows. Indeed, in the longer run it will almost certainly increase them, since the adverse effects of debt crises on banks' confidence will be avoided. Both the borrowers and the banks will benefit from the increased continuity of lending and from avoiding the destabilising effects of pro-cyclical lending behaviour.

3. PROPOSALS FOR REFORM

Growing realisation that the relationship between the IMF and the banks needs to be more fully thought out has generated a number of reform proposals. These fall into basically two categories. The first involves an increase in the degree of direct and formal co-operation or collaboration between the Fund and the banks. The second involves only the indirect and informal collaboration that would be associated with a sharper definition of roles, responsibilities, and areas of specialisation.

Into the first category come proposals for enhancing the flow of information from the IMF to the banks, for providing IMF guarantees, for refinancing or rediscounting commercial loans and for closer co-operation in debt reschedulings.

The idea behind schemes for improving the information flow is, as noted earlier, to enable the banks to make better lending decisions. However, while the provision of additional information – provided that it is accurate and unbiased – is certainly unlikely to result in decisions being less rational, it may not lead to much improvement.

There are a number of reasons for this. First, the information that the Fund can provide to banks depends largely on what information is provided to it by member countries. Indeed, some information may be regarded as confidential by the Fund and may therefore not be made available to the banks. Furthermore, knowledge that information may be made available to the banks may adversely affect the flow of information from countries to the Fund. Second, a good deal of information that is undoubtedly relevant to banks' lending decisions, relating, say, to political stability, either does not exist in the Fund or would, in any case, be treated with circumspection. Third, in reaching decisions about commercial lending it is information about the future that is important. To argue that Fund projections are no worse than anyone else's is not to argue that they are always accurate. To base lending purely on Fund projections may itself therefore involve a substantial risk element. Fourth, specific information may be open to a number of interpretations, and there is no certainty that those given by the Fund and the banks will coincide. Should the Fund then advise the banks how to interpret the information it makes available to them? Probably not, although to some extent this happens de facto through the Fund's own lending practices and, in particular, conditionality.

Realistically, the exchange of more information does not offer a panacea, and it is unlikely that it would have necessarily avoided debt crises in the past.

Guarantees and rediscounting would involve the Fund standing ready to pay back the banks in the event of default. The Fund would essentially buy out the banks. By comparison, refinancing would involve the Fund providing countries with the finance necessary to pay back loans. Although the details of such schemes can vary significantly – for example, refinancing is directly associated with conditionality while rediscounting might not be – they share the common feature that they are basically all ways in which the IMF could support the private banks. While this is their principal advantage, it is also their principal disadvantage, since, as discussed in Chapter 13, they would provide the banks with a risk-reduced environment. They might thereby encourage the banks to overlend, and cause precisely the problems that they are intended to solve.

IMF guarantees could take on various forms. They could be partial or full, and could cover exchange risk or default. Whatever the precise form, there is the question of whether guarantees would merely tie up IMF resources that would otherwise have been lent to developing countries, with the result that there would be no net increase in total financial flows. From a distributional point of view guarantees could be inequitable if they served to increase private bank lending to the richer developing countries at the expense of IMF lending to the poorer ones. Furthermore, care would need to be taken that the IMF did not confer an additional rent to private banks. A scheme might therefore be envisaged which reduced but did not remove the risk. To pay for the reduced risk, banks might be prepared to sacrifice some return. This sacrifice could take the form of a payment to an account within the Fund which would be used to finance the guarantee scheme over the long run.[7] To prevent the existence of IMF guarantees encouraging default by developing countries, access to Fund finance would need to be at a commercial or even penalty interest rate and would need to involve relatively strict conditionality. Thus, this scheme, while not resulting in direct co-operation or co-financing between the IMF and the banks, could involve an additional financial flow from the banks to developing countries and strict conditionality.[8]

The attitude of developing countries to IMF guarantees, redis-counting etc. might be expected to depend on the anticipated pattern of financial flows that would be associated with each, on the terms and conditions involved, and on the expected reactions of both the banks and the IMF. Since it would not necessarily be the case that all individual developing countries would benefit, or benefit equally, under all the various schemes, it is difficult to assess precisely what the general attitude of developing countries would be.

Under a system of co-financing there would almost certainly be dislike of the additional element of conditionality that would be involved. Developed countries that had previously enjoyed access to unconditional private finance might therefore be expected to oppose co-financing, feeling that they were being forced into the Fund. However, if the choice was between an expansion in the availability of finance under co-financing or no expansion, their attitude might change. It is unlikely that countries assessed by the banks as uncredit-worthy would enjoy an additional financial inflow as a direct result of co-financing; indeed, to the extent that co-financing channelled a larger proportion of the Fund's resources to high and middle income developing countries, the effect on low-income countries could be adverse.

Low-income developing countries might also be expected to be unenthusiastic about a system of IMF guarantees, if this were to protect the existing system of private lending at the expense of lending to them. Even if guarantees did not tie up existing Fund resources, but were to be financed by additional contributions, poor countries would no doubt feel that the distribution of the additional finance was inequitable. High and middle income developing coun-tries might also be less than enthusiastic about IMF guarantees, since it might involve prior vetting by the Fund, conditionality and a reduced willingness by the banks to take on unguaranteed loans.

A concern with many of these proposals is not to provide a risk-free environment for the banks. However, as noted earlier, there is a middle path between the 'risk-free' and the 'sub-optimal' lending scenarios. This middle path may well involve some more limited scheme for partial guarantees, or rediscounting at a punitive discount rate. Yet, even in this case, the Fund may not be the ideal institution to undertake such a role, since it would pre-empt the use of scarce IMF resources, and would have adverse distributional consequences, in that there would be fewer resources to lend to the low-income countries which had been unable to attract commercial credit in the first place. The poorest countries could then be crowded out of Fund finance. The Bank of International Settlements (BIS), or the World Bank, is probably better equipped to fulfil the guarantor or rediscounting role.

Indeed, in the midst of a debt crisis the role of the BIS may be vital in providing temporary liquidity while IMF finance is being arranged. It will take some time to negotiate a Fund programme, yet without this the banks are unlikely to be willing to take decisions on their own commitments. At the same time, the Fund may be unwilling to make its own resources available unless it is assured that these will not just be used to pay back the banks. In this situation the BIS may provide a useful 'safety net' source of short term finance while other arrangements are being concluded.

Clearly, it is important to have some mechanism for handling debt crises once they have arisen, and perhaps the Fund should play a more significant organisational role in co-ordinating its own lending policies with those of others than it has in the past. To have a more structured way of dealing with crises would reduce the risks that they would have adverse knock-on effects; and the minimisation of international financial instability is an entirely appropriate activity for the Fund.

Of course, as noted above, in the longer term it is preferable to avoid debt crises, and this objective leads us on to consider the second and more indirect form of co-operation between the Fund and the banks. Indirect co-operation implies a fairly precise definition of the responsibilities of the IMF and the banks and means some specialisation both of function and country involvement.

In low-income countries the IMF should provide both the finance and the adjustment advice, since commercial loans are largely inappropriate for such countries, except to finance projects that are likely to yield a commercial rate of return. Low-income countries require more aid not commercial credit, though in principle this could be in the form of subsidies or guarantees provided by donors on private inflows. As development takes place, the Fund could attempt gradually to wean countries on to private capital markets. Here it would provide invaluable technical assistance, although it would also need to form some view on the sustainable volume of private borrowing.

In the richer and more creditworthy countries the distinction between the financing and adjustment roles would be reflected more clearly in the specifics of institutional involvement, with the IMF providing only a small proportion of the finance, but playing a central role in negotiating an appropriate adjustment strategy. The banks would, on the other hand, provide most of the finance, but would make this available only where a 'suitable' adjustment programme was being implemented.

Co-operation between the IMF and the banks would be dictated by the fact that the appropriateness of any adjustment programme would depend in part on the availability of sustainable inflows of private finance, while these, in turn, would depend in part on the nature of the adjustment programme. Close consultation between the Fund, representatives of the banks and borrowing countries would therefore be desirable.

The Fund should perhaps, however, do rather more than simply form a view on sustainable inflows of private capital. It might wish to be able to set both maximum and minimum limits. Setting the former does not constitute much of a problem; indeed, the Fund has not infrequently employed just such a performance criterion as one aspect of its conditionality. Setting minimum limits as part of Fund programmes is more difficult, since it is not something over which borrowing countries have control, but rather the banks. The Fund would have to rely on bringing some pressure to bear on the banks to reach such minimum lending levels – an activity in which, via the central banks of member countries, it is not without some experience. The contribution that the banks could make to raising the degree of international financial stability would be by ensuring some minimum amount of continuing new lending activity in association with adjustment programmes approved by the IMF. This would be a price the banks would pay for the risk-reducing activities of the Fund. However, the preferable alternative would be for the Fund and the borrowing countries to create an environment in which banks want to lend.

By successful exploitation of the comparative advantage of the IMF and the banks, a virtuous circle could be established under which external benefits would be maximised and external costs minimised; stability would be increased, and confidence restored and maintained.

However, it needs to be stressed that the banks will have confidence in IMF programmes only if these are seen to be successful in strengthening the balance of payments of borrowing countries. If

Fund conditionality is to be given the central role described above, it is vital that it is made as efficient as possible; and this implies modifications to existing practice to make it more flexible and more appropriate to circumstances in individual countries. In certain, though not all, circumstances, there is a case for moving away from the conventional type of Fund programme, which, in particular, concentrates on strictly limited credit creation, to one which emphasises agreement on policies designed to change the underlying real structure of the economy and switch resources into the traded goods sector. Such policies would rely heavily on inducing changes in relative prices (see Chapter 4).

The specialisation advocated above could be achieved in a more direct way by the Fund extending its lending on the basis of resources borrowed, under its own name, from the private capital market. Under such an arrangement the banks would again be effectively providing the finance and the Fund the adjustment input. Ignoring the technical problems, there are a number of broader issues to which direct borrowing would give rise (for a fuller discussion of these, see Chapter 8).

4. THE WORLD BANK

It should also be remembered that the World Bank and other multilateral agencies, as well as central banks and governments in industrial countries, have a role to play in recycling. Indeed, the World Bank has recently introduced a set of three new instruments designed to increase the participation of commercial banks in the financing of Bank projects and to provide better maturities to developing country borrowers than are available from direct borrowings in private markets. Since 1974 the amount of co-financing between the Bank and the private sector has increased quite markedly, yet up to now the Bank and the private banks have entered into separate loan agreements with borrowing countries. Under the new arrangements, and in an effort to supplement existing co-financing, the Bank will participate jointly in loans, but will not have its principal repaid until after the commercial banks have been fully repaid. It will finance any balance of principal left at the end of the scheduled term of commercial loans which results from interest rates being higher than anticipated – the idea here being to allow borrowers' annual debt service payments to be fixed and the maturity of loans to be extended – and it will guarantee the repayment of the later part of loans without initially participating in them directly.[9]

5. CONCLUDING REMARKS

There are important lessons to be learned from the experiences of the 1970s and 1980s about the roles of the IMF and the banks in the intermediation of international finance. The debt problems of the 1980s and the related anxiety over excessive bank exposure in developing countries have followed on the heels of a dramatic increase in private lending in the mid-1970s. This reveals the global unsubtlety of commercial lending, which tends to behave in a pro-cyclical fashion and thereby to increase international financial instability.

The relationship between the banks and the Fund should be seen as but one important part of a much broader picture. A better organised relationship between them should reduce the likelihood of future debt crises and enable those that occur to be handled better. It is unlikely, however, that this improved relationship would eliminate them altogether, since there are a range of other influences, such as trade policy and the conduct of macroeconomic management in the industrial countries that do not currently experience debt problems themselves, over which neither the banks nor the Fund have much control. Nevertheless, closer co-ordination between the banks and the Fund, exploiting the latter's expertise as an adjustment institution, could have the beneficial effects of reducing the likelihood of debt crises and of increasing stability and confidence.[10]

But what form should such co-ordination take? Co-operation cannot be very close, since the Fund and the banks have different institutional objectives. The banks are profit-maximising commercial enterprises and the Fund is not. Nor should too much be expected of additional flows of information *per se*. However, mutual concerns dictate a form of co-ordinated or integrated specialisation. Such co-ordination probably requires a forum in which borrowing countries, the banks, the IMF, and the World Bank would be represented. This might take the form of broadening out conventional Fund negotiations to include representatives of the banks that might be involved, but it might be better achieved under a new discussion framework. Additional regular discussions between the Fund and the banks to analyse global trends as well as their mutual interests and individual responsibilities would also be of positive assistance. Closer co-operation of this kind could be facilitated through the recently formed Institute of International Finance, which is based, along with the Fund, in Washington. Indeed, apart from providing country information to commercial banks, one of the possible functions of the IIF might be to serve as a focal point for dialogue between the international banks and the multilateral lending institutions.

15 Financial Co-operation amongst Developing Countries

Almost all the proposals discussed in this book up to now have involved modifying international financial arrangements within the existing set of North–South institutions. An alternative line of argument runs as follows: since the developed countries are unlikely to make many, if any, changes designed with the purpose of offering positive discrimination in favour of LDCs, the latter should explore financial options that do not rely on the compliance of the North. The purpose of this chapter is to examine a number of these options.[1]

However, the very fact that the discussion is relegated to just one chapter reveals that the conclusion reached here is that the scope for reform in this direction is limited. Certainly, plans which see co-operation amongst developing countries as replacing the need for co-operation between developing and developed countries are rejected. Although frustration with the lack of progress in North–South discussions is understandable, there is little reason to believe that South–South discussions would be any more productive. Indeed, developing countries would sustain significant losses by delinking themselves from existing international financial institutions, and their greatest gain is likely to come from policies which attempt to achieve marginal and incremental reforms within the existing international framework.

A more positive conclusion is that, while not abandoning their attempts to work within the existing system, there may be some scope for closer co-operation between subsets of developing countries. Possibilities for co-operation on this smaller scale should not therefore be ignored.

1. THE PREREQUISITES FOR EFFECTIVE CO-OPERATION

Plans for closer financial co-operation amongst developing countries have to deal with a number of problems. First, they have to identify those deficiencies of the existing arrangements that they are setting out to remedy. Part of the problem here is that some deficiencies may be more transitory than others, and even those that are not transitory may still change in certain ways through time. Policy responses therefore need to be flexible.

Second, plans need to carry the appropriate degree of financial and political backing. There is little point in proposing schemes that require levels of funding and an extent of political co-operation which will simply not be forthcoming. Given that there are fundamental differences between developing countries, not least in terms of their stakes and interests within the existing set of international financial arrangements, a critical issue is whether it is possible to isolate areas where co-operative action can produce an acceptable distribution of benefits.

These problems are nicely illustrated by the OPEC phenomenon. Not only did the rise in the price of oil generate the extra clout for LDCs to push for a new international economic order, but it was also seen as providing the finance for schemes based exclusively in the Third World. However, in practice, the OPEC surplus proved to lack durability and, in any case, questions were legitimately raised concerning the degree to which OPEC countries would use their new found wealth to support Third World countries rather than simply placing their excess reserves on the Eurocurrency markets where the uses of the money depended on the credit policies of the private (and industrial country denominated) international banks.

A third problem associated with plans for financial co-operation amongst developing countries relates to the efficiency of reform. If pursuit of one type of reform involves an opportunity cost in failing to pursue another type, governments have to give considerable thought to where their main effort should be made. It is not just a matter of what countries stand to gain from intra-South co-operation but also what they stand to lose from it. Many LDCs have an important stake in Northern-based arrangements and will be reluctant to risk these in the pursuit of the uncertain benefits that they may derive from Southern-based reforms. This again suggests that the degree of aggregation is important. A continuing theme of this book is that developing countries do not have homogeneous interests in the area of international financial policy. Dissimilar interests will not evaporate under the banner of Third World solidarity. What is needed there-fore is a more painstaking approach that sets out to identify which developing countries have mutual and complementary interests and which do not. The need is for a disaggregated approach to Southern financial reform.

2. THE OBJECTIVES OF CO-OPERATION

The objectives of greater financial co-operation amongst developing countries are very diverse, incorporating both economic and political elements. From a long list of factors, the desire to overcome two related deficiencies of the existing international financial framework may be seen as being paramount to any discussion of South–South solutions.

The first is the inadequacy of LDCs' international reserves and their impaired access to commercial credit. The development of their economies is viewed as being constrained by a shortage of foreign exchange and by the size of the current account deficit that they can finance. As was discussed in Chapter 2, the issue is not clear cut. There are inconsistencies in the theory of reserve adequacy as ap-plied to developing countries as well as there being significant varia-tions amongst developing countries themselves. While the intrinsic instability of the balance of payments and the high cost of adjustment raise the demand for reserves, the high opportunity costs of holding reserves reduces it. In any case, to argue that theory supports the claim that the demand for reserves in LDCs is proportionately higher than in industrialised countries presupposes that their export receipts are most unstable and their costs of adjustment higher, and, as indicated elsewhere in this book, there is some debate over these issues.[2] Furthermore, care has to be exercised not to confuse the demand for reserves to hold, which may be related to the above factors, with the demand for reserves to spend, which may be more appropriately related to the level of development.

What is perhaps more relevant from the point of view of Southern financial co-operation is that the degree of liquidity inadequacy varies *between* developing countries. Again, a more disaggregated approach is appropriate.

The second supposed deficiency is that existing institutions have a pro North–South trade bias which encourages an international division of labour under which LDCs export unprocessed primary commodities and import manufactured goods and which may not be fully appropriate to their needs. This structure of trade has implications for both the trend and the stability of LDCs' balance of payments as their terms of trade decline and are exposed to variations emanating from the business cycle in industrial countries. Intra-South trade is seen as a way of breaking out of these traditional patterns and of encouraging export diversification. Differences in comparative costs amongst developing countries are seen as implying that much of the South would benefit from increased intra-South trade. Yet an increase in such trade is constrained by a lack of finance. Therefore trade measures need to be accompanied by financial reform. It is, then, the claim of those advocating Southern solutions that such reform would overcome the principal deficiencies of the existing system.

3. FORMS OF FINANCIAL CO-OPERATION

Financial co-operation within the South is often encapsulated in proposals for setting up a Southern IMF (although this is really a contradiction in terms) or a Third World or South Bank.[3] Although summarised in this way, the activities of the institution would comprise a number of elements. These normally include, first, some form of clearing union to economise on the use of reserves; second, pooling arrangements, to achieve the same basic objective; third, a payments or credit union which would offer short to medium term balance of payments assistance; and, fourth, a Southern currency or Third World dollar. The details of different schemes vary but these principal purposes are common to most. It is these general aspects which are examined here rather than any specific proposal.[4]

3.1 A clearing union

This is the least ambitious aspect of co-operation. Trade amongst developing countries would be recorded by the union and at frequent intervals would be netted out. Countries would then settle their net balances in convertible currencies. Depending on how frequent the multilateral settlements were, the scheme would involve a small element of intra-South trade credit. The implication of the scheme is that scarce hard currencies would only be needed to finance net imbalances rather than total imports.

3.2 Reserve pooling arrangements

These are significantly more ambitious, since they are a step in the direction of the joint management of reserves, with participating countries depositing a proportion of their reserves with a central reserve pool. The theoretical attractions of the scheme derive from the assumed shortage of reserves in developing economies, their limited access to private capital markets, and the problems associated with using flexible exchange rates. Given these characteristics, which, as has already been noted, more nearly describe the least developed countries than the better-off LDCs, reserve pooling offers a way of using scarce reserves more efficiently.

Any specific level of trade instability can be supported by a smaller pool of reserves than would be necessary if countries held their reserves individually. Since the export base of the South as a whole is more diversified than that for any one Southern country, instabilities are more likely to cancel out at the more aggregated level. By reducing the need for reserves, the opportunity cost of holding the excess reserves is avoided. The benefit from reserve pooling therefore depends on the value of this opportunity cost, which may be seen as the difference between the internal social rate of return on resources and the rate of interest on reserves.

Although attractive for this rather general reason, reserve pooling schemes are subject to a number of difficulties. Countries may be reluctant to give up their independent management of reserves, and may have differing views about the optimum size of the reserve pool. Distributional issues cannot therefore be avoided, since countries which choose to hold relatively large reserves because of the benefits they see from them (perhaps in terms of enhanced creditworthiness), or because they estimate that the opportunity cost of reserve holding is relatively low, may not be anxious to pool their reserves with other countries which have different attitudes. Associated with such differences in reserve management policy will be differences in attitudes to macroeconomic management. Again, countries acquiring reserves by pursuing 'conservative' macroeconomic policies may not wish to pool their reserves with countries whose policies are more expansionary and more inclined to generate deficits and therefore cause reserves to be used. This implies the need for quite a high degree of fiscal and monetary harmonisation amongst the participants, to an extent that may be difficult to arrange.

Aside from these broad issues there are many practical questions. What will determine the size of contributions? What will contributions be denominated in? What will determine the extent to which participants can draw from the pool and how much credit will be extended, at what price and under what conditions? How should any income associated with the management of the pool be distributed? It is more than probable that individual countries within the South will have different views about the appropriate answers to each of these questions.

3.3 A payments or credit union

Although there are similarities between the notion of a reserve pool and a payments union in terms of the range of functions they perform, the latter emphasises more strongly the provision of short to medium term balance-of-payments assistance. The advantages of such provision have already been discussed at length in this book. In summary, they stem from the welfare gains associated with countries being able to select the optimum combination of adjustment and financing when faced with payments deficits, the assumption being that a shortage of finance constrains them from reaching this optimum. In principle, a Southern payments union could operate along similar lines to the IMF, with countries making subscriptions but being able to draw, on a short term basis, beyond the value of these in certain circumstances.

In practice, there are a host of problems to overcome. What will determine the size of subscriptions and their denominations? Will conditionality be attached to drawings and how will this differ from IMF conditionality? In what circumstances will low conditionality finance be made available? Although such questions are familiar in the context of discussion of the IMF, the proposal for a Southern payments union generates other more specific questions as well. Not least, because of its discriminatory basis, it will induce a change in the size and pattern of LDC trade, with there being both trade-creating and trade-diverting effects. The relative sizes of these effects are clearly significant.

Furthermore, there is the question of whether the clash of interests between surplus and deficit countries, as well as between other factions, is likely to be any less within the context of an exclusively Southern monetary fund. There must be severe doubts about this. In addition, there is the question of to what extent the payments union will focus on countries' payments positions within the South rather than overall? Again, will the payments union imply an exchange-rate union? If not, how will the payments problems associated with the third country phenomenon discussed in Chapter 2 be handled?

The mere length of this list of fundamental questions suggests that setting up a Southern payments union will not be straightforward. If a Southern solution exists, it is certainly not an easy solution.

3.4 A Southern currency

Just as the IMF has a General Account which in the main distributes credit, and an SDR Account which creates and allocates SDRs, so it is sometimes argued that any exclusively Southern monetary fund should have the power to create its own currency.[5] The basic idea behind such a scheme is straightforward. If developing countries are reserve-constrained and are, at the same time, subjected to an anti-Southern trade bias, the creation of a Southern currency, to be used in Southern trade, could simultaneously alleviate both problems.

Beyond the basics, however, the proposal raises numerous problematic issues. Will the currency be backed or unbacked? If backed, what will it be backed by? If unbacked, will there be sufficient confidence in it? Will it carry an interest rate on net use and net acquisition and, if so, at what level should this be fixed? Without such an interest rate the incentive to spend the currency will be very great, and this could be inflationary and could alter relative prices within the South, given different income elasticities of demand for the products of different LDCs. Besides, who will eventually hold the assets? Will some designation or reconstitution procedure be required under which countries will have to stand ready to acquire some additional Southern Currency Units (SCUs) and to hold at least a proportion of their allocation in the long run. What factors will determine designation? In any case how will the assets be distributed amongst developing countries in the first place – what criteria will be used?

A further problem is that structural payments imbalances within the South will mean that surplus countries will continually acquire SCUs while deficit countries will be net users. Will surplus countries be prepared to accept this state of affairs? Even if interest were to be paid, this will be in the form of SCUs. However, while additional SCUs might be seen as being of little benefit to such countries, the need to earn SCUs in order to pay interest will reduce the subsidy element to net users. In any case why should surplus countries sell real resources in exchange for SCUs when they might have sold them to industrial countries in exchange for hard currencies?

Another problem relates to the institutional relationship between the reserve-creating part of the Southern monetary fund's activities and its credit-granting part, and the correct balance between reserve and credit provision. Yet another relates to the valuation of SCUs. Will this be linked to the dollar, the SDR, or some other bundle of convertible currencies? Moreover, what will be implications of the valuation method for individual LDCs?

It is not that these problems apply only to a Southern currency. Many of them are quite familiar in the debate over SDRs. The important point is that there is no reason to believe that a Southern currency will *avoid* such problems. If new assets are to be created and allocated to the poorest countries of the world, it would seem better to provide them with general purpose SDRs rather than with limited purpose SCUs. Agreement on some form of SDR link seems no more unlikely from a practical point of view, and the poor country recipients would gain more.

In principle, modifications to the SDR and the introduction of a Southern currency are, of course, not mutually exclusive. But, given the administrative constraints, it would seem likely that a choice is involved in terms of where the emphasis is placed. Furthermore, it needs to be recognised that opting for a Southern solution will reduce still further the chances of developed countries agreeing to a more genuinely international one. However, opting for reforms within the SDR framework does not mean that developing countries will fail to benefit from an extension of trade credit which serves to facilitate the expansion of intra-South trade. A consistent theme of this book is that the sum of benefits from a series of modest reforms may well exceed those from a few grand schemes, which, because of their size and nature, may be difficult, if not impossible, to get implemented.

4. GENERAL CONSTRAINTS ON FINANCIAL CO-OPERATION

Apart from the detailed questions relating to the various forms of co-operation which would have to be resolved, there are some rather more general constraints leading on from earlier parts of this chapter that severely limit the scope for significant evolution in the direction of an exclusively Southern alternative. First, although some LDCs are, without doubt, short of reserves and have little access to commercial markets, others are not. There are then major distributional issues within the South which proposals for Southern resolutions tend to de-emphasise. Figures quoted in Chapter 2 reveal that it is in the low-income countries that the shortage of international liquidity has been most constraining. If the problem is one that is limited to LICs, it is far from clear that the best method of solving it is to establish a Southern institution in which their interests are likely to be dominated by richer LDCs. In any case, what the latter want are measures that serve to protect and extend their access to the capital markets of the North. They might not wish to be associated with proposals that they may feel would be seen as reducing their creditworthiness. Assistance to the LICs, with the concessionary component that this requires, is better handled at the international level.

Second, the presumption that intra-South trade has been discriminated against is open to some debate. Havrylyshyn and Wolf (1982) provide evidence that for 1963–77 there was no obvious bias against such trade. Indeed, they argue that once the weight of LDCs in the world economy, their comparative advantage (which is often competing), their restrictive trade regimes and the liberalising trends in OECD tariff structures are taken into account, the proportion of intra–LDC trade is, in fact, greater than might have been expected. Moreover, they reject the view that, given the slowdown in the growth rate of OECD economies, the North can no longer be an engine for LDC growth. They are unable to find any strong relationship between the growth of developed countries and exports by developing countries, especially since many of the developed countries are themselves important sources of primary products. The correct policy prescription, so they argue, is to optimise gains from international trade through specialisation and exchange irrespective of the distribution of exports or the source of imports. If developing countries want to expand intra–LDC trade, perhaps the first step should be to reduce tariff barriers.

Indeed, given the level of government intervention in the economies of many LDCs, it is extremely difficult to say whether one pattern of international trade is more likely than any other to allow a country to reach its production possibility frontier. Governments intervene both in domestic factor markets and in international final product markets. The consequence of a tangled web of taxes and subsidies, few of which are explicitly directed at correcting 'distortions' which have resulted through market failures or imperfections, is that it is almost impossible to unravel what actually is the domestic resource cost of any particular economic activity. In light of this informational vacuum, it is hard to make unambiguous predictions about the gains which might result from another level of political activism.

Third, if one stops to think about the question of the appropriate institutional structure, then the problems of a Southern IMF are further compounded. Not only will the protracted negotiations over the precise details of the organisation be politically costly and financially expensive, but it is also important to realise that, aside from specific differences over precise arrangements, there are also broad divergences in economic interests, political concerns and ideological perspectives among a group as heterogeneous as 'The Third World', or the 'South'. One cannot fail to be aware of the inertia and political deadlocks which characterise the activities of the EEC, whose membership is relatively more homogeneous and which seems to share a communality of interests much more pronounced than that which 'unites' the South.

Finally, there is the fundamental question of where the money is going to come from, given the evaporation of the OPEC surplus and the debt problems being encountered by many of the better-off developing countries. Although plans for Southern institutions have little problem in stating, in theory, how much capital would be required and who would provide it, there must be huge doubts about whether these potential funders would regard the establishment of such institutions as a high priority use of scarce resources. Neither official nor private sources of finance could be relied upon. The chances are therefore high that any such institution will be starved of finance and will be unable to act on anything other than a very small scale.

5. CONCLUDING REMARKS

Proposals for extensive financial co-operation amongst developing countries rest on a number of premises relating to the nature of problems faced, the community of interest within the South and the best way of going about dealing with problems. However, the discussion in this chapter suggests that each of these premises may be challenged. The political economy of co-operation within the South is revealed as being very much more complex than some its more intemperate advocates seem to suggest. There is no universal set of problems faced by developing countries. The problems facing the poorest ones are significantly different from those facing the NICs. Leading on from this, the specific interests of different developing countries in any form of international financial policy will vary, and these differences will not be concealed or eradicated under the banner of Third World solidarity.

A further implication of this is that most developing countries stand to gain more from *international* financial reform than from intra-South reform. This is true for the NICs anxious to sustain their creditability with the IMF and therefore to maintain their access to private international financial markets, and it is also true for the low income countries since the benefit they would derive from Southern arrangements would be minimised by the reluctance of NICs to participate. Concessionary assistance to LICs is more appropriately dealt with at a global level.

If these observations accurately reflect the perceived private costs and benefits of participating in Southern solutions, it is most unlikely that very much of any real significance will happen.

While co-operation on a smaller scale based on regional trading and financial groupings may in certain cases be economically advantageous and feasible, the pursuit of Third World institution-building on a grand scale would appear to be neither of these. Although in some ways less glamorous, the gradual yet incremental modification to existing international financial institutions and arrangements would seem to offer most developing countries a more efficient way of ameliorating the problems they face.

16 The Way Forward

A number of conclusions emerge from the analysis and assessment of international financial policy contained in this book. The purpose of this chapter is to bring some of them together and to attempt to provide a summary of answers to the questions raised in Chapter 1.

1. GENERAL CONCLUSIONS

Some of the principal general conclusions are as follows. First, there is considerable scope for international financial reform which would be beneficial to the developing world in terms of relaxing its balance-of-payments constraints. It is not the case that all the potential for reform has been fully used up. However, the concept of the 'scope for reform' has a number of dimensions. Not only is there an economic aspect involving whether it is possible to think of schemes that would work to the economic advantage of developing countries, but there is also an important political aspect involving whether the schemes have any chance of being adopted. Developing country negotiators need to be aware of what is and is not feasible, given the current political environment. One of the themes of this book is that a pragmatic approach should be adopted by them. Efficiency dictates that they should use their negotiating skills in areas where there is a chance of being successful. Developing countries will gain nothing from grandiose schemes for a new international economic order if these are not adopted. Indeed on the contrary, there will be a high opportunity cost. Yet significant benefits may be derived from apparently far more modest reforms. Even so, negotiators need to be aware of the fact that the political environment is not static. What seems impracticable today may well become practicable tomorrow. It is perfectly sensible therefore to have a grand design or a blueprint which may help ensure that those reforms that are adopted will be mutually reinforcing, and will move the system towards the envisaged new order. Those who argue that any reforms that discriminate in

311

favour of developing countries will be rejected need to be reminded of the history of the international monetary system, which contains many examples of precisely such reforms.

A second general conclusion is that many developing countries can make out a strong case that they warrant special treatment within the international financial system not purely on developmental grounds but also on the grounds of the size and nature of their payments problems.

However, to group all developing countries together is misleading and does little to advance the interest of any specific sub-group. A disaggregated – though not fragmented – approach to international financial policy is required. As a minimum a distinction has to be drawn between the better-off newly industrialised countries and the least developed countries of Africa and Asia. The difference between these countries not only relates to their levels of per capita GNP but also to various important economic characteristics. Furthermore, the membership of the sub-groups may change over the years. However, a final general conclusion is that while in many areas different developing countries will have different interests, there may still remain certain international financial issues upon which they can speak in unison.

2. A SUMMARY OF SPECIFIC CONCLUSIONS

This section is based on the issues raised in Chapter 1 and gives a brief response to each of the questions posed there in the light of subsequent discussions.

2.1 What should be the Fund's role in its dealing with developing countries?

The Fund has an important role to play in economic development. This role is adequately described by the Articles of Agreement and involves the Fund being both an adjustment and financing institution. Its financing activities are particularly significant for the least developed countries. However, the Fund can play this role without becoming a development agency. In other LDCs the Fund's contribution to adjustment will be relatively more important.

2.2 What should be the nature of the Fund's relationship with the banks in the context of dealings with the developing world?

Unavoidably the relationship will be complex and is likely to differ across countries. In some developing countries the Fund may be largely on its own and will be providing a large proportion of the balance-of-payments finance as well as an important input into the adjustment process. In others it will be a relatively less significant source of finance and its catalytic effect on commercial lending will be more important. Formalised schemes for co-operation in the nature of guarantees or rediscounting involve a range of problems and do not provide the easy panacea that some of their advocates imply.

2.3 What mechanism should be used for providing the Fund with resources?

The existing system based on quota reviews needs to be reformed so that the Fund's activities are not constrained by shortages of finance. The use of subscriptions is preferable both to borrowing from members and to borrowing from private capital markets. However, some of the Fund's activities could be appropriately financed by the further sale of gold.

2.4 Should Fund conditionality be modified to reflect better the needs of developing countries, and, if so, in what ways?

Fund conditionality is at present insufficiently flexible to reflect the various causes of payments deficits in developing countries. The Fund needs to support a richer mix of policies. This is not to argue that strict conditionality should be abandoned. Nor is it to argue that current forms of conditionality are always inappropriate. In some developing countries conventional Fund programmes may be apposite. But, for many of the poorer developing countries, programmes which acknowledge the structural nature of their difficulties would be more cost-efficient in terms of minimising the damage caused to other governmental macroeconomic objectives.

2.5 What is the correct balance between low and high conditionality finance within the Fund?

The answer depends in part on views concerning the appropriate global balance between adjustment and financing, since low conditionality finance does not imply adjustment. There is little chance that views on this issue can be other than subjective. Underpinning it are opinions on the merits and demerits of shock versus gradual adjustment. There is also the question of on which side it is better to err, that of too much or too little finance. Of course the trade-off between adjustment speed and financing is also relevant to the discussion of high conditionality finance, since adjustment would have to be even faster if this source of finance did not exist. Low conditionality finance from the Fund is more appropriate for the least developed countries facing exogenously caused and temporary problems than for the better-off LDCs, since the former countries cannot rely on being able to tap the private capital markets. The question of how much of this type of finance is needed depends on how big this sort of problem is. The recent fall in the availability of low conditionality finance, in part associated with modifications to the CFF, is difficult to substantiate on such grounds. As traditionally operated, the CFF is a more appropriate mechanism for generating low conditionality finance than is the lower credit tranche, because it is based on the external causation of deficits and therefore escapes the problems of moral hazard.

2.6 Is the existing set of IMF facilities satisfactory? If not, what changes should be made to existing ones and what new ones should be introduced?

Potentially the existing set of Fund facilities could make a significant contribution to assisting developing countries in overcoming their payments problems. However, to exploit this potential, modifications are required both to the CFF and the EFF. The BSFF is likely to remain of rather limited usefulness. The changes made to the CFF in 1983 went in the wrong direction and were largely inconsistent with the logic of the facility. The modifications required involve a fuller commitment to this logic, namely, that countries' import capacity should be protected from the effects of temporary payments instability resulting from factors beyond the control of the countries concerned. The changes required to the EFF are even more modest and merely involve its full-hearted application in the context of the reforms to conditionality discussed above.

There is no equally strong argument for an interest-rate facility within the Fund, although there are alternative ways in which the problems caused by unexpected increases in world interest rates could be alleviated via, for example, the incorporation of interest payments in rescheduling exercises.

2.7 What is the best way of dealing with the problem of commodity instability?

The two alternatives are via *ex-post* financial compensation or via buffer-stock schemes designed to stabilise prices. Although not mutually exclusive, the balance of the argument lies in favour of the first approach. Buffer-stock schemes abound with both theoretical and practical difficulties and it is unfortunate that so much attention has been focused on them to the relative neglect of other aspects of reform.

2.8 Is there a case for extending the use of interest-rate subsidies within the Fund, and, if so, how might this be best arranged?

Interest-rate subsidies offer one mechanism through which concessionary assistance can be provided to the least developed countries within the framework of the IMF. Schemes have successfully operated in the past and, in certain ways, are an attractive form of aid provision. Subsidies could be appropriately financed either by donations or by using the Fund's remaining stock of gold.

2.9 In what ways, if any, should the quotas that underpin the Fund's operation be modified?

Under current arrangements quotas are required to fulfil too many, sometimes conflicting, functions. There is a case for moving away from the use of single multipurpose quotas to the use of multiple quotas. Countries' access to Fund credit, receipt of Fund-created reserves and subscriptions would then be based on different sets of criteria. However, care would be needed to ensure that the support from the developed countries, which is vital to the Fund's operations, was not lost in the process.

2.10 Should an SDR link be introduced and would this really benefit developing countries?

SDR allocations to the poorest countries would confer benefits on them even though their use now carries a market-related interest rate. In any case there is no reason in principle why the interest rate charged to low income countries cannot be subsidised. Even developing countries with access to private markets might prefer to receive SDRs because of the lack of conditionality attached to their use. However, there are some arguments for reviewing this feature of SDRs. Many of the arguments mustered against the link spring from a misinterpretation of its likely implications. However, resistance to the scheme needs to be recognised. Even if the hostility is misplaced, it is nonetheless real. Furthermore, it may not only sabotage the chances of the link being accepted but may also damage attempts to establish the SDR or the principal reserve asset in the system. Developing countries will gain nothing from a link which is not activated because there are no further allocations of SDRs. Indeed, they will gain more from a system which, while not incorporating a link, does involve regular SDR allocations.

2.11 How best can the SDR be established as the system's principal reserve asset and can the process be used to benefit developing countries?

Establishing the SDR as the system's principal reserve asset incorporates two elements. One involves making the asset more attractive by increasing its usefulness and liquidity, and the second involves devising a transition mechanism for moving the system from being based on gold and foreign exchange to being based on SDRs. A vital role in this process would be played by a Substitution Account, the operation of which could be modified to include a transfer of real resources to developing countries. As with the SDR link, the details of the arrangements would determine the distribution of the benefits amongst developing countries.

2.12 What are the different interests of different developing countries in international financial reform?

While the low-income countries stand to gain from a structured international financial system based on the SDR, and incorporating a link and interest rate subsidies, the better-off and more creditworthy developing countries will gain more from reform which defends and extends their access to private capital markets.

2.13 Do developing countries share common interests in issues such as the nature of the global exchange-rate regime?

Common interests that unite developing countries do exist. They may all be expected to favour less exchange-rate instability and more economic expansion in industrial countries. Exchange-rate flexibility does create a problem for balance of payments management. Even so, particular aspects of this problem are more significant for some LDCs than for others. Lack of forward cover, for example, may be more of a problem for the least developed countries than for the NICs.

2.14 What approach to achieving reforms is likely to be most successful?

If there are some issues upon which developing countries can unite, would it not be better for their negotiators to concentrate on these and to ignore the more specific and disuniting proposals? It has to be accepted that there is an opportunity cost associated with accentuating any one approach to reform. However, general reforms are certainly not always incompatible with more specific reforms and there is little reason for LDCs to ignore the latter. What is more to the point, different proposals may have more or less chance of being accepted. The political economy of efficient international financial reform is of central significance. Do negotiators push for reforms that give them a small chance of a big gain or for those that involve a good chance of a small gain? It is difficult to provide a clear answer to this question but the choices involved have to be explicitly recognised. The discussion in this book supports an incremental and marginal type of reform rather than one based on grand designs or new orders.

Such an approach would seem likely to maximise the real expected benefits from reform. Developing countries need to survive in the world as it is. However, they also need to have some blueprint upon which reform is based. They should not adopt an ad hoc approach to reform. The existence of such a blueprint will help to ensure that the system evolves, albeit in an incremental fashion, in the direction that they desire. Another important aspect of the political economy of reform is that developing countries need to carry the industrial countries with them. A combative and confrontational approach is least likely to succeed. LDCs need to identify reforms which, while benefiting them, do not impose high costs – or will not be perceived as imposing them – on industrial countries. Ideally, they should be able to present schemes as being to the mutual advantage of developing and developed countries – though, as the Brandt Commission discovered, it is not sufficient merely to claim mutuality.

Although in many respects these guidelines for reform seem to be commonsensical, they have not been complied with. Developing countries have, for example, devoted a disproportionate amount of effort to establishing a programme for commodity stabilisation from which they stand a good chance of receiving only very little benefit. Into the same category come proposals for an entirely new international economic order, of which commodity stabilisation is one part.

2.15 How best can the debt problem of the developing world be handled?

There are no simple solutions to debt problems and many proposals which suggest that there are involve problems of their own. However, there is scope for formalising the way in which debt difficulties are handled. A further consideration is that debt is a distributional issue and schemes for debt relief may crowd out reforms which on equity grounds might be preferred. It is also necessary to look to the future at ways in which the better-off developing countries can continue to gain access to private capital. This may involve new instruments and the development of private secondary markets. But there may also be a role for the official sector and the international financial institutions to play.

2.16 Is there an argument for South–South financial policies?

While it is quite understandable that developing countries are frustrated by the lack of progress in the North–South debate, plans for exclusively Southern arrangements on a grand scale stand little more chance of being successful. Apart from the political problems of reaching agreement amongst the diverse collection of countries which constitute 'the South', there is legitimate doubt about whether many aspects of the Southern solution are desirable on economic grounds. This having been said, on a more modest level there may be scope for greater co-operation between developing countries, for example, in the form of joint ventures and regional trading and financial arrangements, from which the participants would benefit. But these hardly constitute a Southern solution.

2.17 What would be the quantitative significance of the policies discussed?

It is difficult to avoid the answer that 'it all depends'. If, for example, the SDR is established as the principal reserve asset in the system and a link is introduced which directs a significant proportion of any given allocation to low-income countries and if, at the same time, their interest charges on net use are subsidised, they would derive very significant benefits, especially when measured against the size of their economies, the size of their payments difficulties and the size of the financial inflows through other channels. If, on the other hand, the SDR is not so established and the link formula is less advantageous to LICs, and no subsidy is paid, the benefits to them would diminish dramatically. The question then arises as to whether it is worth actively pursuing policies which may generate only a modest amount of assistance. The view taken here is that it is. While it is absolutely vital not to ignore the contribution that domestic policy can make to resolving payments difficulties, beneficial reform at the international level is unlikely to conflict with this, except in the sense of absorbing skilled manpower. Reforms which yield low absolute figures may still be relatively significant to the developing countries which derive the benefits. Furthermore, even though individual policies on their own may make rather small contributions, the sum of these contributions may be significant. Finally, by modifying the structure of the system there may be long-run benefits which are not immediately obvious, not only in terms of the series of short run benefits but also in terms of facilitating and encouraging modifications in the future. There would seem to be nothing gained from losing the momentum of reform.

Notes

2. THE DEVELOPING WORLD: A SPECIAL CASE?

1. The evidence on export instability in developing countries is reviewed in Bird (1982). Not all the evidence points in the same direction but there is considerable support for the claim that export instability is more marked in developing countries.
2. For a fuller discussion of the theory of the demand for international reserves, see Bird (1982), Chapter 5, which also examines the differences between the demand in developed as compared with developing countries. For a more recent empirical study than those referred to in the above reference, see Edwards (1983).
3. Again on this point see Bird (1982).
4. However, the evidence is rather ambiguous. Import coefficients showing the ratio of import values to GDP were as follows for a random sample of low-income countries in 1983: Burma 0.12, Burundi 0.23, Ethiopia 0.20, Haiti 0.40, Kenya 0.10, India 0.27, Pakistan 0.24, Sierra Leone 0.29, Sri Lanka 0.41, and Tanzania 0.18, giving an unweighted average of 0.24. For a sample of better-off LDCs, the coefficients were: Argentina 0.10, Brazil 0.08, Israel 0.59, Korea 0.37, Malaysia 0.59, Portugal 0.44 and Uruguay 0.22, giving an unweighted average of 0.34. Although these averages back up the general claims in the text, there are clearly numerous exceptions.
5. For a review of some of the studies dealing with the question of seigniorage gains, see Williamson (1973).
6. In this respect issues of efficiency and equity reinforce each other.
7. Further discussion of this issue, which suggests that it is not without empirical support, may be found in Heller and Khan (1978).
8. For a fuller discussion of LDCs' own exchange-rate policy, see Bird (1982), Chapter 12, which also contains references to the literature on the subject.
9. A principal example of this is the report prepared by Helleiner (1981) for UNDP and UNCTAD.
10. See, for example, Cushman (1983). But for a rather different assessment, see Goldstein (1984), which finds little evidence to link floating rates with the slowdown in world trade.
11. An example of a plan of this type is Williamson (1983).
12. A clear statement of this point of view may be found in Dornbusch (1984).
13. Thus not all developing countries would be indifferent between a US-based or European-based economic expansion. It might be anticipated that the LDCs of Latin America gained more from the US recovery of

the early 1980s than they would have done from a similar recovery in the principal industrial countries of Europe.

14. The question of how the system may be edged in this direction is taken up in later chapters.

15. They would, of course, also have to be prepared to vote for such additions to international liquidity.

3. THE IMF AND THE DEVELOPING WORLD: HISTORY, RELATIONSHIPS AND RESOURCE USES

1. Sources include: International Financial Statistics, IMF *Annual Reports*, Hooke (1984), Killick (1984), Bird (1982).

2. Committee on Reform of the International Monetary System and Related Issues, *International Monetary Reform: Documents of the Committee of Twenty*, IMF, Washington, 1974.

3. With regard to equity of treatment between developed and developing countries, and since the *Review of Stand-bys* in 1968, the terms of stand-bys do not seem to have raised the criticism that they are of themselves harsher for developing than for developed countries, though there is the criticism that the alleged standard package may be less appropriate for developing countries. The *Review* followed a drawing by the United Kingdom which took the Fund's holding of sterling to almost 200 per cent of the UK quota. There can be little doubt that the conditions attached to this particular upper tranche drawing were significantly and uniquely more lenient than those which had been attached to stand-bys negotiated between the Fund and various developing countries, (de Vries, 1976; Southard, 1979). There were no quantitative performance targets set and no phasing. The Fund defended its position by pointing to the importance of sterling as an international currency.

   Developing countries at this stage endeavoured to persuade the Fund to move towards the uniform adoption of the type of stand-by arrangement that had been negotiated with the UK, incorporating as it did an emphasis on general policy measures and consultation rather than precise quantitative targets. Instead the *Review* confirmed what, in effect, had been standard practice prior to the 1967 UK episode. Quantitative performance criteria were retained for drawings beyond the first credit tranche, and the emphasis remained on the control of credit, though performance clauses were to be limited to 'stipulating criteria necessary to evaluate the implementation of the member's financial stabilisation programme'. Phasing was also retained for such drawings except when the purpose of the stand-by was to maintain confidence in a member's currency. Thus, although developing countries did not achieve the less onerous terms that they ideally wanted, they did ensure that they would not be required to meet relatively harsh conditions as compared with developed countries.

4. Thus Gold (1979) points out that while 'most of the decision is declaratory of the practice that has emerged in the years since 1968 . . . the

decision includes certain new or clarified elements, largely in deference to the views of developing members who feel that the Fund's conditionality has been too severe in relation to them'.
5. This classification may be challenged on the grounds that any tendency to make less use of devaluation would be reflected by the imposition of tighter credit ceilings and this hardly constitutes a weakening of conditionality. Indeed, such a change in emphasis is likely to raise the welfare costs of adjustment. For a further detailed analysis of the change in the nature of Fund programmes, see Killick (1984).
6. It may be noted that the IMF may in certain cases impose restrictions on a country's external borrowing as a condition of Fund assistance.

4. IMF CONDITIONALITY AND ECONOMIC DEVELOPMENT

1. For a further review of the evidence on the causes of payments deficits in developing countries, see Khan and Knight (1984).
2. For a much fuller review of the use of exchange rate depreciation as a tool of balance-of-payments adjustment in developing countries, including an examination of the empirical evidence, see Bird (1984).
3. Trade liberalisation rarely features as a performance criterion (Killick, 1984).
4. The questions are examined more fully in Chapter 5.
5. However, evidence to be presented later casts some doubt on whether devaluation is as frequently advocated by the Fund as is often supposed.
6. See, for example, Reichmann and Stillson (1978) and Reichmann (1978).
7. See Khan and Knight (1981).
8. Out of the sample of thirty IMF programmes examined in Table 4.1 there were ten cases where over-expansionary demand was not mentioned by the Fund as a principal cause of payments problems, and in six of these cases it was not even regarded as a secondary cause. However, there did not appear to be any reduced tendency to set credit ceilings in these cases; the ceilings may of course have been less tight but the evidence did not permit a test of this hypothesis. Looking more closely at the three programmes in 1974–9, where excess demand was not seen as either a principal or secondary cause of payments deficits, in only one case did the programme deviate from the conventional demand side type. This illustrates that while it is unusual for the Fund to support a supply side programme, it is not unheard of. For further details, see Killick (1984).
9. For support of this view, see Killick (1984).
10. See Guitian (1981) and Williamson (1982).
11. For a fairly recent review of the impact of Fund-supported programmes, see Donovan (1983).
12. Examples are Connors (1979) and Killick (1984).
13. Such a finding suggests that the critics' claim that Fund programmes

exert an adverse effect on development may be without much empirical foundation. However, a more adverse effect on growth seems to have been associated with more recent programmes than were examined in the studies cited here.

14. Though, as noted earlier, experience suggests that policymakers in developing countries often put a fairly low priority on economic stabilisation: for example, Jamaica under Manley and Indonesia under Sukarno, as well as various episodes in Latin American countries (Killick, 1984).
15. See Bird (1984) for a more detailed analysis of exchange-rate depreciation in developing countries.
16. The case for such an approach may be found in Schydlowsky (1982). But for a critique, see Laker (1981).
17. See Bird (1984) for a more detailed examination of the issues involved.
18. Some commentators have suggested that Fund conditionality switch completely away from an instrument basis to a target one, see Spraos (1984). However, this approach also has problems in terms of monitoring governmental responsibility, and length of Fund financing, as its advocates concede.
19. Williamson (1982).

5. THE FUND'S LENDING FACILITIES: REFORMING THE COMPENSATORY FINANCING FACILITY AND THE EXTENDED FUND FACILITY

1. A good example of this sort of argument may be found in Dell (1982). For a clear statement of the Fund view, see Nowzad (1981).
2. In practical terms this is precisely what has happened in the 1980s, with the Fund emphasising the need for countries to adjust and the importance of low conditionality finance within the Fund diminishing.
3. See Goreux (1977) for an estimation of the quantitative impact of the 1975 liberalisation.
4. For a report of these findings and a further review of the CFF, see Griffiths-Jones (1983).
5. The only problem with relating repayments to export performance is that the Fund would need to calculate the trend value of export receipts on a continuing basis so that it could be assessed when excesses had been achieved.
6. Raising quotas would increase potential access to all Fund facilities and not just the CFF.
7. The explanation of this may be found in Chapter 6.
8. The argument might also be made that given its apparently structural orientation it was of potentially greatest benefit to the poorest LDCs.
9. For a critical assessment of that rubric, see Williamson (1981).
10. In some respects the IMF's EFF is not unlike the World Bank's structural adjustment loans. A discussion of these is defined to lie outside the

self-imposed terms of reference of this book, but for a good summary of SALs, see Landell-Mills (1981) and Please (1984).

6. COMMODITY PRICE STABILISATION AND INTERNATIONAL FINANCIAL POLICY

1. Supply might also be more assured if price stability encouraged producers to expand output.
2. The analysis of the gains from price stabilisation may be conducted in terms of the size and distribution of the producer and consumer surpluses. Massell (1970) concludes that price stabilisation with costless storage will generate net gains for producers and consumers and that producers will gain more than consumers where stochastic supply variations are more significant than stochastic demand variations, and where the price elasticity of supply is less than that of demand. Such static analysis, however, ignores the dynamic gains from price stabilisation; and these may be more important. For a thorough and refined analysis of buffer stocks which draws on their rick-reducing role, see Newbery and Stiglitz (1981).
3. This has been a consistent theme of Kaldor: see Hart, Kaldor and Tinbergen (1964) and Kaldor (1976). We return to examine this notion in more detail in a later section of this chapter. World economic stability may be defined to cover variations not only in prices but also in output, income and employment.
4. Alterations in the incidence of earnings gains and losses may clearly have consequences for the world distribution of income as between primary-product producing and consuming countries. Depending on the particular configuration of demand and supply shifts and price elasticities, buffer-stock intervention in commodity markets may either redistribute income away from consumers and towards producers or away from producers and towards consumers. There is certainly no *a priori* universal rule which states that buffer-stock intervention will benefit producing countries at the cost of consuming ones.
5. Where future prices could be foreseen with some degree of certainty, arbitrage would tend to stabilise the price around its long term trend level.
6. Again we may note that the belief by producers that the agency will act to prevent price reductions may encourage them to increase supply at any given price, and thus lower the long-run equilibrium price.
7. If private speculators expect the price of a commodity to rise and act accordingly by buying the commodity, this in itself will cause the price to rise. If speculators have elastic expectations, they may take a movement in price as an indication that there will be a further movement in price in the same direction. Action based upon such expectations would tend to be self-fulfilling. Intervention by an agency with accurate information

would not only be price-stabilising but also profitable for the agency concerned.

8. See, for instance, Henderson and Lal (1976).

9. Where a commodity is subject to fairly rapid deterioration, the stock may, of course be frequently turned over. However, the economics of the matter may preclude such a policy even where the physical characteristics of the commodity do not.

10. Details of this agreement, and of others that have relied on some alternative means of commodity regulation, may be found in IMF-IBRD, Joint Staff Study (1969). More specific investigations of the Tin Agreement have been conducted by Fox (1974) and Smith and Schink (1976).

11. Where it is large, sudden and abnormal deviations from trend prices that cause the major economic problems, the size of the buffer stock will have to be correspondingly large: see Kaldor (1976) and Johnson (1976). Smith and Schink (1976) maintain that, in order to have achieved some moderate degree of price stability independently of other factors, the tin buffer stock would have to have been considerably larger than it was. The example of tin illustrates that small buffer stocks are likely to suffer from one or more of three limitations: first, the band of prices that is defended will have to be fairly wide, second, the band will have to follow short-term market trends quite closely, and, third, it will have to be accepted that market prices may frequently move outside the band. In each of these three cases the degree of stabilising influence exerted by the buffer stock will be reduced. Smith and Schink argue further that, in the absence of the US stockpile, conflict between producers and consumers on the International Tin Council (which would then to a larger extent have become a price maker), as well as the problem of financing the larger buffer stock that would have been needed, would have resulted in the collapse of the ITA.

12. Since many primary products are sold in competitive markets, producers tend to be price takers rather than price makers. Action taken by one producer in isolation to increase revenue may not be appropriate from the point of view of maximising the revenue of producers as a group. Maximisation of producer-group revenue might be achieved through cartelisation.

13. The use of commodity arrangements to stabilise or raise prices involves questions both of efficiency and of equity. Generally, since LDCs export more primary commodities than they import, it might be anticipated that they would gain from a relative increase in the price of primary products. However, with any buffer-stocking scheme, the extent to which they would benefit, if at all, would depend on the particular commodities included in the scheme. Schemes for tea, jute and cocoa would tend to favour low-income LDCs most, since exports of these commodities are concentrated in the low-income LDCs, whilst schemes for coffee, copper and sugar would favour middle-income LDCs. Export shares for tin, rubber, sisal and cotton are fairly evenly distributed among low- and middle-income LDCs. The distribution of the costs associated with buffer stocks depends, again, on the commodities covered, the extent to

which increased raw-material prices are reflected in higher prices of manufactured goods. It is quite possible that a non-exporting LDC will lose as a result of an increase in the price of a particular commodity, not only directly, because of the higher commodity price, but also indirectly, because of the higher price of imported manufactures which use the primary commodity as an input. The pattern of costs and benefits associated with buffer-stock schemes will also depend on whether the objective of the buffer stock is to raise or merely stabilise price; clearly, the stabilisation of a price which might otherwise have risen may impose costs on exporting countries. For a full discussion of the distributional aspects of buffer stock schemes, see Michalopoulos and Perez (1977).

14. Kaldor (1964) has advocated a variable export duty or levy, the level of which would be positively related to the level of stocks held. 'The external price would be stabilized by the operation of the export restriction agreement itself, and the purpose of the variable export duty would be to regulate internal supplies so as to keep pace with external requirements, and thus assist in the necessary structural readjustment of the economy.'

15. For a well-argued assessment of commodity backed international currency, see Stewart and Sengupta (1982) chapter 7.

16. See Hart (1976).

17. For an elaboration of this argument, see Grubel (1965). The argument has been challenged: see Hart (1966, 1976). See also Williamson (1973).

18. Kaldor (1976) and Hart (1976) still maintain, however, that a link between the international monetary sector and the real sector which would result from commodity backing would yield benefits in terms of stability which are not generated by fiat systems.

19. With international fiat monetary expansion, LDCs may of course gain indirectly from the expansionist policies thereby encouraged in developed countries: see Grubel (1965).

20. Where unutilised existing warehousing facilities are brought into use, both the private and social costs of the buffer stock scheme will be reduced. Indeed, the social opportunity cost will fall to zero.

21. Commodity coverage may of course also affect storage costs, since some commodities are more cheaply stored than others.

22. This constitutes a financial economy associated with centrally financed buffer stocks. Where individual buffer stocks operate separately, such financial economies are less likely to be forthcoming.

23. Hart, Kaldor and Tinbergen (1964) maintain that 'for the world economy as a whole each unit of income so generated would probably be amplified by a "super-multiplier" (allowing for induced investment) of at least four or five (indeed, the figure may be much larger).' Where developed economies have no spare capacity, the expansionary industrial implications of the buffer-stock scheme will, HKT maintain, be diffused to less developed economies. 'Since the world as a whole is a vast underdeveloped economy – with vast reserves of underutilised and unemployed labour which can be drawn on for employment in industry so long as raw material supplies are available and demand is expanding – it cannot be denied that it is possible to step up the growth of world

manufacturing production sufficiently so as to match any likely increase in the supply of primary products.'

7. INTEREST-RATE POLICY AND INTERNATIONAL FINANCE

1. See the IMF *Annual Report* for a schedule of Fund charges. With high nominal interest rates and a falling rate of inflation, real interest rates rise. The cost of borrowing is of vital significance not only to low-income countries but also to those middle-income countries with large amounts of debt.
2. For a thorough examination of IMF policy with respect to gold and possible modifications to this, see Brodsky and Sampson, (1980), (1981). It may be noted that with price appreciation gold sales by the IMF may confer quantitatively large benefits on the purchasers – almost certainly industrial countries.
3. For a more detailed discussion of factors influencing the optimum path of gold sales, see Chapter 9. The optimum path for the recipients of the related aid is essentially that which maximises their net present value social benefit.

8. FINANCING THE FUND AND REFORMING QUOTAS

1. Horsefield (1970), for example claims that, 'the Fund did not then, nor does it now, rely on any formula for determining quotas'.
2. For details of previous reviews, see de Vries (1983).
3. However, the IMF *Annual Report*, 1983, noted that the deadline involved, 'a considerable acceleration of the normal timetable for completion of a general review of quotas. The acceleration was considered necessary in view of the prevailing international economic and financial conditions and resultant strains on the Fund's resources' (p. 87).
4. It should be noted that although a part of the extra subscription associated with an increase in quotas is paid in reserve assets, a member's reserve position in the Fund (RPF) also increases and this is counted as part of the country's reserves.
5. This option has been used quite frequently by the Fund. In the case of the CFF, for example, the quota limit has been raised from 25 per cent when the facility was introduced in 1963, to 100 per cent by 1979. However, the fall in the relative size of quotas has more than offset this in real terms.
6. Attempts to overcome this problem by using different quotas for different facilities in effect implies not using 'quotas' as such at all.
7. Initially Fund quotas were reviewed every five years, hence the Quinquennial Review. The original Articles provided that 'the Fund shall at intervals of five years' review the quotas of members (Article III, Section

2). In the first Amendment to the Articles (adopted in 1969), Article III Section 2 was changed to read: 'The Fund shall at intervals *of not more than five years*' review the quotas of all members, with these reviews being called General Reviews rather than Quinquennial Reviews. Indeed the Seventh General Review was completed only *three* years after the Sixth Review.

8. The Fund reports that since the Fourth Quinquennial Review, general reviews have comprised the following steps:

   '1. Quota calculations are made using formulas.
   2. The Executive Board decides what the overall increase in the size of the Fund's capital should be, and how this should be apportioned between a general increase in quotas for all members and special increases for some members.
   3. A decision is made on the allocation of special increases among members eligible to receive them.'

9. For a fuller explanation of the pattern of drawings on the Fund, see Killick *et al.* (1984).
10. Details of these schemes may be found in IMF *Annual Reports* for 1982 and 1983.
11. For a review of these, see Bird (1985).
12. It could be argued that the political nature of quota determination negates the relevance of the above analysis. However, this argument is ill-conceived. While recognising that quota changes are ultimately political decisions, the analysis of their optimum value in economic terms allows the impact of politicisation to be assessed. Furthermore, economic analysis provides a useful base point even in political decision-making. If all areas in which politics played an important role were excluded from the scope of economic analysis, there would be relatively little economics left.
13. The old measure was regarded as too simple a measure, which mostly reflected the trend during a period of secularly rising receipts. The new definition of variability equated it to one standard deviation about a moving five-year average over a thirteen year period.
14. Although it has to be recognised that there are important distinctions between having a positive quota but no drawings on the Fund and having a zero quota.
15. See chapter 14.
16. The formula might then look like

$$Q^i = \chi^* \frac{(D - P^f - O^f - R^e)^i}{x} + \frac{Z}{y}$$

where Z is a measure of the structural instability of the balance of payments and $x + y = 1$.
17. See Kenen (1985) for further examination of these points.
18. Some would argue that the Fund's provision of a public good relates to activities not requiring it to lend its own resources and therefore not requiring finance (Vaubel, 1983).
19. For a more involved scheme based on SDRs, see Kenen (1985).

9. RESERVE CURRENCY CONSOLIDATION, GOLD POLICY AND FINANCIAL FLOWS TO DEVELOPING COUNTRIES

1. See, for instance, Grubel (1971), (1973); H. G. Johnson (1970); and Williamson (1973), for a review of some of the problems involved.
2. For the text of the Second Amendment, see Gold (1978).
3. A balance between mandatory and voluntary schemes could also be struck by not requiring participation by those countries with reserves below a certain level or by setting only a minimal level of participation in terms of the proportion of reserve currencies to be paid into the Account.
4. This is strongly argued by V. B. Kadam (1979).
5. A scheme such as the one outlined here may be open to the criticism that the aid element is artificially superimposed. Why not simply introduce a more conventional link between the creation of SDRs and the provision of aid? To some extent this is a valid criticism, particularly if there exists a significant amount of positive hostility towards any reform of the international financial system which directs benefits specifically towards developing countries. It should be noted, however, that schemes involving a Substitution Account represent what is in many ways a logical first step towards making the SDR the principal reserve asset in the international financial system and thereby raising the benefits of a link to developing countries (see later in the text). Furthermore, while the link involves a net addition to total international reserves, the schemes discussed in this paper could operate with either no net addition or even a net reduction. These schemes could therefore operate in circumstances under which a more conventional link would be unacceptable; schemes involving the use of a Substitution Account would mean that the additional financial flow to developing countries could exceed the overall increase in international reserves, something that would be impossible under the more conventional versions of the link.
6. The Account could reactivate the reserve currencies deposited with it by making them either directly available to developing countries or indirectly available through the intermediation of an international development agency. Provided that the recipients of these currencies did not spend the entire amount received in the country of issue, the effect of such a transaction would be to raise the quantity of international reserves. If, on the other hand, the currencies were to be spent in the country of issue, there would be no change in the total quantity of reserves but simply a change in the composition of reserves away from reserve currencies and towards SDRs. Wherever the currencies were to be spent, however, a real resource inflow to developing countries would result. A real resource flow would only fail to materialise if developing countries were to hold 100 per cent of the currencies that they received from the Substitution Account. In these circumstances the total quantity of international reserves would increase by an identical amount. The net addition to reserves would, however, still be in the form of SDRs. In effect, depositors in the Account would be exchanging reserve cur-

rencies for SDRs, and developing countries would be acquiring reserve currencies. Where developing countries were also depositors, the scheme would have the effect of granting them additional SDRs. Where depositors were mainly developed countries, the effect of the scheme would be to change the composition of reserves held by developed countries and to raise the level of reserves in the form of reserve currencies held by developing countries. From the point of view of increasing the degree of international stability, the scheme just outlined would be of little assistance unless an increase in international reserves was appropriate and unless developing countries were less inclined to switch the composition of their portfolio of reserve assets than developed countries. Under such a scheme reserve currencies would initially only assume a less significant relative position as compared with SDRs, they would not become absolutely less important. Either way, the scheme seems to put a higher priority on achieving an extra financial flow to developing countries than on raising the degree of international financial stability.

7. The value of the discount rate will also affect the size of benefits as perceived by developing countries from a reserve currency Substitution Account.

8. To guarantee this, other sources of reserve growth would have to be checked.

9. See Kadam, op. cit.

10. See, for example, Lal (1980).

11. Strong empirical support for the argument that developing countries have been relatively disadvantaged by the revaluation of gold is presented by Brodsky and Sampson (1980).

12. Such an arrangement has been advocated by a number of authors. See, for example, deSilva (1979), Bird (1979), Brandt (1980), and Brodsky and Sampson (1980).

10. THE LINK

1. For empirical verification, see Hawkins and Rangarajan (1970).

2. Williamson (1976) reports that during the C-20's discussions developing countries were able to come up with a common position which involved SDRs being allocated on the basis of quotas that were weighted in their favour. The weighting factor for the least developed countries was higher than for other LDCs.

3. For an explanation and alternative estimations of this, see Helleiner (1974) and Bird (1976). It has also been shown, however, that after a period of time and as soon as the interest due on previous link allocations exceeds the volume of new allocations, the real resource flow becomes negative (Isard and Truman, 1974).

4. Assessment of such changes by LDCs therefore depends significantly on their discount rate. See Bird (1981), where it is estimated that the changes in May 1981 led to a net first year gain to NOLDCs of over 500

million SDRs, but to further diminishing gains which turn negative in 1988 when the summed value of the additional interest payments exceeds the additional expenditure permitted by the cancellation of the reconstitution requirement.

5. For an attempt to take these factors into account, see Bird (1979). The gain from holding SDRs may be seen as the associated security or liquidity that is thereby derived. This may be measured either by the opportunity cost of acquiring a similar quantity of reserves by alternative means, or by the opportunity cost of the adjustment that is avoided. These two measures of the gain from holding SDRs will, however, differ. Taking the former measure, and assuming that the alternative method of reserve acquisition is via the pursuit of expenditure-reducing policies, the size of the related income loss varies inversely with the value of the marginal propensity to import. For those imports which are of producer goods this initial estimate of the impact on national income will have to be multiplied by the value of the marginal productivity of real resources. This approach to the measurement of benefit may also be used to estimate the benefit derived from using SDRs to pay off debts. Taking the latter measure, the gain will further depend on the probability of a deficit occurring to the value of the accumulated SDRs.

The benefit from spending SDRs depends, in the first instance, on the way in which they are spent. If they are spent on consumer goods, the SDR value of the goods, exclusive of interest on the net use of SDRs, gives an approximate indication of the size of the benefit. If, however, they are spent on producer goods, the size of the benefit derived will depend on the rate of return on real resources, after deduction of the interest paid on the net use of SDRs, and deflated by the social discount rate.

It follows that the size of the benefit derived from an allocation of SDRs depends on: the way in which the SDRs are used, either being held (R^H) or spent (R^S); the propensity to import (m), the distribution of imports as between producer and consumer goods $(M^p/M$, and $M^c/M)$; the rate of return on real resources (r); the rate of interest on SDR net use (i); the social rate of discount (d); and the probability of balance-of-payments deficits occurring (P). Expressing the benefit (B^R) as a ratio against the allocation of SDRs received (R) gives:

$$\frac{B^R}{R} = \frac{R^H}{R} \left(\frac{r}{m} \cdot \frac{M^p}{M} + \frac{1}{m} \cdot \frac{M^c}{M} \right) P$$
$$+ \frac{R^s}{R} \left(\frac{r-i}{d} \cdot \frac{M^p}{M} + (1-i) \cdot \frac{M^c}{M} \right).$$

From this expression it may be seen that the size of the benefit from any given allocation of SDRs will vary positively with the values of r, M^p/M, and P, and inversely with the values of i, d and M^c/M.

By making some calculations and some assumptions about the values of these determinants, we may estimate the size of the benefit derived by

LDCs as a group from the SDR facility. Thus, given the following values for the determinants,

$$R^H/R = 0.51$$
$$R^S/R = 0.49$$
$$m = 0.16$$
$$r = 20 \text{ per cent}$$
$$M^p/M = 0.84$$
$$M^c/M = 0.16$$
$$i = 3.5 \text{ per cent}$$
$$d = 10 \text{ per cent}$$
$$\text{and } P = 0.5$$

it emerges that the benefit derived, expressed in terms of nominal SDRs, i.e. ignoring any possible inflationary effects which reduce the real benefit both directly and indirectly via induced policy resources in developed countries, is

$$B^R = R \times 2.37$$

It should be borne in mind, however, that disaggregation would probably reveal considerable differences between LDCs in terms of the benefits that they have derived from the SDR facility. This is because, the way in which SDRs have been used, the rate of return on real resources, the proportion of imports that are accounted for by producer goods, and even the social discount rate are likely to vary as between LDCs.

6. However, to the extent that the link serves to raise national income in industrial countries and thereby developing countries' exports, there might be an additional secondary benefit to LDCs.
7. For a more rigorous presentation of the argument, see Clark (1972), Grubel (1973) and Johnson (1970).
8. Care has to be exercised here, however, since to an extent the interest rate dispersion reflects the likelihood and expected direction of exchange rate variation in a particular currency.
9. This would leave the problem of dealing with a deficit in the SDR Department of the Fund.
10. Other forms of lending to LDCs may involve grace periods that duplicate this SDR effect.
11. Bird (1974) discusses in more detail the relevance of the link to economic conditions in 1974 and 1975 and shows how it could have compensated to a certain extent for the demand deflationary consequences of the oil price rise. The link could, however, be equally relevant to the recessionary conditions of the early to mid-1980s.
12. The debate over the inflation cost of the link has been well documented. See, for instance, Bauer (1973), Kessler (1971), Kahn (1973), Abbott (1975), Maynard (1973), UNCTAD (1965), Dell (1969) and Cline (1976).
13. This of course ignores the fact that unlinked SDRs may be held and not spent.

14. Counter-cyclical international monetary policy might, however, share some of the problems encountered in the pursuit of counter-cyclical domestic monetary policy.
15. For a discussion of these costs and benefits and a review of the literature, see Williamson (1973).

11. PRIVATE BANK LENDING TO DEVELOPING COUNTRIES

1. Much of the literature examines only limited aspects of commercial lending to developing countries, such as the determinants of creditworthiness (Kapur, 1977) and the economics of debt repudiation (Eaton and Gersovitz, 1981). One of the few attempts to provide a fuller examination has been made by Riedel (1983).
2. For a fuller analysis of default, see Eaton and Gersovitz (1981) and Riedel (1983).
3. See Llewellyn (1982) for a review of the evidence on the relationship between interest rates and spreads, and the determination of each.
4. The statistics upon which this claim is made come from *World Economic Outlook*, Occasional Paper No. 21, IMF, Washington, 1983, Tables 25 and 58.
5. Price and quantity variables will move in the same direction following shifts in demand (assuming an upward-sloping supply schedule) and will move in the opposite direction following shifts in supply (assuming a downward-sloping demand schedule).
6. The empirical support for this may be found in *World Economic Outlook*, op. cit.
7. See J. O' Neill (1982).
8. For a useful review and analysis of the evolution of commercial bank lending to developing countries, see again Llewellyn (1982).

12. DEVELOPING COUNTRY DEBT: A REVIEW OF THE POLICY ALTERNATIVES

1. What happens to debt as a proportion of national income depends basically on the relative sizes of the rate of interest and rate of growth of income. Given conditions where both indebtedness and income are increasing, this debt ratio will tend to rise if the rate of interest exceeds the rate of income growth.
2. Technically a distinction needs to be made between rescheduling and refinancing. The latter involves negotiating a new loan of equal amount to the debt due which is then repaid with the proceeds of the new loan. In a sense the distinction is more than simply technical, since the source of refinancing can be other than the original source of the loan, whereas in the case of rescheduling it is the same.

3. For a comprehensive critical review of these proposals, see William B. Cline (1983).
4. Another group of proposals for alleviating the debt problem focus on the overlending of banks as its cause. They therefore advocate a greater degree of regulatory supervision and measures to reduce the book value of old debt in banks' balance sheets. Of course, while it may be true that banks overlent in the 1970s, the problem now is more that of 'under-lending' in response to the newly perceived default risk. The more general problem seems to relate to the intrinsic instability of bank lending.
5. This scheme is the idea of Khatkhate (1966).
6. From amongst the various advocates of using the SDR scheme to assist in alleviating the debt problem, see John Williamson (1984).

13. POLICIES TO ENHANCE PRIVATE LENDING TO DEVELOPING COUNTRIES

1. Chapter 4 involved a discussion of appropriate policies, but see also Killick (1984).
2. For a review of some of the schemes that ha 'e been suggested, see Cline (1984) and Swoboda (1984).
3. Other financial evolutions that have implications for diversification are floating rate notes (FRNs) and Transferable Loan Instruments (TLIs). Details of these may be found in World Bank (1985).
4. For a fairly detailed proposal in this area, see Guttentag and Herring (1984).
5. See, for example, Guttentag and Herring (1983), Rohatyn (1983), Bailey (1983), and Griffith-Jones and Lipton (1984).
6. For a clear statement of the criticism, see Cline (1984).
7. For a fuller discussion of this motivation for lending, see Krugman (1984).
8. For a discussion of such proposals see Lessard (1977).
9. This index could be compiled in a number of ways: it could be based on the prices of the world's traded goods, or it could take the form of a weighted average of consumer price indices or wholesale price indices in major industrial countries (such as those represented in the SDR basket).
10. See, for example, the World Bank's *World Development Report*, for a summary of these regulations. Their existence may be explained in terms of an attempt by host countries to protect their balance of payments as well as the risk perception of the financial authorities of the countries in which the markets are located.
11. For a further discussion of the role of group borrowing, see Williamson (1982). Williamson's paper also examines some of the other issues raised in this chapter.
12. However, if borrowers financed the guarantees themselves, it could also reduce the supply of bonds.
13. There is the possibility that a guarantee fund will be subject to economies

of scale if the size of defaults rises less rapidly than the volume of lending. Assuming, however, that the contributions to the fund grow in proportion to loans, the size of the fund at any one time will vary inversely with the number of defaults. A related problem is that the fewer are the defaults the larger will be the size of the fund's resources but the smaller the need for it, while the larger and more frequent are the defaults the smaller will be the fund's resources, but the larger the need for it. The problem is one of short term instability, since defaulters will be repaying their drawings and over time the size of the fund should expand.

14. THE BANKS AND THE IMF: THE NATURE OF, AND SCOPE FOR, CO-OPERATION

1. Similarly, a country defaulting on a loan will damage bankers' confidence and will impose costs on other countries by reducing their access to finance.
2. Evidence to support this claim is contained in the *World Development Report*, World Bank, Washington, 1982, and in Sidney Dell and Roger Lawrence (1980).
3. Whether attention should focus on the role of the banks or the individual borrowing countries is not purely a question of semantics, since it raises the interesting question of what factors determine commercial financial flows. Are they demand-determined, with the banks passively allowing supply to meet the demand emanating from borrowers? Are they supply-constrained, with the banks rationing credit? Indeed, are they effectively supply-determined, with the banks actively encouraging countries to borrow? There is some evidence to suggest that during the 1970s, and as a general rule, the banks did not *strictly* ration credit, but either allowed countries to borrow what they wanted or even encouraged them to borrow. Since in the event the countries themselves chose to borrow what, in retrospect, were excessive amounts, their role in any explanation of the debt problem cannot be dismissed. From a policy point of view, however, it is useful to be able to influence both the borrowing countries and the banks, since both have a role to play in determining whether or not specific absolute financial flows are 'excessive' in the sense that they lead to debt problems. It is relevant to review the role of the banks irrespective of whether international capital movements have been demand- or supply-determined. In either case, the evidence of debt crises suggests that there is room for reformin $_J$ the bank's lending activities.
4. Supporting evidence may be found in the *World Development Report*.
5. J. Sachs (1983).
6. It is interesting to observe the asymmetrical effects of interest rate changes on banks and borrowing countries. Since banks borrow and lend, it is the value of spread that affects their profits, except to the extent that there is a credit multiplier at work in the Eurocurrency

market. For countries in an unbalanced creditor/debtor role, it is the level of interest rates that is more important, though clearly for countries with substantial reserves the adverse effects of increasing interest rates on them as debtors will be offset to some extent.

7. In the short run, and unless guarantees were financed by additional contributions, it is difficult to see how they could avoid exerting a negative impact on other types of Fund lending.

8. The principal difference between a guarantee scheme and a refinancing scheme is that the former would apply to new private loans while the latter relates to past ones. The idea of rediscounting was discussed in more detail in Chapter 13.

9. For more information on co-financing between the World Bank and the private sector, see 'Co-financing – new World Bank approaches', *Finance and Development*, March 1983.

10. Certain aspects of Fund lending, in particular the Compensatory Financing Facility, which provides finance to offset shortfalls in export receipts, are to some extent automatically counter-cyclical.

15. FINANCIAL CO-OPERATION AMONGST DEVELOPING COUNTRIES

1. For further discussion of the so-called 'Southern solution' see, for example, Pavlic, Uranga, Cizelj and Svetlicic (1983).

2. For a review of the theory of the demand for international reserves as applied to developing countries, see Bird (1982).

3. Discussion of some specific proposals along these lines may be found in the Group of 77 (1984).

4. Steward and Sengupta (1982) provide a useful review of these various financing schemes.

5. A much fuller analysis of the idea of a Southern currency may be found in Stewart and Stewart (1982). For more recent official discussion of the idea, see the Group of 77 (1984).

References

Abbott G. C., 'How Inflationary is the Link Scheme?', *Economia Internazionale*, February 1975.
Bailey N. A., 'A Safety Net for Foreign Lending', *Business Week*, 10, January 1983.
Bauer, P., 'Inflation, SDRs and Aid', *Lloyds Bank Review*, July 1973.
Bird, Graham, 'The Liquidity–Aid Link and the Maintenance of Full Employment and Balance of Payments Equilibrium in Developed Countries', *Economic Notes*, iii, 1974.
Bird, Graham, 'The Informal Link Between SDR Allocation and Aid: A Note', *Journal of Development Studies*, April 1976.
Bird, Graham, *The International Monetary System and the Less Developed Countries*, London, Macmillan, 1978.
Bird, Graham, 'The Mix Between Adjustment and Financing: Geometrical Presentations of Factors Affecting the Different Choices Made by Developed and Developing Countries', *Indian Economic Review*, April–June 1980.
Bird, Graham, 'Financing Balance of Payments Deficits in Developing Countries: the Roles of Official and Private Sectors and the Scope for Co-operation Between Them', *Third World Quarterly*, July 1981.
Bird, Graham, 'SDR Distribution, Interest Rates and Aid Flows', *The World Economy*, December 1981.
Bird, Graham, 'Financial Flows to Developing Countries: the Role of the IMF', *Review of International Studies*, March 1981.
Bird, Graham, 'Developing Country Interests in Proposals for International Monetary Reform' in Killick (ed.), *Adjustment and Financing in the Developing World: the Role of the IMF*, Washington, IMF and ODI, 1982.
Bird, Graham, 'A Role for the IMF in Economic Development', *Banca Nazionale del Lavoro Review*, December 1982.
Bird, Graham, 'Recycling and OPEC: The Need for New Instruments', *Energy Policy*, March 1984.
Bird, Graham, and Orme, Timothy, 'An Analysis of Drawings on the IMF by Developing Countries', *World Development*, June 1981.
Brandt, Willy, *et al.*, *North-South: A Programme for Survival*, first report of the Brandt Commission, London, Pan Books, 1980.
Brett, E. A., 'The International Monetary Fund, the International Monetary System and the Periphery', *IFDA Dossier*, N. S., Nyan, March 1979.
Brett, E. A., *International Money and Capitalist Crisis*, London, Heinemann Educational Books, 1983.
Brodsky, David A. and Sampson, Gary P., 'Gold, SDRs and Developing Countries', *Trade and Development*, no. 2, Autumn 1980.

338

Brodsky, David A. and Sampson, Gary P., 'Implications of the Effective Revaluation of Reserve Asset Gold: the Case for a Gold Account for Development', *World Development*, July 1981.

Clark, P. B., 'Interest Payments and the Rate of Return on International Fiat Currency', *Weltwirtschaftliches Archiv*, 1982.

Cline, William B., *International Monetary Reform and the Developing Countries*, Washington, Brookings Institution, 1976.

Cline, William B., *International Debt and the Stability of the World Economy*, Washington, Institute for International Economics, 1983.

Cline, William B., *International Debt: Systemic Risk and Policy Response*, Washington, Institute for International Economics, 1984.

Colloquium on the Interests of Developing Countries in International Monetary Reform, *Money in a Village World*, Geneva, Committee on Society, Development and Peace, 1970.

Connors, Thomas A., *The Apparent Effects of Recent IMF Stabilisation Programmes*, Washington, Federal Reserve, International Finance Discussion Paper No. 135, April 1979.

Cooper, R. N., 'Currency Devaluation in Developing Countries', in Ranis, G. (ed.) *Government and Economic Development*, New Haven, Yale UP, 1971.

Corea, G., *The International Monetary System and the Developing Countries*, Staff Studies, Central Bank of Ceylon, September, 1971.

Crockett, Andrew D., and Heller, Robert H., 'The Changing Role of the International Monetary Fund', *Kredit und Kapital*, no. 3, 1978.

Cushman, David, O., 'The Effects of Real Exchange Rate Risk on International Trade', *Journal of International Economics*, August 1983.

Dell, Sidney, Report of the Sub-Committee on International Exchange and Payments of Joint Economic Committee, US Congress, Washington, 1969.

Dell, Sidney, *On Being Grandmotherly: the Evolution of IMF Conditionality*, Essays in International Finance No. 144, Princeton University, 1981.

Dell, Sidney, 'Stabilization: the Political Economy of Overkill', *World Development*, August 1982.

Dell, Sidney, and Lawrence, Roger, *The Balance of Payments Adjustment Process in Developing Countries*, New York, Pergamon Press, 1980.

de Larosiere, J., 'The Role of the IMF in Today's World Economy', Washington, Address to the Council on Foreign Relations, 1982.

de Silva, L., 'Gold, the International Monetary Fund and the Third World', *IFDA Dossier*, No. 5, Nyon, March, 1979.

de Vries, Margaret G., *The International Monetary Fund, 1966–71*, Washington, IMF, 1976 (2 vols).

de Vries, Margaret G., 'The Evolution of the International Monetary Fund and How It Relates to the Developing Countries', *International Development Review*, No. 2, 1977.

de Vries, Margaret G., *The International Monetary Fund, 1972–78*, Washington, IMF, 1983.

Donovan, Donal, 'Macroeconomic Performance and Adjustment Under Fund-Supported Programmes: the Experience of the Seventies', *IMF Staff Papers*, June 1982.

Dornbusch, R., 'The Overvalued Dollar', *Lloyds Bank Review*, April 1984.

Eaton, J., and Gersovitz, H., 'LDC Participation in International Financial Markets', *Journal of Development Economics*, March 1980.

Eaton, J., and Gersovitz, M., 'Debt with Potential Repudiation: Theoretical and Empirical Analysis', *Review of Economic Studies*, April 1981.

Edwards, S., 'The Demand for International Reserves and Exchange Rate Adjustments: The Case of LDCs, 1964–72', *Economica*, August 1983.

Fox, W. A., *Tin: The Working of a Commodity Agreement*, London, 1974.

Gold, Joseph, *The Second Amendment of the Fund's Articles of Agreement*, IMF Pamphlet, No. 25, Washington, 1978.

Gold, Joseph, *Conditionality*, IMF Pamphlet, No. 31, 1979.

Goldstein, M., *The Exchange Rate System: Lessons of the Past and Options for the Future*, IMF Occasional Paper Series, No. 30, 1984.

Goreux, L. M., 'Report on Compensatory Financing', *IMF Survey*, 7, March 1977.

Goreux, L. M., *Compensatory Financing Facility*, IMF Pamphlet, No. 34, Washington, IMF 1980.

Griffith-Jones, Stephany, *Compensatory Financing Facility: A Review of the Operation and Proposals for Improvement*, UNDP/UNCTAD, Project INT/P1/06, January 1983.

Griffith-Jones, Stephany, and Lipton, Michael, *International Lenders of Last Resort: Are Changes Required*, Occasional Papers in International Trade and Finance, Midland Bank International, March, 1984.

Group of 77, *Economic and Technical Co-operation Among Developing Countries*, Vols I and II, New York, 1984.

Grubel, H. G., 'The Case Against an International Commodity Reserve Currency', *Oxford Economic Papers*, March 1965.

Grubel, H. G., 'The Demand for International Reserves: A Critical Review of the Literature', *Journal of Economic Literature*, December 1971.

Grubel, H. G., 'Interest Payments and the Efficiency of the International Monetary System', *Economic Notes*, II, 1973.

Guitian, M., *Fund Conditionality: Evolution of Principles and Practices*, Washington, IMF Pamphlet, No. 38, 1981.

Guttentag, J. and Herring, R., 'Commercial Bank Lending to Developing Countries: from Overlending to Underlending to Structural Reform', in Smith, G. W. and Cuddington, J. T. (eds) *International Debt and the Developing Countries*, Washington, World Bank, 1985.

Hart, A. G. 'The Case as of 1976 for International Commodity-Reserve Currency', *Weltwirtschaftliches Archiv*, CXII, 1976.

Hart, A. G., Kaldor, N., and Tinbergen, J., 'The Case for an International Commodity Reserve Currency,' in *Proceedings of the UN Conference on Trade and Development*, Vol. III, New York, United Nations, 1964.

Helleiner, G. K., 'The Less Developed Countries and the International Monetary System', *Journal of Development Studies*, April–July 1974.

Helleiner, G. K., *The Impact of the Exchange Rate System on the Developing Countries: A Report to the Group of Twenty Four*, UNDP/UNCTAD Project INT/75/015, February, 1981.

Heller, H. R. and Khan, M. S., 'The Demand for International Reserves Under Fixed and Flexible Rates', *IMF Staff Papers*, December 1978.

Henderson, P. D., and Lal, D., 'UNCTAD, the Commodities Problem, and International Economic Reform', *ODI Review*, No. 2, 1976.

Hirschman, Albert O., *Strategy of Economic Development*, New Haven, Yale UP, 1958.

Hooke, A. W., *The International Monetary Fund, its Evolution, Organisation and Activities*, IMF Pamphlet No. 37, Washington, IMF, 1984.

Horsefield, J. K. *The International Monetary Fund, 1945–65*, Washington, IMF, 1969 (2 vols).

Institute of Bankers, *The Financing of Long Term Development*, Proceedings of 32nd International Banking Summer School, 1979.

IMF-IBRD *The Problem of Stabilization of Prices of Primary Products*, Joint Staff Study, Washington, 1969.

IMF, *Annual Reports*, 1980, 1981, 1982, 1983.

IMF, Committee on Reform of the International Monetary System and Related Issues, *International Monetary Reform: Documents of the Committee of Twenty*, Washington, 1974.

IMF, *The Monetary Approach to the Balance of Payments*, Washington, IMF, 1977.

IMF, *International Financial Statistics*, various issues.

IMF, *World Economic Outlook*, 1983 and 1984, Washington, IMF.

IMF, *IMF Survey*, 2 June 1978, 4 February 1985.

Isard, P., and Truman, E. M., 'SDRs, Interest and the Aid Link: Further Analysis', *Banca Nazionale del Lavoro Review*, March 1974.

Jayarajah, C.A.B.N., 'Problems and Prospects with Respect to the International Monetary System: Implications of Alternative Exchange Rate Systems for Developing Countries', *Bulletin of Central Bank of Ceylon*, December 1969.

Johnson, H. G., *Efficiency in Domestic and International Money Supply*, Guildford, University of Surrey, 1970.

Johnson, H. G., 'World Inflation, the Developing Countries and An Integrated Programme for Commodities', *Banca Nazionale del Lavoro Review*, December 1976.

Johnson, H. G. and Reichmann, T. M., 'Experience with Stabilization Programmes Supported by Stand-by Arrangements in the Upper Credit Tranches, 1973–75', Washington, IMF, unpublished paper, February 1978.

Kadam, V. B., *Implications for Developing Countries of Current Proposals for a Substitution Account*, UNDP/UNCTAD Project INT/75/015, UN Doc. UNCTAD/MFD/TA/1 1979.

Kahn, R., 'SDRs and Aid', *Lloyds Bank Review*, October 1973.

Kaldor, N., 'Inflation and Recession in the World Economy', *Economic Journal*, December 1976.

Kapur, I., 'An Analysis of the Supply of Eurocurrency Finance to Developing Countries', *Oxford Bulletin of Economics and Statistics*, August 1977.

Kenen, P. B., 'Financing, Adjustment and the International Monetary Fund', mimeo. 1984.

Keynes, J. M., 'The International Control of Raw Materials', Treasury Memorandum, 1942, reprinted in *Journal of International Economics*, no. 4, 1974.

Kessler, G. A., 'Should Development Aid be Linked to SDR Creation?' *The Economist*, CXIX, 1971.

Khan, M. S., and Knight, M. D., *Stabilisation in Developing Countries: A Formal Framework*, IMF Staff Papers, March 1981.

Khan, M. S., and Knight, M. D., 'Determinants of Current Account Balances of Non-Oil Developing Countries in the 1970s: An Empirical Analysis', *IMF Staff Papers*, December 1983.

Khatkhate, D. R., 'Debt-Servicing as an Aid to Promotion of Trade of Developing Countries', *Oxford Economic Papers*, July 1966.

Killick, T., 'Eurocurrency Market Recycling of OPEC Surpluses to Developing Countries: Fact or Myth?', *The Banker*, January 1981.

Killick, T., Bird, G., Sharpley, J., and Sutton, M., *The Quest for Economic Stabilization: the IMF and the Third World*, Heinemann with ODI, 1984.

Konig, W., 'Multiple Exchange Rate Policies in Latin America', *Journal of Inter-American Studies*, January 1968.

Krasner, S. D., 'The International Monetary Fund and the Third World', *International Organisation*, Summer 1968.

Krugman, P., 'International Debt Analysis in an Uncertain World', in Smith and Cuddington, op. cit.

Laker, J. F., 'Fiscal Proxies for Devaluation: a General Review', *IMF Staff Papers*, March 1981.

Lal, D. *A Liberal International Economic Order: The International Monetary System and Economic Development*, Essays in International Finance, No. 139, Princeton University, October 1980.

Landell-Mills, P. M., 'Structural Adjustment Lending: Early Experiences', *Finance and Development*, December 1981.

Lessard, D., 'Risk-Efficient External Financing for Commodity Exporting Countries', *Cuadernos de Economia*, May 1977.

Llewellyn, D. T., 'Avoiding an International Banking Crisis', *National Westminster Bank Review*, August 1982.

Llewellyn, D. T., 'Modeling International Banking Flows: An Analytical Framework,' in Black, J., and Dorrance, G. (eds) *Problems in International Finance*, London, Macmillan, 1984.

Massell, B., 'Some Welfare Implications of International Price Stabilisation', *Journal of Political Economy*, LXXVIII, 1970.

Maynard, G., and van Rijkeghem, W., 'Stabilisation Policy in an Inflationary Economy – Argentina', in Papanek, G. (ed.) *Development Policy in Theory and Practice*, Cambridge, Mass, Harvard UP, 1968.

Maynard, G., 'Special Drawing Rights and Development Aid', *Journal of Development Studies*, July 1973.

Maynard, G., 'The Role of Financial Institutions', in Black, and Dorrance op. cit.

Michalopoulos, C., and Perez L. L., 'Commodity Trade Policy Initiatives and Issues', mimeo, presented at Ford Foundation Conference on Stabilising World Commodity Markets, Analysis, Practice and Policy, March 1977.

Morgan Guaranty Trust, *World Financial Markets*, various issues.

Morley, S. A., 'Inflation and Stagnation in Brazil', *Economic Development and Cultural Change*, January 1971.

Newbery, D., and Stiglitz, J., *The Theory of Commodity Price Stabilization*, Oxford UP, 1981.

Nowzad, B., *The IMF and its Critics*, Essays in International Finance, No. 146, Princeton University, December, 1981.

Nyerere, J., 'No to IMF Meddling', Extract from President Nyerere's New Year Message, 1980, to the Diplomats Accredited to Tanzania, *Development Dialogue*, 1980.

O'Neill, J., 'An Empirical Investigation into the OPEC Surplus and its Disposal', unpublished PhD thesis, University of Surrey, 1982.

Pavlic, B., Uranga, R., Cizelj, B. and Svetlicic, M., *The Challenges of South-South Co-operation*, Boulder, Westview Press, 1983.

Payer, C., *The Debt Trap*, Harmondsworth, Penguin, 1974.

Please, Stanley, 'The World Bank: Lending for Structural Adjustment,' in Feinberg, R. E. and Kallab, Valeriana (eds), *Adjustment Crisis in the Third World*, US–Third World Policy Perspectives, No. 1, Overseas Development Council, 1984.

Reichmann, T. M., 'The Fund's Conditional Assistance to the Problems of Adjustment', *Finance and Development*, December 1978.

Spraos, J., 'IMF Conditionality – A Better Way', *Banca Nazionale del Lavoro Review*, December 1984.

Stewart, F., and Sengupta, A., *International Financial Co-operation: A Framework for Change*, London, Pinter, 1982.

Stewart, F., and Stewart, M., 'A New Currency for Trade Among Developing Countries', *Trade and Development*, No. 2, Autumn 1980.

Streeten, P., 'The Developing Countries in a World of Flexible Exchange Rates', *International Currency Review*, January–February 1971.

Swoboda, A., 'Debt and the Efficiency and Stability of the International Financial System,' in Smith and Cuddington, op. cit.

Taylor, L., *Structuralist Macroeconomics, Applicable Models for the Third World*, New York, Basic Books, 1981.

UNCTAD, *International Monetary Issues and the Developing Countries*, 1965.

Vaubel, R., 'The Moral Hazard of IMF Lending', *The World Economy*, September 1983.

Williamson, John, 'Surveys in Applied Economics: International Liquidity', *Economic Journal*, September 1973.

Williamson, John, 'Generalized Floating and the Reserve Needs of Developing Countries,' in Leipziger, D. (ed) *The International Monetary System and the Developing Nations*, 1976.

Williamson, J., 'Economic Theory and IMF Policies', in Brunner, K., and Meltzer, A. H. (eds) *Monetary Institutions and the Policy Process*, Washington, Carnegie–Rochester Conference Series on Public Policy, 1980.

Williamson, J., *The Lending Policies of the International Monetary Fund*, Washington, Institute for International Economics, August 1982.

Williamson, John (ed), *IMF Conditionality*, Institute for International Economics, 1983.

Williamson, John, *A New SDR Allocation?*, Washington, Institute for International Economics, March 1984.

World Bank, *World Development Report*, various issues.

World Bank, *Coping with External Debt in the 1980s*, Washington, 1985.

Index

and equity, 226–7; *re* inflation, 224–6
benefits to developing countries from, 215–17
case for market-equivalent interest rate, 217–18: link and market interest rates, 218–19
different links, 212–14: developing country preferences, 213, 214–15
South Korea, 88
Streeten, P., 66
Substitution Account, 210–11
demonetisation of gold and, 199–200
developing countries' criticisms, 203: *re* effect on exchange-rate stability, 205; *re* effect on international adjustment, 204; *re* effect on the SDR, 203; *re* financial arrangements of account, 206; *re* global liquidity management, 205; *re* holding of reserves, 205–6
developing country attitudes to, 202–3

financial flows to developing countries, 195–7, 201: estimating, 197–9
key problems, 192–5
role of SDRs, 192

Taiwan, 88
Tanzania, 60
Taylor, L., 66

United Nations Conference on Trade and Development (UNCTAD), 94, 109, 203, 260
Uruguay, 60

Venezuela, 242
debt rescheduling, 260

Williams, J., 49, 50, 65, 94
on global quotas, 172, 173, 174
World Bank, 2, 42, 70, 89–90, 209, 260, 263–4, 268, 284, 295, 297–8
co-financing with private sector, 297
World Development Report, 173